Implementing Enterprise Portfolio Management with Microsoft Project Server 2002

GARY CHEFETZ

APress Media, LLC

Implementing Enterprise Portfolio Management with Microsoft Project Server 2002

Copyright © 2003 by Apress
Originally published by Apress in 2003
Softcover reprint of the hardcover 1st edition 2003

Library of Congress Cataloging-in-Publication Data

Chefetz, Gary.
Implementing enterprise : portfolio management with Microsoft
Project
server 2002 / Gary Chefetz.
   p. cm.
Includes index.
ISBN 978-1-4302-5226-9
1. Project management--Computer programs. 2. Microsoft Project.
I.
Title.

HD69.P75C467 2003
658.4'04'02855369--dc21

2003012532

ISBN 978-1-4302-5226-9   ISBN 978-1-4302-1114-3 (eBook)
DOI 10.1007/978-1-4302-1114-3

Distributed to the book trade in the United States by Springer-Verlag New York, Inc., 175 Fifth Avenue, New York, NY, 10010 and outside the United States by Springer-Verlag GmbH & Co. KG, Tiergartenstr. 17, 69112 Heidelberg, Germany.

In the United States: phone 1-800-SPRINGER, email orders@springer-ny.com, or visit http://www.springer-ny.com. Outside the United States: fax +49 6221 345229, email orders@springer.de, or visit http://www.springer.de.

For information on translations, please contact Apress directly at 2560 Ninth Street, Suite 219, Berkeley, CA 94710. Phone 510-549-5930, fax 510-549-5939, email info@apress.com, or visit http://www.apress.com.

The source code for this book is available to readers at http://www.apress.com in the Downloads section.

Contents at a Glance

Contents

About the Author

Gary Chefetz is the founder of Soho Corp. and MSProjectExperts, which exist to support business and organizations that choose the Microsoft enterprise project management platform. Chefetz has worked with Microsoft Project as a tool since 1995. He has been supporting users of Project and Project Central through the Microsoft communities since the introduction of Project Central in early 2000, and he continues to receive the prestigious Microsoft Most Valuable Professional (MVP) award for his contributions. As an MVP, Chefetz works closely with the Microsoft Project product team and support organizations.

Chefetz is dedicated to supporting Microsoft Project Server implementations through his business efforts and through the newsgroups. Find him online in the Project Pro and Project Server newsgroups at msnews.microsoft.com or e-mail him at gary@chefetz.org.

About the Contributing Author

David Gage, who wrote Chapter 18 ("Customizing the Project Guide") of this book, currently works as a technical consultant providing implementation, training, and custom development services for Microsoft Project Server for Quantum PM. David frequently assists others on the Microsoft newsgroups and has received the Microsoft Most Valuable Professional (MVP) award for his contributions. He holds a master's degree and a bachelor's degree in industrial engineering with a concentration in information systems. He can be contacted by e-mail at dcgage@quantumpm.com.

Introduction

THANK YOU FOR READING my Project Server book. Herein you'll find a complete guide to implementing Project Server 2002 and Project 2002 Professional Edition as an enterprise portfolio management solution. My goal in writing this book is to provide you step-by-step instructions beginning with the planning and requirements gathering process, and culminating in configuring and using your new system.

This systematic approach is the basis for the topical ordering in this book. Although some topics seem, at times, to be orphaned from their broader subjects, this is because they're presented as you need them, when you encounter them during the natural setup and adoption process. Those of you using the book as a topical reference should understand the chronological flow of the book. I don't organize many presentations of the user interface around a page or area itself. In learning about some areas, you'll approach them several times to perform different system tasks. This way, your knowledge develops in context of actual system activity. Following a path guided by the interface wouldn't provide as neat a context.

That last comment took a little poke at the software. Let me disclose up front that there are notes of criticism contained in this book. I must also disclose that I now make my entire living supporting Microsoft Project and that I'm a long-time Microsoft fan. I'm an appreciative Microsoft customer who, as a small business owner with many years in consulting, has relied on Microsoft to make technology that was accessible to me. The bottom line is that I'm extremely prejudiced in favor of Microsoft and Microsoft Project.

I've been working with the Microsoft Project Server technology since the introduction of Project Central, which was introduced and shipped with Project 2000. Project Central seemed like a trial balloon for Microsoft. It certainly put many of its users on trial. If Project Server 2002 demonstrates nothing else, it shows that the Microsoft Project product team focuses on responding to user requests. Each product release shows innovations and improvements requested by the user community. The upcoming 2003 edition is no exception.

As a Microsoft Project Most Valuable Professional (MVP), I answer many questions each week in the Microsoft Project newsgroups. A person posting in the `microsoft.public.project.pro_and_server` newsgroup once asked me a question about content I had contributed to Lisa Bucki's *Managing with Microsoft Project 2002*. He asked why I hadn't warned people in the book about an error condition that could arise during a particular step in the installation. My answer to him was that what I wrote was intended to show him how to install the software without encountering the error; therefore, the information shouldn't be useful to him. Although I say that to you now in advance, I've kept this fellow's comments in mind while authoring this book. I've taken the time to point out many of the errors you might see along the way, including an entire chapter on installation troubleshooting, a real sore spot for many. Nothing, however, replaces the troubleshooting resources that Microsoft provides. These should always be your frontline checks.

In the first chapter I raise some heavy topics regarding achieving management competencies as a prerequisite to the effective application of project management tools such as Project Server. I refer to specific standards in this chapter because they're there in the world to refer to. They aptly describe the management maturities that are required to sustain a managed project practice in an organization. Fortunately, every indication is that a company needs only score somewhere in the middle of the maturity matrix to be an effective tool user. Unfortunately, for many that's a big leap. Weigh both my comments and the research with the knowledge of your organization only you can possess.

This book contains content applicable to a wide range of users. Technical areas of the book present appropriate technical jargon. To approach the installation content, and indeed installation of Project Server, you should be familiar with Microsoft Windows 2000 Server technology and Microsoft SQL Server 2000. Content written on how to use Project 2002 Professional Edition with Project Server assumes that users already know how to use Microsoft Project as a desktop tool. This book doesn't cover basic use of Microsoft Project as a planning tool. When I present topics that seem to be delving into this area, it's because executing them is different in the Project Server environment than it is in the desktop environment.

I hope your Project Server implementation is many ways more pleasant because of reading this book than it otherwise would have been. If you can write to me and tell me that, all the work has been worthwhile.

Take your time with it.

Part One
Project Server Overview and Deployment Planning

CHAPTER 1

Introducing Microsoft Project Server

PROJECT SERVER IS AN enterprise-capable project management automation system designed to support business and industry-specific project management and tracking requirements. It is both an out-of-the-box project assignment tracking system and a platform for business-specific configuration and customization.

Project Server is Microsoft's second-generation server-based project management solution. Its predecessor, Project Central, introduced with Project 2000, offered workgroup-style collaborative features. With Project Server, Microsoft has introduced a more robust architecture that offers enterprise-wide deployment capabilities lacking in Project Central and has added a cadre of features to support its enterprise worthiness.

The combination of Microsoft Project 2002 Professional and Project Server provides a powerful enterprise portfolio management system that is feature rich, but fraught with complexity and challenges. My goal is to help you maximize the feature benefits and minimize the deployment frustrations.

I begin this chapter with a discussion of the product's pedigree and lineage, and then I discuss the Project Server big picture to give you a good idea of what you're getting into when you commit to deploying it in your organization.

Getting Started with Project Server

With the introduction of Project 2002, Microsoft split the Project product line into separate server and client stock-keeping units (SKUs). Project 2000, and all the previous versions of the product, had only one version, and Project Central shipped as a free include on the Project 2000 installation CD. Although the Project Central software was included at no charge, its appearance introduced a new licensing model to the Project line with the requirement of a Client Access License (CAL) for users accessing Project Central via a Web browser.

If you've read Microsoft's marketing material for the Project 2002 product line, you're likely under the impression that there are four distinct products being offered. These products are as follows:

- Project 2002 Standard

- Project 2002 Professional

- Project Web Access

- Project Server

 NOTE Project Web Access is an integral feature of Project Server, which is an Active Server Pages (ASP) application. In other words, Project Server is a Web-based application and structured like a typical Microsoft-based e-commerce application. You can neither purchase nor install Project Web Access separately. Essentially, it's what you get when you purchase a CAL.

Boiling this down, you're left with two versions of the desktop client plus the server application with four different types of software licenses. Choosing between Project 2002 Standard edition and Project 2002 Professional edition is as simple as deciding whether or not you're going to deploy Project Server and, if so, whether it will be a workgroup or enterprise configuration.

The only difference between the two versions of the Project client is how they integrate with Project Server. Simply put, Project 2002 Standard gives you workgroup functionality with Project Server, whereas Project 2002 Professional enables the enterprise features of Project Server. So, if it's a choice between the two client versions, and you have no intention to implement Project Server, choose Project 2002 Standard because Project 2002 Professional is substantially more expensive and offers no additional functionality in absence of Project Server.

Determining Your Licensing Requirements

Whether you implement an enterprise configuration or a workgroup configuration, you'll need to acquire a license for each user of the system. Every user who will create, manage, and update a project plan will require a client license for either the Project 2002 Standard or Professional edition. This largely applies to people who have the title of project manager or who fill that role. It may also apply to resource managers if you intend to have timesheet reporting flow through line managers instead of, or in addition to, project managers. (If you don't understand the distinction between a project manager and a resource manager now, you'll learn about it later.) Finally, you'll need to license a copy of Project for each person who will administer the application. Typically, application administrators are also project managers, so this may or may not increase your head count for licensing.

In addition to your Project Professional or Project Standard licenses, you must acquire a CAL for each person who will use Project Web Access but isn't already licensed to use Project. Each copy of the Project client comes with a CAL for that user instance. The CAL that's bundled with the Project client isn't severable from the client license. Therefore, you may not count these separately. You may, however, use the full client license as a CAL only, but you'll only do this if you've purchased too many full client licenses because the cost of a full license is more than five times the price of a CAL.

Many organizations may find that they have overlicensed Project clients when making the transition to the client-server architecture provided with Project Server and Project 2002. In my experience as many as 50% or more of the Project licenses held by larger companies are being used for the sole purpose of viewing project plans because there is no separate project file viewer available. When transitioning to Project Server, companies have an opportunity to repurpose licensing dollars toward CALs for users who require view-only access to project plans.

Project Server licenses are sold separately. The Project Server license includes a SharePoint Team Services license, which provides the technology for some of the collaborative features of Project Server, including issues management and document repositories. Project Server also includes Microsoft Data Engine (MSDE), Microsoft's free entry-level database engine. MSDE is useful only for very small implementations, so you'll likely need a license for SQL Server and, of course, you must have a license for the operating system (OS) that Project Server will run on: either an edition of Windows 2000 Server or Windows Server 2003.

To take full advantage of the analysis features offered in Project Server, an Office XP license is required on the client machine running Project Web Access. The interactive capabilities of the analyzer views provided in an enterprise deployment of Project Server use Office XP Web components.

If a user doesn't have a copy of Office XP installed, Project Server automatically installs a runtime version of the components the first time a user accesses these views. The runtime version allows the user to see the views, but the interactive drag-and-drop features are disabled, and Office 2000 users will experience the same limitation. You'll need at least one Office XP or higher license installed on a client to create the views.

Determining Your Deployment Configuration

You can deploy Project Server in a workgroup or enterprise configuration. The feature-set difference between the two configurations is seemingly minimal; however, your ability to control the project management environment is vastly different.

In an enterprise configuration, Project Server provides two very important feature differences. Enterprise configurations include an enterprise resource pool and a set of enterprise custom fields and outline codes. These are the foundation for tailoring the application to meet your business needs and enforcing structure and consistency in the project management environment. Both are keys to leveraging the analysis tools that also distinguish an enterprise implementation from a workgroup implementation. An enterprise configuration supports structured portfolio management, whereas a workgroup configuration does not.

Portfolio, Program, or Project?

Assuming that you have an understanding of the term *project*, for the purposes of this book *program* refers to a collection of related projects, and *portfolio* refers to a collection of programs and/or projects within a business unit or across an entire enterprise. Many companies have their own interpretations of these terms. A particular company's interpretations are a reflection of a company's approach to project management. Sometimes this is driven by the sheer size of the organization.

The concept of *portfolio* is malleable. A smaller organization may have a single portfolio of projects, whereas a larger business may conceive of an enterprise portfolio made up of numerous departmental or line-of-business portfolios, each containing its own set of programs and projects. However a business conceives these entities, you can model these in Project Server.

Project Server always requires a database for its own data. Your choices are limited to Microsoft SQL Server or MSDE. Workgroup configurations allow project plans to be stored either in a database or in file shares. In fact, workgroup installations can use most any ODBC-compliant database for project plan storage, including popular platforms such as Oracle and DB2. In a workgroup environment, both the Project client and Project Server connect to the database using a Data Source Name (DSN), which must be configured on both the client and server machine. Although it's possible to save projects to the Project Server database in a workgroup configuration, it's not recommended and may cause problems. A workgroup configuration works well, but it requires additional DSN management, which is an ongoing management process. Data is less secure in this scenario and security can't be managed as granularly as it can be in an enterprise configuration.

Enterprise configurations, on the other hand, leverage Microsoft's OLE DB technology to connect to a single database with security managed through COM+, providing significantly better performance and security management. In order to accomplish these performance gains, enterprise configurations are limited to using Microsoft's SQL Server where all project data is stored in one database repository.

The Project/Project Server Workflow

Project Server's core functionality provides a cyclical assignment and update process between project managers and the team members working on their projects. This workflow is the heart of the management system. Work assignments flow from the plan to resources performing the work and resources report progress data back to the plan.

Project managers and/or planners create project plans in the usual way except that they now build project teams from the enterprise resource pool and they now save plans to a single database repository. Once a manager has created a project plan, work assignments get sent to resources through Project Web Access. A project manager has complete control over the assignment process with the ability to selectively publish or republish assignments as necessary. When a manager sends a work assignment to a resource, Project Server acts like a messaging service. The assignments populate to assignment tables in the database and, if the option is selected, Project Server sends an e-mail notification to the resource with an embedded link to Project Web Access.

Upon receiving the e-mail notification, a resource clicks the link provided in the e-mail and is automatically logged on to Project Server. A personal home page displays a summary status of the user's current activities in the Project environment. This summary includes notices such as the number of new tasks assigned, the number of active issues the resource is responsible for, and reminders about upcoming or overdue status reports. Once notified of new assignments, the resource navigates to the task area to a timesheet view that displays all current and new tasks. The resource then has the option to accept, reject, or delegate the task assignment. Resources also use this view to send progress reports containing completion percentages and/or hours worked based upon the reporting method and periodic basis set for the plan or organization. Resources typically report progress weekly.

Once a resource sends a progress update, the ball is back in the manager's court. The system stages reported data in separate tables pending manager approval. It's important to note that these updates may be flowing to multiple managers if the resource is working on multiple projects reporting to multiple project managers. Managers may approve or reject progress data from team members. Tools provided in the update interface also allow managers to create automation rules for performing these updates. Once accepted by the manager, the progress data flows into the project plan.

Project Team Collaboration Tools

Beyond the core workflow, Project Server provides a complement of features enabling improved team communication. Some of these features are native to Project Server, whereas others leverage integration with SharePoint Team Services.

Status Reports

A status-reporting tool allows managers to establish single or periodic status reports that team members must respond to. The interface provides tools for creating standardized status report formats with an option that automatically consolidates reports submitted by a team. Resources respond to these reports in Project Web Access, which provides rich text editing. Status reports interact with timesheets so that respondents may conveniently insert assignments from their timesheets into their status reports. Status reporting isn't limited to those requested by a manager. Team members may create their own ad-hoc reports and submit them to a manager at any time.

Nonworking Days and Nonproject Time

Project Web Access allows team members to communicate working day changes to their managers such as vacations and personal days. Application administrators can set up categories to capture nonproject working time for overhead tasks such as meetings and maintenance work. Resources report these hours through the timesheet along with task work.

Document Libraries

The system automatically creates Web-based document libraries, provided by SharePoint Teams Services, each time a user adds a project to the server. Managers have the ability to add additional libraries within the individual project libraries to add custom organization the workspace. Users access document libraries through a Web browser, allowing them to upload or download items into the repository. The system captures descriptive information, such as revision state, author name, and dating information, through the upload process. Administrators may extend the information captured by adding fields to the interface using the provided customization tools. Full-text searching is a standard feature and you can link uploaded documents to tasks in the project. Further, tasks in the project itself can be linked to the document and exposed in Web views so that a user browsing the project can click a task field and instantly open the document in a Web view, providing the user has the necessary security permissions.

Issues Management

Like document libraries, the system automatically creates issues lists for each project. Issues lists include a number of data fields that describe the issue, rate its priority, and capture its status and resolution. Users can link issues to affected and resolving tasks. Issues creators assign issues to resources through Project Web Access. Once assigned to an issue, this information articulates to users through their home page in Project Web Access as well as their personal tasks area. Administrators may add fields to capture additional information such as risk-management characteristics.

Automated Reminders and Notifications

Project Server features an automated reminder system that is interactive with almost every function, event, and entity within the system. The notification engine generates e-mail notices for upcoming and overdue task work, and status reports. It also integrates to document libraries and issues, allowing users to subscribe to specific documents and issues triggering notifications when changes to these occur. Each user has the ability to set reminders for him- or herself, and managers have the added ability to set reminders for their resources.

Advanced Analysis

Project Server leverages SQL Server 2000's Analysis Services to provide browser-based access to dimensioned data in OLAP cubes. You can add additional dimensions to the data cubes through the Project interface by adding custom outline codes that group data in a way that is tailored to and meaningful to your business needs. Users familiar with PivotTables in Excel will find that the Analyzer views behave similarly.

What Is OLAP?

The *online analytical processing* (OLAP) technology relies upon a multidimensional view of data. The relational database structure that underpins most transactional applications is two-dimensional. OLAP leverages data cubes based on relational fact sources, which contain preprocessed three-dimensional data typically time-phased and aggregated by business dimension. The advantages of employing OLAP technologies for business analytics include the performance advantages of using preprocessed data and, more important, the transparent enforcement of standardized analytical formulas.

To build Portfolio Analyzer views (see the example shown in Figure 1-1), you drag and drop cube dimensions into data or chart areas. This feature exposes the full range of Excel charting capabilities in the browser interface, and users can view and manipulate data and graphical representations on the fly. Users can coalesce project data across projects, programs, and portfolios, providing the users powerful insight into business trends and issues. Because OLAP data is preprocessed, access to dimensioned data is fast.

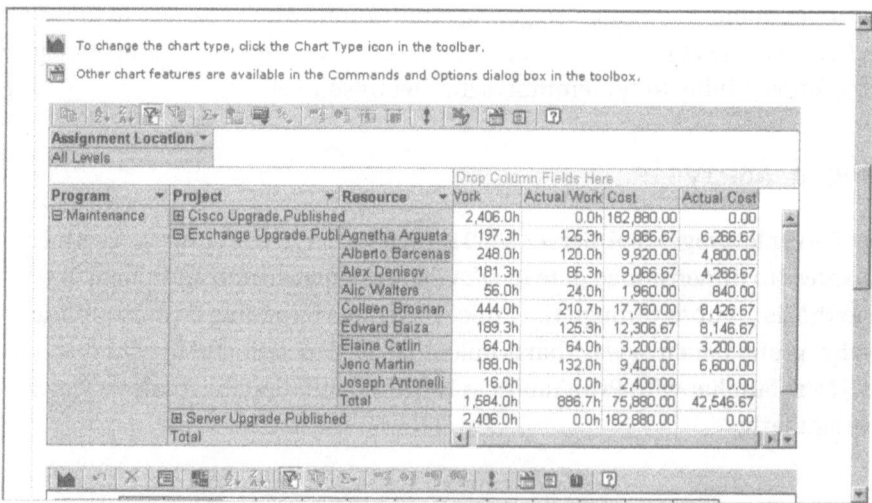

Figure 1-1. Portfolio Analyzer view

Portfolio Modeling

A portfolio-modeling tool provides what-if analysis on staffing changes that can improve utilization and eliminate overallocation of resources, increasing the likelihood of on-time and on-budget completion. Apply analysis to one project or across numerous projects.

Resource Tools

A centralized enterprise resource pool underlies the advanced resource functionality introduced in Project Server. Team-building tools allow managers to quickly slice through a large pool of resources and locate resources by both availability and skills. The addition of custom codes that enable business-specific selection criteria, such as practice groups, location, departmental, or corporate policy attributes that your business may need to address its unique requirements, enhance this capability.

Manual and automated team-building tools simplify the project resourcing process not only by leveraging the custom attributes in the pool, but also by providing instant access to availability data enhanced with graphical representation. Managers can quickly identify available resources with desired characteristics or take advantage of the automated Resource Substitution Wizard. The wizard rapidly analyzes the resource pool to identify skills and availability for staffing a single project or a group of projects. You can save the resulting recommendations as input for manual team building or directly update it into the working plan.

Reporting structures, modeled into the resource pool, enhance security capabilities by accommodating structured access to resource information following the chain of command. Resource managers are easily made a part of the management process.

Choosing to Implement Project Server

Choosing to implement Project Server is only appropriate for organizations that practice or are resolved to practice project management as a required discipline. I cite level-three maturity, as measured by the Carnegie Mellon University Software Engineering Institute (SEI) Capabilities Maturity Model (CMM) or the University of California, Berkeley Project Maturity Model (PMM, see http://www.ce.berkeley.edu/pmroi/assessing-PM-maturity.pdf) as a benchmark. To use the tool effectively, an organization is making a commitment to a manage-by-project discipline. At level three in these maturity models, project plans get created early in the project process and are kept current throughout planning and execution.

CMM and PMM

The *Capabilities Maturity Model* (CMM), developed by the Software Engineering Institute (SEI) of Carnegie Mellon University, describes best practices for organizations seeking to manage excellence in producing software. The University of California, Berkeley *Project Maturity Model* (PMM) echoes the CMM in its steps describing the project management activities and best practices that correspond to building capabilities maturity. Although originally conceived to drive excellence in software development, you can easily extend the CMM to other industries. The ubiquity of software development across all manner of business and its general influence on business management practices go a long way to support this.

The base levels of both models describe an organization that takes an ad-hoc approach to projects; often referred to as "hero-led project management." Companies at this level regard project leaders as "project champions." These terms, or similar expressions, are characteristic of the language spoken in level-one companies. Organizations introduce formal project management at level two, to govern the execution of project work. At level two, an organization makes a commitment to planning all projects. Project plans with work breakdown structures are characteristic of level-two organizations. Unfortunately, the organization may still be struggling with establishing regular update cycles. By the time an organization achieves level three, projects are not only planned, but they are also continuously updated and at any time reflect the current state of the project. Moving through level four, an organization gains the ability to use the data and feedback systems it has built to begin to shorten business cycles and make better project management decisions. Level five is best described as a state where best practice–style management becomes ingrained and autonomic in the enterprise.

Summarizing the characteristics of these models in two paragraphs is a substantial oversimplification. My point in referring to them is that organizations can objectively measure themselves against these accepted standards.

Because Project Server is, at its heart, a progress tracking system, an organization must be committed to tracking its projects before it can derive substantial value from it. Unless your group, division, or company is willing to declare this a requisite for doing business, you will end up repurposing the server in 6 months and shelving the Project Server software. This is not to say that you can't use Project Server in a limited way to deliver business value, but an enterprise implementation of Project Server is overkill for anything less than this level of commitment. Project tracking is not an on-again, off-again practice; either you require it or you do not need to use a tracking tool.

The Benefits of a Project Management Tool

The ability to track project progress is the single largest benefit of installing a collaborative project management tool. Despite Project's popularity as a planning tool, a substantial number of Microsoft Project users fail to use it as a progress-tracking tool. As a stand-alone tool, it does little to promote project tracking. Each plan manager must manually gather this type of input and enter it into the plan. Some businesses employ people specifically to perform this work. Project Web Access timesheets provide the ability to collect progress information directly from the resources who are performing the work.

The predictive analysis enabled by a database full of up-to-date project and up-to-date resource information drives a return on investment for implementing project management software. The ability to recognize future resource demand and track project performance to standardized indices and criteria drives better decision making by line managers and executive managers alike. Perhaps the single most significant benefit of advanced analysis is the ability to identify and respond to project performance failures. Your goal is to know when to make adjustments to scope and resources and know when to kill an unsalvageable effort before costs get out of hand. Managers make these decisions most effectively with data and not by gut. Very few organizations have any, let alone well thought out, criteria for killing a project.

All the additional collaborative features provided by Project Server, such as the easy access to project data through the Web, issues management and document repositories, notifications and reminders, and many more, are the bonus prizes bestowed upon those organizations that can implement and commit to a managed project environment.

Configuring Project for Your Business

As much as Project Server is packed with out-of-the-box features, there's a lot of work involved in configuring Project Server for a specific business. To do it correctly, and without missteps, you must follow a structured implementation approach. If your goal is to have a corporate or even departmental portfolio management system, you should approach this implementation as a project and work through the following implementation phases:

1. Assessment

2. Requirements gathering

3. Installation

4. Configuration

5. Initial load

6. Training

7. Rollout

These phases apply to implementations that are limited to customization through configuration and not by applying custom coding, which would require additional development and quality assurance phases. I recommend that all companies first implement and learn to use the software based on the standard capabilities tailored to the business through configuration only. Approach this by first implementing in a pilot scenario before devising and committing to code changes. A pilot phase is beneficial as it allows you to become familiar with the idiosyncrasies of the software process and reconcile it to your organizational process.

Each of these phases, with its respective activities and deliverables, is important to a smooth and effective deployment. The assessment process is an opportunity for project therapy. It works best when it includes a large cross-section of managers, team members, and stakeholders. The goal is to identify and limit deployment risks, particularly human factors that may affect your ability to implement, while getting a preliminary feel for how to configure your system.

Whether it's the way the finance department likes to see project data, how your team members will interact with the software, or what business stakeholders want from the system, it takes time to methodically identify and respond to these requirements. Because you must make many decisions during installation and setup, and because the output of the system depends so heavily on custom field configuration, it's important to make a thorough effort at requirements gathering and documentation.

Project Server installation is a tedious task with many opportunities for missteps. However, the instructions provided in this book will take the pain out of it for most installers. You must allocate adequate time and attention to platform choices and setup.

Preparing the initial data load for Project Server can take some time as well. These can be more or less trivial pursuits for those who have up-to-date project plans and existing resource pools structured with accurate and consistent data. Alas, this sadly is more often the exception than the rule. You should plan on spending time hunting, gathering, and prodding project and resource information from your enterprise.

Training is necessary. Project Server and Project Professional 2002 together present an entirely new way of working for most project professionals and project teams. You'll need to support the learning curve by properly preparing everyone in your business who will be involved in using the system. Beyond training your project managers, team members, and stakeholders on the tool, most businesses will benefit from project management training. As Microsoft Project and Project Server together support accepted professional standards in project management, project managers using the tool should have experience in the essential disciplines. If your organization is at the bottom of the learning curve, make project management training a prerequisite for Microsoft Project training.

Microsoft recommends rather strongly that companies engage Project Partners, consulting firms that specialize in the Microsoft Project platform, to assist with deployment. As I'm someone who earns his living this way, it may seem self-serving to endorse this recommendation, but it's a wise choice. After working through the life cycle of Project's predecessor product, and after a year of working with Project Server, I'm continually challenged in the field with new surprises. If you follow the recommendations of this book, a do-it-yourself approach is possible, but be prepared to spend more time tackling the learning curve when you take this route.

The Challenges of Moving to a Project Management Tool

As challenging as the tool may be to configure, install, and deploy, these difficulties pale in comparison to the potential organizational challenges you may face. As discussed earlier in the chapter, a high level of organizational discipline is required to succeed with this tool. Organizations introducing time reporting for the first time are likely to meet with resistance from line managers and team members alike. It's beneficial to have a very strong executive-level commitment to this change or have across-the-board grassroots support. Everyone involved in the project process must be committed to using the tool.

For organizations that already have corporate time-tracking systems, a special dilemma arises. Corporate time systems, old and new alike, typically capture time at the project level and not the assignment level. Project Server captures time at the assignment level, so you must make a decision. Which interface will be the corporate standard? Is it possible to transition everyone to the Project Server interface or is a blended approach more applicable? How will these two systems integrate? Will your team accept double entering during a pilot phase and how long is this sustainable before an integration commitment is required?

In organizations climbing through level-two and level-three maturities, the terms "corporate policies" and "corporate politics" are often interchangeable. Referring to the mode of charismatic leadership discussed earlier in this chapter, managers who aren't knowledgeable or comfortable with disciplined project management may become a source of resistance. The introduction of structure and standards often reveals shortcomings in an organization's approach to project work, which generates perceptions that this reflects derogatorily on those responsible. The added transparency of project progress and status may be threatening to managers whose work couldn't be as easily scrutinized without a project management system. Don't underestimate the overhead of organizational change and the pain it often brings. Keep in mind that as difficult as it may be to get Project Server ready for your organization, it may be an order of magnitude more difficult to get your organization ready for Project Server.

Summary

Project Server isn't simply an extension of Microsoft Project, it's a substantial server application that's evolving into a professional services automation tool as well as an enterprise project management system. The complexity of the tool combined with the complexity of project management as a practice makes it a worthy addition to any business's management arsenal. Your approach to implementation must include respect for its complexity and the organizational change it may demand.

An Implementation Framework

AS MUCH AS ALMOST everyone wants to simply install Project Server and immediately begin using it, this is possible in only the most simple workgroup installations where the Enterprise features are not available. Taking a structured approach to your implementation will increase your chances of a successful installation.

In this chapter you'll explore the assessment phase of implementation and the tools that Microsoft provides to help you through the assessment process. The goal is to gain a better understanding of your organization's project process and discover the unique challenges your organization will face when moving toward project management automation.

The Last Entry on the Administration Page

Unless you jumped ahead to Chapter 5 and have already installed Project Server (and even then), you might not know that the last selection on the Project Web Access Administration home page, shown in Figure 2-1, isn't a software function at all. In fact, it has nothing to do with Project Server administration.

Instead, selecting "Implement Microsoft Project in the enterprise" takes you to a splash page within Project Web Access that then links to a section of the Microsoft Project Web site that explains the Enterprise Implementation Framework (EIF). The EIF is, physically, a collection of white papers, instructional documents, and deliverable templates that assist you in the early planning phases of your Project Server implementation. This material describes a structured approach that includes the phases outlined in Chapter 1.

When you read the EIF documentation, you might be impressed by the fact that it stresses the use of a Project Partner to provide consulting services through the implementation process. A warning contained in the EIF Setup and Overview document makes this very clear:

WARNING: The EIF is not a substitute for a proper implementation team. It is critical to a successful implementation that the implementation team has the proper level of technical and project management experience.

Implementing Microsoft Project 2002 Professional and Microsoft Project 2002 Server across an enterprise is not a trivial exercise, and having team members with the proper skills and background is perhaps the single most important factor that determines success. In particular, it is essential to have a senior consultant with at least five years' experience implementing or operating an enterprise project management system (preferably Microsoft Project, Artemis Views, PlanView, Primavera P3e, or TeamPlay). If you do not have such expertise available in-house, go to http://www.microsoft.com/office/project/resources/partners.asp *and, under By Partner Type:, select Solution Provider and then click GO.*

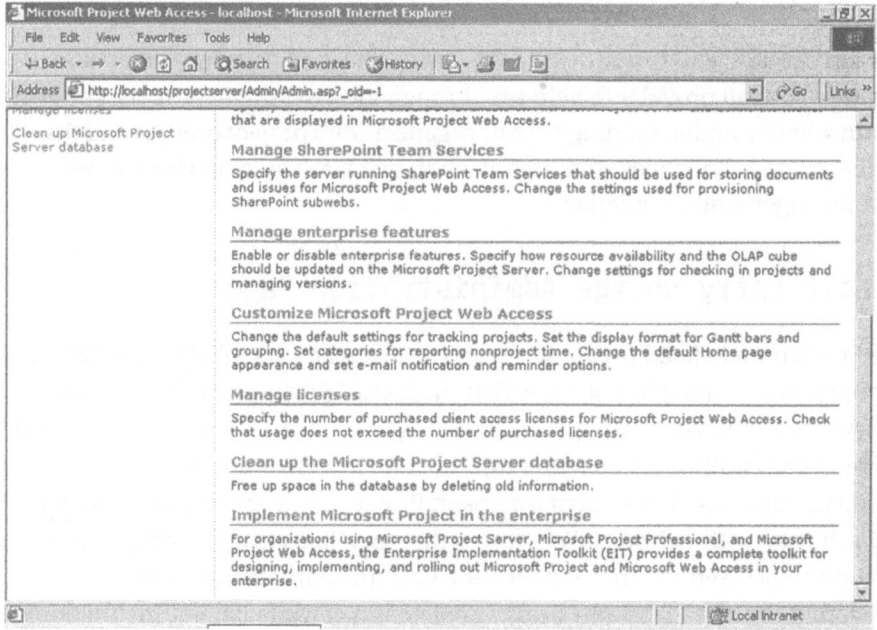

Figure 2-1. The last entry on the Project Web Access Aministration home page doesn't activate a software function.

This is music to my ears, but it may not be to yours. Project Partners are Microsoft Certified Solution Providers. You can log onto Microsoft's Web site to learn more about the partner program and locate a partner, or you can find independent expertise to assist you.

As much as this book is intended to guide you through a structured implementation, it can't entirely substitute for an experienced consultant. There are advantages to professional consulting assistance other than keeping people like me in business, and I point these benefits out as I go along rather than launching a lengthy discussion. Besides, there's plenty of that available in the EIF documentation.

EIF Overview

Download the EIF containing the Enterprise Implementation Toolkit (EIT) from http://go.microsoft.com/fwlink/?LinkId=5897. The 2.4MB self-extracting executable will install the EIF contents to \program files\Microsoft Project 2002 EIF\ unless you change this option in the dialog box shown in Figure 2-2.

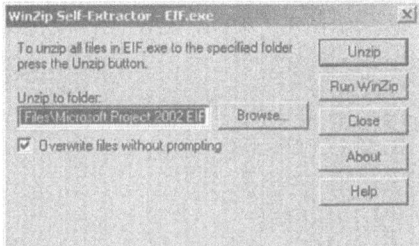

Figure 2-2. Executing the self-extracting EIF file gives you the option to change the default installation directory.

The term "Enterprise Implementation Toolkit (EIT)" appears to be a remnant of a marketing concept of having both a framework and a toolkit, and you arguably get both, but the language is not consistent among all the documents. Although the EIF bundle is surprisingly sloppy in places, it remains an invaluable resource.

EIF Trilogy

Segregating the EIF artifacts into three classifications helps to thresh the wisdom from this resource mélange. Think of the EIF as containing three types of resources: instructional documents, deliverable templates, and white papers. Once installed, you'll find the following contents in your EIF directory.

Instructional documents:

1. EIF FAQ

2. EIF Setup and Overview

3. EIF System Design Guidelines

4. EIT Enterprise Project Overview

Deliverable templates:

1. EIF Interview

2. EIF Project Plan

3. EIF Red Flags

4. EIF Requirements Specification

5. EIF System Design

6. Training-Administrators

7. Training-Executives

8. Training-Project Managers

9. Training-Resource Managers

10. Training-Team Members

White papers:

1. Microsoft Project 2002 Documents Overview

2. Microsoft Project 2002 Enterprise Codes Overview

3. Microsoft Project 2002 Enterprise Project Management Architecture Guide

4. Microsoft Project 2002 Issues Overview

5. Microsoft Project 2002 Notifications Overview

6. Microsoft Project 2002 Project Guide Architecture and Extensibility

7. Microsoft Project 2002 Resource and Skills Management Guide

8. Microsoft Project Server 2002 Architecture and Extensibility

9. Microsoft Project Server Configuration Guidelines White Paper

10. Microsoft Project Server Data Migration

11. Microsoft Project Server Security Architecture and Planning Guide

12. Microsoft SharePoint Team Services Integration Architecture and Extensibility

13. Migration to Microsoft Project Professional 2002

White Papers

The white papers are available redundantly on the Microsoft site. The selections listed in the preceding section pertain specifically to enterprise configurations and represent a slightly expurgated list of all available white papers. You can find a complete list of Project 2002 version white papers at `http://www.microsoft.com/office/project/techinfo/whitepapers/default.asp`. The important thing to keep in mind is that half of the EIF file payload is composed of white papers that are available elsewhere. I strongly recommend that you read the white papers and all of the other documentation Microsoft makes available through TechNet and MSDN, but I do not discuss the white papers included in the EIF bundle here. Instead I focus on the unique information the EIF contains.

Are You Approaching This As a Project?

Examining the deliverable templates and instructional documentation makes one significant first impression: You have a project on your hands. Have you already begun your planning? Have you appointed a project manager for this initiative? Who are your stakeholders? If you don't have the wherewithal to organizationally support your Project Server implementation as a formal project and a model for the business rules driving your implementation, then you should ask yourself why you're implementing project management software. No project management application provides a silver-bullet solution. Project management is a discipline and, as such, adding a tool will confound an organization that hasn't already succeeded in implementing the management disciplines of project management. Your organization must have at least made a commitment to project management disciplines to have reasonable expectations for success.

Instructional Documents

The EIF Setup and Overview document provides a high-level framework for conducting your Project Professional 2002 and Project Server 2002 implementation, as you can connect the process it outlines to its recommended deliverable templates. The EIF System Design Guidelines document is a very compressed, comprehensive guide to the feature-to-organizational use mapping considerations you'll make in pursuing your EIF implementation strategy. It includes detailed instructions for completing the deliverable templates. These two documents embody the EIF strategy and the instructions for its practical use. You also have an FAQ document, which clarifies some of the concepts expressed, and the EIT Enterprise Project Overview document, which is a primer on the Project Server big picture. Consider this last document optional reading if you read the first chapter of this book.

Deliverable Templates

The list of templates can be bifurcated along the lines of training outlines and process templates. The latter group includes a model project plan to govern your implementation effort. An interview question-and-answer template constructed in Excel supports the creation of a Red Flags Report from a Word template and the creation of a requirements specification document from another Word template. The information gathered during the requirements phase is coalesced into a system design document provided as a multitab workbook.

   The other half of the deliverable templates consists of training outlines for the various roles predefined in Project Server. Training is an important step and I endorse its emphasis by these template inclusions. Essentially, the documents are lists of specific Microsoft Project 2002 courseware training modules recommended for each predefined role. The Project 2002 courseware itself is available for download on the Microsoft Web site at `http://support.microsoft.com/default.aspx?scid=kb;en-us;325846`. You must tailor these recommendations to your specific needs, keeping in mind that you may not implement all of the default roles or you may implement other roles not considered by the EIF architects. Training is an important reason to have outside resources lined up for your Project Server implementation.

Enhancing the EIF

The EIF is a model and not an absolute approach. Whether your organization remodels EIF wisdom into its own process or simply uses it as a conceptual baseline to measure the approach of contractors, the EIF is most effective when approached as a rough outline. You must adapt it, enhance it, and mold it to your organization.

Any well-established project practices in your organization that conflict with EIF prescriptions must be reconciled. You should also consider that the overall EIF approach assumes that a full Project rollout occurs after 4 weeks of pilot activity. While this may or may not suit your needs, it's a reminder that the manufacturer's recommendations should be tempered by your own organizational ability to absorb the technology. A strong go/no-go decision point is a legitimate step between piloting and rollout, and some organizations are best served by a slower-paced adoption than the one suggested by the aggressive project plan provided.

Adding and Improving Inception Activities

The EIF doesn't emphasize project inception. It gives short shrift to activities such as determining stakeholders and identifying team implementation roles. These are conveniently bundled into the requirements gathering process. In the absence of a well-understood inception process in your organization, you should give this more time than the EIF suggests. You should have a good organizational understanding of the objectives and reasons for implementing the tool, the complexity of the work, and the organizational pain that you will face in making this decision. Make certain that everyone has the same expectations.

How will your organization go about implementing Project Server? Determining a deployment level is a fundamental decision early in the planning process. Is this a departmental deployment or a cross-departmental deployment? To some degree, determining a potential deployment level for Project Server in your organization is also necessary. Do you structure your configuration for a larger potential, or do you keep it contained? Most organizations benefit from expanded prework and implementation planning.

Adding an Assessment Phase
Incorporating a Red Flags Report

Rather than conducting the interviews to produce the Red Flags Report alone, expand the preparatory steps you take. A go/no-go decision point at the end of this process can spare you wasted effort if it reveals serious obstacles to success. Conducting the interviews has potential therapeutic value and reveals roadblocks as well as opportunities. These revelations may lead you to rethink your deployment strategies; therefore, this exercise offers the most value as an early step in the process. The flowchart shown in Figure 2-3 illustrates a structured approach, incorporating an assessment strategy at inception. This is the high-level process required to take a Project Server implementation to a pilot or proof-of-concept phase.

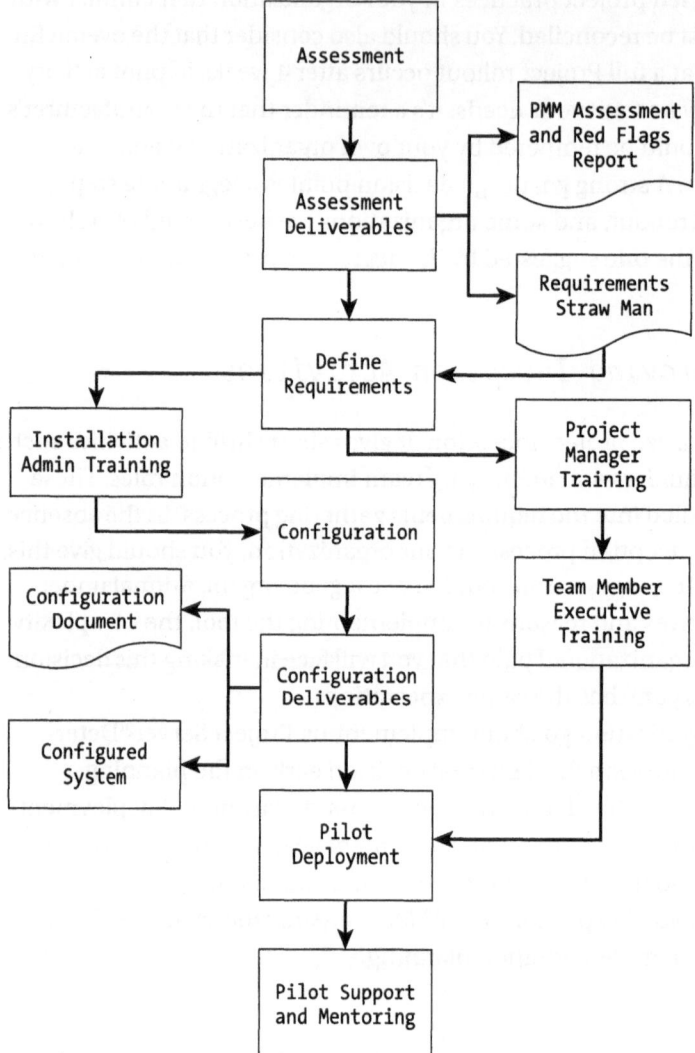

Figure 2-3. Project flow from assessment through pilot

The EIF tacitly drives both assessment and requirements through the single-interview format. In my opinion, initial assessment interviews are most effective when asked in absence of Project Server knowledge to avoid confusing solution capabilities with needs. Requirements discussions, on the other hand, benefit when the participants are familiar with the potential of the tool. It's not entirely realistic to believe that one interview process will fulfill both needs. It's more realistic to expect a good requirements straw-man document as a by-product of the interview process and that additional Joint Application Development (JAD) sessions are necessary to flesh out requirements to a ready-for-configuration state.

A consultant can add significant value to the assessment process. It's often much easier to get interviewees to open up to an independent third party than to a company insider. A nonthreatening interview forum is important to get at disconnects that drive the Red Flags Report. Interviewees should not feel as though they must recite what the interviewer wants to hear.

The assessment phase presents a collateral opportunity to perform some more extensive organizational analysis. Piggybacking the Red Flags interview process onto a Project Management Maturity Model (PMM) and/or Capabilities Maturity Model (CMM) assessment takes advantage of synergies, but requires an additional prework investment. Here, again, the assistance of a consulting firm can be invaluable.

The EIF appropriately emphasizes system documentation by providing both Requirements Specification and System Design templates. It's most important to maintain complete configuration documentation because Project Server is deficient in its presentation of custom information in its administration interface. For instance, custom field names don't appear on the pick lists provided for adding fields to Web views. Therefore, you must have a readable, concise guide to these when performing administration work. You may fall in love with the Excel format of the System Design template, but I think its format is cryptic and awkward. Further, I suggest an evolutionary approach to both the requirements and system design deliverables whereby the requirements document evolves into the design document, keeping the rationale with the specifications.

Simply put, to improve the EIF make sure that your inception process follows your organization's practices or is designed to be a model for your organization, spend more time in the assessment phase and get more value from it, and consider streamlining the documentation process.

Enhancing the Assessment Process

Although the EIF Interview produces good input for the Red Flags Report, the focus is narrow. By adding more depth to the assessment, you can strive to identify underlying causes for the process disconnects identified in the Red Flags Report. To accomplish this, you should add questions focused on project management maturity. If your organization doesn't have a mature project management process, your risk of failure is high. If you don't know what project management maturity is, Harold Kerzner's *Strategic Planning for Project Management Using a Project Management Maturity Model*[1] is the gold standard for understanding the challenges and the benefits.

---

1. Harold Kerzner, PhD, *Strategic Planning for Project Management Using a Project Management Maturity Model* (New York, NY: John Wiley & Sons, Inc., 2001).

To understand the complexity of implementing a process maturity program, in this example the CMM, Diane Burwick provides a comprehensive implementation program framework in *How To Implement the CMM.*[2] Although the material is specific to software development, the underlying management philosophies and process fundamentals contained in the program manual support advancement through either CMM or PMM. Adapting and right-sizing a solution for your business is one of your most significant challenges.

Changing the Format of the EIF Interview

The EIF Interview is an Excel workbook with validations applied to many of the questions. The validations are incidental and tend to be more limiting than they are helpful. For your convenience, I've converted the interview to a Word document, which you can download from http://www.projectserverexperts.com. Many of the validated questions restrict answers to yes or no. This is particularly limiting because sometimes the proper response and good collateral information you may otherwise capture becomes cumbersome, forcing you to add text outside the form margins.

Summary

Having now suggested that you give additional effort to upfront activities, it's only fair that I offer some suggestions for streamlining requirements and your specification process. The next chapter follows an alternative approach to building a requirements document and eventual design specification. Except when you're contemplating extensive customization, you can easily transition the requirements document into a design specification, particularly if complicated customizations aren't included. Moreover, you can adapt and improve it for your organization.

---

2. Diane M. Burwick, *How to Implement the CMM, Second Edition* (Louisville, KY: BPS Publications, 2001).

Requirements Gathering

Using Project Server to its fullest potential requires customization through configuration. Your goal is to map your enterprise to the application and vice versa. Process tools typically impose their own limitations upon their human users, and Project Server is no exception. Consequently, you *must* manage both software configuration and organizational process change, involving all the human resource retraining that implies.

Before you can configure your server, you must know what you're trying to accommodate in the way of process and business rules. To determine these, you coalesce what you've already learned through the assessment phase into the requirements that you'll now gather to flesh out the basis for your configuration. In working along with this chapter you'll fill out a Requirements Template document in Word that I have made available at http://www.projectserverexperts.com/book. The template contains the same tables shown in this book, except that the tables in the template are ready for your input.

Armed with a completed template, your Project Server configuration will proceed smoothly and without the interruptions associated with finding missing pieces that characterize an ad-hoc or otherwise poorly planned installation. Work through the template with the chapter nearby in order to understand the nature of the information you're gathering and how it will be used in Project Server.

A Pilot: Your First Iteration

For most organizations, the most feasible approach to Project Server implementation includes a proof-of-concept and/or pilot phase. Taking the software for a live test drive through some periodic project reporting rituals is the only way to validate its viability in your organization. The process presented in this chapter and the corresponding document templates provided as downloads from http://www.projectserverexperts.com/book represent an *enhanced* framework approach for requirements gathering sufficient to launch a pilot, which then gets extended into a foundation for a full-scale rollout.

Determine Process Improvement Requirements and Goals

Accept that deploying project management software requires process reengineering, even for level-three PMM-competent organizations. Be prepared to give organizational change management a lot of attention. Every time you make a requirements decision, try to imagine how it will play out in your organization. If you can *imagine* a problem, chances are it will happen. Make sure that you anticipate, document, and manage risks from requirements identification through implementation.

Determine Core Requirements

I've grouped the most critical requirement areas for initial Project Server configuration. These are core to getting something more than out-of-the-box up and running. Once you've defined the core requirements, you have enough information to extend this document with configuration-specific information and designs. Noncore requirements support information gathering for features that may or may not be implemented.

Determine Deployment Level

Before you begin to design your customizations, you should define the deployment audience for the application and how application data gets protected across that audience. Doing this well includes keeping things simple yet deep enough to represent current and reasonably certain future requirements. How will you deploy Project Server in your organization? What audience will it serve?

A deployment confined to a single department is straightforward. Outline code values can reflect the department's internal view of the organization. An interdepartmental deployment in which departments share a single portfolio database is designed differently than when multiple instances of Project Server are created on one server. The important thing to know is where to set the margins for your custom structures. If your goal is ultimately to deploy across departments under one portfolio umbrella, then you should represent or at least allow for it in outline code structures that represent your organization.

Define the Project

Microsoft Project largely supports project management practices and assumes familiarity with organizational constructs of organizations that practice this management discipline at least somewhat by the Project Management Institute's (PMI's) Project Management Body of Knowledge (PMBOK). Project Server adopters who want a lighter implementation may still find value in less sophisticated adaptations provided they understand the tradeoffs.

You'll need to define what your organization means by "project." Does your organization's definition of a project match PMI's definition of a project? If not, how does it vary? Will you use projects to track maintenance type of work? If so, what adaptations will be required to accommodate this? Primarily, you want to identify exceptions so that you can deal with them in the configuration design.

Define the Project Organization

Because the primary purpose of project management software is to enhance the project management process, your organizational approach to project management is square one in requirements gathering. I've stressed the importance of the assessment phase and mending the organizational disconnects; this is where you define the future state of the project organization that your Project Server implementation is designed to support while or after you implement the necessary process changes in your organization.

At this point you'll begin using the tables provided in the template document. Remember that it's perfectly OK to modify the tables or establish breaks in them to insert additional explanatory information and narrative content as you feel appropriate.

Table 3-1 contains the key requirements-gathering points for defining the project organization of your company. Often, you'll use "N/A" (not applicable) as an appropriate answer. Make sure you've thought these N/As out carefully.

Table 3-1. Requirements Gathering Points for the Project Organization

REQUIREMENT	VALUE
Total number of active projects to accommodate.	
Near-future number if deployment expansion is a near-term goal.	
Average project size in number of tasks.	
Largest expected project in number of tasks.	
Average project duration (can be expressed in elapsed time or duration units, and note which method you're using).	
Longest anticipated project duration (can be expressed in elapsed time or duration units, and note which method you're using).	
Will external dependencies be used? (Y/N)	
Earned value method used (physical, work, N/A).	
Total number of system users.	
Total number of human resources.	

Table 3-1. Requirements Gathering Points for the Project Organization (Continued)

REQUIREMENT	VALUE
Total number of other work resources.	
Total number of material resources.	
Does the company span multiple locations? (Y/N; if Y, provide details.)	
Do projects span multiple locations? (Y/N; if Y, describe control structure and resource sharing plan.)	
Do location codes exist? (Y/N)	
Will Project Professional users span multiple locations? (Y/N)	
Will Project Web Access users span multiple locations? (Y/N)	
Is this a single locale or multiple language installation?	
Are Master Projects allowed? (Y/N; if Y, explain management strategy.)	
Will the system specify a single currency setting? (Y/N; if yes, provide.)	
Will project managers be allowed to use local base calendars? (Y/N)	
Define date range for long-range resource availability information.	
Define date range for OLAP information and frequency of update.	
Who will be responsible for maintaining resource data?	
Who will be responsible for maintaining project artifacts?	
Who will be responsible for updating resource calendar data?	
Authentication method for the Project Server.	
Minimum password length.	
Require server authentication prior to publishing? (Y/N)	

Define Project-Level Characteristics

After you understand the greater project organizational needs, you must delve into more project-specific requirements. To be effective, you must look for hidden treasures in existing project documents. You're looking for the appearance of repetitive data across multiple reports. How do your users want to see project data expressed? Your challenge is to find project attributes that will help to mold your portfolio presentation. Table 3-2 includes the pointers you'll need to identify requirements in this section.

Table 3-2. Project-Level Requirements

REQUIREMENT	VALUE
Describe project life-cycle phases and the importance of these to management reporting.	
Is there a corporate project numbering system? (Y/N; if yes, specify.)	
Are there accounting codes that are applied at the project level? (Y/N; if yes, specify.)	
Are individual projects aggregated into programs supporting related initiatives? (Y/N; if yes, describe.)	
Are programs aggregated into multiple portfolios? (Y/N; if yes, describe.)	
Are projects identified by client or consumer entity? (Y/N; if yes, describe.)	
Describe other unique identifiers for projects that may be required for reporting or interfaces with other host applications that may apply.	
Describe informational fields to be maintained at the project level.	
Is there a need for archived versions of projects in the data store? (Y/N; if yes, describe.)	

Define the Task Organization

Like seeking characteristics at the project level, hunting down requirements at the task level involves reviewing existing reports and documents. What does your organization wish to track to the task level? Are there accounting or job codes to capture? Review Table 3-3 and include these points in your requirements discussions.

Table 3-3. Task Organization

REQUIREMENT	VALUE
Are there job codes or accounting codes associated with tasks? (Y/N; if yes, describe.)	
What is a typical default task type?	
Is task scheduling effort-driven? (Y/N)	
Is a unique Work Breakdown Structure (WBS) used? (Y/N; if yes incorporate description in text.)	
Describe other unique identifiers for tasks that may be required for reporting or interfaces with other host applications.	

Define the Resource Organization

The consumption of resources drives project cost. Therefore, capturing attributes for the enterprise resource pool is one of the most important requirements-gathering activities. Not only must you understand how resources get acquired for project work, but you must also understand the reporting structures in the organization in order to take full advantage of all of the security features in Project Server.

To help you identify resource organization attributes, look at typical sources of resource information such as the company address book, the Active Directory (if you can access it), and HR information available to you. Review Table 3-4 and record information pertinent to your organization. Identify where your initial resource data will come from.

Table 3-4. Resource Organization

REQUIREMENT	VALUE
Will the Resource Breakdown Structure (RBS) be implemented? (Y/N; if yes, provide RBS definition.)	
Are rate tables required? (Y/N; if yes, provide rate table definitions.)	
Describe other unique identifiers for resources that may be required for reporting or interfaces with other host applications.	
Are skill sets currently defined for resources? (Y/N; if yes, describe or provide reference to attachment.)	

Table 3-4. Resource Organization (Continued)

REQUIREMENT	VALUE
Do location attributes apply to resources? (Y/N)	
Describe other attributes that target resource selection.	
Describe ways that resources are categorized in the company for reporting, management, and accounting purposes.	
Describe the source(s) for resource data.	

Identify Default Working Times and Alternate Calendars

Setting this information up has always been an underlying requirement to using the Project client effectively. With Project Server, you configure working times once at the server and the calendars become available to all users through the system. You must identify calendars required for human resources and nonhuman work resources if you implement them as determined with the guidance of Table 3-5.

Table 3-5. Calendars and Default Working Times

REQUIREMENT	VALUE
Describe the default working times for your company.	
Describe additional calendars required for your implementation for tasks or resources.	
Are resource units adjusted to account for nonproject time in scheduling? (Y/N; if no, describe calendar method.)	

Define Project Tracking Methods and Options

Tracking methods and tracking options determine how resources report on tasks and control the appearance of timesheets for team members. Choosing a tracking method is a core decision driven primarily by the degree to which an organization values accurate effort tracking. In the world of project management maturity, high-achiever organizations track effort. There are, however, organizations that are typically time-to-market driven that don't value effort tracking. For these organizations, a less accurate approach to tracking is good enough.

Does your organization want to track effort as accurately as possible? If so, have resources report hours worked and hours remaining against task work. Use Percent Work Complete only for date-driven planning where tasks planning is predominately a fixed duration. In this case, effort is inferred and calculated by Project Server and is therefore less accurate. In my experience, percentages climb faster earlier in the life of the task than they do later in the life of the task.

If project tasks in your organization's world are predominately fixed work, where you are almost certain that effort doesn't vary, having resources report hours worked only without reporting remaining work or percentage complete might be right for your organization. This approach has the disadvantage of quietly marking tasks complete without manual intervention, because there's no systemic data conveyed to indicate delay rather than completion. Take this approach if you're only looking for a data capture of hours worked. Review Table 3-6 for guidance with regard to capturing your requirements.

Table 3-6. Determining Tracking Methods

REQUIREMENT	VALUE
Will a single-tracking method be enforced or will project managers choose the reporting method for each project?	
Specify the default tracking method.	
Define the default start day of a week.	
Will timesheets span weekly or monthly periods?	
If timesheets will span weekly periods, how many weeks should display in the timesheet?	
If timesheets will span monthly periods, how many reporting periods in a month? (Up to three may be defined—specify start and stop parameters for all specified.)	
Will time entries be made by the day, by the week, or by the time period?	
What is the maximum number of hours a resource may report in a given day?	
Current tasks are defined as tasks that start up to how many days from the current date?	
Will you collect nonproject time? (Y/N; if yes, specify categories.)	

Determine Security Requirements

To determine security requirements, you should bring the organizational chart to the table. Explain how access to project or resource data might be affected by a person's position on the organizational chart. You must define security rules for the Project Server roles you've identified for use in your organization. Consider how these might be defined by a person's role in the project organization as described in Table 3-7.

Table 3-7. Defining Security Requirements

REQUIREMENT	VALUE
Define who has access to all project data across the enterprise.	
By role, describe the criteria by which an executive, project manager, resource manager, team lead, or resource has access to project data.	
By role, describe the criteria by which an executive, project manager, resource manager, team lead, or resource has access to resource data.	
Define special roles of internal or extranet users and the data access they should have.	

Define Training Requirements

Every implementation of Project Server benefits when user training is incorporated into the project. Determine an individual's need for practical Project Server knowledge by his or her role in the system (see Table 3-8). Make your training role-appropriate and deliver it in step with the actual implementation. You should also consider engaging mentoring help at critical points early in the launch, such as the first day that users report progress and project managers accept it.

Table 3-8. Training Requirements

ROLE	NUMBER TO TRAIN
Technical administrators	
Project office administrators	
Project manager	
Team member	
Team leader	
Resource manager	
Executive	
Other/custom	

Project Templates

Project templates are an important inclusion in an enterprise project management system because of the time they save. Templates contribute to standardization in that they provide a fully structured standardized framework, cost model, and resource profile as a starting point. Using a template, a project manager can save weeks of work that he or she would otherwise have to spend creating a base plan for a new project.

If your organization already makes use of templates, you'll want to assess these for improvement for use with Project Server. You must update project templates coming from prior versions to address enterprise custom fields and generic resources as a tool for resource requirements modeling. First identify the project templates, and then update them for import into your new Project Server implementation.

Project Files

Identifying all existing plans for import into the enterprise system is essential. As with templates, it's necessary to determine if these plans require updating and modifying prior to importing them into your new system. In most cases, both templates and project files will require that new information be gathered for values that will now be enforced through the enterprise. Reviewing the material on configuration in Chapters 8 through 12 can help prepare you to understand and anticipate these needs.

Define Noncore Requirements

The topics covered up to this point in the chapter have focused on the core requirements you must work through to achieve a properly considered configuration of Project Server. These requirements are addressed generically in a project management world. The requirement topics I call *noncore* are those that deal with Project Server–specific customizations that you might not immediately identify as something you want unless you first were made aware of their availability.

Library and Issues Customization

SharePoint Team Services pages are customizable using SharePoint administration and, to some degree, using tools in the interface. You may identify nonstandard fields and views within SharePoint screens and apply them to the enterprise.

Menu Customization

Project Server allows you to augment and reorder menus. Specify your required changes to Project Server Web Access Menus in this section of the template.

Project Guide Customizations

The Project Guide is a new feature within the Project client. You can use enterprise customizations to the Project Guide to enforce workflow and process through step-by-step structured interfaces customized using the base functionality provided out-of-the-box. Enumerate customization requirements in this template section.

Custom Gantt Chart Formats

You can control the display of Gantt charts throughout Project and Project Web Access by setting options. You can apply various colors and graphic styles to highlight information or customize appearance. List any nonstandard Gantt formats required in this template section.

Custom Grouping Formats

You may design and save grouping formats for both Project and Project Web Access. List any nonstandard grouping formats required in this template section.

Add System Design Information

To save time, I suggest that after you build your requirements using the template, you save an archive version and then plug in system design information and settings as you determine them. When you add them to the requirements document, the specifications complete a one-source record for use while you create and maintain your configuration. This doesn't apply to requirements that include extensive customizations that include coding or that may demand requirements and specification documentation of their own.

Notifications

Record information relative to your installation in Table 3-9.

Table 3-9. Notification Service Information

REQUIREMENT	VALUE
Default e-mail message	
From address	
Company e-mail address	
SMTP server	
SMTP port	
Daily runtime	

SharePoint Team Services Information

Record information relative to your SharePoint Team Services installation in Table 3-10.

Table 3-10. SharePoint Team Services Information

REQUIREMENT	VALUE
SharePoint Server name	
Port #	
Administration port #	
SSL port	
Database server name	
Database name	
Set server to automatic or manual subweb creation?	
Automatically or manually add users to subwebs?	
Automatically add users to Public Documents subweb project manager role?	

Home Page Content and Link Additions

Record home page links and content links in Table 3-11.

Table 3-11. Home Page Content and Links

REQUIREMENT	VALUE
Specify URLs to add.	
Specify content links to add.	

Server Register

Record your server names and OS in Table 3-12.

Table 3-12. Servers in the Configuration

MACHINE	NAME	OS
Microsoft Project Server		
SharePoint Team Services		
SQL Server 2000 Database Server		
Notification Server (SMTP)		
Analysis Server		
Terminal Services Server		
Other		

Define Custom Fields from Requirements

Once you've finished gathering your requirements, you must translate the custom attribute requirements into enterprise fields and outline codes. Remember that any attribute that you'd like to become a dimension in the OLAP cube must be created as an outline code.

Because custom field names don't publish to the fields list in Project Web Access when building views, it's essential to have an easy-to-read record of your customizations. The format of the grid shown in Figure 3-1 comes from the chapter's accompanying template and is one that I recommend you use to record your field definitions. I use an abbreviation system for representing the codes. (If you're new to Project Server, you may want to read more about custom fields and codes in Chapter 8 before completing your design.)

Field Label	Field	Mand	List	Defit	Description/Notes
Project					
Program	EPOC01	N	PM Methods QA Methods Cnfiguration Infrastructure Consumer Maintenance	None	Identifies Project for Portfolio associations
Sponsor	EPOC02 SH: EROC05	Y	Executive HR Marketing Finance Legal Administration Operations Distribution	None	Department owning the project from the business side
Project Type	EPOC03	Y	Corproate Departmental Enhancement Legacy IS-Internal	None	
Resource					

Figure 3-1. Custom fields design grid

Columns represented include the Field Label, which is the descriptive name you'll give the field. Next, the Field column contains an abbreviation structure for representing specific fields described in the following abbreviation list. The third column tracks whether the field is mandatory or optional. The fourth column contains a value list if one applies, and the fifth column contains a specified default value. Finally, the sixth column is a place to make some notes that further describe your intention for the field.

Enterprise fields come in three flavors: project, task, and resource. In the abbreviations shown in the grid, "E" represents enterprise and "P" represents project. Use "R" and "T" to represent resource and task, respectively. The next two letters in the coded abbreviation are used as follows:

OC = outline code

TX = text field

CO = cost field

NU = number

FG = flag field

DT = date

DU = duration

Follow the first four letters with a number to identify which field number is designated for this use. There you have it, a six-character representation for all of your custom fields.

Lastly, note that in the Field column, some additional entries are added. "SH" indicates that the field "shares" a value list with the field listed on the next line. This will remind you to set it up this way when you actually perform the customizations.

Summary

This chapter provided you with a guide to requirements gathering using the Project Requirements Word template. Download these template files from http://www.projectserverexperts.com/book. Information is organized to speed you through the physical configuration process covered in the next section. Use or change these templates to meet your personal comfort or your organizational requirements.

CHAPTER 4

Designing a Physical Deployment

Enterprise Project Server deployments involve a mélange of technologies that are installed on one server or distributed across many. A single installation may serve a workgroup, a department, or an entire company. To complicate things further, Project Server can be deployed to serve a company under one umbrella or by segregating instances within a single deployment.

In this chapter I sort through the pros and cons of various approaches, from compact implementations to distributed models. I discuss these approaches conceptually here to aid you in your planning process. Chapters 5 and 7 cover the tactics and techniques you'll need to deploy these configurations. Chapter 7, in particular, covers the more advanced material.

Choosing Hardware

Along with the misconception that Project Server is going to be a snap to install, many folks have the notion that it will perform well on any old PC box. Nothing could be further from the truth. Although Project Server seems to be a simple Web application, under the hood it uses power-hungry technologies. Even a small implementation deserves hardware designed for server applications.

When I use the term "server hardware," I'm referring to a box with a backplane, and a minimum of two processors and 2GB of RAM. Your hard drives should be fast SCSI preferably configured in a RAID 5 array. Without the RAID controllers, boxes like this from Dell and Compaq price out at just under $5,000.00 at the time of this writing. This should be your minimum standard. Very large implementations will benefit from using isolated gigabit segments for connectivity between the servers and SQL clusters running on Fibre Channel RAID arrays. Yes, Fibre Channel technology is very high end, and it's applicable only to very large implementations, but my point is that there's fast hardware, and there's really fast hardware.

If you're contemplating a large implementation, one that's intended to serve as many as 1,000 users, expect to dedicate up to five servers to your installation. Project planners, who must update project plans across the Internet or across high-latency and low-bandwidth connections, require a solution such as Terminal Services or a similar technology. You'll need to add a server to support this, too.

Environment Requirements

Enterprise implementations require Windows Authentication within an NT or Active Directory domain. This is essential to a working enterprise configuration. Without a domain, you entirely lose the ability to use SharePoint Team Services (STS) and Analysis Services. Both of these services require Windows Authentication. You also must have a domain to deploy Project Server components, including SQL Server, across two or more boxes. Project Server talks to STS and Analysis Services through COM+ objects that run under Windows identities. These can't be local machine accounts once a second server is added, because one machine's local account isn't recognized by another machine. This is true even when the usernames are the same, as the credentials are passed as *machinename\username*. On the other hand, a domain account is passed as *domainname\username*, which can be resolved by any domain member machine.

Working across multiple domains isn't a problem as long as you establish the proper trust relationships. Without the trusts, you'll run into the same types of problems you encounter with local machine accounts. The credentials will be rejected. I've heard of an implementation that circumvented trusts by using a customized Lightweight Directory Access Protocol (LDAP) solution. Suffice it to say that this is a challenge for very technically skilled folks with plenty of funding, as this isn't a native capability. Generally speaking, it's a good idea to keep all your Project Server boxes in the same domain. Users can access the system from any trusted domain.

Using Project and Project Server Across Low-Bandwidth Connections

Project Web Access, the Web application portion of the Project Server application, can be exposed to the Internet to allow remote users to report progress through timesheets and to view project information. The recommended way to implement Internet connectivity is using basic authentication over Secure Sockets Layer (SSL). Keep in mind that SSL places a heavier load on the IIS server and size your server accordingly if you plan on taking this approach.

In a multiserver environment, both Analysis Services and STS won't be available to the Internet users, as these services require Windows Authentication. You can overcome this by adding a Virtual Private Network (VPN) solution so that users entering from the network have domain credentials to pass to these services. A number of VPN hardware solutions are available, and you can deploy Windows Remote Access Service (RAS) to provide remote users a domain logon. In order to expose any of the OLAP functionality through the Internet, you'll need to set up SQL Analysis Services to respond to HTTP requests. The catch here is that this functionality is available only with the Enterprise Edition of SQL Server, which carries a hefty price tag. Typically, a VPN solution proves to be more economical for smaller companies, and it resolves the access issue for both Analysis Services and STS.

Although Project Web Access is very usable across the Internet or other low-bandwidth connections, Project Professional 2002 remains a Win32 application that requires a minimum of 10MB connections (LAN speed) to perform adequately according to Microsoft's recommendations. Project Professional is simply not very usable connecting to Project Server across the Internet or slow WAN links for that matter. With a VPN solution or via SSL, it can be done; however, opening and saving project plans can be go-out-to-Starbucks-for-coffee slow! This arrangement is painful at best. It's also problematic as latency in the network can cause the user session to timeout the SQL connection. Keep in mind that, once authenticated through Project Server, Project Professional talks directly to SQL Server across port 1433. This can be a substantial problem with your company's security policies! If you're willing to adjust the SQL timeout and suffer the long open and close times, then the way to use Project remotely is to employ the Save offline and Save online features. The best way to overcome this limitation is to deploy Project Professional on Terminal Services, Citrix, or another similar technology.

Scaling Project Server Deployments

Microsoft has provided support for a number of scalability options when deploying Project Server. Both clustering and load balancing can be leveraged, and various components of a Project Server implementation can be distributed across servers to achieve performance gains.

Failover clustering is supported for SQL Server, which adds availability, not scalability. In this type of clustering arrangement, one server responds to user requests while the other server exists to detect a failure in the primary server, taking over the load seamlessly if the need arises. The second server is otherwise idle, so it's common practice to use a lesser box for failover where reduced performance is acceptable in the event of a primary server failure. Clustering is a service available in Windows 2000 Advanced Server or Datacenter Server editions only. This feature isn't available in Windows 2000 Server standard edition. Clustering can also be applied to the application servers running other Project Server components, but this isn't compatible with STS. In other words, if Project Server and STS are installed on the same application server, you can't cluster it.

Microsoft provides *Network Load Balancing* (NLB) as a service in IIS. Using Microsoft's NLB, up to 32 servers can constitute a server farm. You can use hardware solutions from Cisco, F5, and others, and these solutions may not have the same limitation. It's unlikely that a 32-server limitation is a problem unless all your boxes are P2 450 MHz machines. The fact is that, when using current technologies, your system isn't likely to approach the 32-server limit. Inasmuch as NLB also detects failures in the farm, I believe it's a better solution for availability for Web servers than clustering. All the servers in the farm share the load equally, which addresses scalability as well as availability. Of course, you can also load balance clusters!

You achieve scalability in Project Server largely by distributing various application components across multiple servers. The components of Project Server that you can distribute across various servers are as follows:

- *Project Web Access:* The IIS ASP application

- *Project Server database:* The database containing project data

- *SharePoint Team Services:* Provides the document and issues management services accessed through Project Web Access

- *SQL Analysis Services:* Provides OLAP services for Analyzer views and the modeler

- *Microsoft Session Manager Service:* Replaces ASP sessions for Project Server and tracks user sessions

- *Views Notification service:* Handles the updating of information between the Project tables in the database and the Web tables that drive Project Web Access views

Scaling Project Server implementations by distributing these components is fairly straightforward. The first step toward a scaled implementation is to separate the Project Server application server from the database server. Figure 4-1 shows a simple two-server implementation.

The next logical step is to give STS its own box. This is particularly helpful if your teams are making heavy use of the issues and document libraries features. Figure 4-2 shows a three-server implementation.

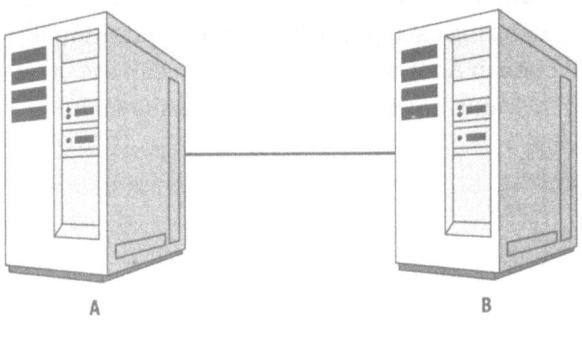

Simple Two-Server Configuration

```
A: IIS, Project Server, SharePoint Team Services
B: SQL Server, Analysis Services
```

Figure 4-1. Two-server implementation

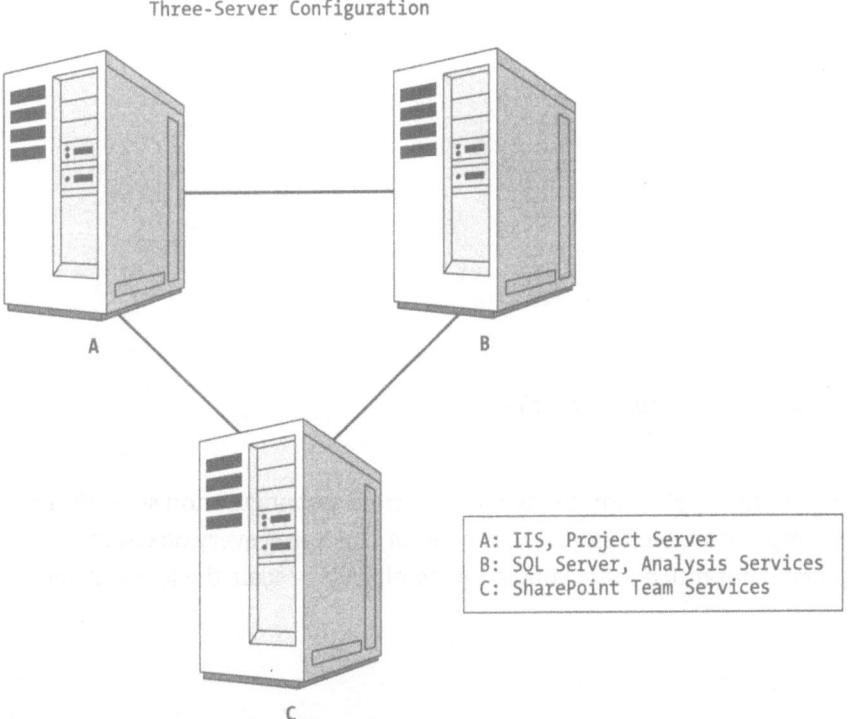

Three-Server Configuration

```
A: IIS, Project Server
B: SQL Server, Analysis Services
C: SharePoint Team Services
```

Figure 4-2. Three-server implementation

Adding a fourth server allows you to offload the Views Notification service, which is a notorious resource consumer. This service gets activated every time projects are saved to the server and during each publish operation. Additionally, it controls the build of the OLAP cube in Analysis Services. As you can see, it's a prime candidate for its own server. A four-box implementation is shown in Figure 4-3.

Four-Server Configuration

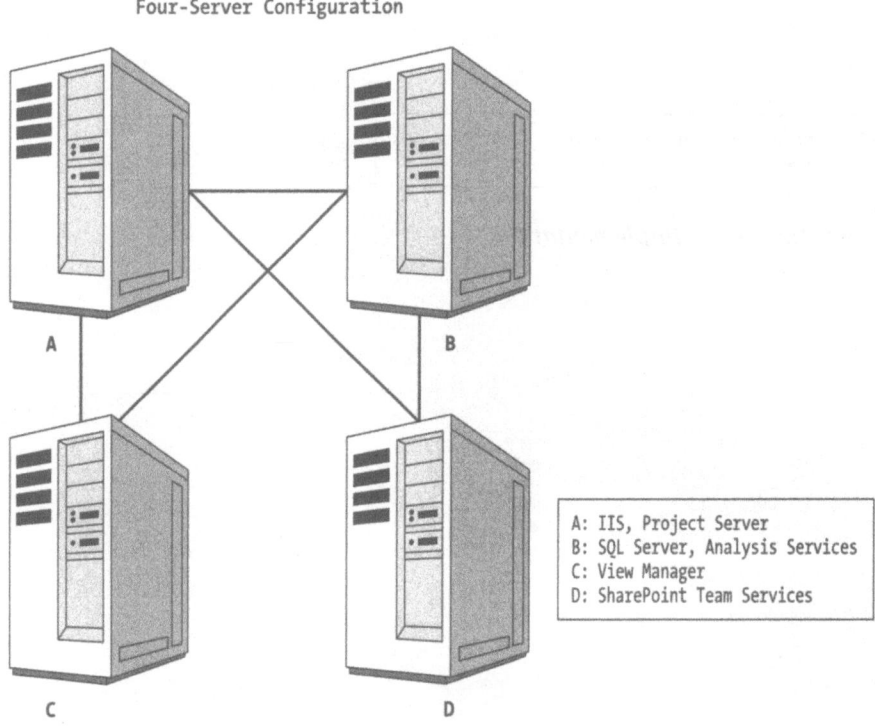

A: IIS, Project Server
B: SQL Server, Analysis Services
C: View Manager
D: SharePoint Team Services

Figure 4-3. Four-server implementation

Scaling out the application to the max will yield a configuration something like the one represented in Figure 4-4. Except for clustering every box in the diagram, there's not much more you can do to physically scale the application environment.

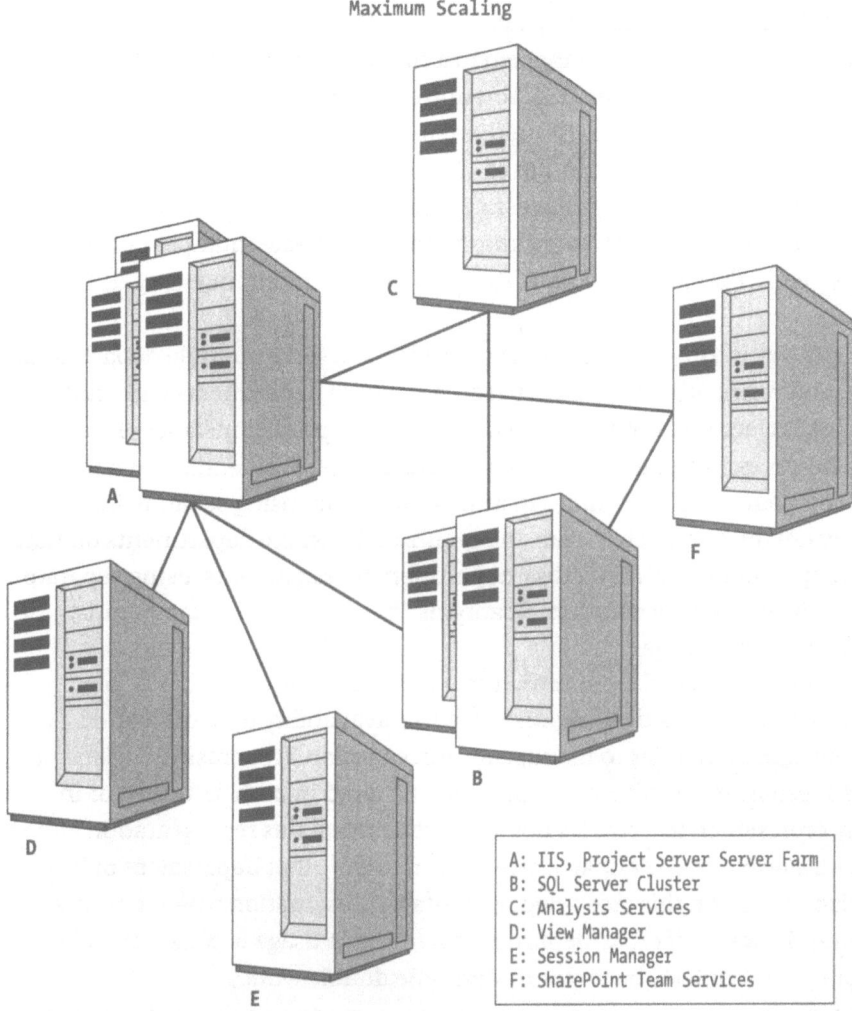

Maximum Scaling

A: IIS, Project Server Server Farm
B: SQL Server Cluster
C: Analysis Services
D: View Manager
E: Session Manager
F: SharePoint Team Services

Figure 4-4. Multiserver implementation

Before you go overboard and order a dozen servers, or faint from the mere thought of it, there are other measures you can take to scale and maximize your implementation's performance. Two significant obstacles to scaling Project Server implementations are STS and the Project Server database itself. The data tables in the Project Server database can't be distributed across multiple servers, so at some point, your SQL Server capacity poses a hard limit on scalability. Here the answer truly is hardware horsepower and connectivity. The number of processors, disk drive speed, RAM, and connectivity between the database server and the application server running Project Web Access are all focal points. Add network interface cards (NICs) to your servers to widen the pipe. This is an inexpensive and easy-to-implement performance tactic.

Only one STS site may be connected to a single instance of Project Server with automatic subweb creation enabled. You don't have the option of farming this service, but you can add servers if you're willing to manage subweb creation manually. Microsoft indicates a maximum of 750 subwebs per server instance. As each project gets its own subweb, this necessarily translates to a 750 active project limit per Project Server instance. The way around this is to create multiple instances of Project Server on the same hardware, except that each additional site gets its own STS server.

This strategy is a no-brainer when you're trying to serve multiple departments across an enterprise. It's often better to serve multiple departments with multiple instances of Project Server rather than one all-encompassing instance. This decision, however, must take resource pool usage into consideration. When departments share many resources in a substantial way, using separate instances is probably not the approach to take. In organizations where departments operate mostly independently with few cross-departmental assignments, using separate instances is likely the best solution. Stratifying Project Server instances must follow resource pool usage.

Where substantial cross-departmental resource usage occurs, multiple instances become impractical because resource availability isn't articulated between instances. In order to manage resource availability across two instances, the shared resources must have assignments mirrored in both instances or in some way represented in both. It's not difficult to create this representation either by blocking a resource's calendar when on loan to the other department or by creating a plan to contain this cross-departmental representation when it occurs infrequently. However, if cross-departmental resource usage is constant and a regular practice, it quickly becomes undesirable double work.

If it's practical for you to implement two or more separate instances, you also overcome the performance issues that crop up when the resource pool approaches 1,000 resources. The larger it gets, the longer it takes to open and save. This is the inevitable consequence of manipulating large datasets.

Strategizing Your Growth Path

Many IT managers are tempted to start with smaller, less powerful servers with the intention of replacing the servers as usage demands. This is a reasonable strategy to a point, but you should take a couple things into consideration if you choose this approach. On the top of this short list is the difficulty involved in migrating STS servers. Avoid this by implementing STS on its own server if you know that's where you're headed to begin with. Make sure the server box you use has the necessary capacity.

The other concern is distributing the Views Notification service to a separate box after you've run your Project Server implementation for a while. In a white paper titled "Best Practices for an Enterprise Deployment of Microsoft Project Server 2002," Lou Lucarelli of Microsoft cautions, "If Views Notification services are off-loaded after your deployment of Microsoft Project Server, then you can run into other serious issues, including updating the registry in the Views Notification server, and provisioning errors." The white paper is available on TechNet and is a must-read for anyone contemplating large-scale implementations. Also see "Distributed Deployment: Microsoft Project 2002," available on TechNet. TechNet links are very long, so I won't include them here. Go to http://www.microsoft.com/technet and expand the Products and Technologies tree until you locate the section on Microsoft Project. Go to http://www.projectserverexperts.com for the latest versions of links cited in this book.

With the exception of the preceding two considerations, it's possible to migrate the database from box to box as it's fairly simple. Adding or upgrading applications servers running IIS is also doable. You can accomplish these types of migrations by using the installation techniques covered in Chapter 5 and under-standing the registry entries covered in Chapter 7.

Summary

Choosing the right hardware and hardware configuration deserves a conscientious planning effort that seeks to identify the future state of the deployment. Wise hardware selections and proper planning will help you to avoid painful service outages and future server migrations.

Part Two
Installation and Installation Troubleshooting

Installing SharePoint Team Services and Project Server

Installing Project Server can be a daunting task, not just the first time but even the third, fourth, or fifth time you attempt it, because there are numerous detailed steps and you must execute many of them manually. By taking the very structured approach I present in this chapter, and following each step and checkpoint in order, installing SharePoint Team Services (STS) and Project Server can be relatively quick and painless. Failure to adhere to these procedures can lead you to many hours of troubleshooting. Indeed, this is a strong warning, but I can't overstate the pitfalls of installation.

In this chapter, I take you through the installation steps for deploying with Project Server, STS, and SQL Server on one box, as well as variances to deploying across two or three servers.

 NOTE These instructions apply to an enterprise implementation and not to a workgroup implementation. I cover advanced scaling techniques as an addendum to the core installation process in a later chapter.

Instructions in this chapter are based on installing on the Windows 2000 Server family. These instructions don't apply to beta or released to manufacturing (RTM) versions of Windows Server 2003. Look for potential service releases in the Microsoft Knowledge Base and TechNet Web sites for the latest information, and check the Apress Web site at http://www.apress.com/book/bookDisplay.html?bID=185 for updates to this book.

Project Server requires a domain to take advantage of all enterprise features. Installations outside of a domain security environment are problematic in a number of ways. STS requires Windows Integrated Authentication; therefore, you must provide at least a local logon for each user on the machine on which STS is running. Project Professional isn't designed to talk to Project Server over the Internet. It's very "chatty," with the database making numerous data calls that return large record sets. This makes it clunky at low bandwidths and frame-relay networks.

Before Beginning the Installation Process

Your server, or servers, are of adequate processor power and memory capacity and are prepared with the Windows 2000 Server operating system (OS) with Service Pack 2 (SP2). One of these boxes has SQL Server 2000 and Analysis Services installed, both with SP2. Any of these servers, which are intended to run Project Server or STS, have IIS installed without any server extensions.

Further, this is the first time you're attempting to install STS and Project Server on these machines. If not, you've read the sections on uninstalling Project Server and STS in the next chapter and have verified that you've completed all the required steps.

For the purposes of this book, I'm assuming that everything is installed in a domain environment and the server that will be running Project Server and/or STS is dedicated to this purpose and isn't running any other applications or Web sites.

 TIP   STS, in particular, doesn't always play well with other applications. The major concern is the unpredictable nature of these conflicts. It's impossible to completely quantify these risks, but my recommendation is to always deploy on dedicated hardware.

Consider any application that uses Microsoft Data Access Components (MDAC) a potential problem. Anecdotally, I've seen issues with BizTalk Server and problems implementing on servers that are also Primary Domain Controllers. There's no official compatibility/incompatibility list, so run other applications at your own risk.

STS is the source of most installation anomalies. Pay close attention to the preparatory steps in getting the server ready for the STS installation, as once you've successfully installed STS, the rest of your implementation is likely to proceed smoothly.

 CAUTION   Don't extend Project Server's version of STS on an existing custom STS site. The Project Server–specific version overwrites the onet.xml file on your STS site and makes other alterations to STS. Therefore, you'll lose any customizations you've already made to the existing site. If you want to test this for yourself, make certain that you first properly back up the STS site.

Before proceeding further, make certain that you have your installation media handy and, if applicable, your license keys for both Project Server and Project 2002 Professional. Keep in mind that some Project Server media types do *not* require activation keys; this varies by license type. It's also very important that you're logged onto the server with a local administrator account. Even if you're logged on as a domain administrator, your account should be explicitly added to the local administrators group or it may not work.

Installation Preparation

Review the Microsoft Project Server Installation Guide in its entirety. This is included on your installation CD as PJSVR10.CHM. Copy the file to your hard drive or a network share and read it from there. Don't try e-mailing it, as most e-mail systems prevent this type of file from being sent. This document contains valuable Project Server technical information. Everything you need to know to successfully install Project Server is contained in this document; however, it leaves many people guessing. Follow the steps I've outlined, but don't overlook the value of the manufacturer's documentation in the process.

Before you begin following my instructions, check your servers against the technology checklist shown in Table 5-1.

Table 5-1. Server Technology Checklist

TECHNOLOGY	VERSION	NOTES
Windows 2000 Server	SP2	Can be either Advanced Server or Server.
Internet Information Services	See Notes	Version 5.0 for Windows 2000.
SMTP Server	N/A	May be any external SMTP, or use built-in IIS capability.
Indexing Service	N/A	Installed and enabled.
SQL Server 2000 Analysis Server	SP2	Server name or named instance using TCP/IP and set to run in mixed authentication mode.

I also assume that you've installed your OSs and database software from original Microsoft-supplied media without any installation or postinstallation modifications. Those who modify their implementations should have the OS talent available to diagnose potential issues, particularly with security changes. Finally, if you're planning on deploying across multiple servers, you're operating in a domain environment and you're using domain logons for authentication.

For a single-server installation, you'll use the same server for Project Server, SQL Server, Analysis Services, and Indexing Service. You may also use the local SMTP service, but this is optional. For a two-server configuration, SQL Server 2000 and SQL 2000 Analysis Services are installed on one box, whereas IIS, Indexing Services, Project Server Web Access, STS, and the optional SMTP Service are on the other box. The box on which Project Server is running also has the Analysis Services Decision Support Objects (DSO) installed on it.

Verifying Installed Technologies

The first step is to verify your installed technologies. The following sections give you the steps for verifying each specific technology.

Verify Windows 2000 Server SP2

To verify Windows 2000 Server SP2, follow these steps. Open Windows Explorer and select Help ➤ Help About. You should see Windows 2000 version 5 SP2.

 **CAUTION** Project Server may not install on Windows 2000 Service Pack 3 (SP3). This has been a troublesome service pack for Microsoft. Install SP3 after you've installed Project Server and STS to avoid problems. If you must install on a server that has had SP3 applied, and you run into difficulties, contact Microsoft Support for an update.

Verify SQL Server 2000 SP2

To verify SQL Server 2000 SP2, follow these steps:

1. Click the Start button and select Programs ➤ MS SQL Server ➤ Query Analyzer.

2. Type **select @@version** and click the Execute (F5) button.

The version should be 8.00.532.

Verify Analysis Services SP2

To verify Analysis Services SP2, follow these steps:

1. Click the Start button and select Programs ➤ MS SQL Server ➤ Analysis Services ➤ Analysis Manager.

2. Right-click the Analysis Services node.

3. Click About Analysis Services.

The version should be 8.0.532.

In order to proceed with the installation, you'll need to record the server names you will be using (see Table 5-2).

Table 5-2. Server Names

SERVER	NAME	FULLY QUALIFIED DOMAIN NAME
STS/Project Server		
SQL Server		
SMTP Server		

Verifying That FrontPage Extensions Are Not Installed

The server that runs STS should *not* have FrontPage Server Extensions installed prior to installing STS. For installations on Windows 2000 Server, you must use the STS version and FrontPage Server Extensions shipped with Project Server. The pre-existence of FrontPage Server Extensions on the server will interfere with the STS installation.

The following sections describe how to verify on various servers that FrontPage Server Extensions aren't installed.

On a Windows 2000 Server, follow these steps:

1. From the Control Panel, launch Add/Remove Programs.

2. Click Add/Remove Windows Components to open the Windows Component Wizard.

3. In the Windows Component Wizard dialog box, highlight Internet Information Services (IIS).

4. Click Details.

5. Verify that the FrontPage 2000 Server Extensions option isn't checked (see Figure 5-1).

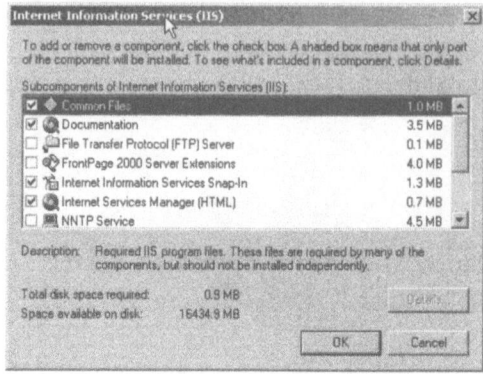

Figure 5-1. Internet Information Services subcomponent details

Checking Security Settings in IIS

In the next step you verify that IIS is configured for STS and Project Server. STS installs on a Web site while Project Server installs as a virtual directory. On Windows 2000 Server, the default Web site is an acceptable target for installing STS and Project Server. Alternately, you can choose to create a new Web site on a different port and install STS onto it. Note that the STS administrative and search sites install on the default Web site.

To check security settings, follow these steps:

1. Launch Internet Services Manager and expand the server.

2. Right-click the Default Web Site and choose Properties.

3. Select the Home Directory tab and verify that Execute Permissions is set to Scripts Only.

4. Select the Directory Security tab, click Edit in the "Anonymous access and authentication control" area, and verify that "Anonymous access and Integrated Windows authentication" is selected.

5. Click Edit in the anonymous access area and verify that "Allow IIS to control password" is checked. Click OK twice.

6. Staying on the Directory Security tab, click Edit in the "IP Address and domain name restrictions" area and verify that Granted Access is selected. Click OK twice.

7. Expand the Default Web Site, if it's not already expanded, click the MSADC virtual directory, and select Properties.

8. Select the Virtual Directory tab and verify that Execute Permissions is set to Scripts and Executables.

9. Right-click msadcs.dll in the right-hand pane and select Properties.

10. Staying on the Directory Security tab, click Edit in the "IP Address and domain name restrictions" area and select the Granted Access radio button. Click OK twice. (See Figure 5-2.)

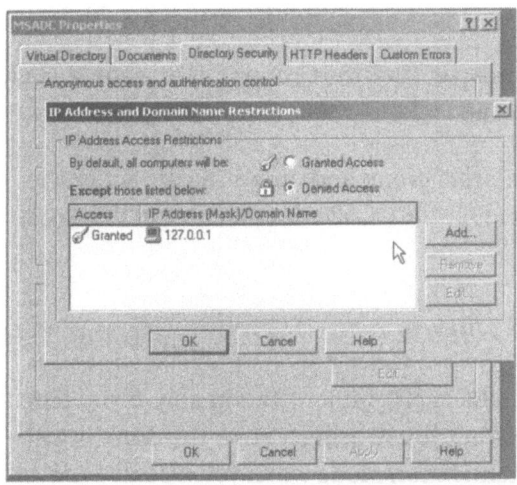

Figure 5-2. By default, IP address and domain restrictions are set to Denied.

Creating Application Accounts

Project Server connects to STS and SQL Analysis Services through COM+. This requires three application identities, one each for the administration and reader roles in STS and one for access to Analysis Services. If you're installing on one computer, these can be local machine accounts. If you're using these accounts to access services on another server, then they must be domain logons. The three accounts should look something like this:

- STS_Reader

- STS_Admin

- OLAP_Admin

To create three local accounts, follow these steps:

1. From the Control Panel, launch Administrative Tools, and then open the Computer Management Console.

2. Right-click the Users folder and choose New User.

3. Follow your company's naming convention and try to use a descriptive name that will let another administrator know what the account is for. Make sure that the "User must change password" option is unchecked and that the "Password never expires" option is checked. Make a note of the name and password for use in installation. Repeat this step for all three accounts.

4. After your new accounts are created, click the Groups folder, double-click the Administrators group, and add all three accounts to the group.

5. Now click the OLAP Administrators group and, repeating the actions in step 4, add the account created for the OLAP administrator to this group.

Verifying SQL Server Settings

Microsoft SQL Server installation defaults to NT Authentication only. If you didn't install the instance of SQL Server 2000 that you're using and/or you don't remember if you selected Mixed Authentication Mode when you installed the instance, follow these steps to make sure that SQL Server is properly configured for STS and Project Server:

1. Open the Enterprise Manager.

2. Expand the Server group.

3. Right-click a server name, and then click Properties.

4. Click the Security tab.

5. Under Authentication, click the SQL Server and Windows option button.

6. Restart SQL Server in order for the change to take effect.

 NOTE   For multiple server installations, make sure that SQL Server Decision Support Objects (DSO) are installed on the system running Project Server.

Installing STS and Project Server

All this work and not bit of STS or Project Server is installed. Having done all this preparation and verification work, your installation of STS and Project Server should now proceed without errors. Before beginning the installation, you should have the following information available (except for the STS administration port, which you won't have until you've completed STS installation).

For STS:

- Database server name

- Web server name

- Web server port

- STS account information

For Project Server:

- Product license key

- Know whether you're using the per-processor or per-seat option

- Project Server database server name

- Project Server Web server name for internal purposes

- Project Server Web server name for external access

- Analysis Server name

- SMTP Server name

- SMTP Server port (typically 25)

- SMTP From address

- Proxy Server name or address (required if you use a proxy server)

- Proxy Server port number

- Proxy Server password

- SharePoint Server name

- SharePoint Server administration port number (varies)

- SharePoint Database Server name

- SharePoint Server SSL port (typically 443)

Now you can proceed with installing STS.

Installing STS

You'll install STS first. Although the published installation procedures allow you to install Project Server first and then add an STS server to Project Server through the Project Server administration interface, more manual steps are involved in installing in this sequence. Be aware that these directions don't include the additional steps required for installing STS after Project Server. If you install Project Server before STS, you should review Microsoft Knowledge Base article Q322235.

 NOTE   STS must be installed from your Project Server installation media. Do not use a copy of STS from your Microsoft Office with FrontPage media.

1. Log onto your system using an administrator account. Insert your Project Server Installation CD into your CD-ROM drive. When the Project Server Installation splash screen appears (see Figure 5-3), select SharePoint Configuration Wizard. If autorun features are disabled on your machine, you can navigate to stswiz.exe manually by opening the Support folder. If you're installing on Windows Server 2003, use setup.exe from your Office XP CD.

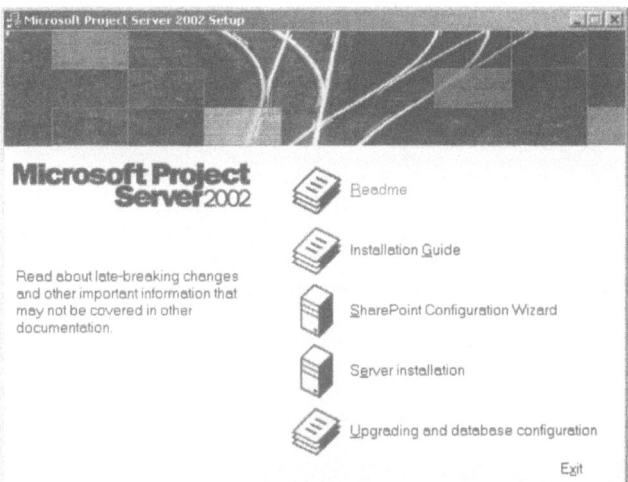

Figure 5-3. Microsoft Project Server autorun installation splash screen

2. Once you've accepted the license agreement, select the Web site on which to provision STS. If you're installing on Windows 2000, you'll likely use the Default Web Site (see Figure 5-4). For Windows Server 2003, choose the new Web site you created.

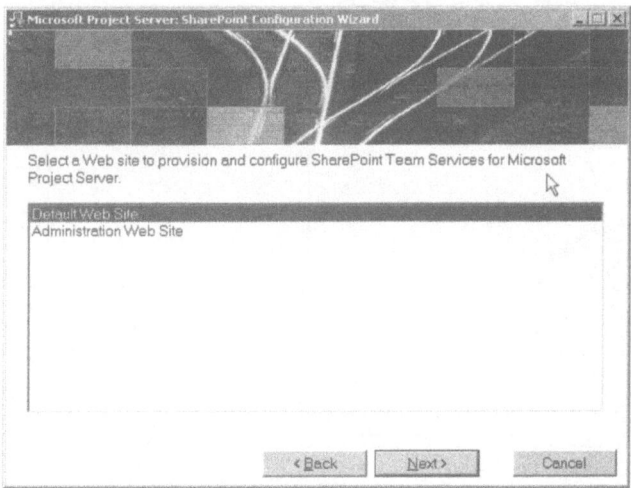

Figure 5-4. Select a Web site to provision for STS.

3. Enter the system administrator (sa) account for SQL Server (see Figure 5-5), which should be SQL Server logon, and click Next when the setup dialog box appears, confirming that you're ready to install.

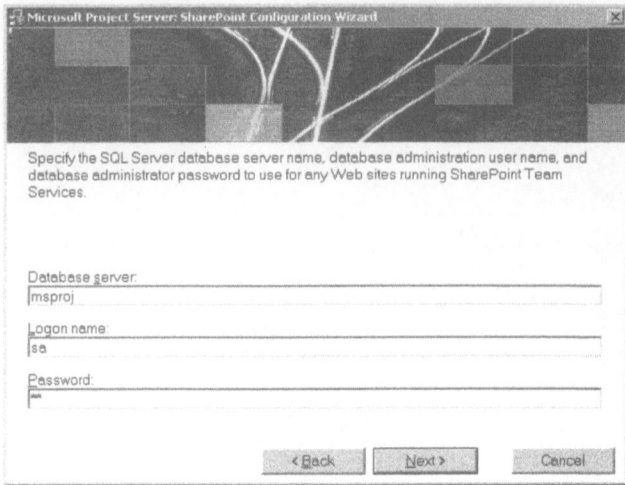

Figure 5-5. Enter the database server name and SQL Server administrator account to use for installation.

4. An install status dialog box displays to let you know that the installation is proceeding (see Figure 5-6).

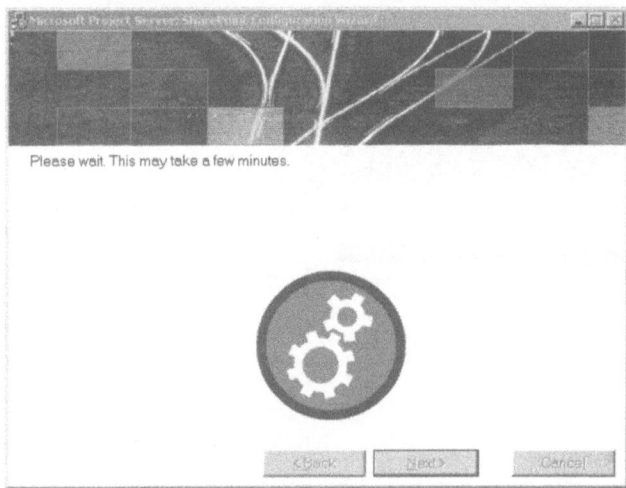

Figure 5-6. The system lets you know that the STS installation is in progress.

5. Record the information in the confirmation dialog box, which contains important information that you'll need to install Project Server (see Figure 5-7), and then click Finish. Note that the database name for STS is slightly different for some installations.

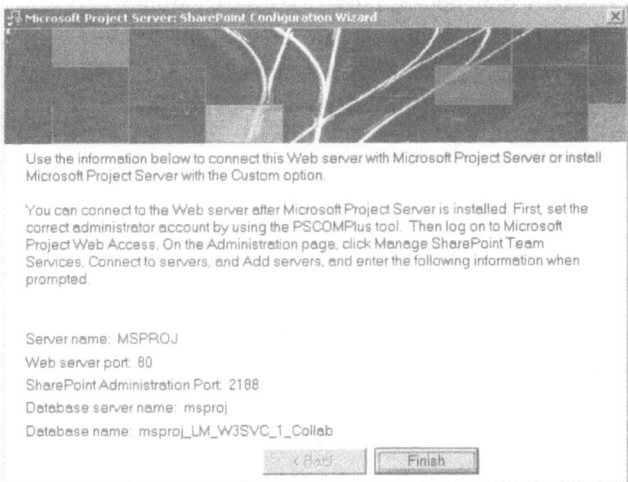

Figure 5-7. Record the information presented when installation completes.

6. Open SQL Server Enterprise Manager and verify the existence of the database name you recorded in the previous step.

Finalizing STS Installation

Before you run the Project Server installation, verify that STS is now running properly. You'll also assign the STS logon accounts their proper roles in the newly created STS database.

1. Click the Start button and select Programs ➤ Administrative Tools ➤ Microsoft SharePoint Administrator. This should take you to Microsoft SharePoint Administration. Verify that the Web site you chose to extend is listed, and that there's no option to upgrade or extend the site. If you see an upgrade or extend option next to the Web site you chose, STS installation didn't complete correctly. See the next chapter for information on troubleshooting STS. Close out of the window.

2. Open SQL Server Enterprise Manager, expand your server, and expand the Security folder. Right-click Logins and choose New Login.

3. Click the search button next to the Name field, select the STS administrator account you created earlier in setup preparation, and click Add and then OK.

4. The account appears in the SQL Server Login Properties dialog box and the system automatically selects Windows Authentication. In the Default Database drop-down list, select the STS database just created. This is typically *servername*_LM_W3SVC_1_Collab for Windows 2000. (See Figure 5-8.)

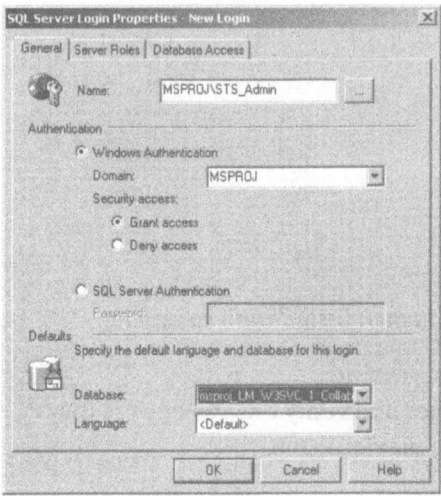

Figure 5-8. The SQL Server Login Properties dialog box

5. Click the Server Roles tab of the SQL Server Login Properties dialog box and select Security Administrators.

6. Click the Database Access tab, select the STS database and db_owner role, and click OK.

7. Repeat steps 2 through 4 for the STS reader account, but skip step 5 and select only public and db_datareader roles on the Database Access tab.

Installing Project Server

It seems as though you've been at this forever and yet you're just now getting around to the main course, but with a solid foundation, this part of the installation is easy.

1. Insert the Project Server CD into your CD-ROM drive and choose Server Installation from the autorun splash screen (see Figure 5-9).

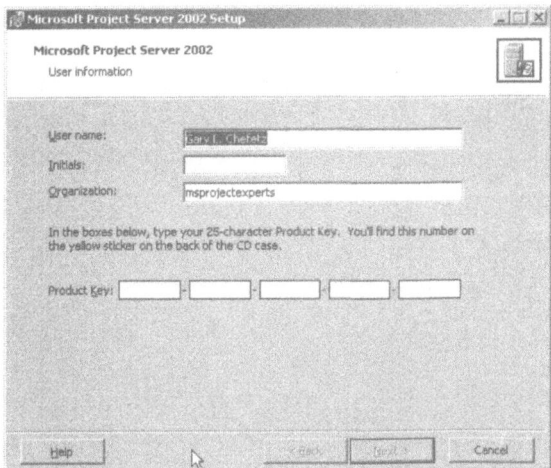

Figure 5-9. The first Project Server installation screen asks for your user details and license key.

2. Accept the end-user license agreement and click Next.

3. Choose Custom and select the directory for Project Server installation (see Figure 5-10).

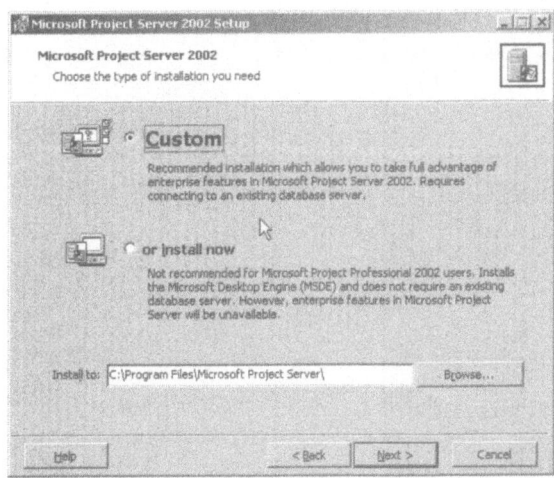

Figure 5-10. Choose Custom for an enterprise installation.

4. Select the "Create a new database" radio button, enter the name of the SQL Server in the appropriate field, and then select the SQL Server Authentication radio button and enter the sa account and password in the fields that are revealed (see Figure 5-11).

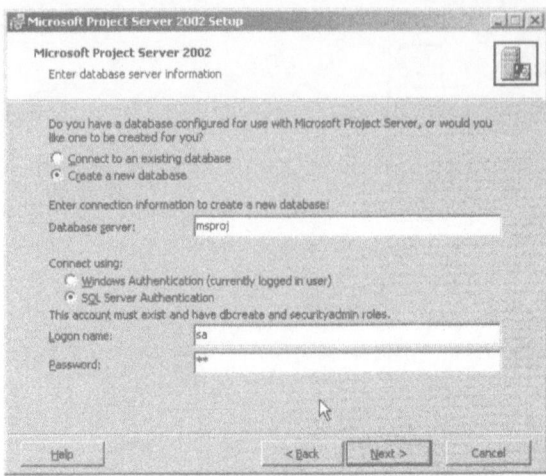

Figure 5-11. Enter the database server and connection account information.

5. Next, enter the Analysis Services information. If the "Enter this information now" radio button isn't selected by default, select it. Enter your Analysis Server name and use the OLAP administrator Windows account that you created during preparation for the logon name. Remember to use the correct format: *domain-name\username* (see Figure 5-12).

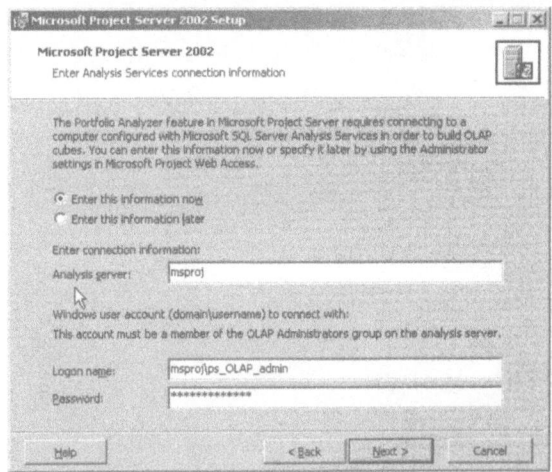

Figure 5-12. Enter the Analysis Services information now.

6. Select the Default Web Site or custom Web site name you want to use (see Figure 5-13).

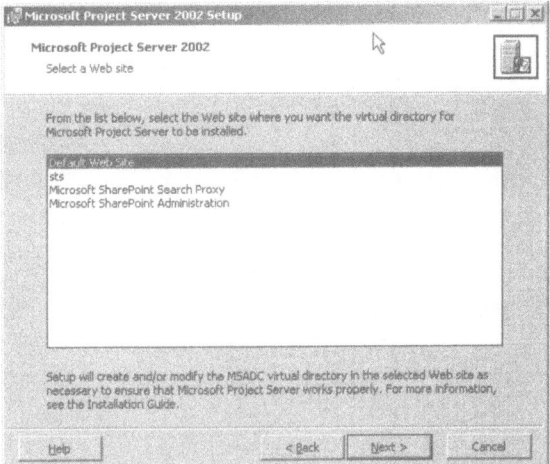

Figure 5-13. Select the Web site for your Project Server installation.

7. You must enter the intranet address for your Project Server. This must be fully resolvable for your internal users, otherwise other links expressed by the system may not function. This information can be changed postinstallation through the administration interface. The extranet information is optional at this time (see Figure 5-14).

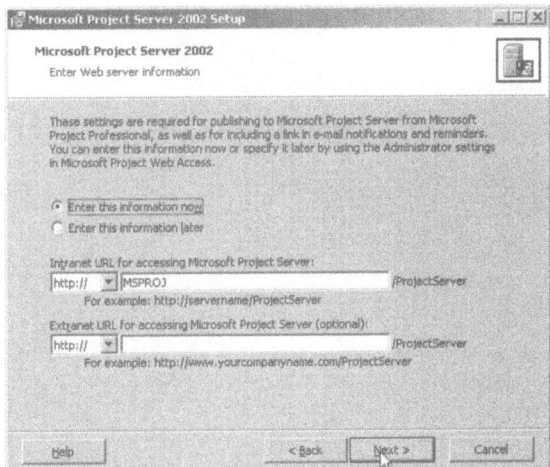

Figure 5-14. Enter the appropriate URL information for your organization.

8. Enter the SMTP information for your organization (see Figure 5-15).

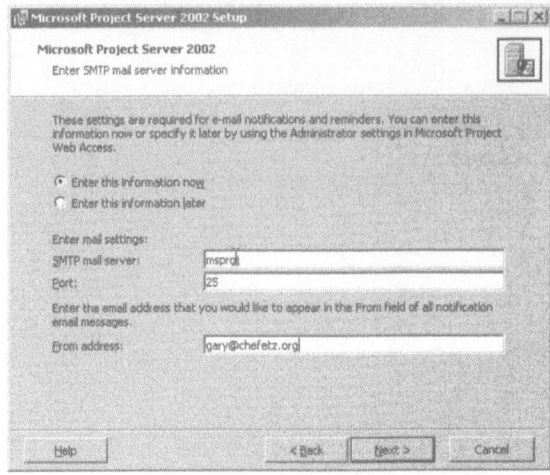

Figure 5-15. Enter the SMTP information for your organization.

9. Enter the connection information for STS. Use the STS **administrator** Windows account you created during preparation (see Figure 5-16). The default port for STS is 80. Your administration port will be different from the one shown in Figure 5-16.

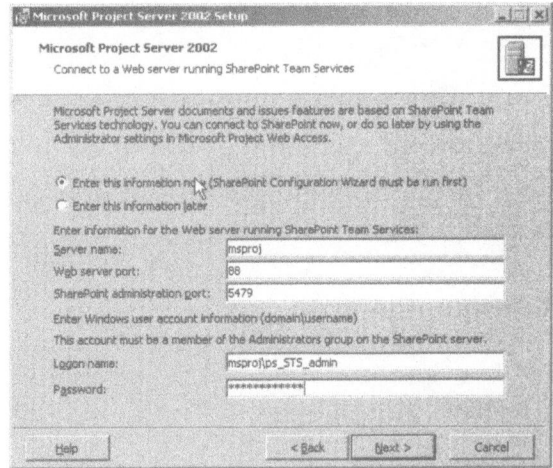

Figure 5-16. Enter connection information for STS.

10. Enter the SQL Server name and the database name, typically *servername*_LM_W3SVC_1_Collab on Windows 2000 Server. On Windows Server 2003, expect the number "1" to be a four-digit number. Use the STS reader account you created during preparation for this logon name (see Figure 5-17).

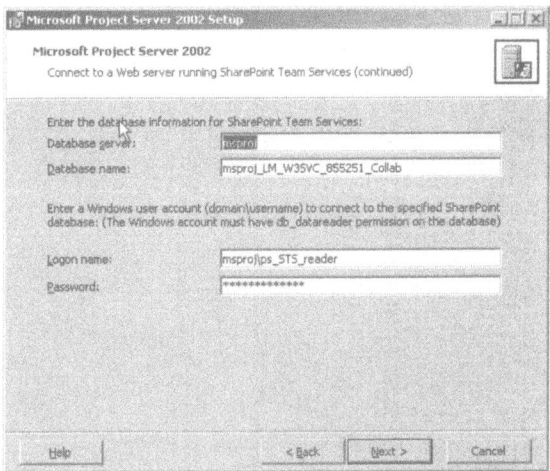

Figure 5-17. Enter the database information for STS and the reader account logon.

11. Because this is an enterprise installation, you must select the Microsoft Project Professional 2002 radio button. Choosing the Microsoft Project Standard 2002 and/or Microsoft Project 2000 radio button to publish to Project Server results in a workgroup configuration (see Figure 5-18).

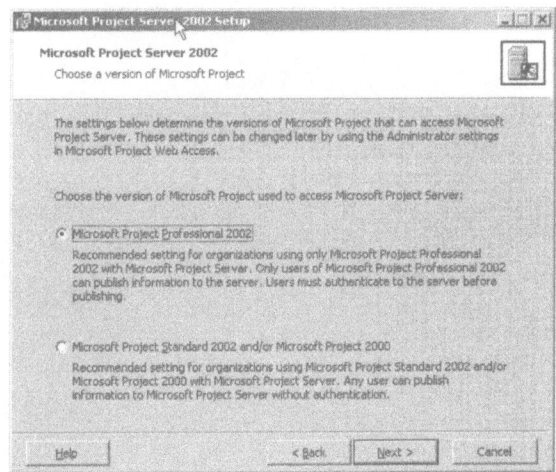

Figure 5-18. Choose Microsoft Project Professional 2002.

12. Enter a password for the Project Server built-in administrator account (see Figure 5-19). You'll use this password to log onto Project Server for the first time.

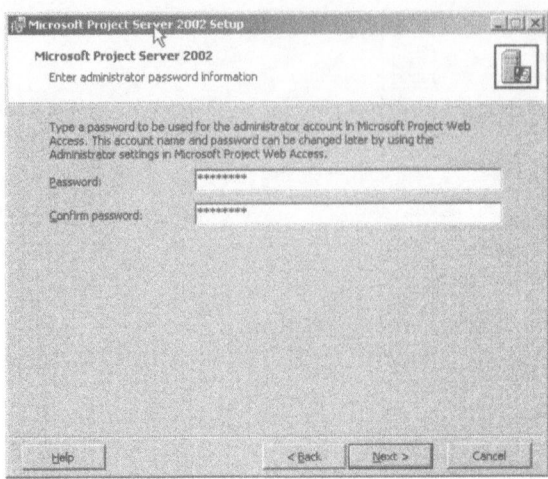

Figure 5-19. Enter a password for the Project Server default administrator account.

13. Click the Install button when Setup dialog box announces it's ready (see Figure 5-20).

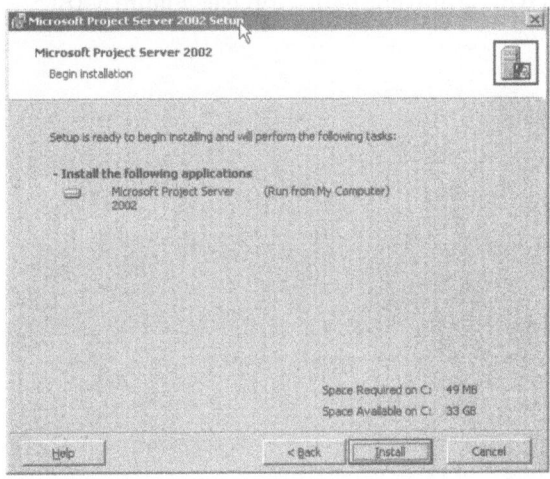

Figure 5-20. Setup is ready to begin.

14. Sit back while the installer displays its status (see Figure 5-21). Go to the next step when the installer announces completion.

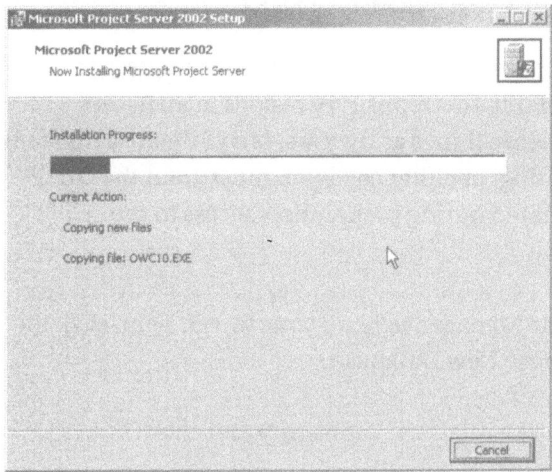

Figure 5-21. Hurry up and wait.

15. Open SQL Server Enterprise Manager and expand the Databases folder. Verify that the Project Server database has been created. If you see ProjectServer0000 rather than ProjectServer for the database name, refer to the next chapter for troubleshooting.

You aren't done—there's more to do. Don't log onto Project Server yet. You'll now move on to postinstallation activities.

Installing the Project Server Update

After you install Project, install the Microsoft Project Server 2002 Update released August 20, 2002. This update addresses a security issue with the Office Web Components included with Microsoft Project Server 2002. Download the update from here: http://office.microsoft.com/downloads/2002/ps1001en.aspx.

Postinstallation Steps

Your collaborative project management system is almost ready to begin accepting your business configuration; however, a few installation steps remain. These include some work on the server(s) and installing the Project Professional client on your workstations. Each of these steps, described in the following sections, has potential pitfalls. Try to avoid them.

Migrate the Analysis Services Repository

It's generally accepted good SQL Server management practice to migrate the Analysis Services repository. By default, this repository resides in an Access (.mdb) file. You have the option to leave things as they are, but you gain significant performance advantages by migrating. In either case, you must grant the OLAP administrator identity that you created during preparation access to the repository.

1. Start SQL Server Enterprise Manager, expand your server, right-click the Databases folder, and choose New Database.

2. Give the database a name like Analysis_Repository and click OK.

3. Expand the Databases then expand the Security folder. Right-click Logins, and select New Login.

4. Use the search button next to the Name field to locate the OLAP\Administrators group and select it. Click Add and OK.

5. Select the new repository database as the default database for the login.

6. Click the Database Access tab, select the new repository database, and select the db_owner role for this database. Click OK.

7. Click the Start button, select Programs ➤ Microsoft SQL Server ➤ Analysis Services ➤ Analysis Manager, and expand the Analysis Services folder in the Console Root.

8. Right-click the server and choose Migrate Repository. (Note: If the server isn't connected, connect to the server first.)

9. Choose SQL Sever 7.0 OLAP Services format. The Installation Guide recommends that you use the "Analysis Services native format," which translates to this choice (see Figure 5-22).

10. Enter the name of the SQL Server (see Figure 5-23).

11. Select the database from the drop-down menu (see Figure 5-24). Click Finish.

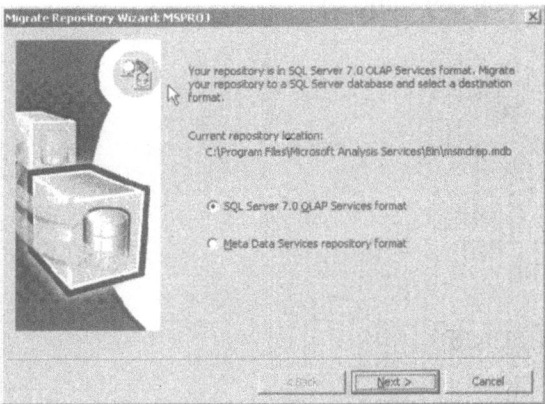

Figure 5-22. Select the migration format.

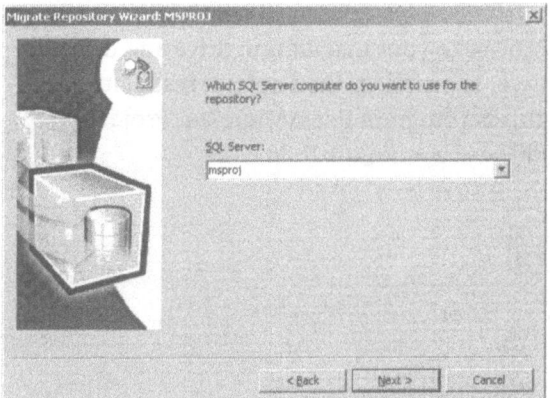

Figure 5-23. Enter the SQL Server name.

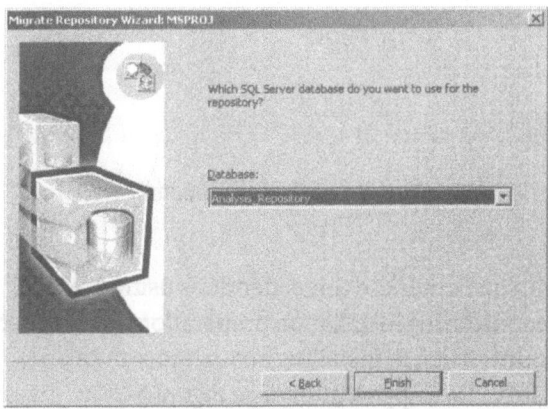

Figure 5-24. Select the database.

12. Seeing Figure 5-25 should bring you some joy!

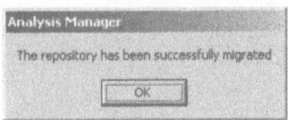

Figure 5-25. Even more than OK!

Initializing COM+ Identities

To establish the impersonation identities for COM+, you'll use the COM+ tool shipped with Project Server as PSCOMPlus.exe. This is an important step to enable articulation between Project Server and STS and between Project Server and OLAP Services.

1. Use Windows Explorer to browse to your installation drive and directory where Microsoft Project Server is installed. On a default installation as described in this chapter, this is \Program Files\Microsoft Project Server\Bin\1033\PSCOMPlus.exe (see Figure 5-26).

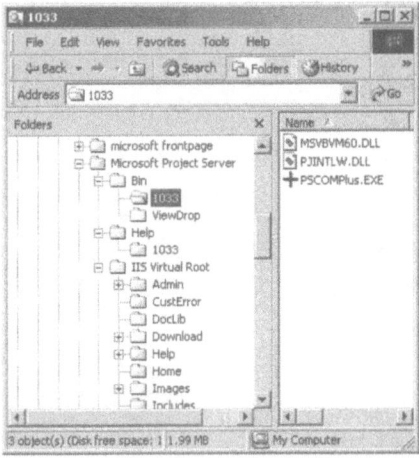

Figure 5-26. Windows Explorer view of the default installation directory structure

2. Double-click the COM+ icon and enter the three identities using the local administrator accounts created during installation preparation. Remember that these are domain accounts if you're installing across more than one box. Click the Create\Update COM+ Apps button (see Figure 5-27).

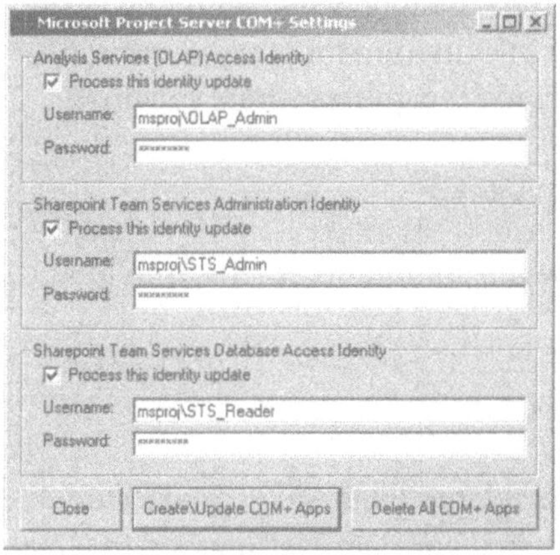

Figure 5-27. COM+ Settings dialog box

3. The system will display an alert box notifying you that components are running in COM+.

Running Proxycfg.exe

Project Server uses the XML HTTP protocol to talk to STS. To enable the protocol, you must configure the server to talk through the network proxy server if one exists, or configure it with a spoof setting if no proxy server exists. You must complete this step whether you use a proxy server or not—even if both Project Server and STS are installed on the same server. Running the WinHTTP proxy configuration utility (proxycfg.exe) is another potential trouble spot in the Project Server installation process. See the troubleshooting guides in the next chapter if you have problems with this.

TIP Running the COM+ utility can wipe out the proxy configuration. Always run proxycfg.exe after you run the COM+ utility, and always run it each time your run the COM+ utility.

---

1. Click the Start button, select Run, and enter **cmd** in the Run dialog box. Click OK.

2. At the command prompt type **cd \Program Files\Microsoft Project Server\BIN**. Note that this is the default path; your actual installation path is the one you selected in a previous step.

3. If you have a network proxy server, type the following command in the presented format, substituting your information for proxy-server and optional-bypass-list. Be sure to include the quotes where specified.

```
proxycfg -d -p "http:-proxy-server" "<local>"
```

4. If you don't have a proxy server, type the command exactly as follows, including the quotes:

```
proxycfg -d -p "FakeProxy:80" "*;<local>"
```

To see what your results should look like, refer to Figure 5-28. Make sure that you have entries for all three values. To verify that your new settings are in effect, start and stop IIS by typing **iisreset /stop**. Wait for the service to stop. Then type **iisreset /start** and wait for the service to report a successful start. (Note that there is a space between iisreset and the slash.)

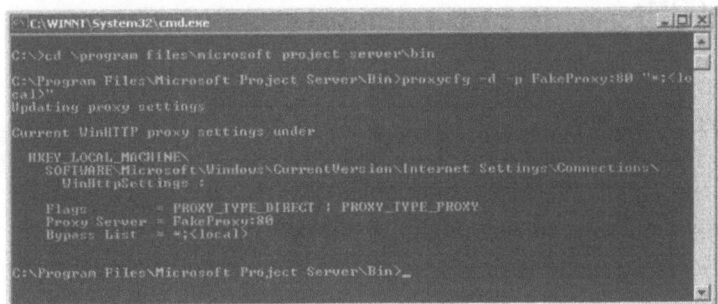

Figure 5-28. Command window after running proxycfg.exe

Verifying Project Server/STS Interoperability

Before moving on to configuration, verify that Project Server is talking properly to STS. To do this, log onto Project Web Access for the first time as per the instructions that follow. Web Access sends two ActiveX downloads to the browser the first time you log on. Therefore, it's important that you're logged on with an account that has the right to install software. You should set your browser security to allow ActiveX downloads.

1. Open a browser and type in the URL for your Project Server. Enter http://machinename/projectserver, where *machinename* is the name of your server.

2. In the Project Web Access logon screen, type the username **administrator** and enter the password you provided during installation (see Figure 5-29). Click Go.

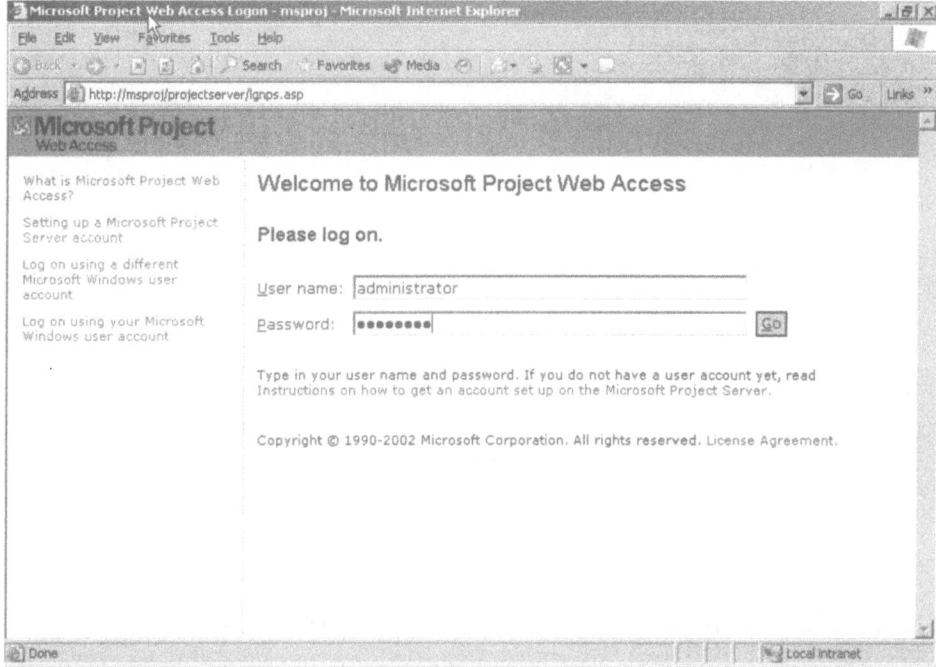

Figure 5-29. Project Web Access logon screen

3. Accept the end-user licenses agreements as they're presented. The system reports that it's downloading controls, and you're then logged on and the Project Web Access home page displays.

4. Once the Project Web Access home page loads, click Documents on the main navigation menu across the top of the page.

5. When the View and Upload Documents page for library selection displays, click the Public Documents link (see Figure 5-30).

6. You'll next see an alert box, as shown in Figure 5-31. This is displayed because you logged on using the Project Server administrator account, which isn't a Windows logon. Because you're already logged on the server as an administrator, you can ignore this warning and click OK.

7. The View and Upload Documents page will display. Choose the Shared Documents library (see Figure 5-32).

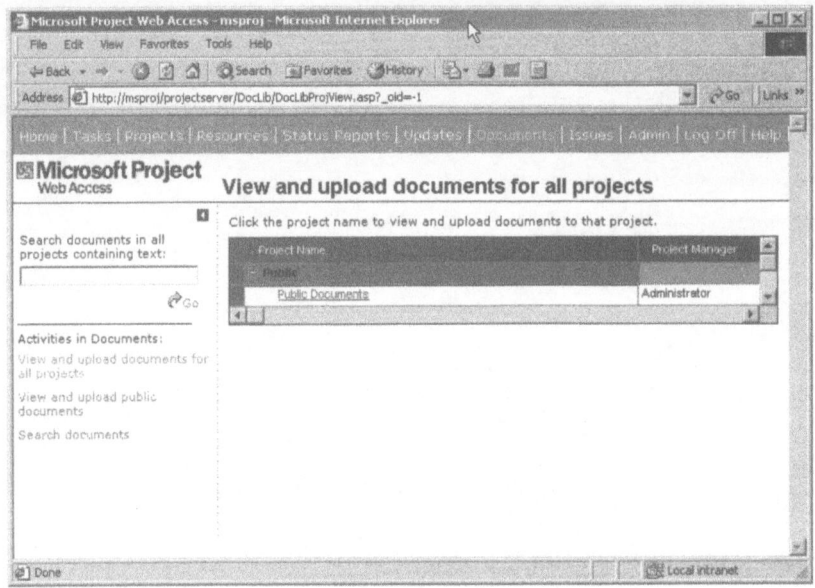

Figure 5-30. View and upload documents for all projects.

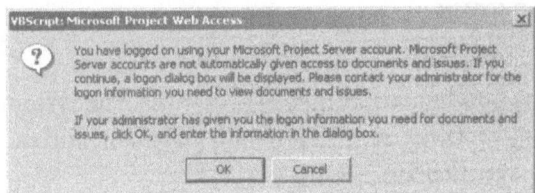

Figure 5-31. You can ignore the alert box warning at this time.

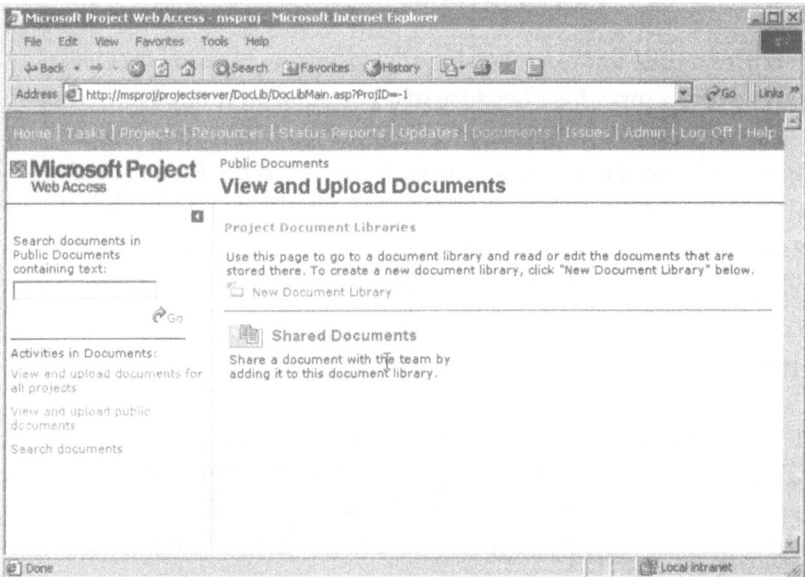

Figure 5-32. Document library selection screen

8. The Shared Documents library should now open, as shown in Figure 5-33. If you see an error message instead, refer to the next chapter for trouble-shooting information. Otherwise, you're ready to move on.

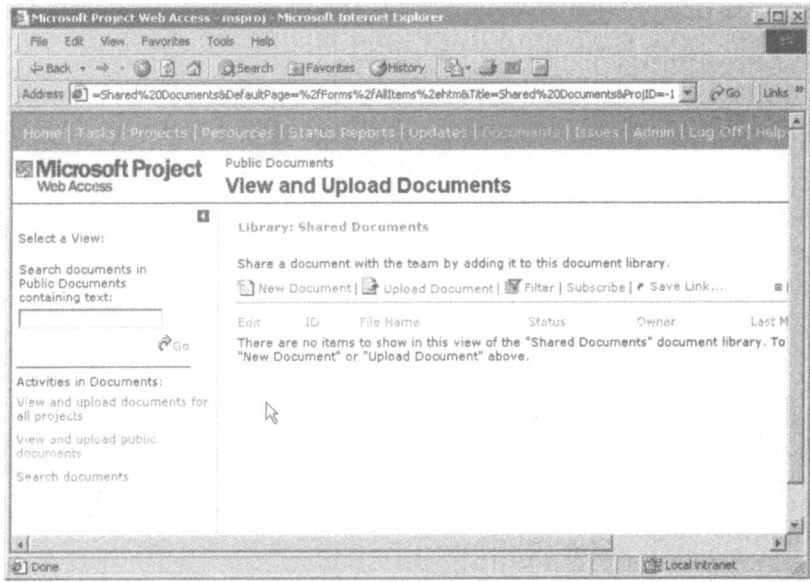

Figure 5-33. Document library page

Installing Project Professional

Installing the project client on your workstations doesn't require any special know-how. I've included it as a topic here because of a potential anomaly. Numerous users of the Microsoft Project newsgroups have reported connection failures between Project Professional 2002 and Project Server when the Project Professional client is installed before the first access to Project Web Access is made. In the name of prevention, it might be a good practice to log onto Project Web Access before installing Project Professional on your workstations.

Installing SQL Decision Support Objects

When you install Project Server on a separate machine from SQL Server, you must install the SQL DSO on the machine running Project Server. To install DSO on your Project Server machine, place your SQL CD in the server's CD-ROM drive. From the autorun splash screen, select client tools and follow the direction from there.

Summary

Installing Project Server and its supporting technologies correctly is a complex set of simple tasks. Executing the steps outlined in this chapter will almost always guarantee you success. After you install the OS and SQL Server technologies, installing Project Server and STS should take about an hour.

Installation Troubleshooting

Allowing for the possibility that, for some reason, you didn't follow the installation routine outlined in Chapter 5 to the letter, I've included undocumented and advanced tips and tricks for installation troubleshooting in this chapter. I offer these as an enhancement to, not a substitute for, the Microsoft Knowledge Base (KB) available at `http://support.microsoft.com/default.aspx?scid=fh;EN-US;KBHOWTO`. As the approach to installation outlined in Chapter 5 avoids many of the situations listed here, you'll be well served reading through this chapter entirely if you've picked up this book to troubleshoot an installation that didn't follow the Chapter 5 method.

Troubleshooting SharePoint Team Services Installation

I address SharePoint Team Services (STS) installation issues first, as these are the ones you're most likely to confront. The purpose of this discussion is to help you solve the more esoteric problems, but I cover the more common issues first by way of elimination. Make sure that none of the following situations applies to you before you delve into the advanced topics in this section.

"Run-Time Error 76" or "Could Not Create the Subweb"

The existence of FrontPage 2000 Server extensions on the server at the time you install STS will cause this error. Only the 2002 version of the extension will work; this is installed with the STS installation that comes with Project Server. This error message is covered by KB article 32302. Make sure that you review and follow the STS uninstall recommendations later in this chapter before you attempt to resolve this issue. Note that there are other resolutions for the "Could Not Create the Subweb" error that might apply to your situation if you aren't receiving the "Run-Time Error 76" message, which is unique to the cause outlined in KB article 32302.

1. Uninstall STS according to the instructions that appear later in this chapter.

2. Click the Start button, select Settings ➤ Control Panel, and double-click the Add/Remove Programs icon.

3. In the Add/Remove Programs dialog box click Add/Remove Windows Components in the left navigation pane.

4. Highlight Internet Information Services in the Windows Components Wizard as shown in Figure 6-1, and click Details.

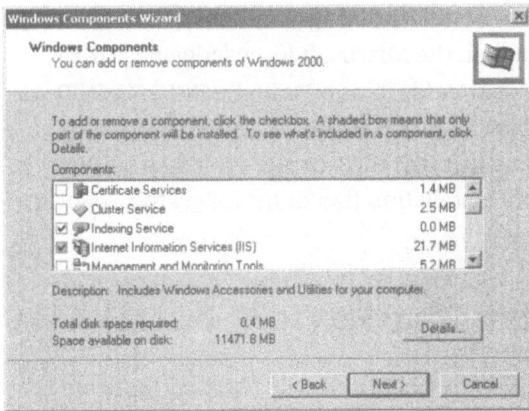

Figure 6-1. Windows Components Wizard

5. In the Internet Information Services (IIS) dialog box, uncheck the box for FrontPage 2000 Server Extensions, as shown in Figure 6-2.

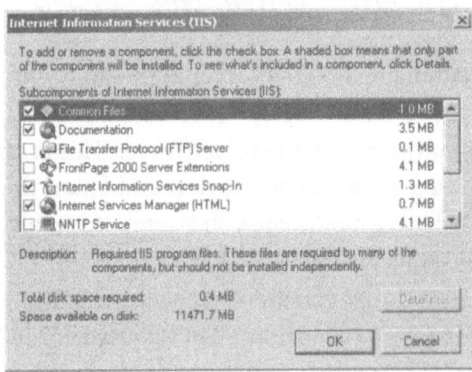

Figure 6-2. Internet Information Services (IIS) dialog box

6. When the installer completes, click the Start button, select Run, and enter **CMD**.

7. Type **IISRESET** at the command prompt.

8. Reinstall STS.

Errors Adding an STS Server After Project Server Installation

This error is common as many users attempt to install Project Server without first reading through the Project Server Installation Guide. When STS is installed after Project Server, there are configurations that must be made. These are well documented in KB article 322235. The error manifests itself in three variants: In addition to the errors shown in Figures 6-3 and 6-4, the error "VBScript: Microsoft Project Web Access Error occurred when creating subweb. Subweb does not seem to exist" may appear.

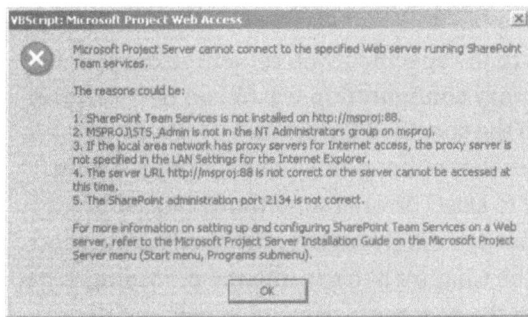

Figure 6-3. "Cannot connect to the specified Web server" error

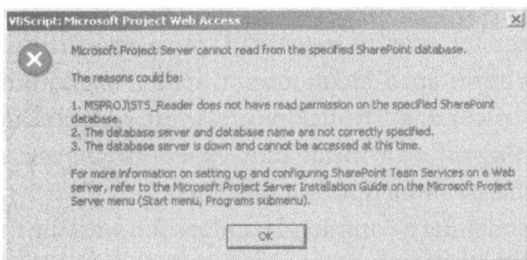

Figure 6-4. "Cannot connect to the specified SharePoint database" error

There are three key installation/configuration points to Project Server integration with STS. These are as follows:

1. You created identities for SharePoint to connect to its own database (separate from the Project Server database). These are among the local administrator identities that you (should have?) created during installation configuration and are the identities that will be used by COM+. Adding these to the SharePoint database is a manual installation step and commonly missed by inexperienced installers.

2. You ran the COM+ utility provided on your installation drive at drive:\Program Files\Microsoft Project Server\Bin folder or the path you specified at installation. The existence of the accounts and the manual steps in database installation are requisites for running the COM+ utility as referenced in the preceding point. (Note: This includes the OLAP administrator identity covered in Chapter 5.)

3. You were successful in setting the server's proxy settings by running the proxycfg.exe file provided at drive:\Program Files\Microsoft Project Server\Bin\1033 folder.

The occurrence of the "Connect to the specified Web server" error type, as shown in Figure 6-3, indicates that proxy configuration wasn't run or wasn't run successfully. The "Cannot connect to the specified SharePoint database" error type, as shown in Figure 6-4, indicates that either point 1 and/or point 2 were missed. The "Subweb does not seem to exist" error is sometimes caused by an unsuccessful proxycfg.exe run or other seemingly mysterious circumstances. Refer to instructions in provided in the Chapter 5 to execute the preceding installation steps. Familiarize yourself with the next topic to avoid known pitfalls.

Successfully Troubleshooting Proxycfg.exe Issues

In the last section, I referred to "successful" and "unsuccessful" proxycfg.exe runs. There are times when proxy settings errors are difficult to spot, appear to take but don't, or stop working after a period of working. The flakiness of these settings can lead you to one of your most frustrating software installation experiences if you don't pay close attention to the troubleshooting tips described here.

Those of you who aren't used to opening a command window and working in a DOS environment may be thrown by the fact that there isn't a lot of error handling. The command to be typed has four segments. The first is the command itself, **proxycfg**, which invokes the proxycfg.exe file. Next there are switches **-d** and **-p** followed by a proxy server name and bypass list, both of which require you to type quotes around them. Leaving out the quotes on one can cause the settings to fail in a more subtle presentation than you might notice at first glance. With that in mind, be very careful about your syntax and pay attention the system output after you press Enter. Make sure that what you thought you typed for the values of proxy server and the bypass list displays as the values on the screen. When in doubt, do it again with the next precaution in mind.

I've seen significant public discussion conducted over the value to use when typing a fake proxy server name, which Project Server documentation specifies as the standard when proxycfg.exe is run in absence of a Proxy Server. Numerous users have reported that using a variant to the command specified solved a proxy setting issue. The Project Server Installation Guide specifies this as

```
Proxycfg -d -p "proxyserver" "<local>"
```

The variant suggested is

```
proxycfg -d -p "FakeProxy:80" "*;<local>"
```

In reality, neither choice is more valid than the other. The illusion that one is a better choice than the other is actually the therapeutic effect of typing a different Proxy Server name. When proxy settings are entered correctly but don't appear to work, rerunning the proxycfg command and changing the name of the Proxy Server may be required to get the system to refresh the settings. (It's apparently possible for the system to ignore the proxycfg command when the proxy server name isn't changed.) When in doubt, rerun proxycfg using a different name and then switch it back to what you actually want.

Running the COM+ utility is one event that can cause the proxy settings to stop functioning. Project Server documentation would lead you to believe that the order in which you run COM+ and proxycfg doesn't matter, but sometimes it does. Rerun proxycfg with a new proxy server name when you can no longer connect to a SharePoint server after running the COM+ utility. Creating additional sites using the Site Editor tool, covered in Chapter 7, can also cause this problem. It's likely that there are other causes not covered here.

"Could Not Create the Subweb" and Complete Installation Fails

A variant to a cause for this specific error message occurs during installation for unknown reasons. Anecdotally, I suspect the Office XP Web Components SP2 is one potential cause of this error. On affected systems, when running stswiz.exe STS software installation completes to the point that the installation wizard extends the Project Server customizations to the STS Web site and then fails. STS characteristically works when a server is in this state and you can create through the native STS Web interface. Only the Project Server wrapper fails to install.

For systems that experience this issue, it's possible to work around the problem by installing STS in debug mode and stepping through the installation to the point where the wizard creates the MS_ProjectServer_PublicDocuments folder on the default Web site. Intervening by manually creating the folder at the correct step point can get the job done. A clean uninstall is a requisite to reinstalling STS in debug mode. You must complete all the steps outlined later in this chapter in the section "Uninstalling STS" prior to attempting a reinstall.

Resolving Project Server Installation Issues

Project Server itself is typically an easy installation. Once you've moved past the integration quirks with STS, Analysis Services, and SMTP, installing the Project Server application software is remarkably trouble-free most of the time. In fact, most situations are related to reinstallation and not first-time installation when a structured process is followed for the first time.

Project Server Database Created with "0000" Extension

When you verify the creation of your Project Server database and you discover that four zeros (0000) have been appended to the name of your database in SQL, you missed the manual database uninstall steps. Refer to the uninstall discussion later in this chapter.

When You Can't Connect to Project Server Through the Browser

There are circumstances that can prevent you from connecting to your Project Server instance with the Project Professional client. These problems often relate to security applied to the workstations by your IT department. When problems relate to specialized security, determining the nature of the problem can be quite tedious. If this is happening on a widespread basis in your organization, look to security policies first. The largest culprit here is changes to registry security on the workstations. Beyond these very esoteric problems in the realm of security, you can take some obvious troubleshooting approaches.

Unable to Download ActiveX Controls on Client

In order for Project Web Access to download the Project Server ActiveX controls at the time of first logon, a client machine must at least have "Run ActiveX controls and plug-ins" enabled and "Download signed ActiveX controls" must be set to at least Prompt, if not Enable, under directory security for your Trusted Sites zone. Further, the user logged onto the workstation must have permission to install new software; otherwise, the ActiveX download for Project Server will fail.

Your first approach should be to try the basic troubleshooting techniques, as follows:

1. Make sure that your Project Server site wasn't configured with an invalid name such as with spaces or an underscore in the URL. If you find this is the case, try again after deleting and re-creating it.

2. Passing the first test, in your browser, select Tools ➤ Internet Options, click the Security tab, and select the Trusted sites icon. Click the Sites button and uncheck the "Require server verification (https:) for all sites in this zone" check box if you're not requiring SSL. Type the URL for the site in the appropriate field in the dialog box. Be certain to use the full form beginning with "http://". This will add the Project Server instance to the Trusted site zone and assist in troubleshooting. For an illustrated version of these instructions, see the "Unable to Make Project Server a Trusted Site" section later in this chapter.

3. While you're still in the Options dialog box, click the Security tab, and then click the Trusted sites zone. Click the Custom level button and make sure that signed ActiveX objects are enabled for download and installation. Also make sure that the account with which you're logged onto the client machine has software installation privileges. This is a gotcha for users attempting to install on a corporate test system with proper authority.

4. On the Connections tab, click LAN Settings and make sure that "Automatically detect settings" isn't checked on your client. If you're using a proxy, enter it manually.

5. Find the downloaded programs file on your client and remove the project server ActiveX objects if either PJ10enuC Class or PJAdoInfo2 Class is installed.

6. Finally, if the Project Professional client was installed before you logged onto Project Web Access for the first time, complete step 5 and uninstall the Project Professional client, then reboot. Access Project Web Access through the browser before you attempt to reinstall the Project Professional client.

Project Server public newsgroup contributor David Cheslow reported a possible client-side fix when ActiveX download fails when the aforementioned configuration is verified. This may or may not help you, but it's nondestructive to at least verify these settings.

1. Delete the ActiveX objects if any were partially installed from the down-loaded program files directory.

2. Click the Start button and select Run.

3. Type **RegEdt32** (typing **RegEdit** won't work).

4. Expand to HKEY_LOCAL_MACHINE/Software/Classes.

5. Choose Security ➤ Permissions from the menu.

6. Select the allow check boxes for Read, Full Control, and Allow inheritable permissions. Click OK.

It's my current assumption that if you run into a problem like this, it's because your company alters the registry for security purposes. Problems like this are difficult to troubleshoot when they arise.

Web Access Pages Display a VBScript Error or Continuously Report "Loading Data"

This error occurs most often because something is amiss with the MDAC installation. If you've implemented a default IIS installation, your Web site should contain an MDAC installation, and if you've correctly performed the postinstallation steps outlined in Chapter 5, your MDAC should be configured correctly. If you don't recall having manually set a DLL's IP restrictions to Granted on this directory, this is a likely cause in your case. Another possibility is the use of the URL Scan utility. If you're using the URL Scan utility, refer to KB article 316398. Otherwise, this error occurs most often on systems that have had changes made beyond the default OS installation described in Chapter 5.

Symptoms include the following:

Problems with this Web Page might prevent it from being displayed properly or functioning properly. In the future, you can display this message by double-clicking the warning icon displayed in the status bar.

Line: n

Error: Internet Server Error: Object/module not found

Code: 0

URL: `http://ServerName/ProjectServer/TasksPage.asp`

or

VB Script: Microsoft Project Web Access

An error occurred while trying to access the resources stored on the database. Either there are too many resources, or the Microsoft Project Server may not have the correct DSN configuration. Contact the server administrator.

or

Cannot Create Business Objects

The first two messages are most likely to occur due to issues on the server, whereas the third error scenario occurs most often because of client-side issues. One way to make this determination is to test the system using various clients. If all fail, the problem is most likely on the server. If some clients connect, client-side issues are most likely.

It's entirely possible, but not likely, that the MSADC virtual directory wasn't created or that MDAC isn't installed on your server at all. The more likely cause is that directory security hasn't been properly configured on the msadcs.dll located in the MSADC virtual directory. Verify this first by opening Internet Services Manager and expanding the Default Web Site. Click the MSADC virtual directory, right-click the msadcs.dll, and select Properties. On the Directory Security tab, click the Edit button next to IP and Domain Restrictions and make sure that Granted Access is selected. After you make the change, try accessing the site again. For more information on re-creating MSADC on your server, see KB article 321357.

If the msadcs.dll has the proper Granted Access configuration, then the next step is to upgrade or reinstall MDAC. To do this, search the software downloads section on the Microsoft Web site. Download and install the latest version for your OS. Do the same for the client if you're receiving the "Cannot Create Business Object" error. Even though you may have a current OS, some third-party vendors have older versions of MDAC overwrite newer ones when installing their software. Typically, upgrading to the latest version of MDAC has no effect on the offending application and clears up the issue on the client.

When Project Professional Doesn't Connect to Project Server

When you log onto Project Server from Project Professional 2002, the "Cannot Connect" error is displayed. There are a couple of causes not mentioned in the error message and not documented by KB articles. After you eliminate the causes listed in the error message, consider the following conditions:

"Cannot Connect" Error

In some instances, you'll receive the "Cannot Connect" error as follows:

Cannot connect.

Microsoft Project was unable to establish a connection with the selected Microsoft Project Server. This could be caused by a loss of network connectivity, invalid username or password, lack of an enterprise global template, problems with the Microsoft Project Server or database, or your Microsoft Project Server may have enterprise features enabled.

Symptoms

The Project Professional client fails to connect to the Project Server despite the fact that the Test Server Connection functionality in the Project Server Account Creation and Maintenance dialog box reported success.

Cause 1

The default language setting on the client is set to a language other than English and Project Server hasn't been configured for multiple language support as defined in TechNet under "International Server Deployment: Microsoft Project 2002" (http://www.microsoft.com/technet/treeview/default.asp?url=/technet/prodtechnol/project/project2002/reskit/ps02/psdply/psntldpl.asp).

Resolution

Set the client default language to en-us or execute the steps outlined in the previously mentioned TechNet article.

Cause 2

Project Professional was installed prior to logging onto Project Web Access for the first time. It seems that some client systems react badly when Project Professional is installed before the user has logged onto Project Web Access.

Resolution

Here's what you must do to correct this problem:

1. Uninstall Project Professional.

2. Reboot.

3. Delete the two Project Server ActiveX objects PJ10enuC Class and PJAdoInfo2 Class if they were installed or partially installed from the Downloaded Programs file folder typically in the Windows directory of Windows XP.

4. Log onto Project Web Access and accept the ActiveX downloads.

5. Reinstall Project Professional.

Unable to Make Project Server a Trusted Site

The first time you log onto Project Server from Project Professional, the system detects whether or not the URL is in your Internet Explorer's Trusted sites security category. Normally you can select the option to make Project Server a trusted site from the logon dialog box. Occasionally, the automation fails and you must do this manually in your browser. To perform this step manually:

1. Open Internet Explorer.

2. Navigate to Tools ➤ Internet Options.

3. Select the Security tab and click the Sites button, as shown in Figure 6-5.

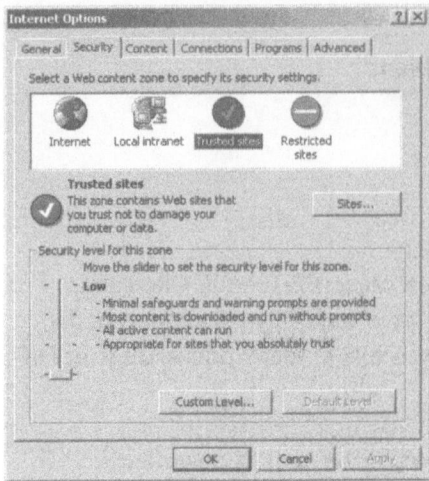

Figure 6-5. Internet Explorer Internet Options dialog box

4. In the Trusted sites dialog box (see Figure 6-6) uncheck the "Require server verification (https:) for all sites in this zone" option if you haven't installed an SSL certificate on your server.

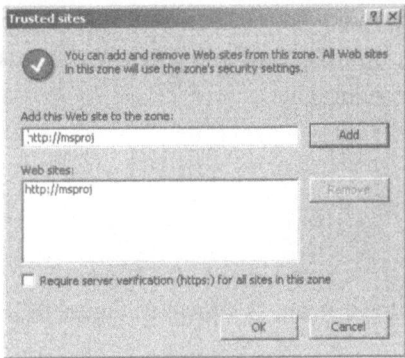

Figure 6-6. Trusted sites dialog box

5. Fill in the name of the site and click Add.

Uninstalling STS

A clean STS uninstall is a prerequisite to getting a second chance to install. Therefore, I've included it in this troubleshooting chapter. The steps you are most likely to miss are the manual ones. To uninstall STS from your server, follow these steps:

1. Click the Start button and select Settings ➤ Control Panel.

2. Double-click the Add/Remove Programs icon.

3. Select Microsoft SharePoint as shown in Figure 6-7 and click the Remove button.

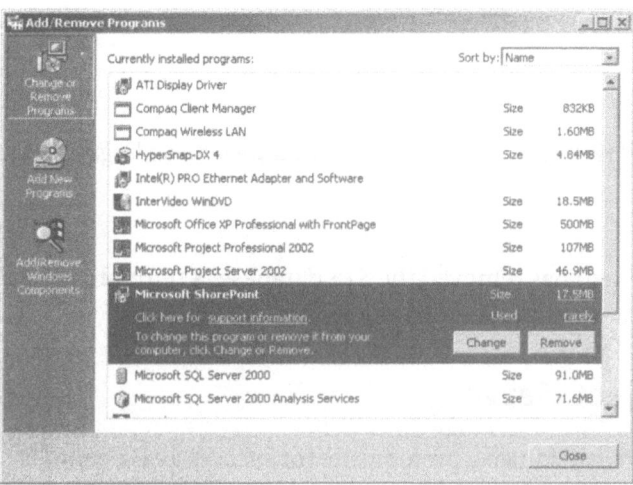

Figure 6-7. Highlight Microsoft SharePoint to select it for uninstall.

4. When the uninstall process completes, stop IIS by opening a DOS command window and typing **iisreset /stop**.

5. When the system reports a successful stop, navigate to drive:\Program Files\Common Files\Microsoft Shared\Web Server Extensions\50 and delete the contents of the folder.

6. Restart IIS by typing the command **iisreset /start** at a command prompt.

7. In SQL Enterprise Manager, verify that the STS database has been deleted.

8. Open Internet Services Manager, expand the Web site on which you installed STS, and manually remove any lingering STS subdirectories, including the MS_ProjectServer_PublicDocuments folder. A typical Default Web Site tree is shown in Figure 6-8.

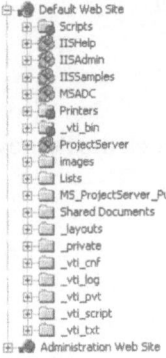

Figure 6-8. Typical Default Web Site tree. You must manually remove lingering STS folders.

9. Verify that the system has removed the STS database. A normal uninstall should remove the database. If not, remove it manually.

Uninstalling Project Server

A clean Project Server uninstall is also a prerequisite for success at a second-chance installation. Once again, the steps you're most likely to miss are the manual ones. To uninstall Project Server from your server, follow these steps:

1. Click the Start button and select Settings ➤ Control Panel.

2. Double-click the Add/Remove Programs icon.

3. Select Microsoft Project Server 2002 and click the Remove button.

4. Once the uninstall process is complete launch SQL Enterprise Manager.

5. Expand the Databases folder on the Server tree.

6. Right-click the ProjectServer database and select Delete.

7. Expand the Security folder and select Logins.

8. Right-click the MSProjectServerUser user and select Delete.

9. Right-click the MSProjectUser user and select Delete.

NOTE   Removing the residual Project Server database and logins prevents the four zeros (0000) from being appended to the new database and login names after you reinstall Project Server.

Backing Up and Restoring Project Server and STS

After installation you should back up your newly installed system. You can use the method I present in this section to back up your implementation or you can use commercial tools to automate this process. To do this you must back up the Project Server and STS databases and the STS subwebs.

Backing Up

To back up Project Server and STS, perform the following steps:

1. Open SQL Enterprise Manager and expand the Server folder, then the Databases folder.

2. Right-click either the Project Server or STS database and select All Tasks ➤ Backup Database to open the SQL Server Backup dialog box, as shown in Figure 6-9.

3. Click the Add button in the Destination section to open the Select Backup Destination dialog box.

4. You must provide a file name for the backup or use the Backup Device option to select a device destination for the backup. In this example I use a file name, as shown in Figure 6-10. Click OK twice to run the backup.

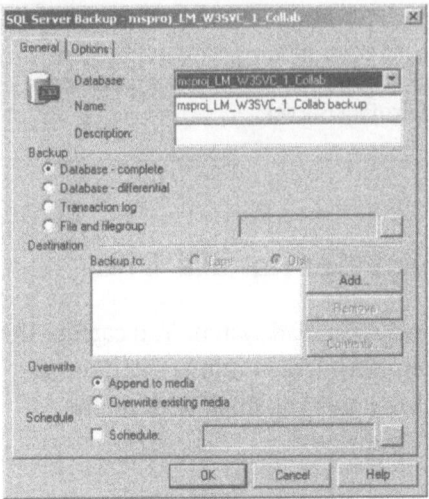

Figure 6-9. The SQL Server Backup dialog box

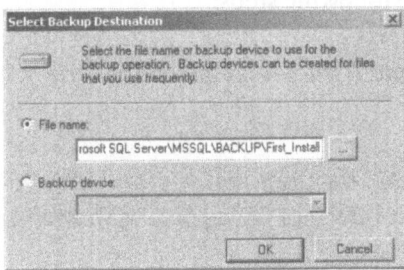

Figure 6-10. Provide a file name for the backup.

5. Repeat this process for the Project Server or STS database.

6. Make a backup copy of all of your STS subweb folders and their contents from drive:\intepub\wwwroot or the appropriate parent directory for your system.

Restoring

To restore Project Server and STS, perform the following steps:

1. Open SQL Enterprise Manager and expand the Server folder, then the Databases folder.

2. Right-click either the Project Server or STS database and select All Tasks ➤ Restore Database to open the SQL Server Restore database dialog box, as shown in Figure 6-11.

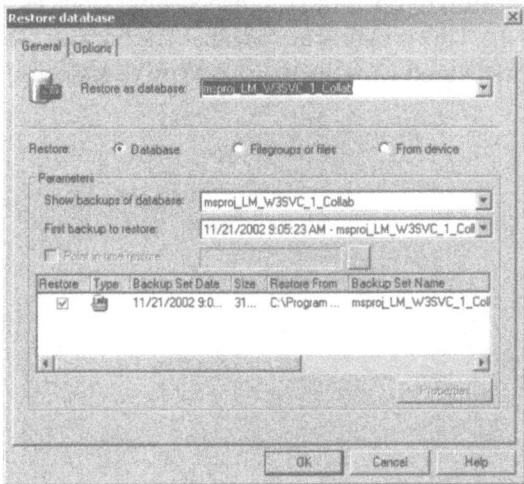

Figure 6-11. SQL Server Restore database dialog box

3. Select the backup file from which to restore and click OK.

4. Repeat these steps for the Project Server or STS database and then copy the backed-up STS subwebs to restore the STS server state that matches the database.

Restoring to a Different Server

You can migrate a Project Server installation from server to server by restoring your backup files onto a different destination server. The easiest way to accomplish this is to install STS and Project Server according to the installation instructions outlined in Chapter 5. Once you've completed your installation, you can migrate another server's data onto it by extending the restore procedure as follows:

1. Open SQL Enterprise Manager and expand the Server folder, then the Databases folder.

2. Right-click either the Project Server or STS database and select All Tasks ➤ Restore Database to open the Restore database dialog box shown in Figure 6-11.

3. Click the From device radio button to open the Choose Restore Devices dialog box shown in Figure 6-12. This is necessary because the backup file you'll be using isn't already associated with the database you're restoring it to.

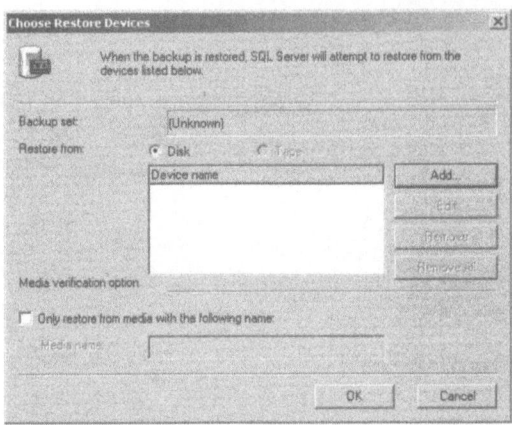

Figure 6-12. Choose Restore Devices dialog box

4. Click Add to open the Choose Restore Destination dialog box shown in Figure 6-13. Use the browse button to locate a file or select the backup device option if your file is located on tape or the like. Click OK to restore the backup.

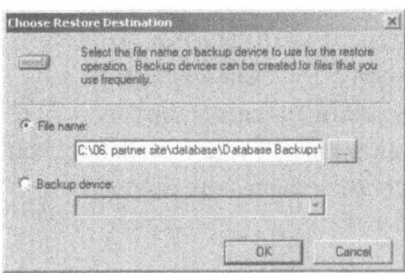

Figure 6-13. Use the browse button to locate the file.

5. At this point it's necessary to make changes in the database to resynchronize logins and connection information. Open SQL Enterprise

Manager, expand the ProjectServer database, and select Users. If they exist, delete both the MSProjectServerUser and the MSProjectUser logins.

6. After you delete the existing accounts, right-click Users and select New Database User to open the Database User Properties – New User dialog box. Select MSProjectServerUser from the drop-down list and select MSProjectServerRole for Permit in Database Role.

7. Repeat the previous step, this time selecting MSProjectUser and the corresponding MSProjectRole.

8. The STS database requires similar tweaking. This time expand the STS database in SQL Enterprise Manager. Click Users and delete the STSAdmin and STSReader accounts if they exist.

NOTE These instructions are dependent on the assumption that you've created the STS COM+ identities as outlined in Chapter 5, that you've correctly assigned the database access initially, and that the database being restored has the same name as the backup. If this isn't the case, refer to these instructions before proceeding.

9. After you delete the existing accounts, right-click Users and select New Database User. Select the <machinename>\STSAdmin account and select db_security admin in the Permit in Database Role.

10. Repeat the previous step, selecting the STSReader account and checking db_datareader for Permit in Database Role.

11. Rerun the PSCom+ tool by navigating to the installation drive:\Program Files\Microsoft Project Server\Bin\1033 and double-clicking the File icon.

12. Click the Start button, select Run, type **CMD**, and click OK. Change to the X:\Program Files\Microsoft Project Server\Bin directory, where "X" is your installation drive. Type the proxycfg command appropriate to your system, keeping in mind the lessons you learned in the "Successfully Troubleshooting Proxycfg.exe Issues" section earlier in this chapter.

13. In SQL Enterprise Manager, expand the ProjectServer database and select Tables on the expanded tree.

14. Right-click the MSP_WEB_STS_SERVERS table and select Open Table ➤ Return All Rows. Delete the record for the current STS server Log onto Project Web Access on the new server using an administrator account. From the Admin menu, select Manage SharePoint Team Services.

15. Log onto Project Web Access on the new server using an administrator account. From the Admin menu, select Manage SharePoint Team Services.

16. Click Add Server and fill in the appropriate information in the "Add a Web server running SharePoint Team Services" screen, as shown in Figure 6-14. Scroll down to verify the COM+ identities and click Save Changes. If the update isn't accepted, recheck your entries. If you are still unsuccessful, refer to the "Successfully Troubleshooting Proxycfg.exe Issues" section in this chapter.

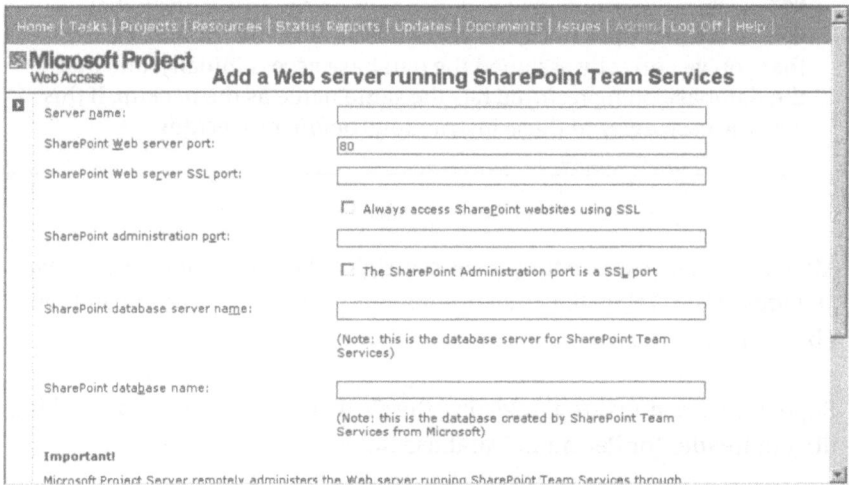

Figure 6-14. Add the STS Server through the Project Web Access Administrator interface.

17. In SQL Enterprise Manager, expand the STS database, right-click the UserInfo table, and select Open Table ➤ Return all Rows. Change the machinename\Administrators entry to the correct machine name.

CAUTION   There's an additional step when the database isn't running under a domain. Completing step 17 may require additional work if the database hasn't been restored from one machine to a new machine running in the same domain. If local machine accounts are used for authentication, then it will be necessary to manually modify all of the user entries in the UserInfo table to reflect the correct logon machine name.

18. Rebuild the OLAP cube on the new server according to the directions in Chapter 12. You'll also need to re-create your Analysis views, unless your new machine name and cube name are identical.

Summary

Carefully following the installation instructions in Chapter 5 should help you avoid the need to spend a lot of time studying this chapter. If you're picking up where someone else left off, or you didn't get a copy of this book in time, then the troubleshooting techniques in this chapter will help you get your implementation running.

Advanced Installation Techniques

This chapter covers the tools and techniques for creating stratified and scaled implementations. I covered multiserver installations and Project Server instances conceptually in Chapter 4 because they have a significant impact on hardware selection. Here I focus on the physical techniques to implement the server strategies discussed in Chapter 4.

Creating Multiple Project Server Instances

In my professional practice implementing Project Server for corporate America, I've made it a standard practice to create at least one additional Project Server instance in all of my implementations. I've found that my clients are eager to "play" with their new technology once it's implemented. Further, all companies have an immediate and ongoing need for training as new users are added to the system. A second site provides a training/sandbox environment that can meet this need without placing the production environment in jeopardy. Once you've established the second site, it's very easy to take a snapshot of production and move it to the sandbox.

Any additional site you create is subject to the same domain control as your first site. It uses the same identities to access the Project Server and SharePoint Team Services (STS) databases as the first site. Only one set of these identities is available for all sites, despite the fact that they connect to different Project Server and STS database instances. In other words, all the instances that you create are part of the same security group.

Downloading the Site Editor Tool from Microsoft

Microsoft provides a handy tool that's essential to this process and is available for download from the Microsoft Download Center. Type **http://download.microsoft.com** in your browser to reach the Download Center. Once you've accessed the home page, select Microsoft Project in the Product/Technology selection box and type **site editor** in the keywords entry box. Click the result link and follow the directions to download the editsite.exe file to your computer. While you're on the Microsoft site, you should also have a look at the Knowledge Base article related to this tool; however, as of this writing, the directions contained in it are inadequate. See article Q320231 at http://support.microsoft.com/default.aspx?scid=kb;en-us;Q323021.

Capturing Passwords from the Registry

Project Server uses two internal identities to talk to the Project Server database. MSProjectUser and MSProjectServerUser are the two SQL identities created during the initial installation. These get created with very strong passwords, which you'll need to provide when you create the additional sites. Follow these steps to find the passwords for these identities in the registry:

1. Click the Start button, select Run, and type **regedit**.

2. Navigate to HKEY_LOCAL_MACHINE\Software\MicrosoftOffice\ 10.0\MS Project\WebClient Server.

3. Record the passwords as shown in Figure 7-1 and close the registry.

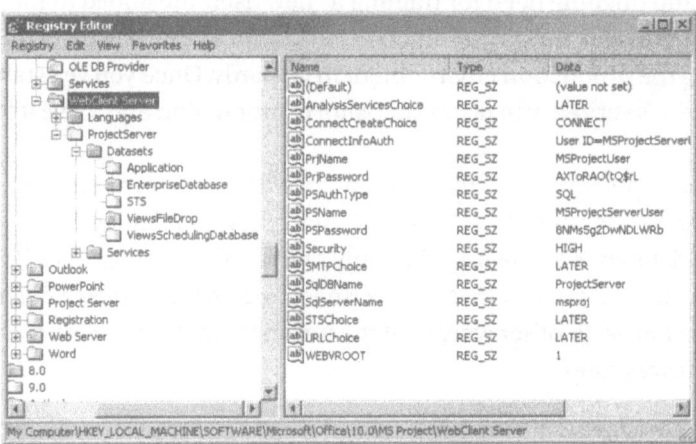

Figure 7-1. Registry entries for Project Server

TIP You can copy the passwords and paste them into a Notepad document for holding while you complete a number of other tasks that you must finish before you'll actually need the passwords. Make sure that you properly identify the account that the password belongs to in your document. Double-click the password key you want to copy and copy it from the Edit String dialog box. Right-click the highlighted value and choose Copy, or highlight the value and use the keyboard shortcut Ctrl+C. Be careful not to delete or alter the password or you'll break your installation.

Creating a New SharePoint Team Services Site for Your New Project Server Instance

Adding a corresponding STS site for your new Project Server site is a slightly more manual process than creating the first STS site. Chances are you used your default Web site for the first site, so you'll create an additional Web site by opening Internet Services Manager and selecting Action ➤ New ➤ Site to open the Web Site Creation Wizard. Select Next from the splash screen. Enter a description in the first entry screen shown in Figure 7-2.

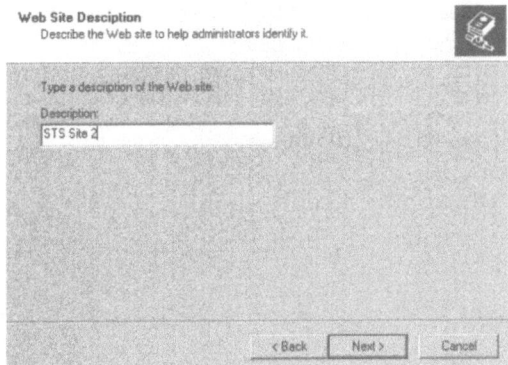

Figure 7-2. Type a description for your new Web site.

Unless you're binding the site to an IP address, set the port for the site in the IP Address and Port Settings dialog box to 71 or another unused port, as shown in Figure 7-3. Click Next when you've completed your entry.

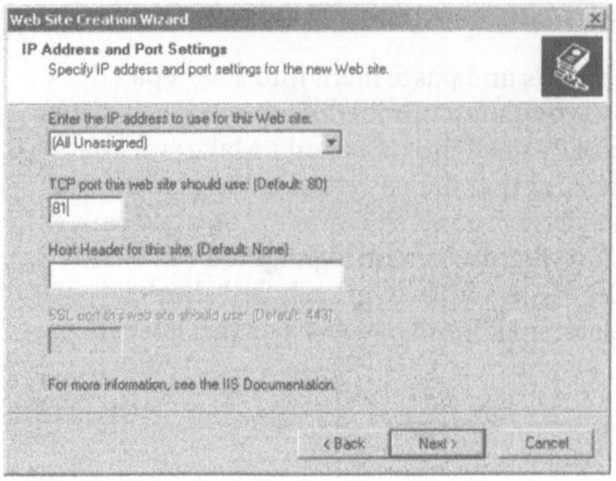

Figure 7-3. Enter a port number for the new site.

Next you must provide a physical path where the site folders will reside. Keep in mind that STS sites grow with documents. Many organizations use small boot partitions and install data files on other partitions and drives. Select a location that can handle the growth over time. See Figure 7-4 for details, and make sure that you've already created the directory for your new site if you don't want to put it in an existing directory.

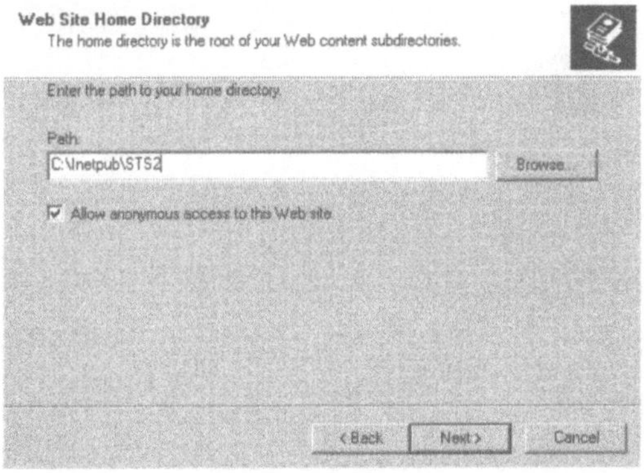

Figure 7-4. Select a target directory.

You're now presented with Access Permissions options. Select Read and select Run scripts. Do not select Execute, Write, or Browse. The proper selections are shown in Figure 7-5. Click Next to continue, and then click Finish to complete the process.

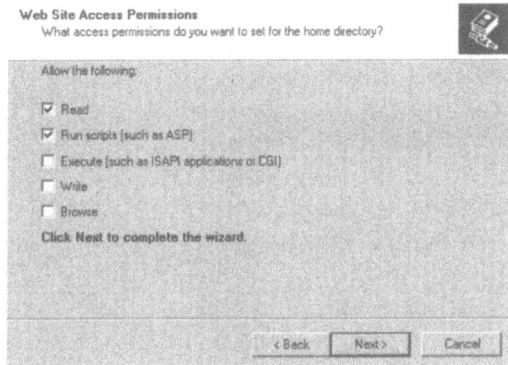

Figure 7-5. Select site access permissions options.

Extending the New Site for STS

The next step is to extend your new Web site for STS. To do this click the Start
button and select Programs ➤ Administrative Tools ➤ Microsoft SharePoint
Administrator. Alternately, type the URL with the Admin port number if you know
it. The Microsoft SharePoint Server Administration home page displays. In the
Virtual Servers section, as shown in Figure 7-6, you see your existing STS site
showing as extended as well as your new site and any other site on the server that
hasn't yet been extended with STS. In Figure 7-6 the Default Web Site is already
extended and three additional sites are eligible. Click the Extend link to the right of
the site to extend STS onto the site.

    After you click Extend, the Extend Virtual Server page displays. Enter the
database information, as shown in Figure 7-7, and select the "SharePoint-based
Web site" radio button. Once you've entered the correct information, click Submit
to process the site.

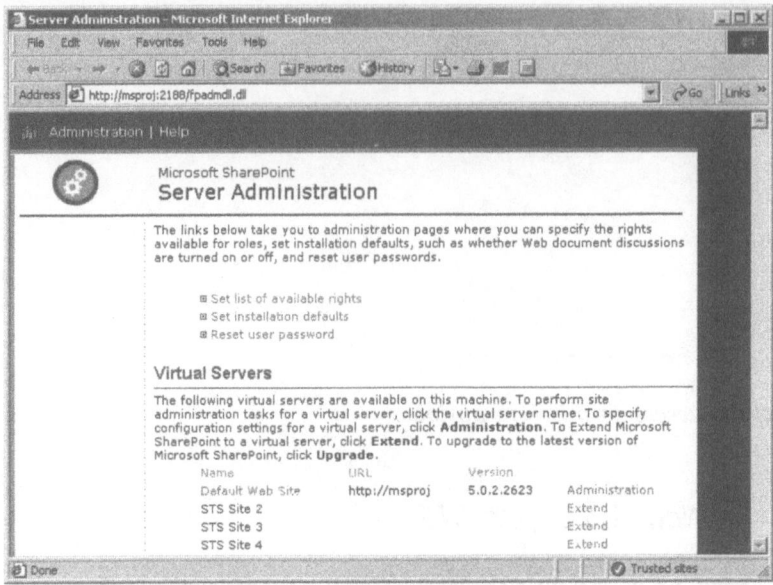

Figure 7-6. Select the site to extend by clicking the corresponding Extend link.

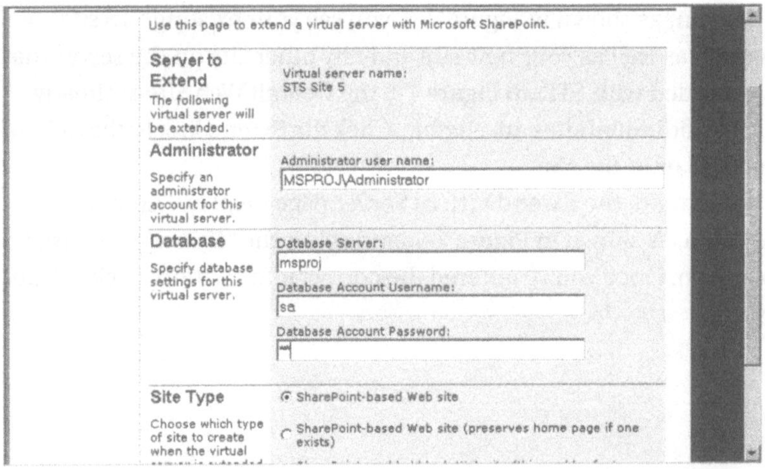

Figure 7-7. Enter the database information and click Submit.

While the system processes the request, it will display the familiar animated sprocket GIF. When the processing is complete, the Server Administration page will redisplay, showing your new site as extended (see Figure 7-8). If you open SQL Server Enterprise Manager, you'll now see an additional STS database. Note that the number sequence on the database may not be incremented by one.

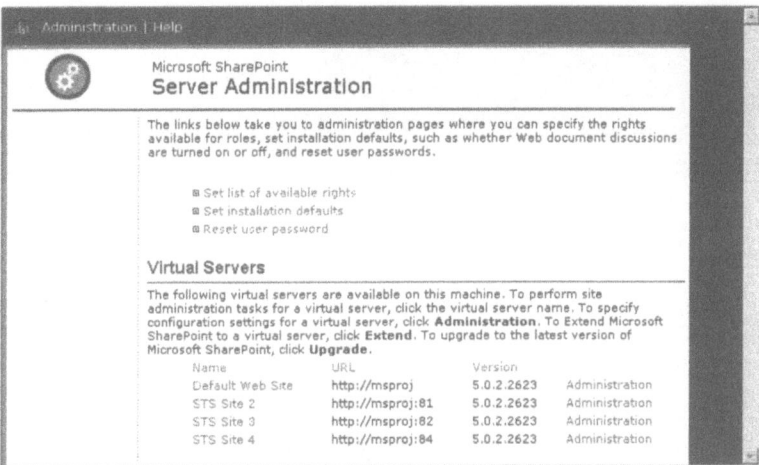

Figure 7-8. The Microsoft SharePoint Server Administration page showing the newly extended site

Provisioning the STS Site for Project Server

Now that you've extended the site for SharePoint, you must now provision it for Project Server. This adds Project Server–specific modifications to the site. To do this, you'll run stswiz.exe, which you may recall using to install STS the first time. Launch stswiz.exe from your installation CD. Navigate to the Support folder to locate the executable. From the splash screen, select the "Provision Additional SharePoint Web sites for Project Server" option and click Next.

The site selection screen displays next (see Figure 7-9). Select the site you want to provision and click Next twice to provision the site. If you make an error or select an ineligible site, the system will report errors when you click Next on the first screen.

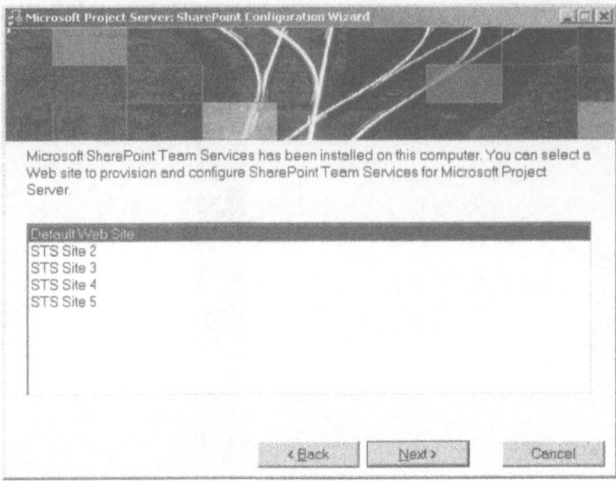

Figure 7-9. Select the site you want to provision.

When it's finished provisioning, the system will display the information for your new site. After the initial installation, you wrote this information down to provide during or after the Project Server installation. Do the same now, particularly the database number and the site port number so that you can keep these sorted out later.

Creating a Database for Your New Site

As you may have already noticed that, unlike the initial installation, adding additional Project Server instances is a manual process. The difference is that by now you've acquired some experience with the technology so it's less daunting, if not less tedious. The next step is to create a blank database for your new site. To do this, follow these steps:

1. Open SQL Server Enterprise Manager. Expand your server until you can see the folders. Right-click the Databases folder and select New Database.

2. In the General tab of the Database Properties dialog box, enter a name for your new database. Something like "projectserver2" will work fine, without the quotes, of course. You can use the Data Files tab to determine the location of the database if you want to change from the default and do the same with the transaction log on its tab. Click OK to create your new database.

Now you have a decision to make. You can populate the database in two ways. The first option is to restore a good Project Server database over the new one you just created, and the second option is to run the database creation scripts. The former option is fast and easy, and it works if you already have a backup of your original empty Project Server database or if you want to copy your nonblank version onto your new site. Note that restoring a Project Server database that already contains projects along with restoring the related SharePoint sites is more involved than the instructions given here. The second option isn't as difficult as it might sound, because Microsoft has thoughtfully provided a command file to run all the scripts outside of the normal Project Server installation routines. In either case, now is a good time to back up your existing Project Server database. You need the backup to use for the restore for the first option, and you need the backup to protect yourself against accidental missteps during the second approach.

Running Database Scripts Using Setupdb.cmd

The setupdb.cmd file is in the Scripts.SQL folder in the Microsoft Project Server Directory. By default, this is drive:\Program Files\Microsoft Project Server\Scripts.SQL. To run the scripts, open a command window and change directories to the directory noted previously. Type the following command, substituting your server name for dbServer and your new database name for databasename; use any SQL account with dbo rights and substitute the appropriate password for password. Don't include the quotes.

```
Setupdb "dbServer" "databasename" "sa" "password"
```

The scripts will begin to run, displaying a continuous stream of data as shown in Figure 7-10. This is normal. When processing is complete, the system will report "SetupDB.cmd completed. Press any key to continue." Your new database is now ready for your new Project Server site. The only difference between this database and the one you created during the initial installation is that the administrator password for this new site is blank. This is because you didn't run the entire install program, which inserts the password into the administrator account.

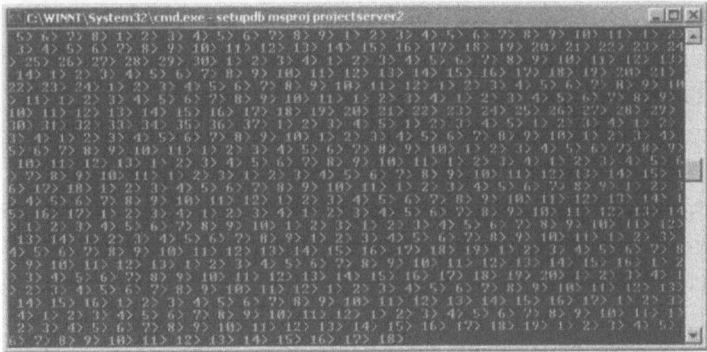

Figure 7-10. A stream of data flows after you start the setupdb.cmd process.

Adding the Project Server Internal Identities As Users in the New Database

Now that you've prepared the database, you must add the MSProjectServerUser and MSProjectUser accounts as logons to the database. Open SQL Enterprise Manager and expand your server, expand the Databases folder, and expand your new database. Right-click Users then select New Database User. In the Database User Properties – New User dialog box, select the MSProjectServerUser account from the Login name drop-down selector at the top of the dialog box, as shown in Figure 7-11. Select the MSProjectServerRole under Permit in Database Role. Repeat these steps for the MSProjectUser, selecting its corresponding role in the database, MSProjectUserRole.

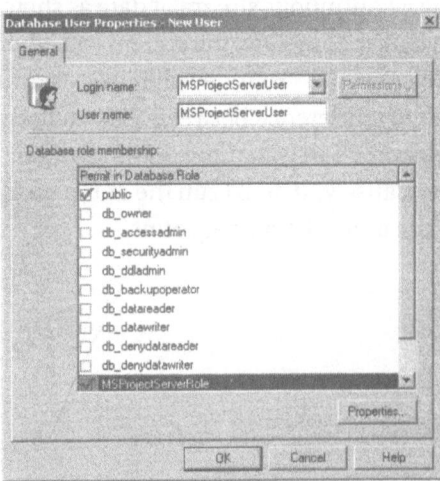

Figure 7-11. Add the internal identities and roles to the new database.

Adding the STS Admin and Reader Accounts to the STS Database

Repeating the steps in the previous section for your new Project Server database, you must add the STSAdmin and STSReader accounts as logons to your new STS database. Assign the STSAdmin account to the db_securityadmin role and the STSReader account to the db_datareader role.

Using the Site Editor to Create the New Virtual Directory

It's now time to use the Site Editor you downloaded in the first step. Start Windows Explorer, navigate to the location on your hard disk to which you downloaded the editor, and unzip the files. Once the files are extracted, navigate to your Program Files directory and find the folder Microsoft Project 2002 Resource Kit. The sub-folder ProjectServerSiteEditor contains the extracted editsite.exe. Double-click the file to start the Site Editor, as shown in Figure 7-12.

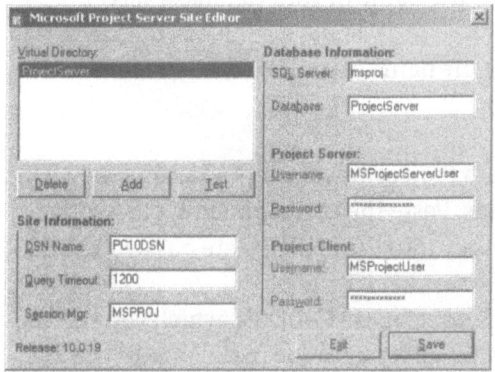

Figure 7-12. Microsoft Project Server Site Editor main screen

Note that the Site Editor doesn't register itself on the Windows taskbar, which means you'll need to go hunting if you open windows on top of it. The main display shows the details for your existing site, which is selected by default. To add your new virtual directory, click Add to open the Create a new site dialog box, as shown in Figure 7-13.

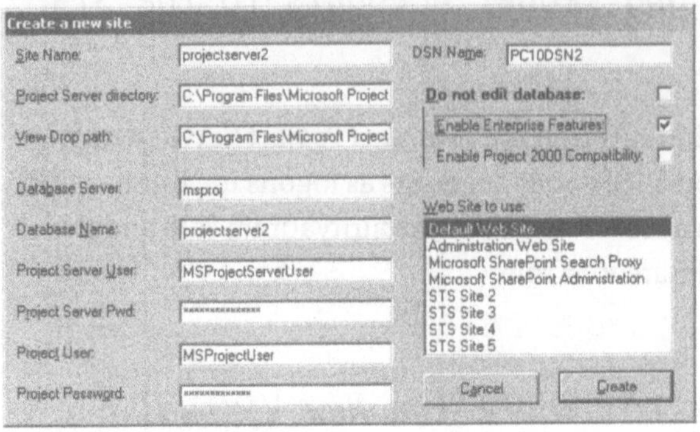

Figure 7-13. The Create a new site dialog box

In the Create a new site dialog box, type a name for the new virtual directory in the Site Name box. The example in the figure is projectserver2. In the Project Server directory and View Drop path fields, verify that the paths to the Microsoft Project Server and View Drop folders are correct, and then continue with the remainder of the fields.

1. In the Database Server field, type the name of your database server.

2. In the Database Name field, type the name of the database you created for your new site.

3. Enter the names of the Project and Project Server users accounts shown in the figure in their respective fields. Paste the corresponding passwords that you harvested from the registry into the appropriate password field.

4. The first Data Source Name (DSN) created is PC10DSN, which you can see under system data sources on your server or in the main page of the Site Editor. You'll create a new DSN for your new site. The tool does this for you automatically; you must provide a unique name for it. I add a number to the DSN name to indicate which site it's for, as shown in Figure 7-13.

5. Select the Enable Enterprise Features check box.

6. Lastly, select a Web site for your new virtual directory. You can add this to your default Web site or any other Web site that has both scripts and executables enabled.

Once you've entered all the information, click the Create button to create your new site, which takes only a moment. When your new creation completes, open a browser window and log onto your new site, entering **Administrator** for your username and leaving the password field blank. If your new site doesn't open correctly, review all the instructions contained in this section. If necessary, refer to Chapter 6.

The Site Editor tool is useful for site maintenance, as it gives you graphical interface access to information and settings for your site stored in the registry. The tool is useful for making changes to existing sites as well as for creating new sites.

Connecting Your New Project Server Site to Its STS Site

While you're logged onto to your new Project Server site with the administrator account, click the Admin menu and select Manager SharePoint Team Services. If you created the database by running the SQL scripts, the Connect to servers page will display in Project Web Access, as shown in Figure 7-14. If you used a database restore to initialize the database, you must first remove the pointer to the server, as it will be pointing to the server registered to the site that you backed up from. See the server removal instructions that follow.

Figure 7-14. Manage SharePoint Team Services ➤ Connect to servers

Click Add Server to open the "Add a Web server running SharePoint Team Services" administration page, as shown in Figure 7-15. Use the information you recorded. Notice that there's only one SharePoint Team Services administration site per server. All sites share the administration site.

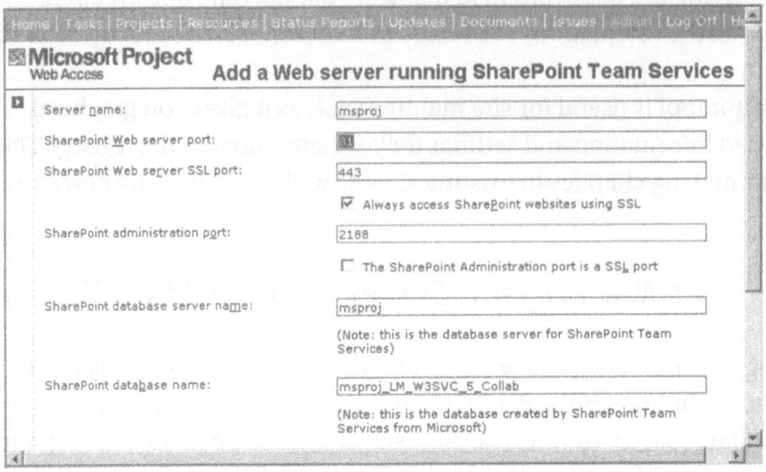

Figure 7-15. Add a Web server running SharePoint Team Services.

When the system has completed processing the request, the Connect to servers page redisplays with the new server information displayed, as shown in Figure 7-16. At this point it's good to see for yourself that the connection is working properly. There aren't any issues to browse yet, but you can click through to the Public Documents Library and open it to verify that Project Server is talking to STS.

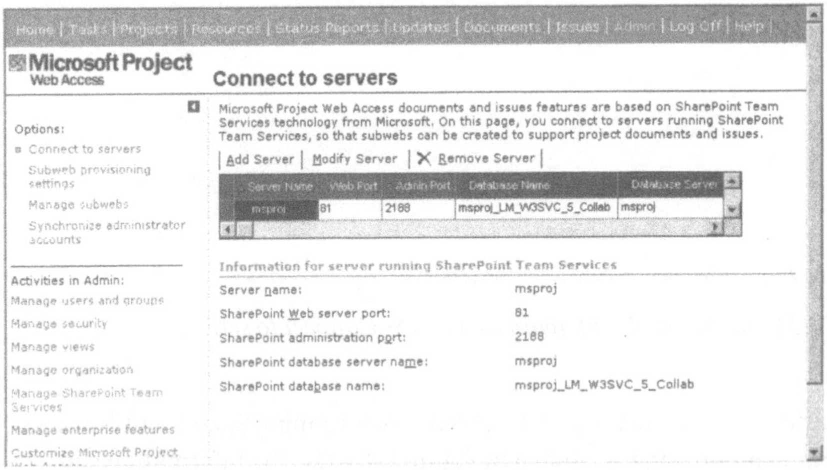

Figure 7-16. Connect to servers after adding an STS server.

TIP   If the server connection is rejected, rerun the proxycfg.exe utility and follow the troubleshooting guide in Chapter 6.

Removing an STS Server

Referring back to the previous image, Figure 7-16, note that the Connect to servers page allows you to modify or remove a server entirely. If you used the SQL restore method to create your new site, and the database backup contains an STS connection record, delete it by highlighting the record and clicking Remove Server. To make changes to an existing record, clicking Modify Server will open an entry page titled Modify Server that is identical to the Add Server page.

Understanding Registry Keys That Relate to Your Project Server Installation

The Microsoft Project Server setup process creates registry entries that identify the locations of various components and contain information necessary for the Project Web Access application to connect to its data stores. You should also be aware of registry keys pertinent to your STS and SQL Server installations, as it may become necessary for you to manipulate these.

Project Server Registry Keys

Registry keys for Project Server are created under HKEY_LOCAL_MACHINE\ Software \Microsoft \Office \10.0\MS Project\WebClient Server. Under the Web-Client Server key, entries are created under Languages and the virtual directory name that you gave your Project Server installation. By default, this is equal to "projectserver" (without the quotes). Figure 7-17 shows the registry expanded, revealing two Project Server sites on the machine. In this case, registry keys are created under two virtual directories, ProjectServer and projectserver3. This information is taken from the Microsoft Project 2002 Resource Kit, which is available on TechNet at http://www.microsoft.com/technet/treeview/default.asp?url=/ technet/prodtechnol/project/project2002/reskit/default.asp.

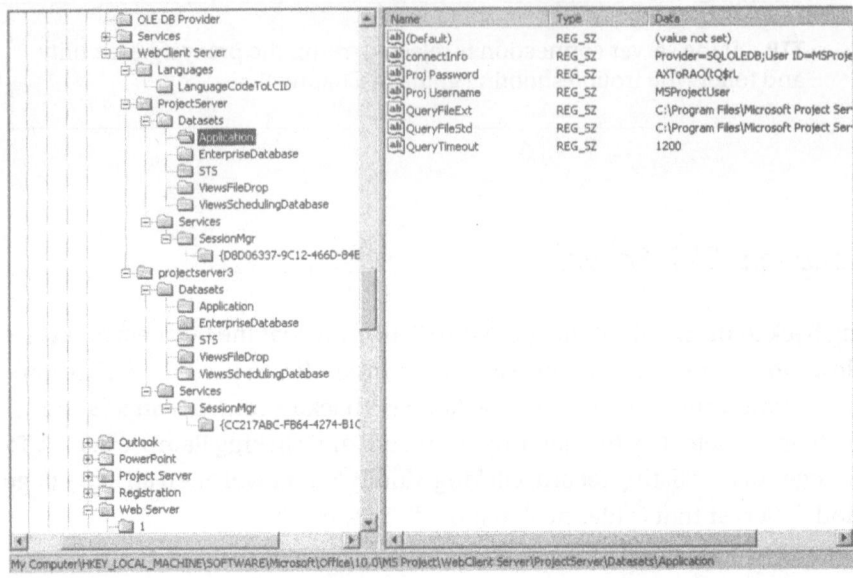

Figure 7-17. Registry expanded to reveal two Project Server instances

\Datasets Keys

The \Datasets key contains the physical data locations for Microsoft Project Server. The subkeys to \Datasets include the keys presented in the following sections.

\Application

This key contains the connection information for the Project Server database corresponding to the named virtual directory.

- *connectInfo:* Stores the database connection string for the Microsoft Project Server database. The string contains the following key/value pairs separated by a semicolon:

  Provider = SQLOLEDB;

  User ID = MSProjectServerUser;

  Password = The database password;

  Persist Security Info = False;

  Initial Catalog = ProjectServer;

  Data Source = <SQL Server Name>

- *Proj Password:* The password for the user specified in Proj Username.

  Value = Password set during installation

- *Proj Username:* The database user identity with which Microsoft Project Professional connects to the Microsoft Project Server database.

  Value = MSProjectUser

- *QueryFileExt:* Points to the Microsoft Project Server extended SQL Query Library.

  Value = <drive>:\Program Files\Microsoft Project Server\Bin\QYLIBSQL.sql

- *QueryFileStd:* Points to the Microsoft Project Server standard SQL Query Library.

  Value = <drive>:\Program Files\Microsoft Project Server\Bin\QYLIBSTD.sql

- *QueryTimeout:* The amount of time the component will wait for the SQL Server.

  Value = 1200

\EnterpriseDatabase

This key contains information specific to the enterprise features of the Microsoft Project Server database.

- *DSN:* The views processing engine uses this DSN to access the Microsoft Project OLE DB provider.

  Value = PC10DSN (default)

- *UserName:* The username associated with the preceding DSN.

  Value = MicrosoftProjectServerUser

- *Password:* The password for the previously specified UserName.

  Value = <system assigned Password for UserName>

\STS

This is the key that contains connection values for Microsoft Project Server to connect to the STS database.

- *connectInfo:* Stores the database connection string for the STS database. The string contains the following key/value pairs separated by a semicolon:

Provider = SQLOLEDB

Integrated Security = SSPI

Persist Security Info = False

- *QueryFileExt:* Contains a pointer to the extended Microsoft Project Server SQL Query Library.

  Value = <drive>:\Program Files\Microsoft Project Server\Bin\QYLIBSQL.sql

- *QueryFileStd:* Contains a pointer to the standard Microsoft Project Server SQL Query Library.

  Value = <drive>:\Program Files\Microsoft Project Server\Bin\QYLIBSTD.sql

ViewsFileDrop

This key contains the location where the views processing service receives new view files.

- *connectInfo:* Contains the path to where the views processing service listens for new publish action view files.

  Value = <drive>:\Program Files\Microsoft Project Server\Bin\View Drop\

ViewsSchedulingDatabase

This key contains connection information for the views scheduling database.

- *connectInfo:* Contains the database connection string for the Microsoft Project Server database. The string contains the following key/value pairs separated by a semicolon:

  Provider = SQLOLEDB;

  User ID = MSProjectServerUser;

  Password = The database password;

  Persist Security Info = False;

  Initial Catalog = ProjectServer;

  Data Source = <SQL Server Name>

- *QueryFileExt:* Contains a pointer to the extended Microsoft Project Server SQL Query Library.

  Value = <drive>:\Program Files\Microsoft Project Server\Bin\QYLIBSQL.sql

- *QueryFileStd:* Contains a pointer to the standard Microsoft Project Server SQL Query Library.

  Value = <drive>:\Program Files\Microsoft Project Server\Bin\QYLIBSTD.sql

\Services Keys

The \Services key contains configuration information Microsoft Project Server services. The Configuration key has two subkeys, which I describe in the following section.

\SessionMgr

This key contains a GUID for a name. The (Default) entry in the GUID folder points to the server running Session Manager.

\Languages Keys

The \Languages key contains the languages supported by the current Microsoft Project Server instance.

- *defLCID:* Stores the locale ID (LCID) for the Project Server default language.

- *LCIDXXXX: XXXX* equals the LCID of the first language supported by the Microsoft Project Server instance.

- *LCIDXXXn: XXXn* equals the LCID of the *n*th language (2 through *n*) supported by the Microsoft Project Server instance.

Distributing Project Server Components

Project Server supports horizontal scaling by allowing you to offload some of the resource-intensive software services onto their own application servers. By way of review of Chapter 4 the following Project Server components may be distributed:

- *Project Web Access:* The IIS ASP application

- *Project Server database:* The database containing project data

- *SharePoint Team Services:* Provides the document and issues management services accessed through Project Web Access

- *SQL Analysis Services:* Provides OLAP services for Analyzer views and the modeler

- *Microsoft Session Manager Service:* Replaces ASP sessions for Project Server and tracks user sessions

- *Views Notification Service:* Handles the updating of information between the Project tables in the database and the Web tables that drive Project Web Access views

You can distribute some or all of the Project Server core application services to one or more application servers. You build an application server by using the Microsoft Project Server Distributed Setup Tool to install Project Server services on top of IIS. You should first establish your Project Server full installation on the primary Web server before you use the tool to build application servers.

Downloading the Distributed Setup Tool

Microsoft provides a tool to assist you with your distributed application setup. You'll find this tool at the Microsoft Download Center at http://www.microsoft.com/download. The actual link is too long to cite. Select Microsoft Project as your product and search on the keywords **distributed Setup**. Download the 6MB .exe file and run the self-extracting installation. The file prjsbox.msi is added to a subdirectory of Program Files called Microsoft Project 2002 Resource Kit. This directory is created if it doesn't already exist.

Using the Distributed Setup Tool to Create an Application Server

Install the self-extracting file on your new application server. Navigate to the Distributed Setup Tool subfolder of the Microsoft Project 2002 Resource Kit folder and double-click prjsbox.msi. In the User information box, enter your username, initials, and organization as you entered them for Microsoft Project Server. After you accept the license agreement, the Microsoft Project Server Distributed 2002 dialog box shown in Figure 7-18 displays. The drop-down lists allow you to select to run all from your computer, or you can selectively choose services to install. For this example I'll move all the services onto one application server. Therefore, I'll set all services to run on my computer.

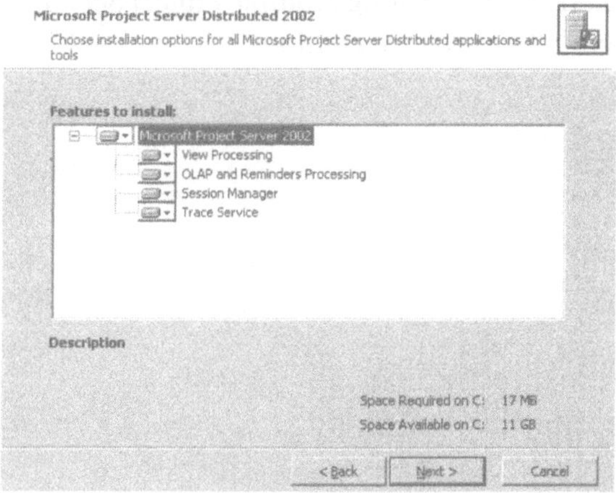

Figure 7-18. Microsoft Project Server Distributed 2002 dialog box

Click Next to move to the database information entry dialog box shown in Figure 7-19. Enter the database server name and the database name from your original installation. Click Next when you've entered the information completely.

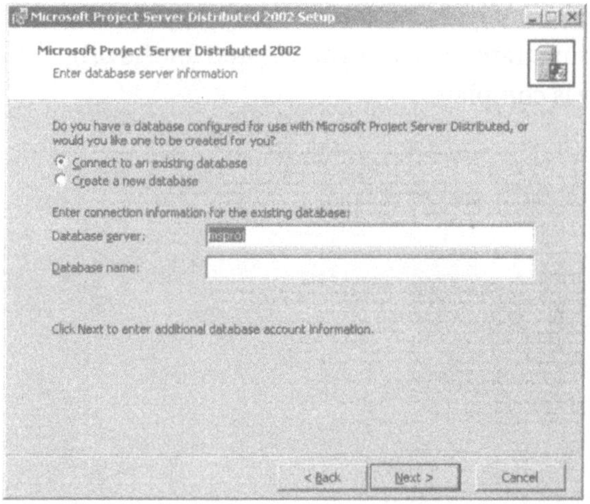

Figure 7-19. Enter the database server and database information.

The system displays the database account information dialog box shown in Figure 7-20. The installation routine created these accounts on the first server. The names are typically as shown in Figure 7-20, but they may vary for your system. Harvest the usernames and the corresponding passwords from the registry according to the instructions contained in the "Creating Multiple Project Server Instances" section earlier in this chapter. Click Next to continue.

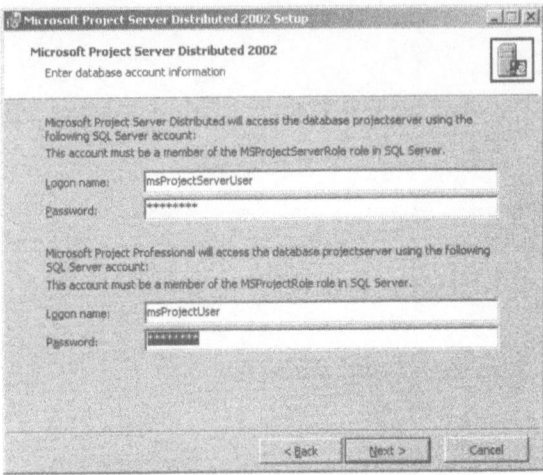

Figure 7-20. Enter the database account information.

Enter the Analysis Services server name and the domain account information for the COM+ identity used to access Analysis Services in the dialog box shown in Figure 7-21. This is the OLAP administrator account you created for the original setup. Click Next when your entry is complete.

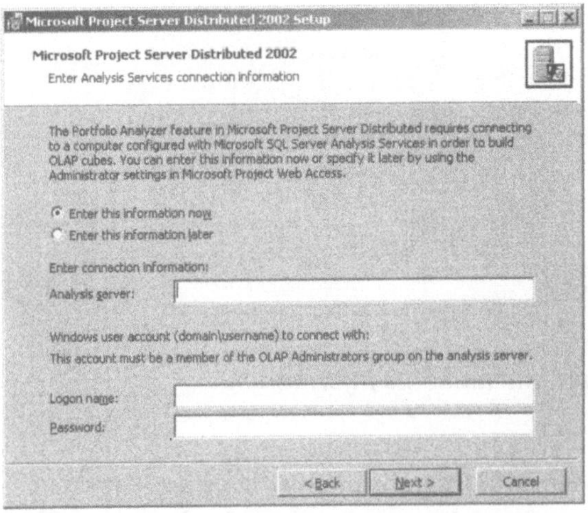

Figure 7-21. Enter Analysis Services information.

Enter the SMTP mail server information in the next dialog box, and complete the SMTP Mail Server, Port, and From Address fields. This is the same information you entered in Microsoft Project Web Access. To view this information in your current installation, select Admin ➤ Customize Microsoft Project Web Access ➤ Notifications and Reminders. Click Next and then click Finish to install core services on your application server. When the Microsoft Project Server Distributed Setup Tool completes, the system displays a confirmation, as shown in Figure 7-22.

Figure 7-22. The Distributed Setup Tool reports success.

For the final step in this process, create a new domain logon. Then, open Windows Explorer and navigate to the installation drive. Expand the Program Files\Microsoft Project Server\Bin\ViewsDrop\ directory. Right-click this folder and share it as a public share. Make the domain user account you created a user of the folder, and under Properties grant Change and Read permissions to the user account.

Creating an Application Server Manually

Another approach to building an application server is to install a full version of Project Server instead of running prjsbox.msi. To manually install core services on an application server, enter the correct database information during the installation, but select "Enter this information later" for all of the optional features except SMTP and Analysis Services if these are required for the services you intend to have running on your application server. For example, this information is required for an application server running the Views Notification service. After you install the full version, start Internet Services Manager and navigate to the Microsoft Project Server virtual directory on the new application server; delete it.

Implementing the Application Server

Once you've created an application server, it's necessary to point the original server at the new application server. You accomplish this by editing the registry on the first server to point it at the new server, and then stopping and disabling the services on the original server. In this chapter's example I'm moving all the core services onto one server. You can use these directions to point your original Project Server at two or more application servers, observing the limit of one server, or server cluster, per service.

Point to the Services Running on the New Application Server

Click the Start button, select Run, and type **regedit**. Expand the registry key HKEY_LOCAL_MACHINE\Software\Microsoft\ Office\10.0\MS Project. Refer back to Figure 7-1 for visual guidance. Under the \WebClient Server\ <Virtual Directory>\Services\SessionMgr folder, open the folder that has the GUID for the server running Microsoft Project Server, as shown in Figure 7-23. Double-click the (Default) registry entry, and change the value to the name of the new application server. The current value will be the current Microsoft Project Server computer.

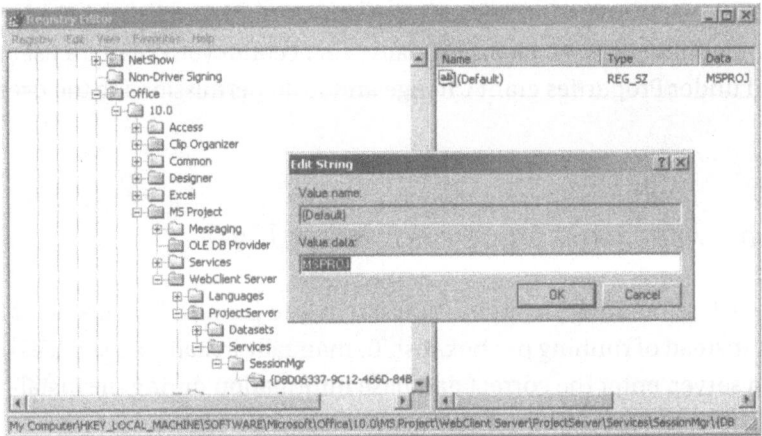

Figure 7-23. Enter the name of the new application server in the default string.

Working again from the MS Project folder in the registry, under \Services\ Configuration\Views Notification\ folder add the following registry entry by right-clicking the folder and choosing new string value:

Type = String

Name = ForwardUNC

Value = pathname to the ViewsDrop directory on the designated notification processor on the application server

Shut Down the Services on the Original Server

Once you've completed the registry changes, you'll need to shut down the services running on the original server. To do this, click the Start button and select Settings ➤ Control Panel. Then open the Administrative Tools folder and launch the Services tool as shown in Figure 7-24. Locate the services beginning with "Microsoft Project."

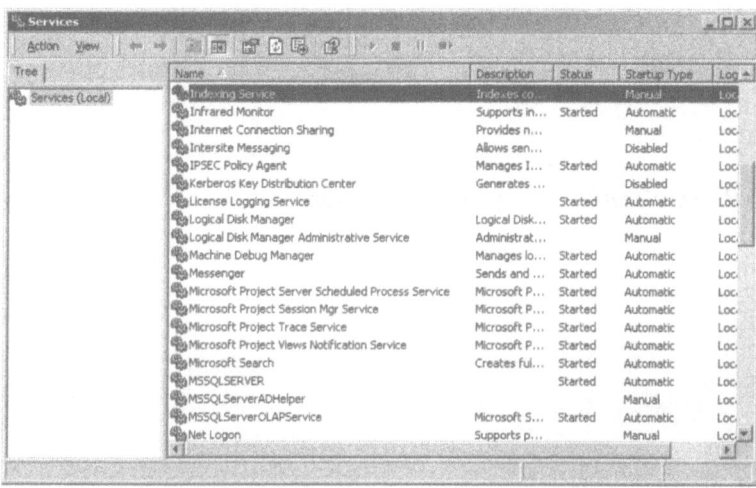

Figure 7-24. Locate the services in the Services dialog box.

Open the Microsoft Project Server Scheduled Process Service properties dialog box by double-clicking the service. On the General tab, click Stop to stop the service as shown in Figure 7-25. If this service isn't needed, use the Startup type drop-down selector to select Disabled to prevent this service from running when the server is started. Click OK. Repeat this process for the Project Session Manager Service as required.

Next, you'll need to change some properties on the Microsoft Project Views Notification service. Open this service as you did the previous services, and then click the Log On tab, as shown in Figure 7-26. Click the This account radio button and enter the username and password for the user granted Change and Read permissions that you created in a previous step.

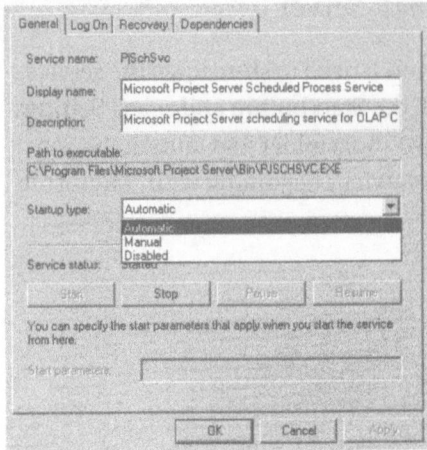

Figure 7-25. Stop the service and change the Startup type.

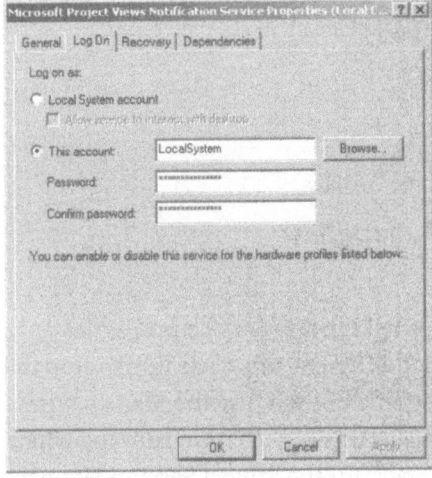

Figure 7-26. Enter the domain logon you created earlier.

Restoring an STS Implementation to a Different Server

A Microsoft TechNet article titled "Migrating Web Sites Based on SharePoint Team Services" describes most of what you need to know to accomplish an intersystem STS restore. You can find this article by expanding the Products and Technologies tree on the TechNet site (http://www.microsoft.com/technet) to SharePoint Team Services and then expanding the Deploy category.

An alternate approach to restoring an STS server for a Project Server is to simply back up all the numbered subwebs and nothing else. Instead of migrating the system, you can re-create it and then restore the contents to the subwebs. In this process, you install a new instance of STS on a server by running the stswiz.exe file. See the section that covers this process in Chapter 5. After re-creating the STS server, you must connect it to the instance of Project Server it will serve.

Use the Project Server Admin interface from Admin ➤ Manage SharePoint Team Services ➤ Connect to Servers to delete the old STS connection and add the new one. Alternately, you can edit the record directly in the MSP_WEB_STS_SERVERS table in the database. Similarly, you must remove all the STS subwebs either by using a SQL script to update the MSP_WEB_PROJECTS table WPROJ_STS_SUBWEB and WSTS_SERVER_ID or by deleting them one by one using the Manage Subwebs interface.

The next step is to re-create the subwebs one by one from Admin ➤ Manage SharePoint Team Services ➤ Manage Subwebs dialog box, as shown in Figure 7-27. Select each project from the drop-down list and click the Create Subweb button. After you create all the subwebs, run Synchronize Users for each site and then copy the contents from the backup folders to the new STS site. Although this process is extremely tedious, it works best to re-create the STS environment for a Project Server.

Figure 7-27. Manage SharePoint Team Services subwebs.

Summary

Building Project Server systems that support hundreds of users or multiple departments requires scaling your hardware by adding servers. You now know how to add instances and servers to your Project Server implementation, allowing scaling through multiple approaches. Building systems like this takes some practice. Make sure that you're comfortable with standard installation techniques before you tackle a distributed system. Consider seeking experienced help if you have any doubts about your own technical skills in this regard.

Part Three
Configuring Project Server for Your Organization

Getting Started with Project Server Configuration

Before your newly installed Project Server can start providing you with business value, you must configure it for your specific needs. As a prerequisite to plunging into configuring your implementation, you must develop some knowledge of the basics. You perform configuration activities in both Project Web Access administration and using the Project Professional client. Therefore, you'll need a fundamental understanding of both interfaces.

Finding your way around and understanding your options presupposes that you also understand the language of Project Server. I begin this chapter with a review of the major terms and the concepts that underlie an understanding of Project Server's approach. Then I move on to cover the basic configuration manipulations and where they're found in the Project Professional or Project Server menus by touring the necessary interfaces.

This chapter has a significant secondary focus on enterprise custom fields and enterprise outline codes. You'll learn the importance of their use and how to create and modify them for an enterprise configuration, as well as how to understand and manipulate essential global values as an important foundation for building your portfolio model in Project Server.

Understanding Project Server's Language

Two constructs you must immediately understand to grapple with Project Server configuration and management are "enterprise project" and "enterprise resource." Very specific criteria establish the enterprise pedigree of a project or a resource. You must learn these.

Enterprise Project

A project is an *enterprise project* when one of the following two conditions is true:

- The project was created using the Project Professional client while connected to a Project Server with enterprise features enabled.

- The project was imported to the enterprise using the Import Project to Enterprise Wizard.

No other method of creation is possible. Many Project Server novices will attempt to open a project in Project Professional from a drive or file share while connected to a Project Server thinking that they can then publish it to the server. Depending on server settings, the Project Server may actually accept the publishing command; however, a well-configured sever doesn't permit a mix of enterprise and nonenterprise projects and should reject these with an error advising that the users are attempting to publish a nonenterprise project. Users who attempt this are unwittingly attempting to publish a project that appears to Project Server to reside in a directory not within in its database. All enterprise projects are stored in the Project Server database.

Enterprise Resource

A resource is an *enterprise resource* when one of the following two conditions is true:

- The resource was created within Project Professional client after acquiring write access to the enterprise resource pool.

- The resource was imported to the enterprise using the Import Resource to Enterprise Wizard.

Like its enterprise project counterpart, a rigid requirement is in place for creating an enterprise resource. You may have already noticed that Project Web Access has its own user account creation and management interface; you may not be aware that this interface provides access to logon and account type information only. Know that having a Project Web Access account doesn't necessarily make a user a resource. Executive users, for example, will likely not have an enterprise resource record. Understand that there's a difference between "user" and "resource" in the Project Server vernacular.

Check In and Check Out

The terms *check in* and *check out* apply to the enterprise global file, enterprise projects, and enterprise resources. A user may check any of these out for editing in a manner such that others may have only read access to these items until they're checked back in. Check in and check out are not offered through the services that STS provides, including documents and issues in Project Web Access. Likewise, there's no version control through these services either.

Understanding Publishing in Project Server

There are four primary table groups in the Project Server database. The first table group consists of project data. Project Professional saves project information to a collection of tables labeled with the prefix "msp_." These are the Project data tables. A near duplication of these, with the prefix "msp_web_," are the tables used to articulate data through Project Web Access. Project data is saved to the ms p_ tables, but Project data is published to the msp_web tables. One of the remaining two table groups contains the cube data prefixed with "msp_cube." The last group contains the view tables used by Project Server when processing the business and presentation logic in the application. Finally, a nominal fifth group is identified as containing the application settings for Project Server and its connections to its member services.

   The important concept to understand is that Project data remains local to the Project tables until a specific publish action is taken to move the data to the public view (into the msp_web tables), which is expressed as publishing the data. This is true for data seen in the various views area of Project Web Access, the timesheet, and the personal Gantt views. In other words, a resource can be assigned to a task in the project but not be aware of the fact through the Project Web Access interface because the project manager hasn't yet published the assignment. Understand that saving a project isn't tantamount to publishing it; however, there are options within the Project Professional interface to trigger project publishing automatically when save actions are taken. I cover these options in the examination of the Project Professional client and look more closely at the database in other chapters.

Understanding Enterprise Global Concepts

Two global entities are ever-present in Project Server conversations: the *enterprise global*, sometimes referred to as the *enterprise global template,* and the *enterprise resource pool.* I call them "entities" because despite the fact that we refer to these singularly, they're actually information collections consisting of numerous data tables and relationships.

You may already have figured out that the enterprise resource pool contains all information pertaining to enterprise resources. Remember that there's a distinction between an enterprise resource and a Project Web Access user. Often, managers and stakeholders are Project Web Access users, but they aren't resources in the pool. Enterprise work resources always get a Project Web Access logon, though these aren't always used. For instance, a machine tracked as a work resource isn't likely to use its logon account.

The enterprise global contains all of the field customizations, plus all of the organizer artifacts covered later in this chapter. When each user connects to Project Server, the enterprise global contents get loaded into cached memory from the server into the user's session. Any changes made to the global file are immediately available to all users upon logging onto the system. The enterprise global is an important foundational element to enforcing a uniform standard for program management.

Essential Knowledge for Working with the Enterprise Global and Enterprise Resource Pool

Although both the resource pool and the enterprise global are governed by check in and check out requirements, these are implemented slightly differently in each case. When opening the resource pool for adding and editing, you can select specific resources to check out, leaving other resources available for others to edit. The global file, on the other hand, is an all-or-nothing proposition, as only one person may edit it at a time.

Checking out resources doesn't affect anyone's ability to use these same resources for team building, assignments, or any other normal project management functions. It only precludes more than one user from attempting to edit resource details such as rates or personnel information for the same resource at the same time. You don't need to check out any resources in order to add resources to the enterprise resource pool; nonetheless, the user must complete the checkout screens to acquire permission to add resources.

Only one person may check out the enterprise global at one time. You must open the global file before making changes to enterprise custom fields or other project objects if you want to include the changes to these in your enterprise global. Until you open the enterprise global, you'll be able to view enterprise fields, but you won't be able to make changes to them. The most important thing to keep in mind when making enterprise global changes is that the changes you make in your session aren't available to anyone until you've saved the changes and closed the enterprise global and until each user has logged on and cached the values contained in the enterprise global after you made changes. This applies to you, the author of the changes, as well. You must completely exit out of Project Professional and restart the application to recache the enterprise global containing the changes you saved. It's best, therefore, not to make changes to the enterprise global when the system is in use.

 WARNING There's no way to refresh the contents of the cached global on your workstation without exiting and restarting the Project Professional client. This applies even to a Project Professional client running on the server machine itself.

Throughout the configuration activity instructions contained in this book, I refer to opening the enterprise global or opening the enterprise resource pool. You should refer back to this topic and the instructions contained in the following section if you need to refresh your memory on enterprise global etiquette.

Opening the Enterprise Resource Pool

To open the enterprise resource pool, launch Project Professional and follow these instructions:

1. Select Tools ➤ Enterprise Options ➤ Open Enterprise Resource Pool. The Open Enterprise Resources dialog box shown in Figure 8-1 displays.

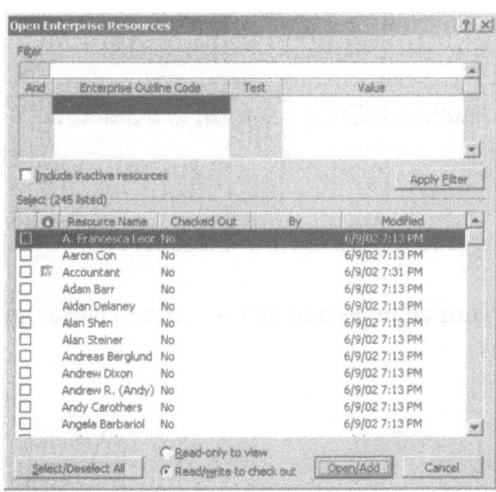

Figure 8-1. The Open Enterprise Resources dialog box

2. Select the resources that you want to check out by clicking the individual check box next to the resource name or optionally by using the Select/ Deselect all button.

3. Click the Open/Add button.

4. The resource pool selections you made will now open in a Resource Sheet view. The title bar across the top of the Project Professional screen will now read "Microsoft Project – Checked-out Enterprise Resources" as shown in Figure 8-2.

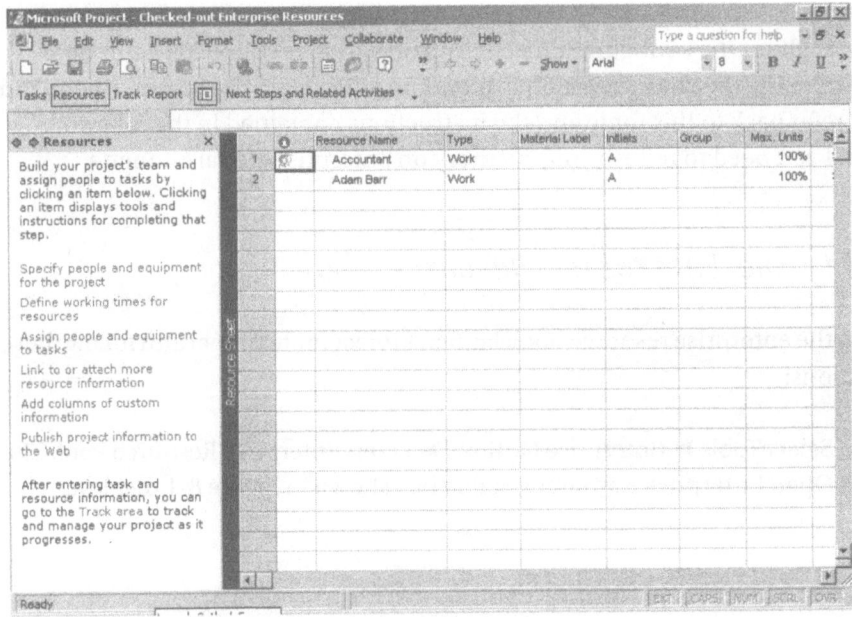

Figure 8-2. The Checked-out Enterprise Resources dialog box open to a Resource Sheet view

5. You're now ready to make changes to the checked-out resources.

6. Always use File ➤ Save to save your changes and File ➤ Close to close the file and check in your resources.

Opening the Enterprise Global

To open the enterprise global, launch Project Professional and follow these instructions:

1. Select Tools ➤ Enterprise Options ➤ Open Enterprise Global. The screen shown in Figure 8-3 displays. The only visible evidence that the file is actually open is the title bar on top of the screen, which reads "Microsoft Project – Checked-out Enterprise Global."

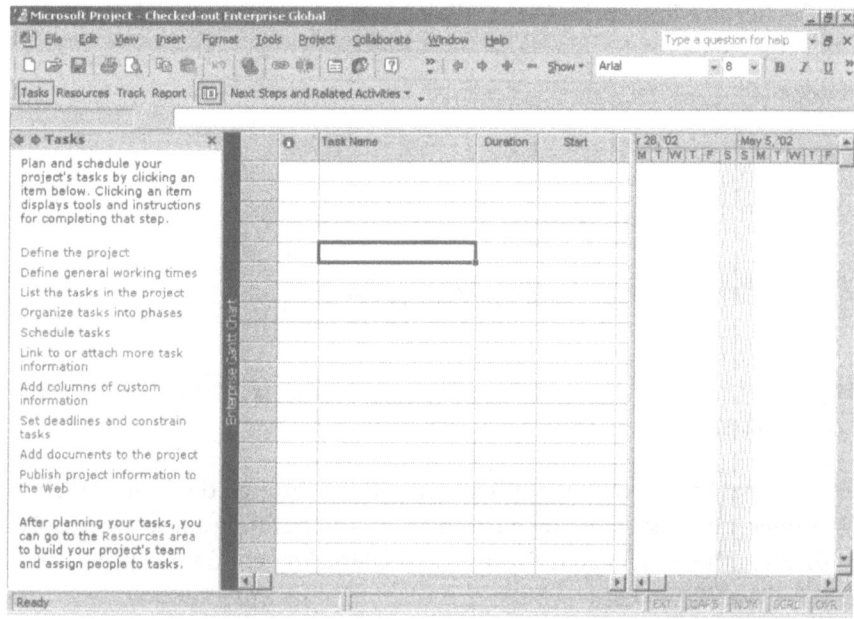

Figure 8-3. You can see that the enterprise global is checked out by looking at the title bar.

2. Always use File ➤ Save to save your changes and File ➤ Close to close the file and check in your resources.

Backing Up and Restoring the Enterprise Global

It's always smart to make a backup of the enterprise global before you check it out to make changes. There's no telling what can happen during a global file editing session. You never know what type of distraction my lure you away from your desk, causing you to risk exposure to accidental system shutdowns and the like. The point is to make backing up the enterprise global a habit.

Fortunately, Project Professional makes backing up the enterprise global easy. From the Tools menu, select Enterprise Options ➤ Backup Enterprise Global. A typical Save As dialog box is displayed that allows you to select a location on your drives or network connections to save the file, which is stored as an .mpt file. To restore a backed-up enterprise global from a file, from the Tools menu select

Enterprise Options ➤ Restore Enterprise Global. The Restore Enterprise Global dialog box displays, as shown in Figure 8-4. Heed the warning about the irreversibility of your actions. Select the administrator account as appropriate. Click the Browse button to open the typical file dialog box to locate the backed-up file you wish to restore. Click the Restore button in the file dialog box and then the Restore button in the Restore Enterprise Global dialog box to complete the operation.

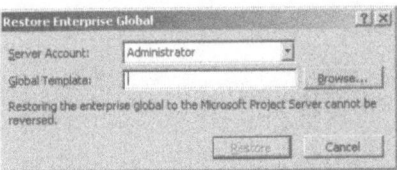

Figure 8-4. The Restore Enterprise Global dialog box

Getting Familiar with the Project Web Access Administration Interface

You control global Project Server application options through the Project Web Access interface, although creating custom fields and building a resource pool is handled through the Project 2002 Professional client. You configure application options in Project Web Access through the Admin menu and interface.

The organizational structure of the Admin menu is confusing. You must cull specific functionality from a hodgepodge of menu selections. The nine selections in the left navigation pane in Figure 8-5 are repeated in the page body (some of these are cut off in the figure) with descriptions. Table 8-1 contains the nine high-level menu choices and the submenu selections that they contain in the Admin interface. Note that the Implement Microsoft Project in the Enterprise selection covered in Chapter 2 isn't counted in this list.

Figure 8-5. All Project Web Access Admin menu selections are represented in the left pane.

Table 8-1. Project Server Admin Menu Organizational Structure

ADMIN MENU SELECTION	SUBSELECTIONS
Manage users and groups	Users
	Groups
Manage security	Categories
	Security templates
	User authentication
Manage views	Views
	DSNs for views
Manage organization	Features
	Menus
Manage SharePoint Team Services	Connect to servers
	Subweb provisioning settings
	Manage subwebs
	Synchronize administrator accounts
Manage enterprise features	Features
	Update resource tables and OLAP cube
	Check in enterprise projects
	Check in enterprise resources
	Versions

Table 8-1. Project Server Admin Menu Organizational Structure (Continued)

ADMIN MENU SELECTION	SUBSELECTIONS
Customize Microsoft Project Web Access	Tracking settings
	Gantt Chart formats
	Grouping formats
	Nonproject time categories
	Home page format
	Notifications and reminders
Manage licenses	N/A
Clean up Microsoft Project Server database	N/A

The Project Web Access Admin menu organizational structure doesn't group functionality in the way you're likely to use it. You need to consider multiple menu selections when attempting to set system options and the same is true for maintenance routines. I've taken a functional approach to organizing selections into four categories:

- *Manage application options:* This category includes selections that manipulate features and feature options that address global selections and system behaviors and don't require frequent manipulation.

- *Application maintenance:* Day-to-day and occasional maintenance routines, including the management of user accounts, are included in this category.

- *Manage security:* This category includes all functionality to manage the security functions and templates that underlie data and user security.

- *Manage collaboration services:* This category includes managing services provided by STS and SMTP connections.

If this helps you to make sense of the selections available to you, use Table 8-2 as a roadmap to locate the functionality you're looking for.

Table 8-2. Categorizing Menu Selections by Working Category

WORKING CATEGORY	MENU LOCATION
Manage application options	Manage organization ➤ Features
	Manage organization ➤ Menus
	Manage enterprise features ➤ Features
	Manage enterprise features ➤ Versions
	Manage enterprise features ➤ Update resource tables and OLAP cube
	Manage views ➤ Views
	Manage views ➤ DSNs for views
	Customize Microsoft Project Web Access ➤ Tracking settings
	Customize Microsoft Project Web Access ➤ Gantt Chart formats
	Customize Microsoft Project Web Access ➤ Grouping formats
	Customize Microsoft Project Web Access ➤ Nonproject time categories
	Customize Microsoft Project Web Access ➤ Home page format
Application maintenance	Manage users and groups ➤ Users
	Manage enterprise features ➤ Check in enterprise projects
	Manage enterprise features ➤ Check in enterprise resources
	Manage licenses
	Clean up Microsoft Project Server database
Manage security	Manage users and groups ➤ Groups
	Manage security ➤ Categories
	Manage security ➤ Security templates
	Manage security ➤ User authentication
Manage collaboration services	Manage SharePoint Team Services ➤ Connect to servers
	Manage SharePoint Team Services ➤ Subweb provisioning settings
	Manage SharePoint Team Services ➤ Manage subwebs
	Manage SharePoint Team Services ➤ Synchronize administrator accounts
	Customize Microsoft Project Web Access ➤ Notifications and reminders

The point to the reorganized view is that you must bounce around the menu to perform tasks in any of these working categories. When you're configuring Project Server, for instance, you must consider selections under four top-level selections. I describe the uses for each of these selections in depth when I cover the relevant related topics in this book. For the purposes of beginning a discussion on configuration, a high-level understanding of the Admin interface is all you need. To that end, I offer you one last table on the topic. Table 8-3 contains brief description of each selection in the Admin interface in its natural order.

Table 8-3. Admin Interface Selections

MENU/SELECTION	DESCRIPTION
Manage users and groups ➤ Users	Add, modify, and deactivate users. Set user password, global permissions, and categories. Merge accounts applies to nonenterprise resources only.
Manage users and groups ➤ Groups	Add, modify, and delete groups. Set global permissions and categories, and users for a group.
Manage security ➤ Categories	Add, modify, and delete categories. Select users, projects, resources, and views that belong to the category. Set global permissions and security relationships for category.
Manage security ➤ Security templates	Add, modify, and delete security templates that can be used to set global permissions for roles defined as groups.
Manage security ➤ User authentication	Set authentication standard for system, minimum password length, and an authentication option applicable to some workgroup installations to allow Project 2000.
Manage views ➤ Views	Add, modify, or delete views displayed in Project Web Access.
Manage views ➤ DSNs for views	Applies to workgroup installations only.
Manage organization ➤ Features	Turn system features on or off globally. Set base intranet and extranet addresses to be used in constructing URLs expressed by Project Server.
Manage organization ➤ Menus	Add, change, delete, or reorder menu selections within Project Web Access.
Manage SharePoint Team Services ➤ Connect to servers	Add, modify, or remove an STS server connection.
Manage SharePoint Team Services ➤ Subweb provisioning settings	Manipulate automation settings for STS subweb creation when projects are published to Project Server.

Table 8-3. Admin Interface Selections (Continued)

MENU/SELECTION	DESCRIPTION
Manage SharePoint Team Services ➤ Manage subwebs	Create, edit, or delete subwebs and their data records.
Manage SharePoint Team Services ➤ Synchronize administrator accounts	Publish Project Server administrator accounts to STS server.
Manage enterprise features ➤ Features	Enable or disable certain enterprise features in Project Server.
Manage enterprise features ➤ Update resource tables and OLAP cube	Set parameters for automated OLAP cube generation and publication of resource availability data to the system.
Manage enterprise features ➤ Check in enterprise projects	Feature to unlock a project record inadvertently left in a checked-out state.
Manage enterprise features ➤ Check in enterprise resources	Feature to unlock a resource record inadvertently left in a checked-out state.
Manage enterprise features ➤ Versions	Add, modify, or delete project save versions allowed on the server.
Customize Microsoft Project Web Access ➤ Tracking settings	Specify default and/or locked-down reporting methods for the system. Select timesheet settings.
Customize Microsoft Project Web Access ➤ Gantt Chart formats	Set formats for Gantt charts that can be associated with Project Web Access views.
Customize Microsoft Project Web Access ➤ Grouping formats	Set grouping styles that can be applied to Project Web Access views.
Customize Microsoft Project Web Access ➤ Nonproject time categories	Set up the nonproject collection buckets that appear on the timesheet.
Customize Microsoft Project Web Access ➤ Home page format	Allow the user to add simple links and content to the Project Web Access home page.
Customize Microsoft Project Web Access ➤ Notifications and reminders	Set up a connection to a mail server and determine base message, and set time for daily notifications to run.

Getting Familiar with Configuration Selections in Project 2002 Professional Edition

Now that you have inklings about the Admin interface in Project Web Access, it's time to explore the desktop client's substantial role in configuration. You can perform certain configuration work only in the Project Professional client. This includes the customization of fields and outline codes as well as enterprisewide customizations to the Project Professional interface. Most important, understand that very little project or resource data gets changed through the Project Web Access interface. This is primarily a Project Professional function.

At the bottom of the tools menu, shown in Figure 8-6, three selections, Organizer, Customize, and Enterprise Options, come into play for configuration.

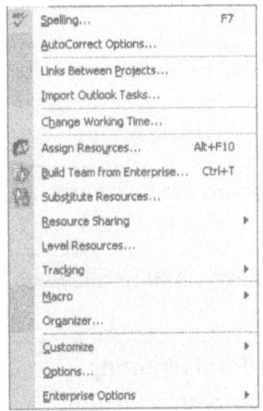

Figure 8-6. The Tools menu

Four of the five selections on the Customize menu, shown in Figure 8-7, pertain to enterprise configuration. The Fields selection refers to nonenterprise fields and is therefore not relevant to this discussion. Enterprise fields, on the other hand, is a selection you'll make often during the initial configuration. This is where you create custom enterprise outline codes and fields. Changes made to the Toolbars and Forms selections are globally available for all users. Published Fields refer to the fields that users see on their timesheet.

Figure 8-7. The Tools ➤ Customize menu

The Enterprise Options menu, shown in Figure 8-8, reveals a number of selections that you'll use constantly when configuring and building your system. The menu items Open Enterprise Global and Open Enterprise Resource Pool are used to update custom information contained in these information entities. The import wizards launched by the selections Import Project to Enterprise and Import Resources to Enterprise are essential to a speedy initial system data load. The Backup Enterprise Global and Restore Enterprise Global options aren't configuration-specific functions; however, you'll use them periodically during configuration as insurance against missteps.

Figure 8-8. The Tools ➤ Enterprise Options menu

Another menu selection you'll use on the Tools menu to perform system-wide customization is Change Working Time to add and modify calendars. This simply becomes a global operation when you check out the enterprise global.

Those of you who have exercised Project client customization in the past will already be familiar with the Organizer shown in Figure 8-9. In previous versions you used it to copy project artifacts from project to project or into and out of the global.mpt file. Now it is also useful as a conduit for importing custom artifacts into the enterprise global, including

- Views

- Forms

- Calendars

- Groups

- Toolbars

- Tables

- Reports

- Modules

- Filters

- Maps

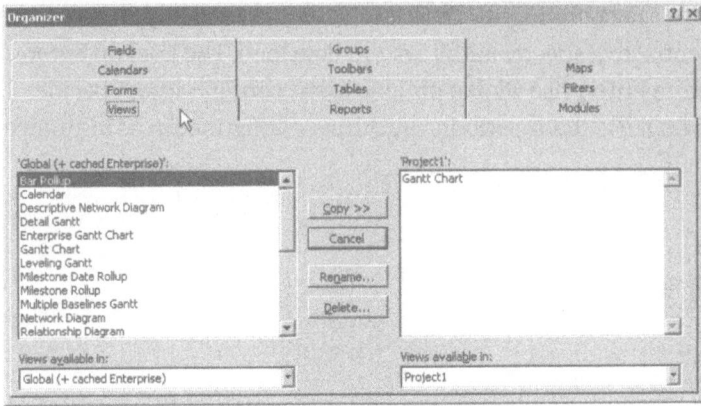

Figure 8-9. The Organizer interface

Understanding Custom Outline Codes and Custom Fields

You must mold the raw functionality provided in Project Server to shape and channel information to your organization's specific requirements. Although the built-in generic information streams provide useful tracking and statistical data, you accomplish a more meaningful presentation of information by seeding the database with custom attributes. These exist in Project Server as custom fields and custom outline codes, which come in two flavors: enterprise and local. Those of you familiar with field customization will find that the process for customizing enterprise fields is the same as it is for local fields in prior versions of Project. The most striking difference is the lack of enterprise finish and start fields. These remain available as local fields.

You manage enterprise fields and outline code definitions centrally. Only administrators or users specifically granted permission can modify these. Modify local custom fields and outline codes on an individual project basis. Local fields and codes aren't available across projects except that these may be moved from one project to another through the Organizer, as shown in Figure 8-9. In the figure, I copied the view "new gantt" from the Long Hill Development plan to the Data Recovery Service plan. You accomplish this by opening both plans from Project Server and then launching the Organizer.

Project Server configuration focuses on enterprise custom fields and outline codes. The most important distinction between custom enterprise fields and custom enterprise outline codes is that enterprise outline codes publish to the OLAP cube as dimensions. Thus, your ability to craft Analyzer output to meet

specific requirements is supported exclusively by enterprise outline codes. Consequently, outline codes will usually follow reporting vectors and you'll use them
liberally in your configuration design.

Traditionally, Microsoft Project has offered a complement of fields and outline
codes definable at the task/assignment and resource levels. Both remain available
as local field sets, and now as enterprise fields and outline codes. New with Project
Server are project-level fields and outline codes, which facilitate flexible portfolio
designs.

Why Enterprise Fields and Outline Codes Are Important to Your Configuration

Project stakeholders and management often have difficulty accessing project facts
traditionally buried in charter and scope documents. Project Web Access gives you
the opportunity to capture and display this information in convenient views that
can bring the metadata associated with a project to the public eye, information as
mundane as what stage the project is at in the corporate approval process, stakeholder names, and contact information. Of course, you can also share the charter
document through STS, but that might be too much clicking and searching for
some. In the Project Center view shown in Figure 8-10, I added the custom outline
codes Location and Performer to enrich the view.

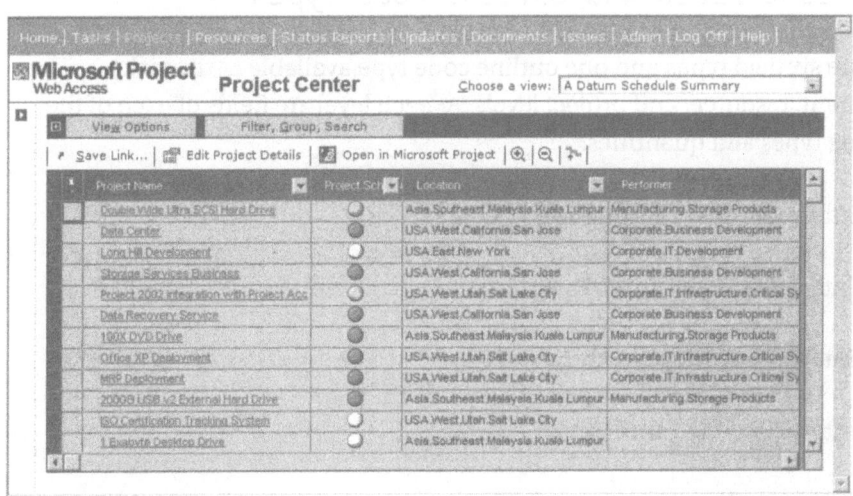

Figure 8-10. Project Center view displaying custom field data information

The Analyzer view in Figure 8-11 shows the power of outline codes when using
OLAP cube data. Because I attributed resources by practice group, you're able to

see the resource loading across these classifications and you're able to drill down to the individual resource within each group. If you desire, you could expand the time data to quarters. Without the custom attributes, this display wouldn't be possible. The power of these tools relies heavily on custom data.

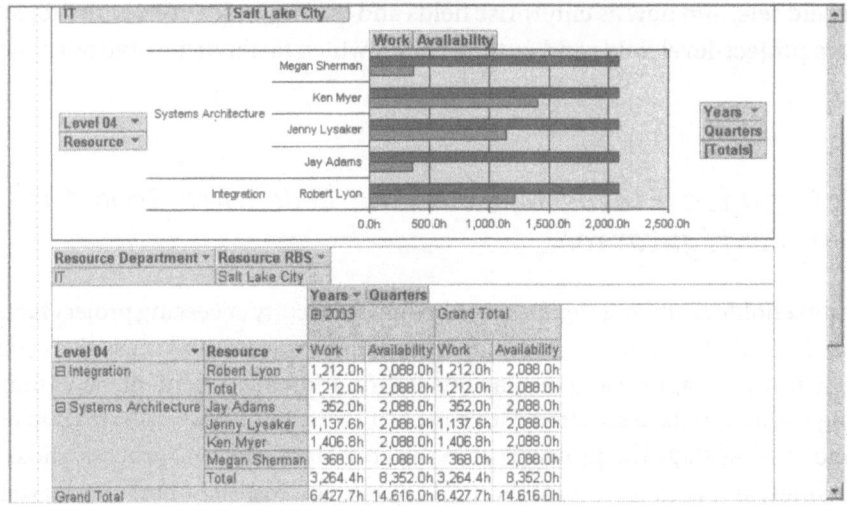

Figure 8-11. Analyzer view displaying demand and actual work by practice group

Enterprise Field and Outline Code Types

There are six field types and one outline code type available at the task/ assignment, resource, and project levels. At each level are fields of each of the following types and quantities:

- Enterprise *Cost* 1 through 10

- Enterprise *Date* 1 through 30

- Enterprise *Duration* 1 through 10

- Enterprise *Flag* 1 through 20

- Enterprise *Number* 1 through 40

- Enterprise *Text* 1 through 40

- Enterprise *Outline Codes* 1 through 30

Defining Enterprise Fields and Outline Codes

To define an enterprise field or outline code, you must first check out the enterprise global. Once you've done so, navigate to Tools ➤ Customize ➤ Enterprise Fields. The Customize Enterprise Fields dialog box opens as shown in Figure 8-12. Open the Custom Fields tab. It's shown again in Figure 8-13 with the Custom Outline Codes tab exposed.

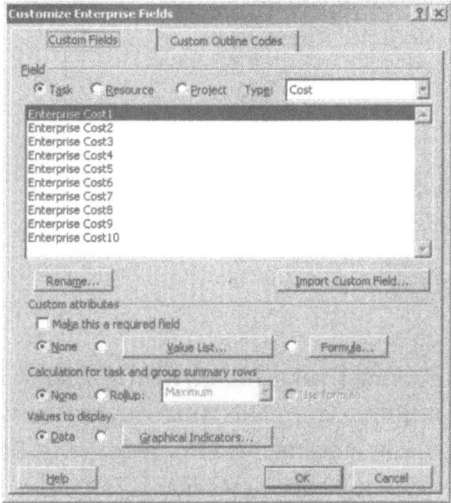

Figure 8-12. The Customize Enterprise Fields dialog box with the Custom Fields tab open

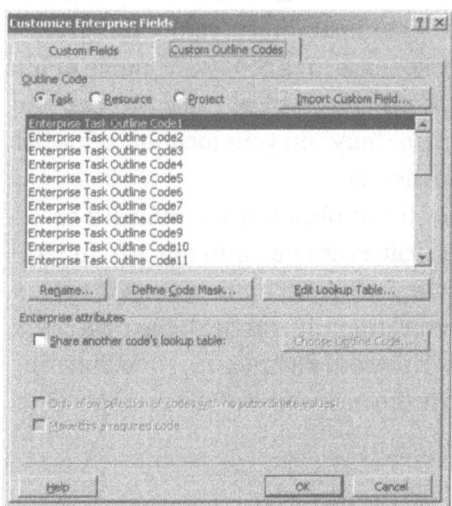

Figure 8-13. The Customize Enterprise Fields dialog box with the Custom Outline Codes tab open

Customizing Enterprise Fields

Referring back to Figure 8-12, you can see that each field has it own set of attributes. First make a selection to customize a field for Task, Resource, or Project by clicking the corresponding radio button. Select a field type and click the Rename button. The Rename Field dialog box appears to accept the input of a new name. In the example in Figure 8-14, I rename Enterprise Project Text6. Type the name of your new field and click OK. In the example, I've entered the name **Project Manager**. Next, determine whether the field will be required. If this is a required field, select the "Make this a required field" check box.

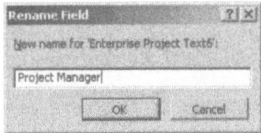

Figure 8-14. Renaming your new custom field

Making a field required forces users to provide a value before writing a record to the database. In other words, if you have required task fields, you can't save new tasks to a plan without a value provided. Similarly, required resource fields must be completed when saving resource data; likewise for project level fields. You must give required fields careful thought. First, it must be reasonable to expect that users will have values for required fields when they encounter them. Second, you must anticipate exceptions to validated values when you opt to use them.

In the case of required resource fields, you must consider whether you have applicable values for generic resources if your configuration includes them. For instance, a required location field doesn't make sense for a generic resource unless you're creating the resource as geographically specific. Typically this isn't the case, so you must include a value such as "generic" or "any" on your location value list. This caution applies to custom outline codes as well.

Control the contents of your new field by the application of a value list or formula. Once a value list is set for a field, all values entered into the field must adhere to the list values. Without a value list and value list options set, the user is free to enter any text up to 255 characters in the example text field. Click the Value List button to open the Value List dialog box shown in Figure 8-15. Note that the name Project Manager contained in quotes is the new name of the example field.

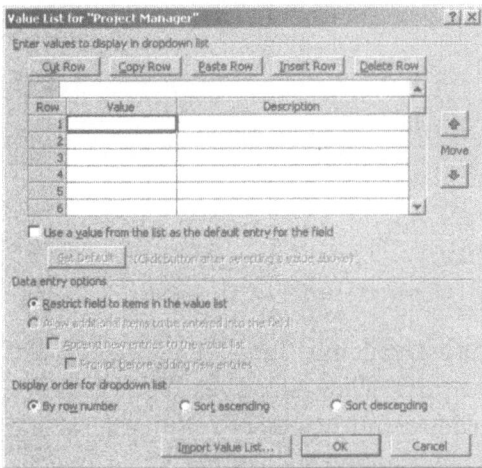

Figure 8-15. Custom field Value List dialog box

Setting a value list enhances your control over the field by optionally forcing validation of all input. Establishing a value list allows you to set a default value for the field.
To do this, check the box immediately under the value list grid in the Value List dialog
box after you've highlighted the selection to use. This turns the display of the value to
red. Type in your values and descriptions in the entry grid provided. The descriptions
are for administrative purposes and aren't visible elsewhere, so don't sweat them.

Don't let the dialog box fool you; the option to allow additional items to be
entered into the field applies only to local fields, not enterprise fields. Use the
display order for drop-down list selections to control the ordering of drop-down
displays when the user encounters them.

> **TIP**   Although you can select a sort order for custom fields, outline
> codes always observe an alphabetical sort. Therefore, if you're con-
> structing a value list that you want to display in a specific order, you'll
> need to work around this behavior by prefixing your values with num-
> bers in sequence or creating a prefix using alphabetical characters such
> as "a-," "b-," and so on.

Click the Import Value List button at the bottom of the Value List dialog box to
activate the Import Value List entry dialog box shown in Figure 8-16. In the first
drop-down box, select from one of the open project files. Select the Checked-out
Enterprise Global file to import a value list from another global file field. Then,
select the field containing the value list you wish to import. Click OK once you've
made your selection or click Cancel to exit.

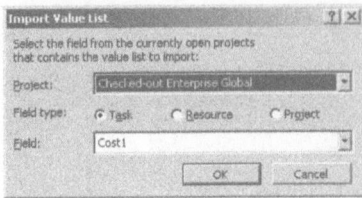

Figure 8-16. The Import Value List dialog box

After you've defined an optional value list, you must choose how the field will behave in views. Here the Customize Enterprise Fields dialog box allows you to choose the calculation behavior. You also determine whether to display the actual data from a field or a graphical indicator representing the data. Selecting a calculation option for your new field allows you to control the way the values roll up to task summary rows and group summary rows in Project views. Rollup options apply to all custom fields except text fields and don't apply to custom outline codes. When you select the Rollup radio button, you must also choose a type in the corresponding drop-down box. (Refer back to Figure 8-12.)

Understanding Rollup Methods for Enterprise Custom Fields

Once you select the Rollup radio button, the rollup drop-down list becomes available for you to make a selection. Your choices vary by field type. I enumerate the number fields, the selections, and their applicability in Table 8-4.

Table 8-4. Enumeration of Custom Field Rollup Types

ROLLUP TYPE	COST	DATE	DURATION	NUMBER	FLAG	TEXT
Average	X		X	X		
Average First Sublevel	X		X	X		
Count All				X		
Count First Sublevel				X		
Maximum	X	X	X	X		
Minimum	X	X	X	X		
Sum	X		X	X		
AND					X	
OR					X	

Now that you know which rollup method applies to each specific field type, the following explanations of the rollup methods will help you choose the appropriate method for your new field. Keep in mind that there's no particular right or wrong answer here—these choices must follow the function you intended for the field.

- *Average:* Causes the rollup to be an average of all nonsummary values beneath the summary row.

- *Average First Sublevel:* Causes the rollup to be an average of both the non-summary and summary values on just the first level of subtasks or grouped tasks.

- *Count All:* Causes the rollup to be a count of all summary and nonsummary items beneath the summary row.

- *Count First Sublevel:* Causes the rollup to be a count of both the summary and nonsummary tasks on just the first level beneath the summary row.

- *Maximum:* The rolled-up value will be the maximum value of values beneath the summary row.

- *Minimum:* The rolled-up value will be the minimum value of all values beneath the summary row.

- *Sum:* Sets the rolled-up to value to the sum of all nonsummary values beneath the summary row.

- *AND:* Is applicable to enterprise flag fields only. When selected, it indicates that the rollup should be a logical AND of all the flag values appearing beneath the summary row. For example, if all flags in the subtasks are set to Yes, then the rollup in the summary task is Yes; if any flags in the subtasks are set to No, then the rollup in the summary task is No.

- *OR:* Is applicable to enterprise flag fields only. When selected, it indicates that the rollup should be a logical OR of all flag values appearing beneath the summary row. If any flags in the subtasks are set to Yes, then the rollup is Yes.

- *Use Formula:* Applies the same formula to the summary row as it does the subordinate rows when a formula applies to the custom field, rather than rolling up the values in the column.

Using Formulas to Display Calculated Data in Custom Fields

Calculated fields provide a very flexible way to influence the output of Project Professional views and reports, and Project Web Access views. Use calculated fields to perform compound financial calculations such as net present value or to build business-specific key performance indices (KPIs). Tap them to make alternative data available conditioned to a specific business interpretation to accommodate nonproject standard displays of duration and effort facts. Keep in mind that enterprise custom fields can reference other enterprise custom fields or any built-in Project field, but they must not reference local fields, which aren't reliable data sources.

Click the Formula button in the Customize Enterprise Fields dialog box (refer back to Figure 8-12) to open the Formula dialog box. Shown in Figure 8-17, the Formula dialog box provides graphical tools for building formulas, such as the simple one in the figure where one cost field is subtracted from the other. If you prefer, you can type in the formula directly. The system represents operators as buttons for quick clicking, and fields and functions are inserted using pull-down menus. The navigational structure of the pull-down menus is very intuitive and logically categorized.

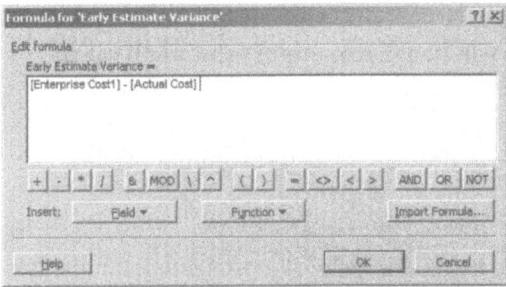

Figure 8-17. Build a formula using the interface tools or type it in directly.

Displaying Graphical Indicators in Custom Fields

Graphical indicators give a powerful, popular, and eye-pleasing impact to both Project Professional and Project Web Access views. You'll always see these used liberally in sales-pitch demonstrations given by Microsoft staffers and Project Partners. Project and Project Server both display graphical indicators as set through the field customization interface. Click the Graphical Indicators button in the Customize Enterprise Fields dialog box to launch the Graphical Indicators dialog box shown in Figure 8-18. The example shows a Project-level field defined to display a simple red, yellow, and green stoplight-type indicator based on three simple values.

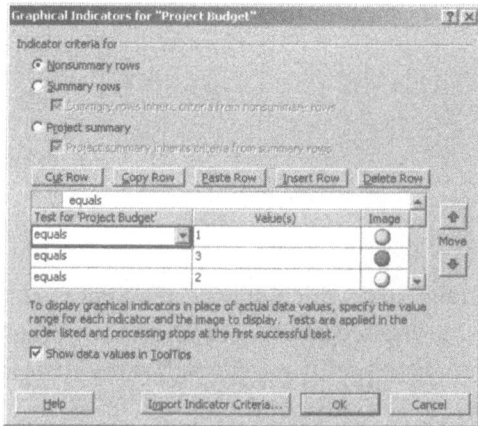

Figure 8-18. The Graphical Indicators dialog box

As a project-level field, it's intended for views that will display project records. Therefore, it makes sense to define this for nonsummary rows as the Project Budget indicator in the sample will apply to projects as a whole. Notice that you can also choose to set this for summary rows or the project summary row. In these cases, you also determine whether the summary rows inherit criteria from the nonsummary rows. Another thing to keep in mind is the effect this inheritance can have on graphical indicators based on the rollup method when a graphical indicator applies to a calculated field.

Along with editing tools, the test grid populates using pull-down menus. You can apply the following tests to the specified values:

- Equals

- Does not equal

- Is greater than

- Is greater than or equal to

- Is less than

- Is less than or equal to

- Is within

- Is not within

- Contains

- Does not contain

- Contains exactly

- Is any value

You may apply these tests to the Value(s) field, which may be a Project standard or enterprise field, or a literal value entered by the user. The "is any value" test yields a positive result in all cases, making it useful as a catchall at the bottom of the list to display an indicator to represent a value not otherwise defined or other. The fact that you would place this at the bottom of the list brings up a very important point about graphical indicator tests. These prosecute from the top down. Not only must you keep this in mind while structuring your test logic, but you can also use it to your advantage.

In the example shown in Figure 8-18, number 1 displays green, number 3 displays red, and number 2 displays yellow. In this case, the order these appear in the list is inconsequential with the exact test. It should be noted in this case that any value occurring in the field that isn't 1, 2, or 3 exactly would cause no indicator to display. Changing the example to use the "is greater than" test for all of these values would cause all values above 2 to display the yellow indicator and the red indicator to never display. This is because after meeting the test for being greater than 3, the value would then meet the test for being greater than 2, changing it ultimately to yellow.

You can choose from 17 distinct graphics. Some are available in only one color, whereas others are available in many colors. Use the check box at the bottom of the Graphical Indicator dialog box to determine whether the data value underlying the graphical display will show in a pop-up display when the user hovers a mouse over the indicator in a view.

Customizing Enterprise Outline Codes

Renaming an enterprise outline code is done in exactly the same way as renaming a field. Outline codes are different from other fields, as they can accommodate a flat value list or hierarchical structure. Like custom fields, outline codes may be set as required. Unlike custom fields, outline codes may not be defined using calculations and graphical indicators, and outline codes require that you define a code mask before defining a value list. The *code mask* determines the allowable structure of an outline code value by setting a sequence of code segments and determining their allowable length. You select which character separates the code segments. An option also allows you to set an outline code to accept only selections on the tree with no subordinate values.

Click the Define Code Mask button on the Custom Outline Codes tab of the Custom Enterprise Fields dialog box to launch the Outline Code Definition dialog box shown in Figure 8-19. In the sequence box, you may select Numbers, Uppercase letters, Lowercase letters, or Characters. By selecting any of these, your values must adhere to the type specified. Selecting Characters gives you the most flexibility, as you may use any character in defining your values. You select the length for the code segment using the pull-down menu. This gives you the choice of limiting the segment to a number value on the list or a number you type into the field, or you may choose to set the segment to any, which allows any number of defined characters in the definition.

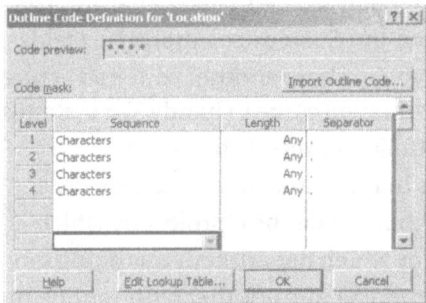

Figure 8-19. Use the Outline Code Definition dialog box to construct a code mask.

Separators for code segments may be the dot, dash, plus sign, or forward slash. Choose these from the pull-down menu. The system also accepts other special characters, such as those found above the number keys on a keyboard. Once you define the code mask, click the Edit Lookup Table button in the Outline Code Definition dialog box to activate the Edit Lookup Table dialog box shown in Figure 8-20. Note the indenting controls in the upper toolbar. Use the indenting tools to create subordinate values. Indenting in pick-list displays is turned on or off by checking or unchecking the "Display indenting in lookup table" check box.

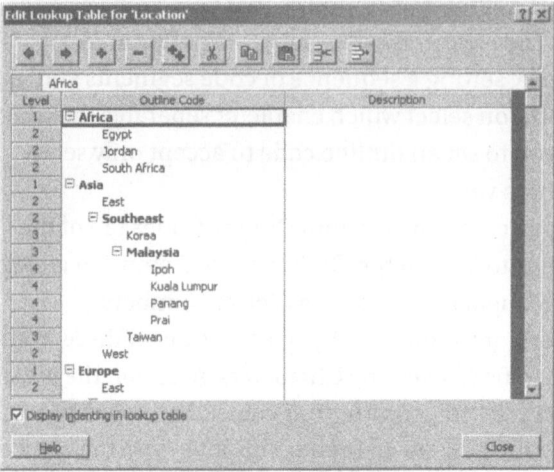

Figure 8-20. The Edit Lookup Table dialog box

One of the most useful features of outline codes is their sharing nature. The option to share another code's lookup table on the Customize Enterprise Fields dialog box (refer back to Figure 8-13) allows you to share another code's structure. You'll likely find a number of occasions when this will come in handy. For instance, many companies will want to slice their portfolio of projects based on department. It's possible to want to slice this in more than one way. Let's say a company wants to define a project-level attribute to define a project by which department it primarily benefited and again by which department was doing most of the work. One outline code representing producer and another representing the consumer will share one lookup table.

Deleting a Custom Field or Outline Code

There are two ways to approach this. The first is to open the enterprise global and open the field to modify and then clear all the custom attributes, including the new name. The other approach is to open the enterprise global, then launch the Organizer (covered earlier in this chapter) and delete the custom field using the Organizer.

The Publishing Process and Enterprise Custom Fields

An unexpected quirk that comes along with Project Server's data publishing process is that custom fields aren't immediately available in Project Web Access. If after a new field is defined, an administrator then checks in the enterprise global and proceeds directly to Project Web Access Admin interface and modifies a view to display the new field, chances are the new field won't immediately show in the view at all or won't show valid data. New graphical indicators, for example, will show default or null value data rather than an indicator until you republish an existing project. Similarly, fields may not appear in a freshly modified Project Center or Resource Center view until you publish a project to the server, causing the new field customization to appear as well.

The RBS and Reserved Enterprise Resource Outline Code 30

Enterprise Resource Outline Code 30 is reserved for the Resource Breakdown Structure (RBS). Although the RBS provides the same useful functionality as other outline codes, this one is unique among all others because of its interplay with security. The RBS is used to define a resource manager's relationship to a resource. A resource manager's ability to see project and resource data is determined by subordination in the code values. These constructs are very powerful in controlling some Project Server security relationships. I'm calling it out here to make you aware of its special role. I cover this extensively in Chapter 10.

Summary

You now have the foundational knowledge with which to proceed with your configuration. The administration interface guidance and field customization rules in this chapter will serve you well as you proceed. Refer back to these as needed.

CHAPTER 9

Configuring Project Server Application Options

In the previous chapter you learned the basics you need to proceed with configuration. Assuming that you've done your requirements homework, you should be ready to dive in. The order in which you do things, to some degree, makes a difference. I suggest that you approach things in this order:

1. Create custom fields.

2. Set application options.

3. Configure security.

4. Import resources.

5. Import projects.

6. Build custom views.

Beginning with your field customizations makes sense because you'll need these to apply to your resources and projects, and because your custom views are likely to be dependent on them. It's time to introduce a model for this configuration discussion, as it's much easier to understand examples when they come together as a whole.

I expect that about half this book's readers are involved in the information technology (IT) field. IT challenges beg for project-based solutions. An IT department for a growing company serves as the deployment example for this and the rest of the chapters in this part. The example is oversimplified, but deep enough to demonstrate the power of the solution when configured correctly.

In this chapter you'll learn how to set Project Server's application options to best serve your company's needs. I assume that you've created your custom fields. The fields shown in Table 9-1 make up the custom fields and outline codes configured in your sample system.

Table 9-1. Custom Fields and Outline Codes for an Example IT Department

FIELD LABEL	FIELD	MANDATORY	VALUES	DEFAULT	NOTES
Project					
Program	EPOC01	N	Process Imp, Supply Chain, HR Sys, WinXP Upg,Whse Upg, Maintenance	N/A	Describes program the project belongs to
Sponsor	EPOC02	Y	Gen Business, Finance, Logistics, HR, IT, Purchasing, Marketing, Stores	N/A	Consumer of project work product
PM	EPOC03	Y	J. Murray, K. Patel, M. Berg		
Phase	EPOC04	Y	Request, Approved, Discovery, Design, Development/Quality, Delivery, Complete		
Resource					
Location	EROC01	Y	LA, Chgo, NYC, Balt, Buffalo	N/A	
Skill	EROC02,SK	Y	Proj Mgr, Anal Mgr, Q/A Mgr, Sys Mgr, Architect, DBA, Analyst, P/A, P/A Lead, Q/A, Q/A Lead, Sysop, Sysop Lead, Security, Security Lead, SME, Stakeholder		
System	EROC03, SH:EPOC02	Y			
RBS	EROC30	Y	Dev Mgr > Dev, Q/A Mgr > Q/A, Sys Mgr > Sys, Anal Mgr > Anal		
Task					
Phase	ETOC01, SH:EPOC04	Y			

Setting Options for Enterprise Features

Your logical first step is to make sure that, at a high level, Project Server behavior is configured to your requirements. You access the screen shown in Figure 9-1 by clicking the "Manage enterprise features" link from the Admin menu in Project Web Access.

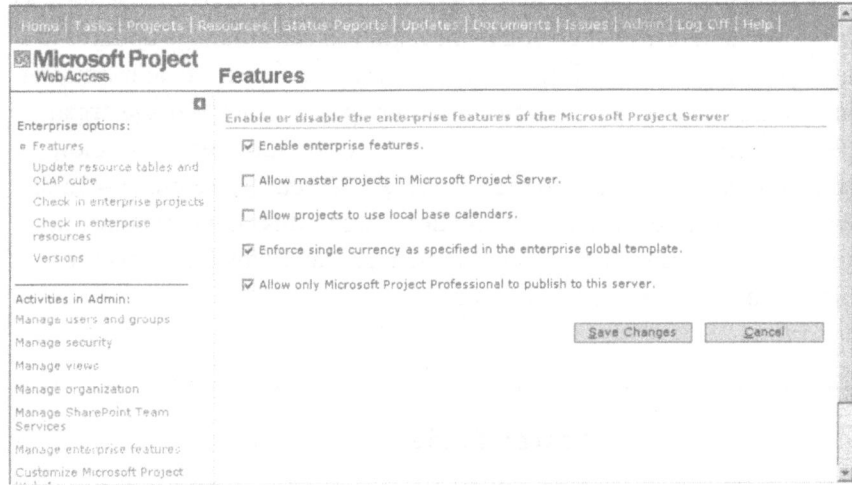

Figure 9-1. The "Manage enterprise features" area

Make sure that the submenu Features is selected to reveal five check-box settings:

1. Enable enterprise features.

2. Allow master projects in Microsoft Project Server.

3. Allow projects to use local base calendars.

4. Enforce single currency as specified in the enterprise global template.

5. Allow only Microsoft Project Professional to publish to this server.

The first and last options in the list have a large impact on Project Server behavior. In the purest sense, the tightest enterprise configuration would have both option 1 and option 5 checked. With this combination, you enable enterprise features and the server is set to accept projects from Project Professional only. It's possible to uncheck the last option and enable enterprise options at the same time, but the results are that the projects saved to the server from Project

Professional will be enterprise enabled, whereas those saved from versions other than Project Professional won't be enterprise projects. Microsoft doesn't support this type of configuration, and it's beyond the scope of this book.

Allowing publishing of master projects to the server is problematic. First, Project Server theoretically diminishes the need for master projects. Second, master projects cause doubling of work values when published to Project Server. I recommend that you use master projects on-the-fly if you really need to see a view like this. Save copies of your project files, create the master project outside the auspices of the server, and toss it when you're through. You can't manage updates to a master plan using the Project Web Access interface. If you do wish to allow master projects in your installation, you must set another option under Manage organization ➤ Features from the Admin menu. You must select the check box "Allow master projects to be published to Microsoft Project Server." (See Figure 9-4 in the "Setting Base URL Paths for Your Server" section later in this chapter.) Selecting this option allows your users to publish from master plans, which renders the system vulnerable to doubling assignments.

Master Project

In Microsoft Project terms, a *master project* is a project that contains two or more inserted projects. You create these by opening a new project plan, and then selecting the Insert menu and choosing Project. From here, the system allows you to navigate to an existing project and insert it into the current plan as a subproject.

The other two check boxes you encounter control global behaviors for the system. If checked, option 3 permits your project managers to define and select their own base calendar for a project. You want to enable this feature if your company is managing projects with calendar requirements that vary by project and aren't easily standardized. Enforcing a single currency (option 4) is another option that determines whether the system permits multiple currencies for costing. In all likelihood, you'll want your system configured exactly as shown in Figure 9-1, with a single currency enforced and the local base calendars option unchecked. Click Save Changes to save the settings you've chosen.

If you determined that your company will use versions to accommodate saving more than one version of a plan to the server, then you'll configure them by clicking Versions in the submenu. Click the Add Version button to add a new version. Create your version by providing a name for it, which you should keep short because it shows up as a file extension in project names. Choose whether it's an archived version or not and select a Gantt Bar style for the version in Project Web Access displays, as shown in Figure 9-2. The difference between an archived version and a nonarchived version is that a nonarchived version can continue to be changed and used for modeling. You can save a nonpublished over a published version to make it the current working version. Archived versions are snapshots in time and they're stored for informational purposes only.

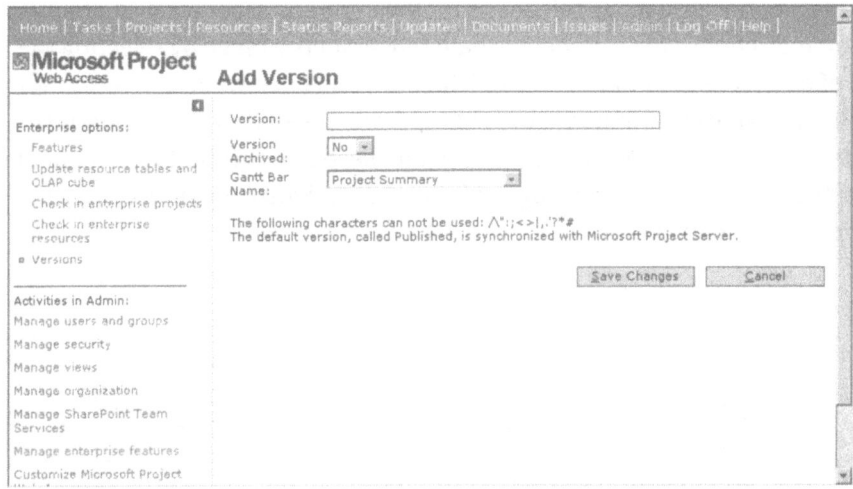

Figure 9-2. Add a new version to your server configuration.

Setting Options for OLAP and Resource Availability Tables

OLAP data and extended resource availability data are available through the Project Web Access interface. You determine how far this data extends into the future and how often it gets refreshed by setting these options in your system. OLAP and availability data options also appear under the "Manage enterprise features" area. If you're configuring your Project Server for the first time and haven't loaded your resources and plans yet, you can skip this configuration for now. Without resources or project data, there's not much for the system to publish at this point anyway.

Click the "Update resource tables and OLAP cube" link from the "Manage enterprise features" navigation menu to open the OLAP settings page. This particular page has a lot of text at the top that attempts to describe the functionality listed. Here's the deal: Data gets pushed to the cube and the cube gets built at the frequency and time you set. To begin with, you must provide the name of your Analysis Server and you must name your cube if this is the first time you're building the cube. You may also choose to deal with only the cube or only the resource tables when you use the interface.

The system pushes data to the cube and the resource availability tables based on the settings you choose. The cube build process is slow and consumes system resources when it runs. Most administrators set this to run at a time of day when the system is idle, as performance degradation can be substantial. In selecting your time, make sure that you choose a time that doesn't conflict with other periodic chores that touch the same server or database such as nightly backups.

Figure 9-3 shows a section of the "Update resource tables and OLAP cube" page displaying the date range selections for the cube and resource availability tables. You may choose to set a specific date range; set the range by selecting the number of days, weeks, or months to look forward and backward; or select a radio button that automatically includes everything from the earliest project start date to the latest project end date found in the system. Resource availability is definable only as a fixed date range or by using the look back and forth a number of days, weeks, or months feature.

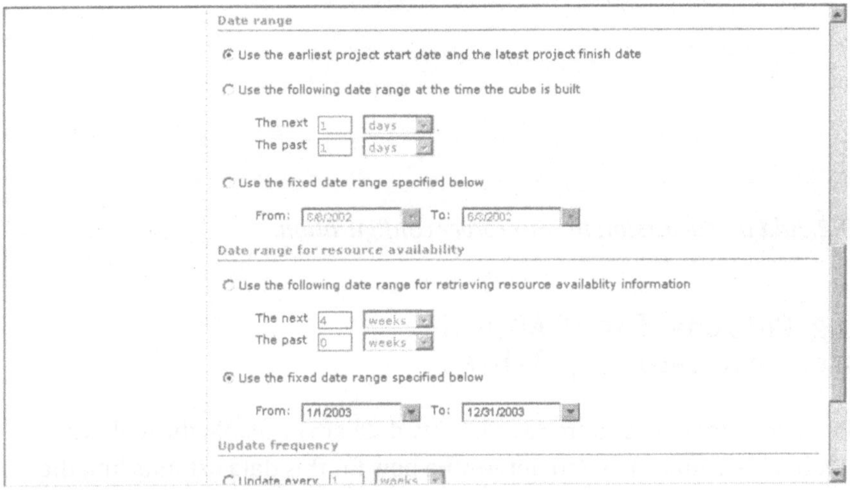

Figure 9-3. Set the OLAP cube and resource availability options.

Lastly, you must set the update frequency. There are strong arguments for setting this daily and weekly. Where system activity is brisk and project status is changing frequently, a daily build might be the best selection. If you have a slower-paced project environment and updates are occurring on a weekly basis, then you might want to choose a weekly build. The first time you build your cube, you'll want to select the option "Update only when specified" and click the Update Now button. If you don't force the build of the cube, the cube won't build until the next time it comes due based on your settings. You must force the build to discover whether you have any setup or authentication issues with the cube build.

Consider the accuracy of your planning before selecting to encompass a distant future range. If you don't have well-developed plans, the value of the data you'll see will be questionable. I present these settings here because they're contextually part of the settings in this section; however, building the cube before data is in the system is premature. I dig deeper into the cube build at the point where you've added data to the system in Chapter 12.

Setting Base URL Paths for Project Server

Project Server's notification engine allows you to configure reminders for your users and for your users to configure reminders for themselves, and generates e-mail notices that contain links back to specific functional areas in Project Web Access. In order for it build the URLs correctly, it must have a source for the base URL of the server both on the intranet and on the extranet. The intranet URL is set for the first time from information you provided during installation.

To set your server's address information, select Manage Organization from the Admin menu. Select Features from the submenu, if it isn't already selected (it's the normal default selection, as shown in Figure 9-4). Scroll to the bottom of the page and enter the correct URL information for your configuration. Note the "Allow master projects to be published to Microsoft Project Server" check box on this screen. It's grayed out because master projects haven't been allowed under the "Manage enterprise features" options. Once you set it there, you must also check this box to activate master project publishing in your installation. You'll also notice the features grid on this page, which I cover extensively in Chapter 11.

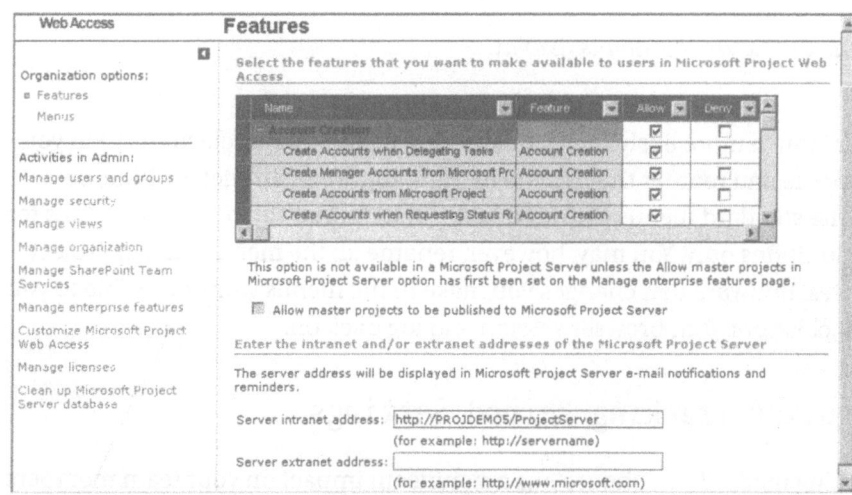

Figure 9-4. Enter your server's URL information.

Configuring Project Web Access Menus

Changing the ordering and layout of your Project Web Access screens isn't likely to be at the top of your first-time implementation task list. However, it's a useful way to tailor Project Server to your specific needs. Although the tools provided allow you to rename and reorder the existing menus, you may not change the pages that they point to. Figure 9-5 shows the menu customization interface, which you can reach by selecting Menus from the "Manage organization" screen. Add hints for your users by filling in the Custom ToolTip field. This will cause the text you type in to display when a user hovers the mouse pointer over the selection. By default, these aren't set for any menus in Project Server.

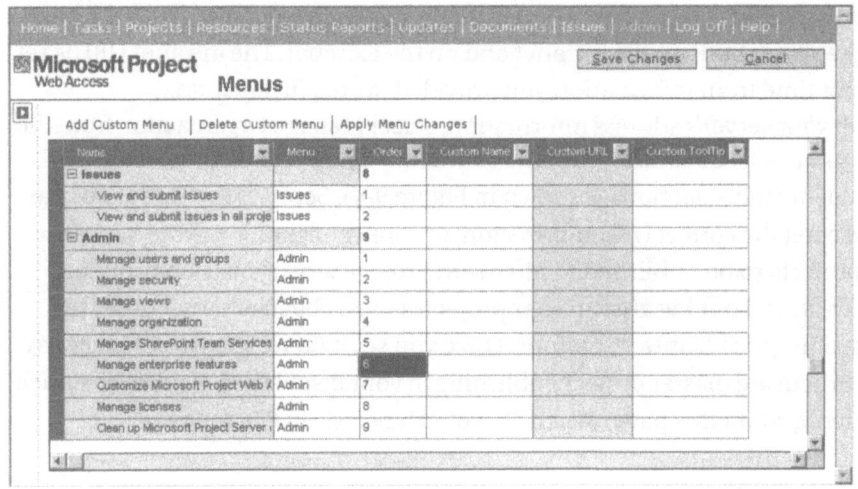

Figure 9-5. Configure the Menus display.

You're much more likely to use this feature to add menu selections than you are to rename and reorder them. Keep in mind that you can't delete, hide, or redirect the standard menus provided in the system. You can define new URLs for custom additions only. You may, however, rename all the menu items in Project Web Access. Be aware that changes you make to the menus won't be visible to you until you close out your browser session and log back on.

Configuring Tracking Method Settings

The tracking method you choose has a significant impact on your team members and their interaction with their timesheets. Not only do some of these options control what data a resource reports, but they also determine the appearance of the timesheet. In Chapter 3 I discussed the organizational indicators for identifying a tracking method preference. You must understand the interface impact to decide on tracking method settings.

Your first decision is whether to configure Project Server to provide a default tracking method that an individual project manager may change or to lock down the tracking method to the default type only. Figure 9-6 shows the upper area of the Tracking settings interface in Project Web Access that you reach by selecting Customize Microsoft Project Web Access ➤ Tracking settings from the Admin menu. Lock down the system to a single tracking method by selecting the radio button "Force project managers to use the progress reporting method . . ." specified previously for all projects under the "Lock down defaults" area.

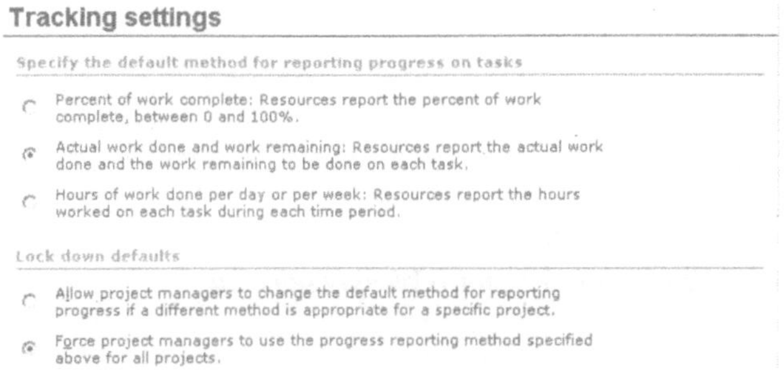

Tracking settings

Specify the default method for reporting progress on tasks

○ Percent of work complete: Resources report the percent of work complete, between 0 and 100%.

◉ Actual work done and work remaining: Resources report the actual work done and the work remaining to be done on each task.

○ Hours of work done per day or per week: Resources report the hours worked on each task during each time period.

Lock down defaults

○ Allow project managers to change the default method for reporting progress if a different method is appropriate for a specific project.

◉ Force project managers to use the progress reporting method specified above for all projects.

Figure 9-6. The Tracking settings interface in Project Web Access

Most organizations choose to force project managers to use the default tracking method in an enterprise implementation. The consequence of not locking this down is potentially confusing resources with a timesheet displaying tasks that follow different tracking methods. In this scenario, a resource must know how to report progress three different ways. Generally, simplicity and uniformity are more desirable. In certain implementations where project teams are static entities, multiple reporting methods may be a viable option. Project Server defaults to "Percent of work complete."

The important difference between tracking methods is the information collected by each one, which varies by method.

- *Percent of work complete:* Resources may enter the percent of work complete and the percent of work remaining.

- *Actual work done and work remaining:* Resources may enter the actual work completed and the work remaining on a task.

- *Hours of work done per day or per week:* Resources may enter hours by day or week and work remaining.

You can base time-period settings on a weekly or a monthly frequency. Certain options change according to the frequency selection. Figure 9-7 shows the "Time period settings" page with Weekly selected, and Figure 9-8 shows the "Time period settings" page with Monthly selected. In both cases, the "Week starts on" selection is set by choosing from the pull-down menu provided.

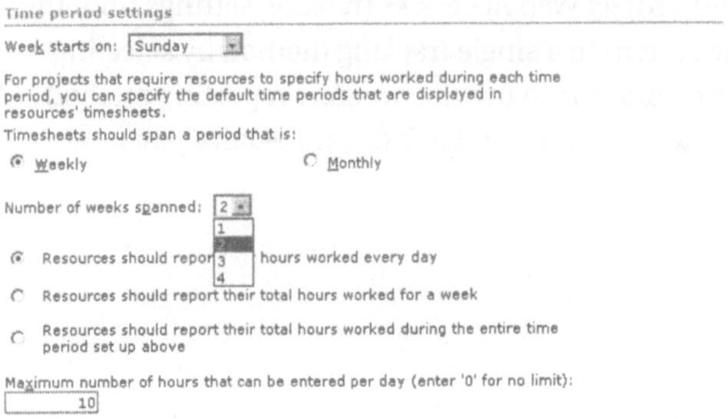

Figure 9-7. The "Time period settings" interface with Weekly selected

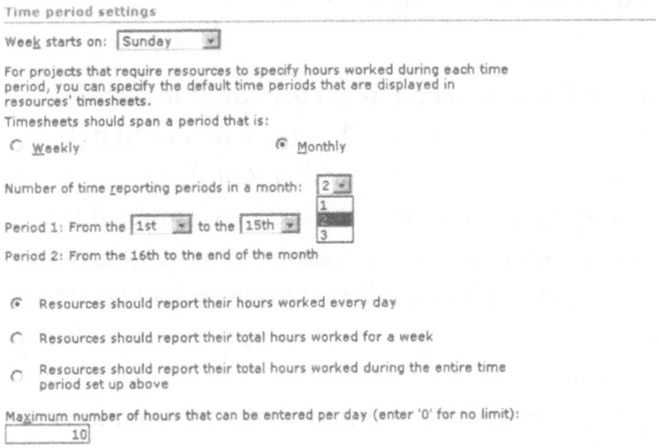

Figure 9-8. The "Time period settings" interface with Monthly selected

When you select a weekly span, you may set the number of weeks spanned on the timesheet view from 1 to 4. When you select a monthly span, semimonthly reporting periods are modeled by selecting up to three reporting periods and building the start and stop rules using the Period selection pull-down dates. With either span selected, you must choose one of three radio buttons to determine how the timesheet will accept hourly input.

Selecting the "Resources should report their hours worked every day" option causes the timesheet to provide daily input cells for time entry within the format specified by the span period and number of periods spanned. Figure 9-9 shows a weekly timesheet with a 1-week span with daily reporting selected.

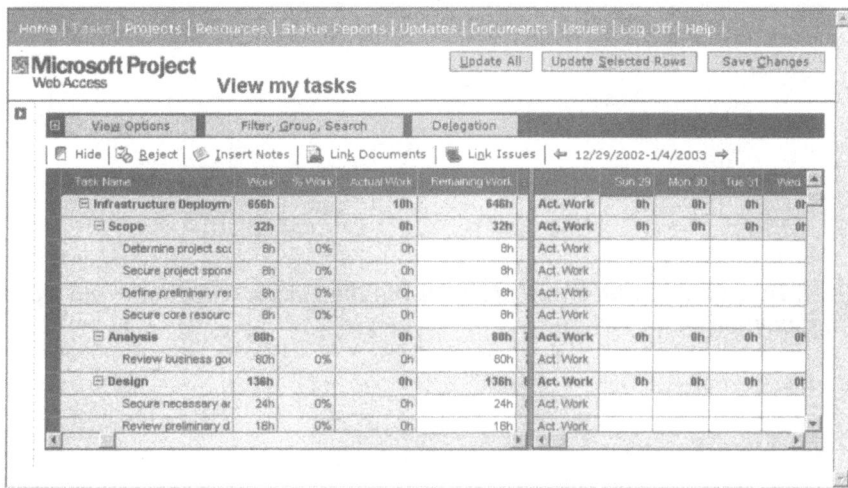

Figure 9-9. Timesheet view with daily reporting configured

Selecting the "Resources should report their total hours worked for a week" option opens weekly entry cells on the timesheet for resource hour entries. Figure 9-10 shows a weekly timesheet with a 2-week span with weekly reporting selected.

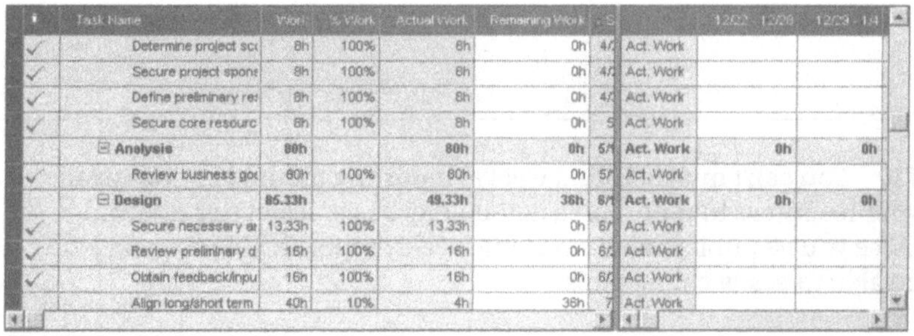

Figure 9-10. Weekly reporting accepts the total for a week at a time.

Using the "Resources should report their total hours worked during the entire time period set up above" option, you can force the input cells to represent the total by time period. This is the setting to gather totals for nonstandard periods such as semimonthly. Figure 9-11 shows this option selected along with "Actual work done and work remaining" selected as the tracking method. Figure 9-12 shows the same span options selected with "Percent work complete" selected as the tracking method.

i	Task Name	Work	% Work	Actual Work	Remaining Work	Start	Finish	Update Sent	
	Align long/short term	80h	0%	0h	80h	9/18/2003	10/2/2003	NA	Act. Wc
	⊟ Budget	168h		18h	168h	10/2/2003	10/24/2003	NA	Act. Wc
	Develop budget base	40h	25%	10h	30h	10/2/2003	10/9/2003	NA	Act. Wc
	Align budget request	40h	0%	0h	40h	10/7/2003	10/13/2003	NA	Act. Wc
	Align budget request	40h	0%	0h	40h	10/9/2003	10/16/2003	NA	Act. Wc
	Present long/short ter	24h	0%	0h	24h	10/16/2003	10/21/2003	NA	Act. Wc
	Secure multi-phase/v	24h	0%	0h	24h	10/21/2003	10/24/2003	NA	Act. Wc
	⊟ Finalization/Validation	60h		0h	60h	10/24/2003	11/18/2003	NA	Act. Wc
	Secure resources ba	40h	0%	0h	40h	10/24/2003	10/31/2003	NA	Act. Wc
	Finalize detailed desi	16h	0%	0h	16h	10/31/2003	11/4/2003	NA	Act. Wc
	Secure approval to p	4h	0%	0h	4h	11/18/2003	11/18/2003	NA	Act. Wc

Figure 9-11. Time entry for an entire period using the "Actual work done and work remaining" method

i	Task Name	Work	% Work	Actual Work	Remaining Work	Start	
	⊟ Pilot	84h		76h	8h	6/30/2	Act. Work
✓	Select infrastructu	8h	100%	8h	0h	6/30/2	Act. Work
✓	Review deployme	16h	100%	16h	0h	7/1/2	Act. Work
✓	Communicate impe	2h	100%	2h	0h	7/3/2	Act. Work
✓	Deploy infrastructi	24h	100%	24h	0h	7/3/2	Act. Work
✓	Test infrastructure	8h	100%	8h	0h	7/8/2	Act. Work
✓	Release to produc	2h	100%	2h	0h	7/9/2	Act. Work
✓	Obtain feedback	16h	100%	16h	0h	7/10/2	Act. Work
	Evaluate pilot feed	8h	0%	0h	8h	7/14/2	Act. Work
	Determine readiness	8h	0%	0h	8h	7/15/2	Act. Work
	⊟ Post Implementation	24h		0h	24h	8/18/2	Act. Work

Figure 9-12. Time entry for an entire period using the "Percent work complete" method

TIP You can't mix daily and weekly reporting methods. If you want your resources to report on a day-by-day basis, select this up front. Once you've published plans using weekly reporting blocks, you won't be able to easily change this.

Setting the maximum number of hours a resource may report per day limits the daily input to the number entered. Nondaily entries are restricted by the aggregate total of the number of working days in the period multiplied by the daily limit.

Finally, in its own section not shown in any of the preceding figures is an option to set the current task definition in number of days. This allows you to set the timesheet to display tasks that are due to start within the number of days set in the option.

Configuring Gantt Chart Formats and Grouping Formats

You can customize the appearance of the personal Gantt chart by customizing its Gantt Chart format or customize the timesheet by configuring its grouping format. Gantt Chart formatting and Grouping formats are discussed in Chapter 12 as they apply more acutely within the scope of the views discussion.

Configuring Nonproject Time Categories

According to the Project Server Nonproject Time Categories interface shown in Figure 9-13, "You can change the default nonproject time categories, delete existing categories, or create your own." Project Server doesn't install with predefined nonproject time categories. Therefore, changing the default is creating your own.

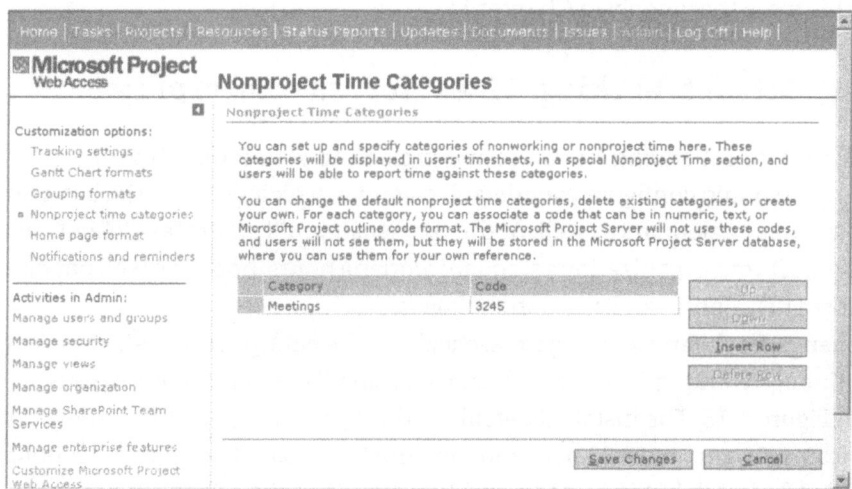

Figure 9-13. The Nonproject Time Categories interface

From the Admin menu, choose Customize Microsoft Project Web Access ➤ Nonproject time categories. To define a nonworking time category, simply click in the blank row under category and type a name, and then optionally enter a code. Click Save Changes to make the category instantly available in your users' timesheets as shown in Figure 9-14. In the example shown, the category Meetings is now visible in the timesheet view, which doesn't yet contain any tasks.

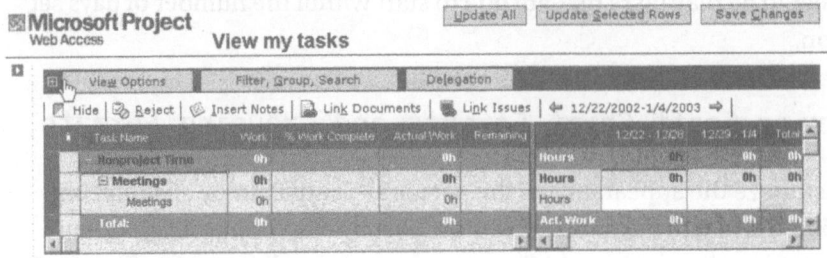

Figure 9-14. Nonproject time categories appear in the timesheet.

It's important to note that nonproject category data isn't readily accessible through out-of-the-box views in Project Server. You must mine this data using SQL and present it through custom views or data access pages. You can also view it in Analyzer views, but not without advanced customization there as well. If you choose not to use this feature, don't define any categories and they won't appear in the user interface. An alternative is to use a project for reporting overhead tasks, which has the potential to impact availability settings in your resource pool. I discuss this more thoroughly in Chapter 11.

Setting Default Working Times for the Enterprise

Before you can begin adding resources and projects to your Project Server database, you should configure your default calendar, which serves as the basis for task and resource calendars as well. At the very least, you'll adjust the default calendar to reflect your organization's standard working hours, hours worked per day, days worked per month, and standard holidays.

To change the default working time, check out the enterprise global and select Tools ➤ Change Working Time. The Change Working Time dialog box displays, as shown in Figure 9-15. The installed default settings provide for an 8-hour day worked from 8:00 a.m. to 12:00 p.m. and then from 1:00 p.m. to 5:00 p.m. An hour is scheduled for lunch between noon and 1:00 p.m. To make a change to time settings that apply globally to all dates, it's very important that you remember to highlight the calendar days by clicking the column headers. In the figure, the Monday and Tuesday columns are highlighted this way. As you can see, I've selected the columns. Make sure that yours are selected too or you'll end up with unexpected results. These settings drive scheduling.

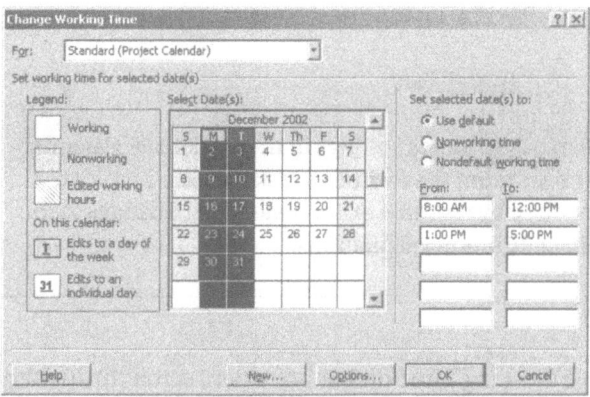

Figure 9-15. The Change Working Time dialog box with the Monday and Tuesday columns selected

Click the Options button in the Change Working Time dialog box to open the Options dialog box, and then select the Calendar tab as shown in Figure 9-16. If you made any changes to the standard calendar, they may be out-of-synch with the Calendar tab. The data on this tab determines how Project calculates duration. Therefore, if your settings on this tab are out-of-synch with the Change Working Time options, you may see confusing durations reported in Project views. This isn't to say that Project's handling of durations is not confusing all in itself; however, incongruities in these settings makes it much worse. You can set the options on the Calendar tab by checking out the enterprise global and then selecting Tools ➤ Options ➤ Calendar tab.

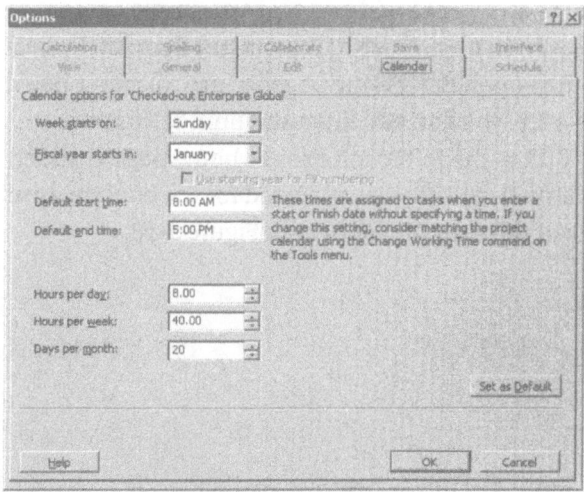

Figure 9-16. Settings on the Options ➤ Calendar tab determine how Project calculates duration.

Duration

Project calculates task duration based on the settings in the Options ➤ Calendar tab. Durations displayed in the duration field within a task view are based on these settings and aren't overridden by resource or task calendars. Changes to the default working time don't affect duration calculations.

While you have the Change Working Time dialog box open, scroll through the coming year and mark each organizational holiday as nonworking time. To do this, find the date of a holiday, click it, and then click the "Nonworking time" radio button to mark the date as nonworking. This action turns the cell gray in the display. You can also create additional base calendars for the enterprise by clicking the New button.

If you're familiar with Project, then you might be surprised to learn that the only enterprise base calendar available on installation is the standard calendar. If you work offline, the 24-hour and night shift calendars you may be familiar with are available, but not in the enterprise. You can create these types of calendars for the enterprise. The best approach is to configure the standard calendar first and base all your new calendar creation on the standard calendar after you enter the organization's holidays.

Adding Simple Home Page Content and Links

The Project Web Access interface allows you to add two types of simple content to the home page display. From the Admin menu, select Customize Microsoft Project Web Access ➤ Home page format to open the "Home page format" display shown in Figure 9-17. As shown in the figure, you can add links and links to content.

In the preceding example, a link to the Microsoft Project home page is added under links and the Microsoft Home Page URL was specified for the content area set at 250 pixels high. The results of this addition appear in Figure 9-18.

Figure 9-17. Home page format controls

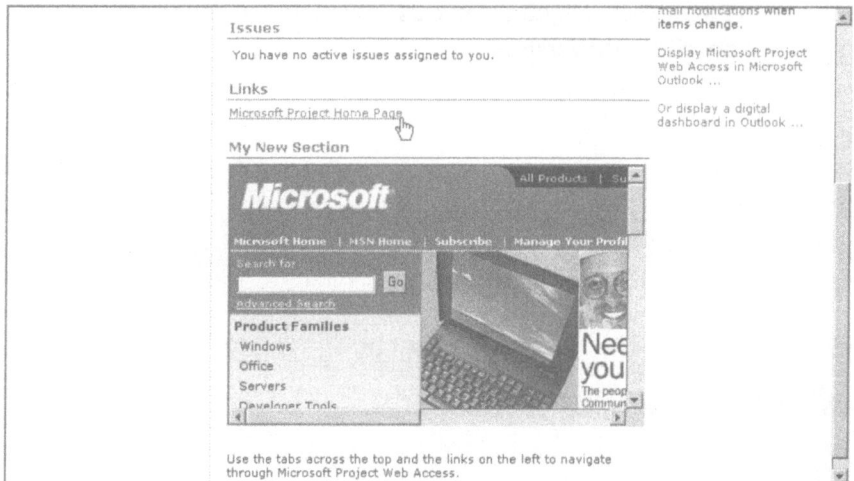

Figure 9-18. Home page with additions

Establishing Project Versions

Before your server will accept various saved versions of projects into the database, you must create the versions through the Admin interface. The default version of any project saved to the server is dot-published, where "dot" is a period (.) character. You may define additional versions as archived or nonarchived, the difference between the two mainly being that nonarchived versions may be edited whereas archived versions may not.

Be clear that because the published version is the system's default version, all projects that are saved to the server are visible within the system views to the extent that their assignments have been published. You must always use the published version for reporting and tracking, as data doesn't flow to any other version in the system. You may use versions for planning and then save an alternate nonarchived version as the new published version by overwriting the currently published version. In this way, you can leverage versions during the planning process.

Another substantial use for versions is in the Portfolio Modeler where nonarchived versions of projects are available to create portfolio models for what-if analyses. I cover the Portfolio Modeler at length in Chapter 16. Archived versions are useful for preserving historic snapshots of project plans and project templates. Maintaining current archived copies of templates is particularly important, as these are vulnerable to inadvertent changes.

To create a new version, select "Manage enterprise features" from the Admin menu, and then select Versions from the left submenu. This displays the Versions interface shown in Figure 9-19. Highlight an existing version to delete or modify it. To add a new version, click Add Version.

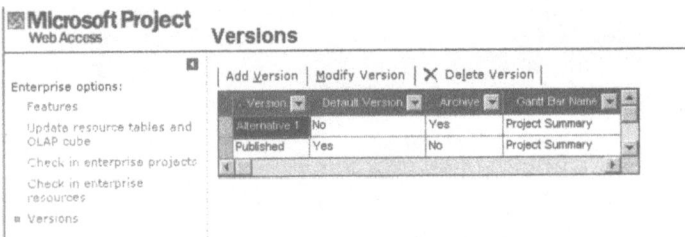

Figure 9-19. The Versions interface

Clicking Add Version opens the Add Version interface shown in Figure 9-20. You provide a name for the version, determine whether it's an archive or nonarchive version, and select which Gantt Bar to use when displaying the version.

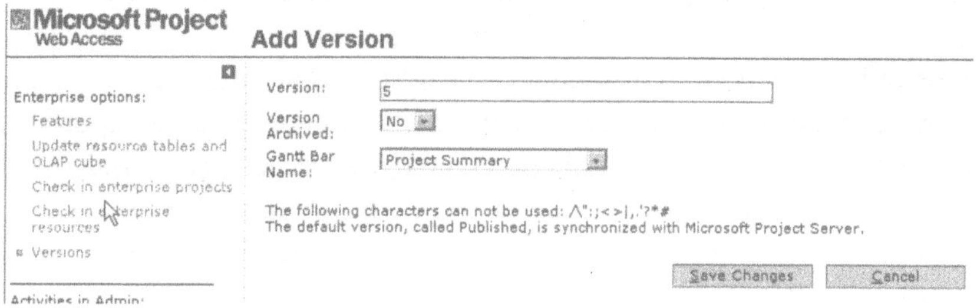

Figure 9-20. The Add Version interface

Specifying User Authentication and Password Length

Project Server supports both Windows Integrated Authentication and its own internal Project Server Authentication. Although Project Web Access can run without a Windows logon, documents and issues functionality provided by STS requires Windows Authentication. You must install multiple servers within a domain/Active Directory context, so the use of Windows Authentication is largely required for enterprise configurations.

From the Project Web Access Admin menu, select Manage security ➤ User authentication to open the User authentication options page shown in Figure 9-21. Note that you have a choice of three option states: Mixed, Windows Authentication only, and Microsoft Project Server authentication only. The default installation value is set to Mixed.

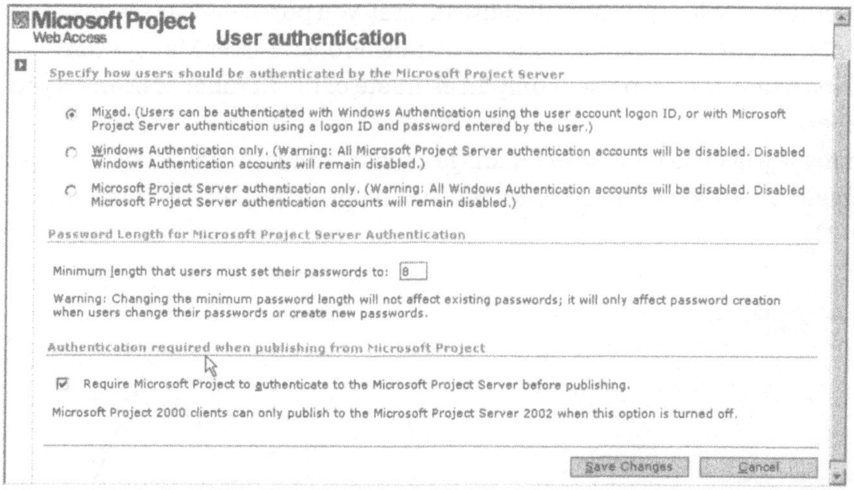

Figure 9-21. User authentication options

In an enterprise environment, your practical choices are either Mixed or Windows Authentication only. Before you select to convert from Mixed to Windows Authentication only, consider the consequences. The built-in administrator account is a Project Server account. Project Server accounts are rendered disabled upon acceptance of the change. It's incumbent upon you to prepare for this by assigning full administration privileges to any number of Windows accounts. I recommend establishing both domain and local logon–based accounts with Project Server admin privileges.

Set your password length to your organizational preference by changing the value in the Minimum length field in the Password Length section. Deselecting the option to require Microsoft Project to authenticate to Project Server is for workgroup configurations only. This should remain unchanged in an enterprise implementation.

Managing Your Licenses

A housekeeping chore you need to attend to is setting the number of licenses for the system. To my knowledge, you enter these into the administration page in Project Server on the honor system. Project Server will count all work resources as Project Server users whether or not these represent actual users of the system. Therefore, if you use work resources to define machinery and equipment, you'll need to inflate the number of licenses you enter by the number of nonhuman work resources you're trying to represent. Normally, the number of licenses you purchase are counted as one each per Project Professional license plus the total number of Client Access Licenses (CALs) purchased separately or bundled with your server software if applicable. Because the way you purchase CALs is based on number of machines, the calculations used in the Project Server Manage licenses page are inaccurate and represent only an estimate of the number of licenses you should own.

To enter the license total, select Manage licenses from the Project Web Access Admin menu. The Manage licenses administration page displays, as shown in Figure 9-22.

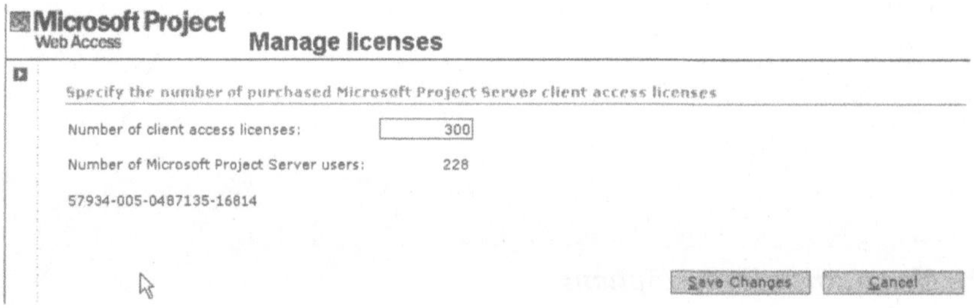

Microsoft Project
Web Access
Manage licenses

Specify the number of purchased Microsoft Project Server client access licenses

Number of client access licenses: 300

Number of Microsoft Project Server users: 228

57934-005-0487135-16814

Save Changes   Cancel

Figure 9-22. The Manage licenses administration page

Summary

The flexibility of Project Server's built-in application options comes at the cost of some complexity. Understanding the topics in this chapter prepares you to configure your own system. Once you've made any necessary adjustments for your organization, you're ready to tackle security in the next chapter.

Configuring Project Server Security

Among your most important configuration efforts is mapping your organizational security requirements to Project Server's security constructs. You must give yourself time to understand the underlying concepts so that you can apply them in a way that meets your requirements and enables easier maintenance.

Project Server provides a flexible set of security management tools. At first glance these may seem obscure and complex. In this chapter, I'll do my best to render these approachable. In previous chapters, you've learned the language of "enterprise" in Project Server. Now it's time to tackle Project Server's language of "security." In this introductory section, I list the terms you'll come across when you read the Project Server documentation and include brief explanations to get you started. Although the term "permissions" is also used as a stand-alone concept, I've chosen to work with one term, "global permissions," because in practice there seems to be no discernable difference between the two.

Topping the following list is "authentication methods," which I covered amply in the previous chapter, so look there for anything more than the honorable mention below. Each of the succeeding topics makes up the subject matter of this chapter.

- *Authentication methods:* As covered in Chapter 9, Project Server uses Windows Integrated Authentication as well as its own built-in authentication system.

- *Global permissions:* A collection of permissions that grant access to security objects.

- *Group:* A collection of permissions that can be assigned to a user.

- *User:* An individual logon account in Project Server.

- *Category:* A collection of security objects and, to a more limited extent, permissions that can be assigned to a user or group.

- *Security object:* Software functions, views, and project and resource data, collectively.

- *Security rules:* Access permissions that may be assigned based on Project Server relationships. (I think of them as relationship-based security roles.)

Global Permissions Essentials

The most important concept behind Project Server permissions is that they have three potential value states: allowed, not allowed, or denied. This is an important construct in Project Server. When you encounter permissions in the Admin interface, each of the 58 (57 that apply to enterprise configurations) individual permissions has two check boxes associated with it, one for Allow and another for Deny. You may choose to check either Allow or Deny to explicitly assign either value, or you may check neither of them to indicate an implicit state of not allowed.

The difference between not allowed and denied is that when the former is the state for a user by virtue of membership in a group or category, it doesn't preclude being granted permission in another group or category. On the other hand, when a user is denied in any one group or category, the value inherited by any other group or category relationship is moot.

In other words, there's precedence to these values as follows, in order from strongest to weakest:

- Denied (the Deny check box is selected)

- Allowed (the Allow check box is selected)

- Not allowed (no check box is selected)

The two explicit states override the implicit not allowed (absence of the selection of the Allow and Deny check boxes) state. For instance, if a user is a member of group 1 and group 2, with group 1 containing a not allowed state and group 2 containing an allowed state, the user is allowed to perform the activity. Denied trumps allowed in all cases. If a user belongs to two groups, and in one group a specific permission is allowed and in the other it's denied, the user doesn't have permission.

The fact that permissions are cumulative gives you a lot of flexibility in taking a layered approach to granting permissions. Every bit of time you spend designing your security approach will yield manifold maintenance benefits in managing your system.

Controlling Global Permissions (aka Features) Globally

When is a permission not a permission? Give up? When it's a feature! In the last chapter I glossed over the Admin ➤ Manage organization ➤ Features option because it's more germane to security discussion. The list of so-called features that you may manipulate from the interface, shown in Figure 10-1, is identical to the list of permissions you may set in Groups, Categories, and Users. Simply put, it's the master security list of permissions. Turn it off here and it doesn't matter what values you chose in Groups, Categories, and Users.

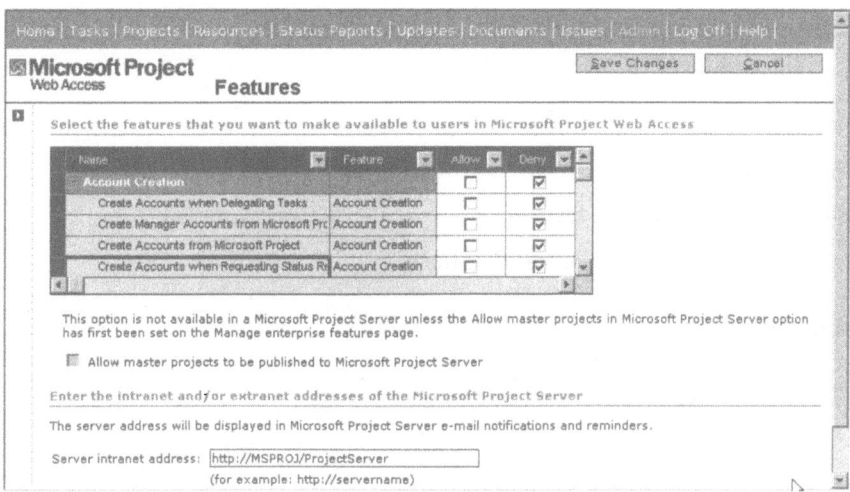

Figure 10-1. Features administration interface

As Figure 10-1 shows, the four account creation selections (covered later in this chapter) under Account Creation are explicitly denied. This is the default state for these upon installation. All other features are set to Allow in the interface. Only account creation is denied by default.

The Project Server features displayed here are organized into 11 categories. Note that the last category pertains to workgroup configurations and isn't covered here. If a feature is denied or not allowed in this display, it won't be available to any user of the system at any time regardless of his or her individual, group, or category permissions.

The presentation of these options in the Features interface lists the feature categories and their individual selections. A categorical sort isn't a pleasantry provided when presented for selection in groups. Here's how it reads as you scroll down through the features list:

Account Creation

Create Accounts when Delegating Tasks

Create Manager Accounts from Microsoft Project

Create Accounts from Microsoft Project

Create Accounts when Requesting Status Reports

Administration

Manage enterprise features

Customize Microsoft Project Web Access

Manage users and groups

Manage security

Manage licenses

Manage views

Manage SharePoint Team Services

Clean up Microsoft Project Server database

Collaboration

View Issues

View Documents

Enterprise Portfolio Management

Save Enterprise Global

Save Project

Read Summary Assignments

New Project

Edit Enterprise Resource Data

Open Project Template

Backup Global

Open Project

See Enterprise Resource Data

New Resource

Save Project Template

Read Enterprise Global

General

Set Resource Notifications

Change Password

View Home

Set Personal Notifications

Go Offline

Status Reports

Manage Status Report Request

View Status Report List

Submit Status Report

Tasks

Hide Task from Timesheet

View Timesheet

New Project Task

Delegate Task

Transfer Calendar Entries

Change Work Days

To-Do List

Create and Manage To-Do List

Publish To-Do List to All Users

Assign To-Do List Tasks

Transactions

Manage Rules

Manage Calendar Changes

Manage Task Changes

Views

View Documents and Issues

View Project View

View Portfolio Analyzer

View Project Center

View Resource Center

View Assignments View

View Models

View Resource Allocation

See Projects in Project Center

See Projects in Project Views

See Resource Assignments in Assignment Views

Workgroup

Publish/update/status

Working with Permissions in Groups and Categories

All of the features listed in the last section are permissions that can be allowed, not allowed, or denied at the group level. An individual user inherits permissions from groups to which he or she is assigned. Once again, the rules of precedence apply when a user belongs to more than one group. A feature denied in one group disables that feature for the user across the board, regardless of permission settings in another group and so on. You control your Project Server application security environment by adding, deleting, or modifying groups and categories.

The presentation of permissions in the group management interface is divided in two, with 8 of the enterprise 57 permissions presented in the Categories section and the rest presented in a section titled "Global Permissions." Figure 10-2 shows a portion of the Add/Modify Group interface and the line between permissions groupings. To reach this screen, select "Manage users and groups" from the Admin menu, and then select Groups ➤ Add or Modify.

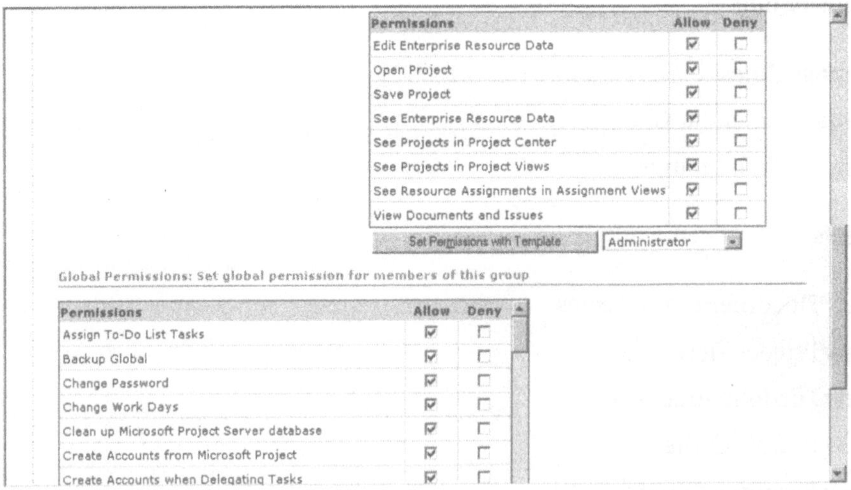

Figure 10-2. Permissions set at a group level

Two important characteristics distinguish the subset of eight permissions from the broader group. First, these specific permissions are very high level. They refer to broad-stroke functions within Project Server. All of these permissions have subordinate permissions in the second, larger set of permissions. In other words, denying permissions in the subset of eight permissions overrides some permissions that may be granted in the second, larger group. For example, the See Projects in Project Views permission, when denied, overrides the permission to View Project View in the subordinate group. Second, the high-level eight permissions are also available to set in Categories. Therefore, these can also be overridden between a group and category.

Besides setting permissions, you can manage user membership to a group and group-to-category associations through the Add/Modify Group interface, as shown in Figure 10-3. Because you set permissions primarily through group membership, the Modify Group dialog box is the place to determine who may take what specific actions in Project Server. What data users can take the action on, however, is primarily accomplished through category management. Finally, you can set a digital dashboard link for a group through group maintenance.

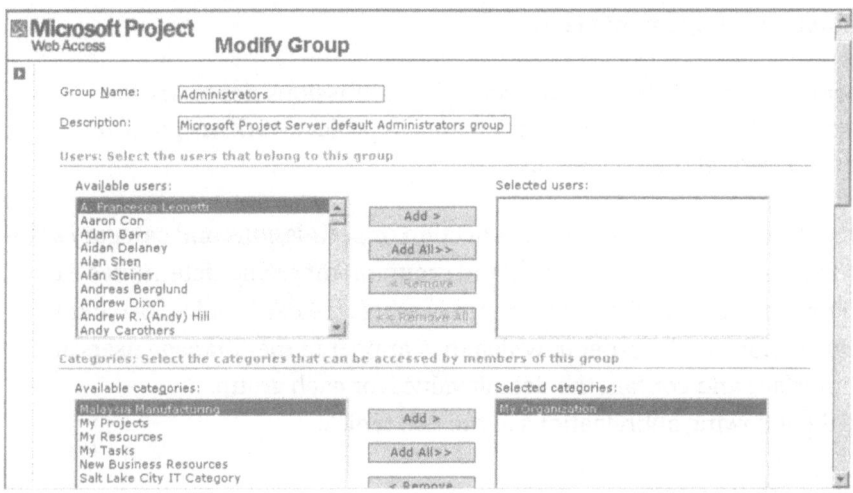

Figure 10-3. You add users to groups and manage category associations through the Add/Modify Group interface.

The Project Server installation process creates seven predefined groups. You can create as many as you want. These default groups are as follows:

- *Administrators:* By default, administrators have blanket access to everything in Project Server that isn't disallowed by global settings.

- *Executives:* Intended for upper-level management, this group doesn't have the ability to open, save, or edit projects or resources. However, this group generally has view access to everything.

- *Portfolio Managers:* This group has a superset of permissions typically granted to project managers, with some system maintenance functions enabled that are usually reserved for administrators, such as managing views and enterprise features.

- *Project Managers:* Project managers have liberal permissions to project management functions but don't have administrative-type access or the ability to use Analyzer output.

- *Resource Managers:* This group has permissions tailored to maintaining resource information and managing resources but not project plans.

- *Team Leads:* The Team Leads group is primarily used to give team members permissions that are in addition to those granted through Team Members group membership. These are largely in the form of privileges to use Project Center and assignment views.

- *Team Members:* This group provides the permissions necessary for resources to become active participants in project work assigned and tracked through Project Server.

Each of these groups has its own collection of permissions and category associations. The combination of category and group membership determines what data a user has access to and how the user may access the data. Tables 10-1 and 10-2 list the permissions in the order in which they appear in the "Manage users and groups" interface and contain the default values for each group.

I use the following abbreviations in the two tables:

Admin = Administrator

Exec = Executive

Port Mgr = Portfolio Manager

Proj Mgr = Project Manager

Res Mgr = Resource Manager

T Lead = Team Lead

T Mem = Team Member

A = Allowed

D = Denied

NA = Not allowed

Table 10-1. Default High-Level Permissions States for Groups

PERMISSION	ADMIN	EXEC	PORT MGR	PROJ MGR	RES MGR	T LEAD	T MEM
Edit Enterprise Resource Data	A	NA	A	NA	NA	NA	NA
Open Project	A	NA	A	A	NA	NA	NA
Save Project	A	NA	A	A	NA	NA	NA
See Enterprise Resource Data	A	A	A	A	A	NA	NA
See Projects in Project Center	A	A	A	A	A	A	A
See Projects in Project Views	A	A	A	A	NA	A	A
See Resource Assignments in Assignment Views	A	A	A	A	A	A	A
View Documents and Issues	A	A	A	A	A	A	NA

Table 10-2. Default Global Permissions States for Groups

PERMISSION	ADMIN	EXEC	PORT MGR	PROJ MGR	RES MGR	T LEAD	T MEM
Assign To-Do List Tasks	A	A	NA	A	A	A	A
Backup Global	A	NA	NA	NA	NA	NA	NA
Change Password	A	A	A	A	A	A	A
Change Work Days	A	NA	NA	NA	NA	NA	A
Clean up Microsoft Project Server database	A	NA	NA	NA	NA	NA	NA
Create Accounts from Microsoft Project	A	NA	NA	A	NA	NA	NA
Create Accounts when Delegating Tasks	A	NA	NA	A	NA	NA	NA
Create Accounts when Requesting Status Reports	A	NA	NA	A	NA	NA	NA
Create and Manage To-Do List	A	A	NA	A	A	A	A
Create Manager Accounts from Microsoft Project	A	NA	NA	A	NA	NA	NA

Table 10-2. Default Global Permissions States for Groups (Continued)

PERMISSION	ADMIN	EXEC	PORT MGR	PROJ MGR	RES MGR	T LEAD	T MEM
Customize Microsoft Project Web Access	A	NA	NA	NA	NA	NA	NA
Delegate Task	A	NA	NA	A	NA	NA	A
Go Offline	A	A	A	A	A	A	A
Hide Task from Timesheet	A	NA	NA	A	NA	NA	A
Log On	A	A	A	A	A	A	A
Manage Calendar Changes	A	NA	NA	A	NA	NA	NA
Manage enterprise features	A	NA	A	NA	NA	NA	NA
Manage licenses	A	NA	NA	NA	NA	NA	NA
Manage organization	A	NA	NA	NA	NA	NA	NA
Manage Rules	A	NA	NA	A	NA	NA	NA
Manage security	A	NA	NA	NA	NA	NA	NA
Manage SharePoint Team Services	A	NA	NA	NA	NA	NA	NA
Manage Status Report Request	A	A	NA	A	A	NA	NA
Manage Task Changes	A	NA	NA	A	NA	NA	NA
Manage users and groups	A	NA	NA	NA	NA	NA	NA
Manage views	A	NA	A	NA	NA	NA	NA
New Project	A	NA	A	A	NA	NA	NA
New Project Task	A	NA	NA	A	NA	NA	A
New Resource	A	NA	A	NA	A	NA	NA
Open Project Template	A	NA	A	A	NA	NA	NA
Publish To-Do List to All Users	A	A	NA	A	A	A	A
Publish/update/status	A	NA	A	A	NA	NA	N
Read Enterprise Global	A	NA	A	A	A	NA	NA
Read Summary Assignments	A	NA	A	A	A	NA	NA
Save Enterprise Global	A	NA	A	NA	NA	NA	NA
Save Project Template	A	NA	A	A	NA	NA	NA

Table 10-2. Default Global Permissions States for Groups (Continued)

PERMISSION	ADMIN	EXEC	PORT MGR	PROJ MGR	RES MGR	T LEAD	T MEM
Set Personal Notifications	A	A	A	A	A	A	A
Set Resource Notifications	A	A	A	A	A	A	NA
Submit Status Report	A	A	NA	A	A	NA	A
Transfer Calendar Entries	A	NA	NA	NA	NA	NA	A
View Assignments View	A	A	A	A	A	A	NA
View Documents	A	NA	A	A	A	A	A
View Home	A	A	A	A	A	A	A
View Issues	A	NA	A	A	A	A	A
View Models	A	A	A	NA	NA	NA	NA
View Portfolio Analyzer	A	A	A	NA	NA	NA	NA
View Project Center	A	A	A	A	A	NA	A
View Project View	A	A	A	A	A	NA	A
View Resource Allocation	A	A	A	NA	A	NA	NA
View Resource Center	A	A	A	NA	A	NA	NA
View Status Report List	A	A	NA	A	A	NA	A
View Timesheet	A	NA	NA	A	NA	NA	A

Project Server installs with four default categories: My Organization, My Projects, My Resources, and My Tasks. The permissions assigned to these categories and their default values are contained in Table 10-3.

Table 10-3. Default Permissions States for Categories

PERMISSION	MY ORGANIZATION	MY PROJECTS	MY RESOURCES	MY TASKS
Edit Enterprise Resource Data	A	NA	A	NA
Open Project	A	A	NA	NA
Save Project	A	A	NA	NA
See Enterprise Resource Data	A	A	A	NA
See Projects in Project Center	A	A	NA	A

Table 10-3. Default Permissions States for Categories (Continued)

PERMISSION	MY ORGANIZATION	MY PROJECTS	MY RESOURCES	MY TASKS
See Projects in Project Views	A	A	NA	A
See Resource Assignments in Assignment Views	A	A	A	NA
View Documents and Issues	A	A	NA	A

Setting Permissions with Security Templates

To make your life easier and to support better standardization of permissions set-tings, Project Server provides security templates you can use to set permissions in Groups and Categories. Refer back to Figure 10-2 and observe the Set Permissions with Template buttons below each permissions display frame. Security templates allow you to manage group permissions based on templates.

Project Server provides a default security template for each default group. To add or modify security templates, from the Admin menu select Manage security ➤ Security templates to reveal the interface shown in Figure 10-4. Clicking a tem-plate in the grid displays a summary of its properties below.

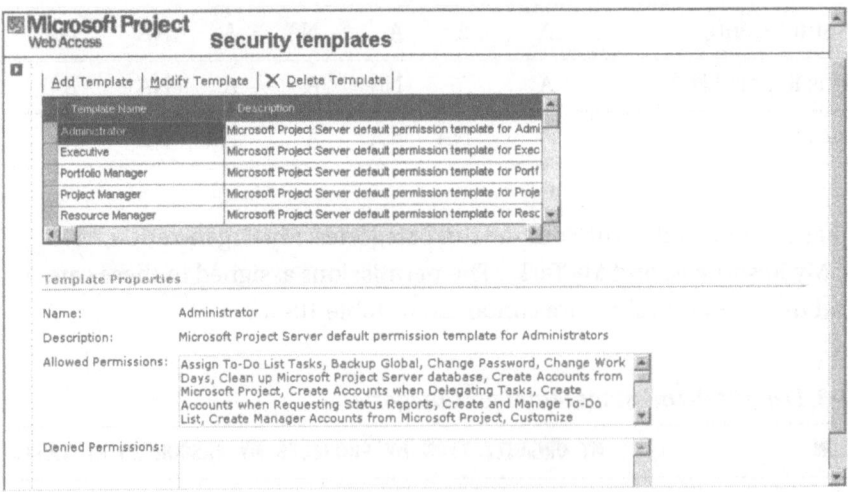

Figure 10-4. Security templates interface

Click Add Template to open the Add New Template dialog box shown in Figure 10-5. The dialog box allows you to name and describe your new template. The system conveniently provides the ability to select an existing template to clone. This feature's greatest worth is in preserving prior configurations for fallback. It's always smart to copy a template for purposes of backing it up before you alter it. Of course, you'll also want to use this feature to jump-start new templates for any new custom groups you create.

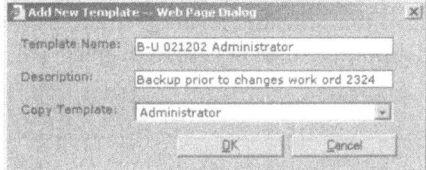

Figure 10-5. The Add New Template dialog box

After you click OK, you'll return to the display shown in Figure 10-4. Now, to modify the newly cloned template, highlight it in the grid display and click Modify Template. The Modify Template administration page displays. Here again you see the entire global permissions display in its nicely sorted presentation, as shown in Figure 10-6.

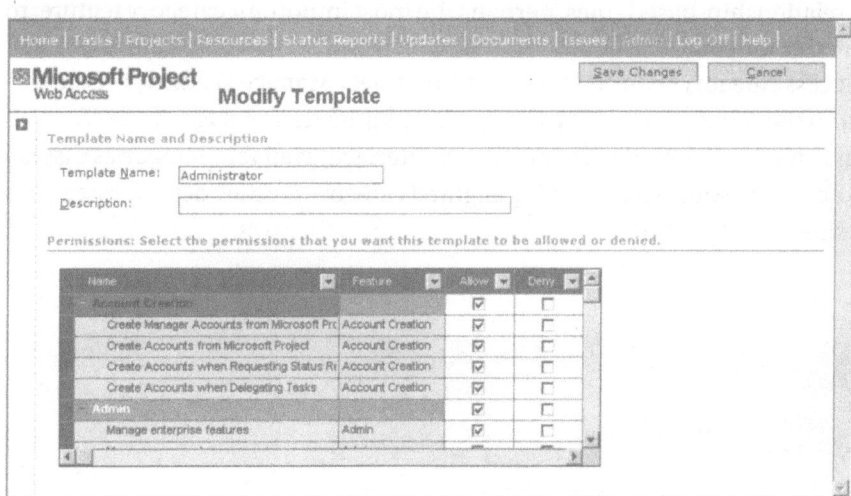

Figure 10-6. The Modify Template administration page

K.I.S.S. My Security

The old "keep it simple, stupid" rule applies here. Your goal in using groups and categories is to simplify your schema as much as possible and leverage the relationship-based security rules in categories to automate user access to project data and software functions.

Working with Categories

To a large degree, your ability to manage category configuration determines your success with simplicity. Categories connect groups and individual users to project views and data. You may assign individual users and groups to categories as well as individual projects. When you begin to approach categories at an individual level, however, you cross the border into high-maintenance territory. Instead, your goal is to use relationship-based rules, perhaps the most important category feature, to automate this for you.

To access category maintenance routines, select Manage security ➤ Categories from the Admin menu. The Categories administration page displays, as shown in Figure 10-7. Like the Modify Group interface, available categories display in a grid above the summary of the highlighted category. All four default categories are also shown in the figure.

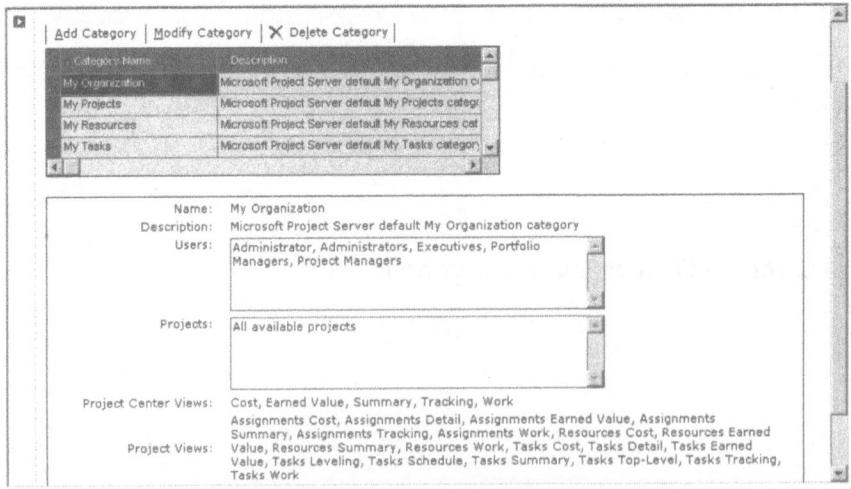

Figure 10-7. The Categories administration interface

Project Server's default categories the necessary complement to the default groups to connect their permissions with data and software functions. Here's a summary of these categories:

- *My Organization:* Includes blanket access to just about everything in Project Server, from projects and resources to views and Analyzer models. The default users of this category are Administrators, Executives, Portfolio Managers, and Project Managers.

- *My Projects:* Connects users who manage plan data to their own data by implementing access based on the users' relationship to a project. The default users of this category are Project Managers, Resource Managers, and Team Leads.

- *My Resources:* Exists to connect resource managers with their resources' data. The default user of this category is Resource Managers.

- *My Tasks:* Designed to connect Team Members with their task data. The default user of this category is Team Members.

Whether you choose to add or modify a category, the maintenance interface is the same. You define each category by the following six characteristics:

- *Category Name and Description:* Accepts input accordingly.

- *Users and Groups:* Determines the users or groups associated with this category.

- *Permissions:* As covered under the previous topic.

- *Projects:* May specify all projects, projects specified manually, or projects specified by relationship-based security rule. Detailed project views are also specified in this area.

- *Resources:* May specify all resources, resources specified manually, or resources specified by a relationship-based security rule. You specify Assignment and Resource Center views in this area.

- *Project Center Views:* Specifies the Project Center and Portfolio Analyzer views, as well as manually specified Analyzer models or models by relationship-based security rule.

The first two characteristics in the list are intuitive, and I've already covered the third. That leaves the interesting and useful category attributes that boil down to projects, resources, and views. Collectively, these are the objects you control through categories. Keep in mind that no matter what object you expose through a category, corresponding permissions must also allow a user to take the action that accesses the data granted in the category.

Selecting either to open or to modify a category, or choosing to add a new category, opens identical displays except for the screens labeled Modify Category and Add Category, respectively. As shown in Figure 10-8, the Projects section of the Categories interface allows you to specify both projects and views. Specifying views is simple: You simply use the Add or Add All button to move the available views from the left to the right. In Figure 10-8, I used the Add All button to move all the views into the category. This manipulation technique applies to the following two characteristic groups as well.

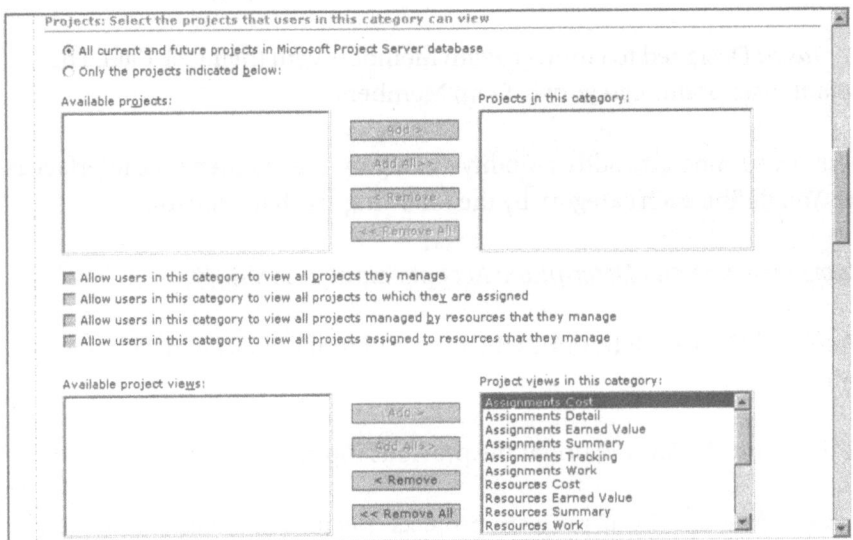

Figure 10-8. The Projects section of the Categories administration interface

Note that there are no available projects to add manually in Figure 10-8. This image is from a fresh installation. In the example, I've selected the "All current and future projects in Microsoft Project Server database" radio button. This is the way the system defines the My Organization category by default. If you were to select the "Only the projects indicated below" radio button instead, then you would have the option to either manually specify projects or specify projects by relationship-based rules, or both. The definable rules are as follows:

- *Allow users in this category to view all projects they manage:* Allows any user or group associated with the category the ability to access projects for which the user or group is the project manager.

- *Allow users in this category to view all projects to which they are assigned:* Allows any user or group associated with the category to view projects in which the user or group has assignments.

- *Allow users in this category to view all projects managed by resources that they manage:* Allows any user or group associated with the category the ability to see projects in the system when the resources that the user or group manages have projects they're managing in the system.

- *Allow users in this category to view all projects assigned to resources that they manage:* Allows any user or group associated with the category the ability to see projects in the system when the resources that the user or group manages have assignments in a project.

The Resources section of the Categories interface follows a similar structure to the Projects section discussed previously. Figure 10-9 is shot from a server with an established resource pool; therefore, in the example you can see that the Available resources area is populated.

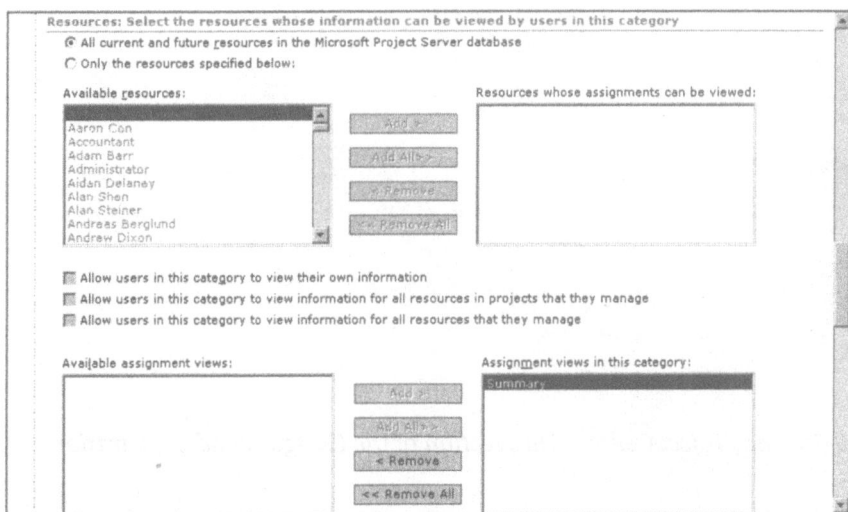

Figure 10-9. The Resources section of the Categories administration interface

The example also shows the default value for My Organization. In addition to the visible part in the figure, a section for Resource Center views isn't shown. When you want a category to specify access to resources via relationship-based security rules, you may select from the following check boxes:

- *Allow users in this category to view their own information:* Grants access to users to see their own data.

- *Allow users in this category to view information for all resources in projects that they manage:* Allows project managers to view resource information for resources that have assignments in plans that they manage.

- *Allow users in this category to view information for all resources that they manage:* Establishes access to resource data based on a management role.

The final section of Categories administration interface is titled Project Center Views. The options contained in this section, part of which is shown in Figure 10-10, control access to Project Center views, Portfolio Analyzer views, and models. Figure 10-10 doesn't show the Project Center views portion. These views are handled the same way all other views are handled.

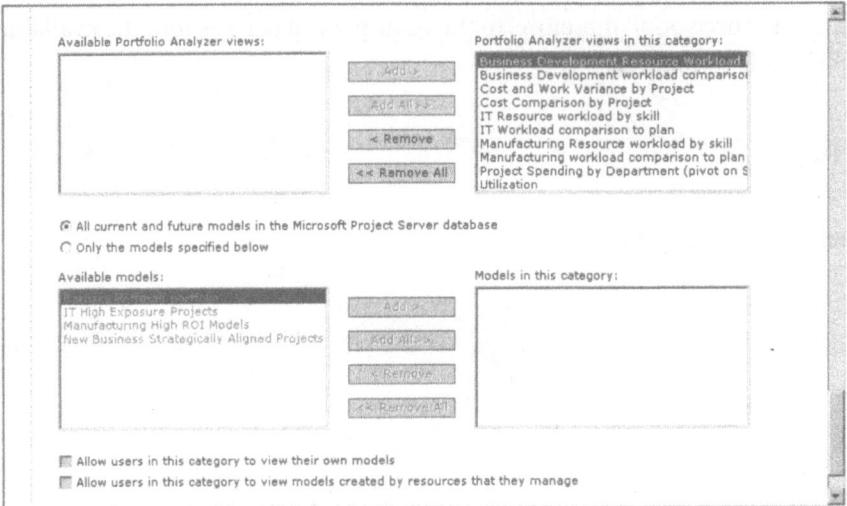

Figure 10-10. The Project Center Views section of the Categories administration interface

No precooked Analyzer views are provided with Project Server. Therefore, you'll have little to be concerned with until you've loaded data in the system and built some Analyzer views. It's interesting that only Administrators and Executives have permission to see these by default. You'll need to consider how to structure permissions for your organization and make the appropriate changes. Analyzer views are a big hit in the Project office, and project managers like them, too.

Models don't come into play until you have data loaded and have created them. Once you or your users have built models, you control access rights through category selections. Once again, you have some relationship-based security rules as well as the blanket All selection to enable your users.

- *Allow users in this category to view their own models:* If a user isn't granted access through an All selection in a category, this selection is required if a user is to have access to models of his or her own creation.

- *Allow users in this category to view models created by resources that they manage:* Grants access to models to a Resource Manager based on reporting values established in the system.

Understanding the Group/Category Cross-Connect

Group and category values interplay to define a user's access in the system. A good example of how you can leverage this structure is the default My Organization category. Administrators, Executives, Portfolio Managers, and Project Managers are members of this category by default. The category settings provide sweeping access to portfolio information. In every section, "All current" is selected and all views are exposed, yet these users have very different access based on settings in their individual groups.

As I mentioned before, there are also more direct relationships between permissions set in Groups and the security objects controlled by Categories. Not all permissions are tied directly to category objects this way, but many are. Table 10-4 lists the category sections and their related permissions.

Table 10-4. Category Objects and Related Permissions

CATEGORY OBJECT	RELATED PERMISSIONS
Projects	Save Project, New Project, Open Project Template, Open Project
Project Views	View Project Center, View Project View, View Assignments View, View Portfolio Analyzer, See Projects in Project Center, See Projects in Project Views, See Resource Assignments in Assignment Views, Read Summary Assignments
Resources	Edit Enterprise Resource Data

Table 10-4. Category Objects and Related Permissions (Continued)

CATEGORY OBJECT	RELATED PERMISSIONS
Resource Views	Read Summary Assignments, View Resource Center, View Resource Allocation, View Assignments View, See Resource Assignments in Assignment Views
Project Center Views	View Project Center, See Projects in Project Center, View Models, View Portfolio Analyzer

The important thing for you to remember is that there are cross-relationships between categories and groups. Moreover, there are dependencies within these entities. For instance, granting a user access to Project Views is useless without also including both category and group permissions for access to the Project Center, where users access the views. I must stress again how important it is to take your time designing your configuration for the sake of ease of management and perhaps your sanity over time.

Working with the Resource Manager Relationship

One of the more mysterious Project Server features—mysterious because most folks simply don't get it from reading the Help files or find the coverage of it on TechNet—is the Resource Breakdown Structure (RBS). I mentioned this in the discussion of custom fields in Chapter 8, and here's where it comes into play.

The RBS, Enterprise Resource Outline Code 30, identifies reporting structures that enable the resources-I-manage relationships when defining access to projects, resources, and views in categories. The RBS is also a blank slate out of the box, so the onus is on you to design and configure it for your organization. Keep in mind that outline codes can be hierarchical, and that's what you need for this purpose. The simple rule is that everyone who is a resource manager has access to resources tagged with a value that's on a subordinate leaf of the hierarchy.

Depending on requirements, an RBS will reflect a reporting structure. If it's the responsibility of various resource managers within the organization to maintain their own resource data, then a design such as the one shown in Figure 10-11 might fit the requirement. In this structure, the analysis manager will be seen by the system as an analyst's manager providing that the person who is the analysis manager and the corresponding analyst are attributed correctly in the resource pool. You'll learn more about this in the next chapter.

Figure 10-11. A sample two-level RBS

The example in Figure 10-11 shows how a two-level structure appears in a drop-down selection list. Though the example structure gives each manager the right to edit reporting resource data, it doesn't define a relationship above the manager level; therefore, the administrator is the only one who can edit the data for the managers.

The scope of your deployment largely determines the complexity of your RBS. If you're deploying a single implementation across many departments, and each department distributes resource maintenance to its manager, your RBS structure may have many top-level branches with many descending levels. On the other hand, if your installation is for a single department, and only one person is responsible for handling resource data, then you may not have a need for an RBS at all.

The key is to assess the value of the RBS to your organization. Is the relationship-based security rule, enabled by the RBS, useful to you as it was intended? If you can hijack it to accomplish something entirely different, that's OK, too. Remember that users granted access to data and views through relationship-based security rules require corresponding permissions.

All About User Accounts

Most of your account creation will occur when you create your resource pool, which is the subject of the next chapter. For users not in the enterprise resource pool, you'll create accounts using the Admin interface. Additionally, you'll need to update users, whose accounts you create through the resource pool, to add group membership beyond the default Team Members group. By default, accounts created through the enterprise resource pool receive Team Members group membership only. You change these values through this interface.

To add new user accounts or to modify existing ones, select Manage users and groups ➤ Users from the menu to open the Users administrative interface shown in Figure 10-12. The interface allows you to select a user to modify from a drop-down list or switch to the grid style view you've seen everywhere in the interface so far.

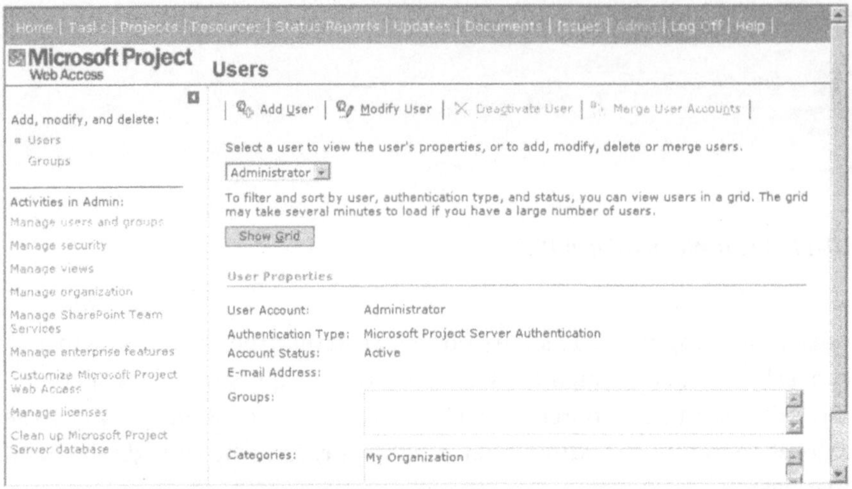

Figure 10-12. Administration home page for managing users

You may add, modify, or deactivate users but not delete them. The merge function applies only to nonenterprise resources or user accounts. Deactivation doesn't remove a resource from the resource pool; rather, it simply deactivates it, preventing project managers from using the resource for project assignments.

Select a user to modify and then click Modify User or click Add User to open the Edit or Add screen, respectively. The Add User screen, shown in Figure 10-13, contains fields to determine the user's authentication type, name, e-mail address, and Windows account if applicable. It's very important to use the format *domainname\username* when you enter a Windows account. If you're entering a local machine account, you substitute the machine name for the domain name.

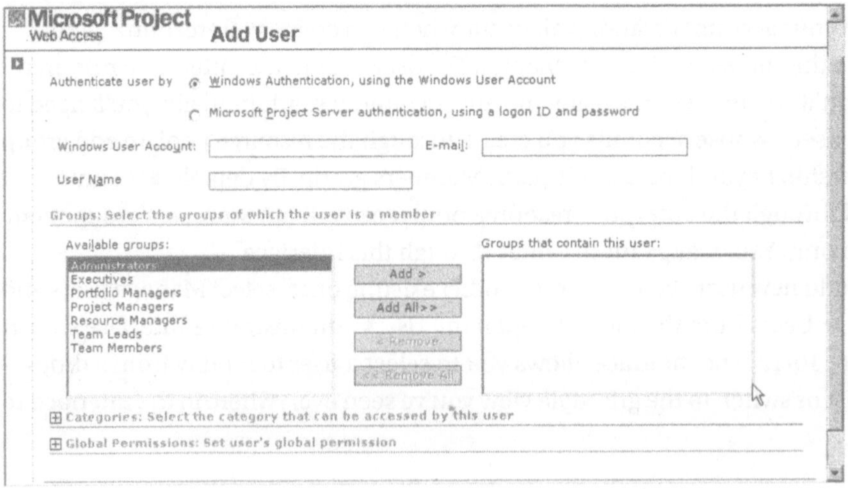

Figure 10-13. The Add User administration page

Scrolling down the page, you can see that the interface also allows you to set group and category membership for the user, as well as the user's individual global permissions. I recommend that you not manipulate permissions at the individual level. Again, this is a step across the threshold to more manual maintenance. Don't forget that you can also accomplish assigning users to groups and categories through each of those interfaces.

If you do run into a situation where you want to delete a resource, Microsoft has published a stored procedure that you can download with instructions for its use in the Project Resource Kit on the TechNet site.

Summary

You manage Project Server's security through a complex web of permissions and security object access. The information contained in this chapter should give you a comfort level in approaching your configuration. At the risk of sounding pedantic and redundant, give this task enough time to keep your design simple.

CHAPTER 11

Building an Enterprise Resource Pool

Building a well-structured enterprise resource pool enables you to use Project Server's important new resource management features. I've mentioned some of these already. Project Server's new resource management technology builds on the resource engine Microsoft acquired from E-Labor.

Outline codes play a major role in crafting your portfolio, and the enterprise resource pool is no exception. The promise of meaningful output from the system is completely dependent on these. Before proceeding with building your pool, you should have created your outline codes and custom fields. You should also know where your existing resource data is coming from, whether you create it manually or import it.

Whether you pull this data from Active Directory, Exchange, Outlook, Excel, or from any other source, chances are you'll be doing significant manual updating. This is mostly due to the fact that the outline codes and custom fields you'll use are very likely to be new constructs to your organization. Those that aren't new to your organization may come from disparate sources. I'll admit to some degree of pessimism in the previous statement, but I recommend that you give thought to this when allocating time to build your pool.

The Importance of the Pool

Defined in simple terms, *resources* are the people, equipment, and material required to execute a project. Defined in accounting terms, resources are the elements of project direct costs. As such, resource pool attribution drives the ability to track activity-based project costs as well as material consumption. Project cost drives meaningful performance measures in the system that yields the data that can enhance business decision making. What are you in this for, anyway?

Your Cost or Mine?

Resource cost tracking is always a hot topic of debate in project management forums. Generally, in discussions centering on the sensitive nature of cost data, the greatest concern is how to shield this from the eyes of contractors, resources, and project managers. I always ask, why on earth dump actual cost figures into a project management system?

I suggest to you, instead, that the cost representation in a Project Server implementation produce consistency in labor and material expense reporting so that the built-in indices in the system are relationally representative of actual cost, but the cost totals don't necessarily equate to actual cost. Using true or near-true costs for materials isn't, generally, as sensitive an issue as human resource cost, so approach this as you see fit. Consider attributing human resources by using a loaded labor rate or a fractionalized representation applied consistently across the pool. You might choose, for instance, to enter $1.00 for everyone's pay rate. This would be enough to cause the earned value calculations in Project to calculate along with their indices, the Schedule Performance Index and the Cost Performance Index. Of course, the cost index isn't true, and in this case it makes no differentiation between resources as to cost. You can enhance this approach by making $1.00 the mean cost and using $.75 and $1.25, respectively, to add three dimensions to resource cost. The point is, no matter what cost approach you use, as long as it's consistent, you can use the percentages of cost produced by the system at any rollup level to infer actual cost from financial journal sources.

What you get for your effort is the ability to use Project Server's built-in Earned Value Analysis (EVA) calculations, which include key performance indices that measure performance across your portfolio. If you agree that ultimately the value of an automated project management system is to deliver business intelligence, then you'll want to leverage these standard indices rather than inventing your own.

Framing this in project management best practices terms, you choose the projects in your portfolio based on cost/benefit or return on investment (ROI) analysis. Then you continuously recalculate the value of your program and periodically review the profitability of the program based on performance as measured against standards. One such standard you can use is net present value (NPV). You use the output of Project Server to determine the current NPV of the individual projects, programs, and initiatives in your portfolio. It doesn't matter if you also condition your NPV calculation with strategic weightings; what matters is that you measure and calculate consistently so that the output is reliable and accepted as a standard in your organization. You can build an NPV calculation in a project-level enterprise field that calculates NPV using system output and some additional input fields, and then display it in a continuously recalculated Project Center view.

Besides providing a cost basis for standardized project performance measures, the enterprise resource pool accommodates more prescient resource management needs, such as short-term and long-range staffing demand projections. A well-attributed pool also supports easier team building with tools that slice through large resource pools to identify resources with the skills, availability, and other user-specified characteristics for the job.

Local vs. Enterprise Resources

You may create resources in Project Server at the enterprise or local plan level. *Local resources* exist within an individual plan and aren't part of the enterprise resource pool. I discourage you from using local resources, as Project Server always attempts to create a user account for local resources. This typically results in system errors unless you've altered the default settings on account creation under Manage organization ➤ Features, as discussed in the previous chapter.

You have tighter control over the system when all your resources are managed through the enterprise resource pool. If you've given sufficient consideration to generic resources, a project manager is never without adequate fodder for temporary resource representation. Because you can't stop project managers from entering local resources into their plans, without implementing custom code, this becomes a training and policy issue. Determine a definite workflow for your organization's handling of resource creation.

Understanding Enterprise Resource Types

Project represents resources of two primary types: work and material. With Project Server, a hybrid of work resources and generic resources is now available. Work resources always include your human resources and you may use work resources for scheduling equipment or other nonconsumable fixed-asset resources you don't classify as materials.

- *Work resources* are actual resources you apply to tasks. The system tracks availability of work resources and contains the necessary attributes to support skill-set matching and resource demand and availability management.

- *Generic resources* are pseudo work resources that represent actual resources in a plan. You use generic resources to model staffing demand and for use in skill-set matching and resource substitution. Generic resources don't accumulate availability.

- *Material resources* are consumable resources that typically represent materials or supplies used during the execution of a task. Material resources are defined in units to suit your requirements and don't participate in availability calculations.

TIP   Because the system has no way to distinguish between nonhuman and human work resources you define, it will count every work resource as a Project Server user in calculating its internal license count requirement. Add as many of these to your license count as required. Consider adding an enterprise resource outline code to distinguish between human and nonhuman resources to separate these two categories in Project views, reports, and Analyzer views.

Your Resource Availability Decision Is Due

For effort-driven planning, the best way to account for individual resource availability against the project standard calendar is by adjusting the resources' availability by percent or by units as per your preference, not by applying resource calendars. This can occur at the time you make an assignment by adjusting it manually, or by taking advantage of the resource's default value.

If you don't care about collecting nonproject time, the simple solution is to set each resource's individual availability to a percentage that allows for your anticipated average for nonproject work. If you want to collect nonproject work, there are both advantages and disadvantages to approaching it through a project plan rather than the nonproject time buckets provided in the system.

How you account or whether you account at all for nonproject time is important requisite information to setting the resource default value in the enterprise resource pool. In Chapter 10 when I discussed nonproject time a la Project Server, I noted that this decision had a potential impact in resource pool settings. This is it—time to make the decision.

A Plan for Nonproject Time

The disadvantage of the nonproject time buckets captured by Project Server is that they escape scrutiny before updating to the database. The fact that they're then invisible without custom coding or database modifications makes the choice of a project plan solution rather appealing. Whether you use one plan or a number of plans will depend upon who you want to approve the reported hours. Using a project plan(s) to collect nonproject hours from resources is an option if you understand the impact and manage it.

If resource managers are responsible for updating this type of information, a possible solution is to have each resource manager maintain a nonproject work plan. The point is to structure this to what works for your organization and what's practical with the system. Remember that whoever is supposed to accept the updates must own the assignment in the plan to establish that flow. With that in mind, design accordingly.

I recommend taking a very simple approach to establishing maintenance tasks and keep these as generalized as possible. Try to limit the tasks to three or four maximum. A timesheet gets unfriendly when it scrolls too long. Consider the psychology of your users in making these decisions.

Structure the plan using fixed duration–type tasks. Make sure that your plan has an accounting-based time frame so that the start and end reflect a calendar or fiscal year—whichever is most appropriate for your situation. You can do this by using *e-days* for duration, which denote elapsed days in Project.

Assign the appropriate resources to the maintenance tasks in the plan so that the cumulative total of the maintenance tasks equal the percentage of resource time that you would otherwise have deducted for default availability had you chosen not to track nonproject work. In other words, if you would have normally discounted availability to 80% for the average user, make sure that your cumulative assignments sum to 20%. Of course, set resources default availability to 100% unless other factors apply. Resource assignments in this type of plan should be set to "demand" to avoid the possibility of being accidentally altered by the Resource Substitution Wizard. More on this later.

Setting Up Skill Codes and Other Resource Keys

Scale is everything in approaching skill sets and other attributes specifically designed to help project planners quickly identify appropriate and available resources. Project Server provides tools that instantly sift through hundreds or thousands of resources to locate one that has the preferred attributes for the job. If your organization doesn't have hundreds or thousands of resources, then you may take a very light-handed approach to this capability or opt to ignore it completely.

The system matches skills through enterprise resource outline codes. Although it's possible to set multiple outline codes as participants in the matching process, this approach is less flexible than using a single code for skill matching. Because you can apply filters to the results of skill-set matches, they're best suited for narrowing down a result set. Therefore, skill-set matching is very effective at a fairly high level, provided that precooked filters are provided and that planners are properly trained in the use of ad hoc filters in the team-building tools.

Skill-set matching in Project Server uses exact-match-only logic. Therefore, it's difficult, if not impractical, to represent a lot of complexity in skill-set modeling. It's impractical because of the number of generic resources that are required to model skill combinations and it's just too darn specific. Don't confuse skill-set matching in Project Server with an application that manages skill sets. Look elsewhere for that, like your sophisticated HR application that came with your enterprise resource planning (ERP) system. If your company is among the very few that have skills management automation in place, chances are you'll need to dumb down the attribution to suit Project Server skill-set matching.

I recommend that you employ broad-level matching for skills because of their absolute nature. Use filters in the Project Web Access interface to narrow resource selection. This delivers the greatest flexibility and is the easiest to manage conceptually and physically. The built-in ability to save filters and perform ad hoc filtering to augment skill-set and availability matching delivers a very effective resource matching solution.

Providing thoughtful attribution values as filters to enhance Project Server's team-building tools is your challenge. If you're working with a large resource pool, it's possible to build a significant matrix of attributes for team building. Distributed organizations want location codes; larger organizations want seniority codes and secondary skill identifiers. The only limit to your scheme is that eventually you'll run out of custom outline codes. Remember that once you create a new attribute, you obligate yourself to provide a value for it for each resource in your pool.

The following example uses a very simple model to identify resources. One outline code is used to represent skills. The skills represented are as follows:

- Architect

- Business Analyst

- Business SME

- DBA

- Executive

- Infrastructure

- Other

- Programmer/Analyst

- Project Manager

- QA

- System Analyst

- Stakeholder

- Sysop

Note that these are deliberately set at a high level. Discounting Stakeholder, Other, and Business SME, because they exist to identify noncore resources, this skill code immediately divides the resource pool by 10. In a pool containing 200 resources, 10 slices yields an average of 20 resources to choose from based on skill matching alone. You can quickly reduce the number of eligible resources by considering availability, but two additional attributes provide even finer slicing in the selection. The second is actually a repeat of the first with a different name. More remarkably, you're sharing a value list with the enterprise project outline code, Sponsor, that you originally defined as a project-level attribute.

Primary System Knowledge

- Finance

- Gen Business

- HR

- IT

- Logistics

- Marketing

- Purchasing

- Creative

Secondary System Knowledge

- Finance

- Gen Business

- HR

- IT

- Logistics

- Marketing

- Purchasing

- Creative

The simplicity of the preceding example belies its usefulness. It very naturally follows the way the sample organization taps resources. The project managers locate resources sought first by role, then by system knowledge, and always according to availability and priority. The duplication of the code to represent primary and secondary knowledge demonstrates how you can best create multi-value constructs using outline codes.

Opening the Resource Pool

The check-in and check-out processes for the enterprise resource pool are different from the enterprise global in that you don't necessarily check out the entire pool all at once, whereas with the enterprise global it's an all-or-nothing deal. The menu path to approaching the enterprise resource pool is the same as the enterprise global. While you're logged onto Project Server with administration privileges through the Project Professional client, select Tools ➤ Enterprise Options ➤ Open Enterprise Resource Pool to display the Open Enterprise Resources dialog box shown in Figure 11-1. Take this approach to add individual resources to the pool as well as to edit existing resource data.

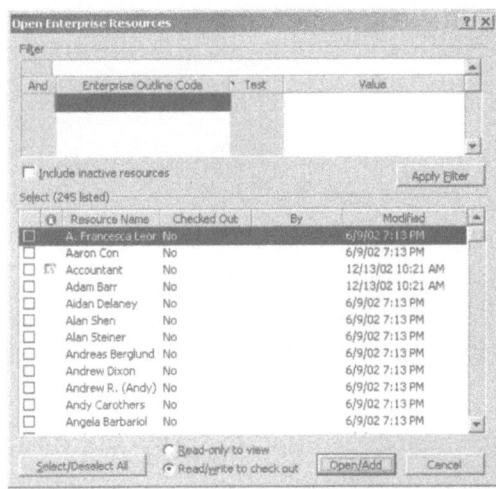

Figure 11-1. The Open Enterprise Resources dialog box

The dialog box allows you select or deselect all resources by using the Select/Deselect All button, or you may select resources individually or select none to open the pool for additions only. When you check out a resource, you lock it for editing by anyone else, but you don't preclude scheduling or assignment activities from continuing with the resource. Whether or not you select a resource, clicking the Open/Add button opens the Resource Sheet view in Project Professional with the title Checked-out Enterprise Resources, as shown in Figure 11-2. In the example, I chose to check out a resource.

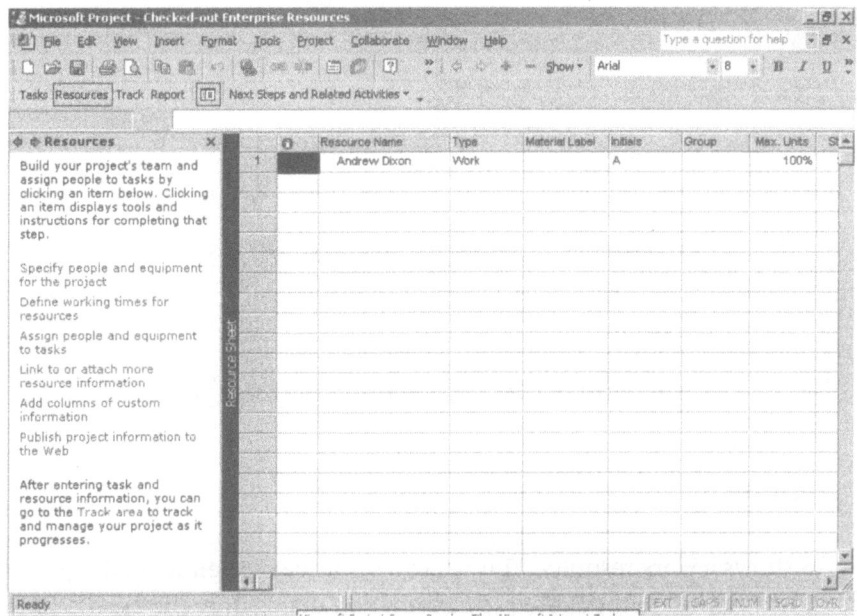

Figure 11-2. The enterprise resource pool opens to the Resource Sheet view in Project Professional.

Working with Individual Resources

Once the enterprise envelope is open, experienced Project users will find that working with resources in Project Server is almost identical to working with resources in Project 2000. Of course, generic resources are a new and welcome twist. The default Resource Sheet view is limited in that it doesn't expose all the fields that you need to work with. You have the option of creating new views or altering the default Project Professional views if you prefer. Simply double-click a resource to open the Resource Information dialog box shown in Figure 11-3 to edit specific resource information.

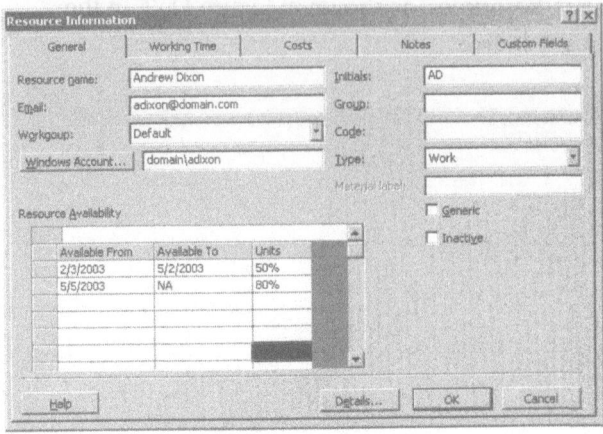

Figure 11-3. The General tab of the Resource Information dialog box

Work Resources

Figure 11-3 shows a work resource. You select a resource type either in the Resource Sheet view or in the Resource Information dialog box. The Type field is on the right side of the dialog box. You know this isn't a generic resource as the Generic check box is unchecked. As I mentioned previously, a correct e-mail address and Windows account are essential for human work resources. If you're using a work resource to represent equipment or other asset usage, you won't specify Windows authentication; instead, you'll use Project Server authentication.

When working with a human resource, you may enter the Windows account or pull it from an available address book. If you have Outlook or any other Messaging Application Programming Interface (MAPI)–compliant mail client installed on your workstation, for instance, clicking the Windows Account button will give you options to connect to your address book in Outlook or Notes. Note that a mail client must have a Windows mail profile in order for Project to find it on the workstation. Lotus Notes, for instance, doesn't create a Windows mail profile during installation; you must do this manually.

Making an entry into the first Units field sets the maximum units for the resource to the entered amount. You may contour availability by making time-bracketed entries into the Resource Availability grid in the lower-left quadrant of the Resource Information dialog box's General tab. The system accepts up to 25 entries. The Group and Code fields are available, and they do show up in Project Center and Resource Center views, but you can't apply value lists to these and they require adherence to Project templates to control their labels globally for the organization.

Use the Working Time tab to mark a resource's calendar for vacation time. This is required for all your resources on an ongoing basis. Initially, your goal is to represent accurate near-term availability for your resources. The interface on this tab is identical to the one you used to set the default working time in the enterprise global.

Edit any of the five rate tables for the resource on the Costs tab. You can time phase each of these by setting ascending effective dates similarly to the way you create availability contours in the previous figure. Enter the standard and overtime rates, if applicable, in the appropriate rate table in the Costs tab display, as shown in Figure 11-4. Note that you can set a cost-per-use instead of or in addition to an hourly rate. Choose your cost accrual settings. The default cost accrual is Prorated, which distributes the cost evenly across the timeline. Select Start to accrue the cost at the beginning of the assignment or End to accrue the cost at the end of the assignment.

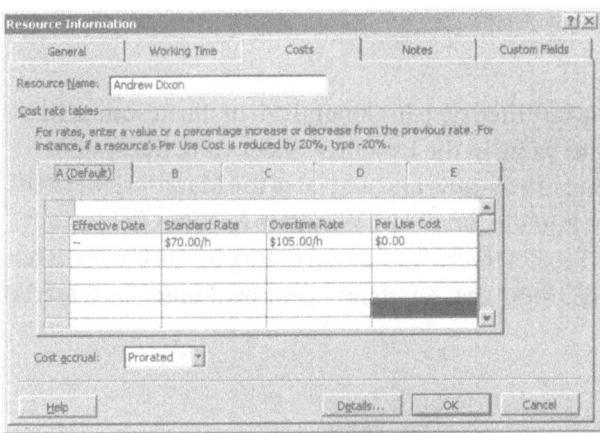

Figure 11-4. The Costs tab of the Resource Information dialog box allows you to date stage rates.

The Custom Fields tab is new in 2002. This tab accepts entry into enterprise custom fields. Be aware that this display contains enterprise fields only; standard custom fields don't show up in the Custom Fields tab shown in Figure 11-5. You can use the rich-text features to add notes to the resource record through the Notes tab. Use this tab to present additional information about resources.

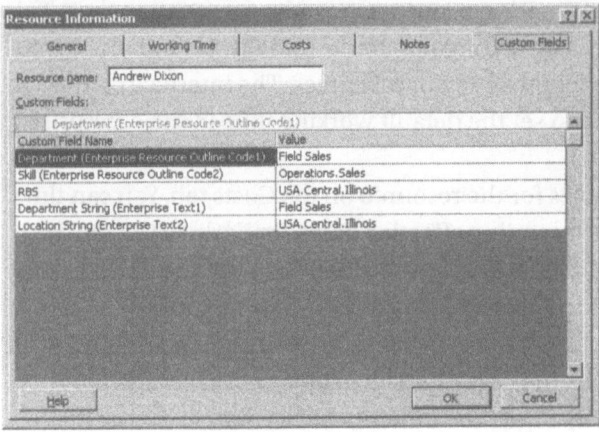

Figure 11-5. The Custom Fields tab of the Resource Information dialog box

Material Resources

When you select Material as the resource type in General tab of the Resource Information dialog box or you set this value in the Resource Sheet view, the system disables availability and working time inputs and activates the Material label field. The system also disables input into the Email and Windows Account fields, as shown in Figure 11-6. Whereas Project tracks human inventory in work units, it has no predefined units for material resources. You define your own units for material resources.

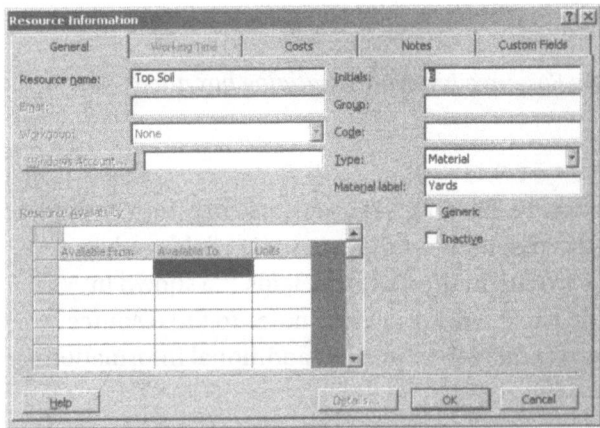

Figure 11-6. The General tab of the Resource Information dialog box for material resources

The Material label field allows you to define your own consumption units corresponding with the costs that you set. For instance, top soil for a construction project might be labeled "yards," and an electronic component for a product might be labeled "each," or "assembly." The point is to make the label correspond to the cost. As with work resources, you may define multiple rate tables and time-phased rates as well as per-use costs for material resources.

Generic Resources

Generic resources support key resource features in Project Server. They drive skill matching in the Team Builder and Resource Substitution Wizard, and they're essential to rich enterprise project templates. Generic resources serve as placeholders for actual resources before actual resources are determined.

Unfortunately, you can't use generic resources in the system to measure demand or availability, as these aren't calculated by the system. This limits their value beyond early planning phases.

Generic resources are useful for modeling costs. When you assign them to tasks in project plans, Project calculates costs based on the rates set in the resource pool. Setting up generic resources is nearly identical to handling other work resources, save the Generic check box shown in Figure 11-6. In a resource view such as the Resource Sheet, you set this value by exposing the Generic column in the view, which offers and accepts values of yes and no.

....

Using Generic and Material Resources with Required Enterprise Fields

When you define both generic and material resources, you must provide a value for any enterprise custom field or outline code that you marked as required. It's very important to provide values for generic and material resources when defining your fields and outline codes. Otherwise, you're likely to run into the errors shown in Figure 11-7. If you attempt to enter a value on the fly, you'll also see the error illustrated in Figure 11-8.

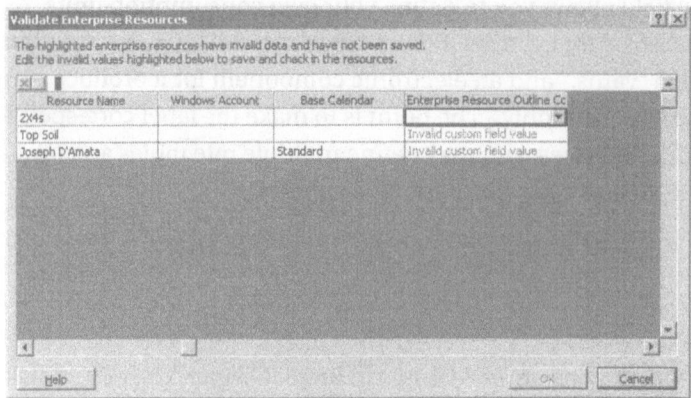

Figure 11-7. The system validates enterprise resources for required field values.

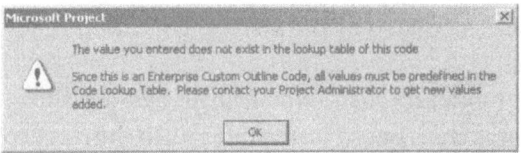

Figure 11-8. Attempting to set enterprise field values on the fly generates an error.

Coalescing Your Resource Pool Input

Although Project provides a conduit for importing resource data directly into the enterprise resource pool from foreign data sources such as .xls or .csv files, I suggest that you promise yourself not to do this. It's inefficient and potentially dangerous in that you have a much higher risk of corrupting your database with the direct method. Instead, gather your resource pool data in a simple Project .mpp file until you're certain that the data is ready for importing into the pool.

Using a Project file provides two benefits. First, you have an opportunity to catch bad data characters—data that might be uniquely acceptable to Excel, for instance, but cause Project to choke—without affecting your production database. Second, it's the easiest way to establish importable custom field and, in particular, outline code data. This approach works when resource data is acquired from a foreign system and is a natural for organizations that have their resource information in existing file-based resource pools or distributed across existing project files that will be imported into the system.

Organizations that already have a resource pool and well-established project management system need only make a copy of the pool for export purposes. Now is a good time to clean up the existing data for typos, name changes, and the like. Add the new enterprise attributes and their values to the resource pool file by mirroring those using local custom fields. These will be available to map in the import wizard during the final import process.

Organizations that have resources defined across project plans, but not in resource pools, should first consider whether there's enough consistency in the plans to make the effort of obtaining the data worthwhile. The most important consistency to look for is the resource naming convention. If resource naming isn't consistent across plans or cost rates vary, the value of using them for input diminishes. You also want to verify that they contain enough information to make them worthwhile. Accurate Windows accounts and e-mail addresses are highly valued here. If your plans pass this test, the approach to take is to create a new resource pool from existing projects:

1. Start Project Professional and choose to work offline. Working offline avoids the possibility that you might accidentally take a publish action or that you might prematurely generate user accounts in Project Server.

2. Working with the default Project 1 file, from the File menu, open a project plan containing resources that you want to harvest.

3. Cut and paste from one resource view to the same view in the new pool file.

Next, clean up the data by repairing minor inconsistencies and omissions, and then add the new attributes and values.

If you're not starting out with an existing collection of Microsoft Project plans, and project management is new to your company, you can find any type of data source to begin with, such as a resource listing in Excel or Access, or you can simply choose to enter your resources by hand. Consider your resource naming convention in light of Project's default alpha sort, which makes no distinction between a first name and a last name in the Resource Name field.

Adding Resources from Active Directory or Your Company Address Book

Project Professional articulates with the company address book and Active Directory whether connected to Project Server or not. If you use this feature when connected to Project Server, then the application will begin making assumptions about the resources that you enter. When you have the enterprise resource pool open, the system will assume that these are new enterprise resources and add them directly to the pool. If the enterprise resource pool isn't open, the system will automatically mark the new resources as local. When you're using this feature early in the process to build an interim pool, work with Project Professional offline from Project Server.

From the Resource Sheet view in Project, select Insert ➤ New Resource From ➤ Active Directory, as shown in Figure 11-9.

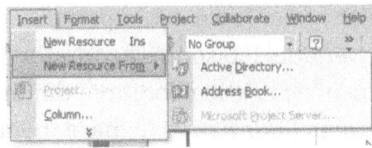

Figure 11-9. Insert menu selections from a resource view.

An Active Directory explorer opens. At the top of the dialog box shown in Figure 11-10 is a drop-down selector with which you can select from various Active Directory trees. The figure was shot on a stand-alone computer, so the selector isn't active as presented.

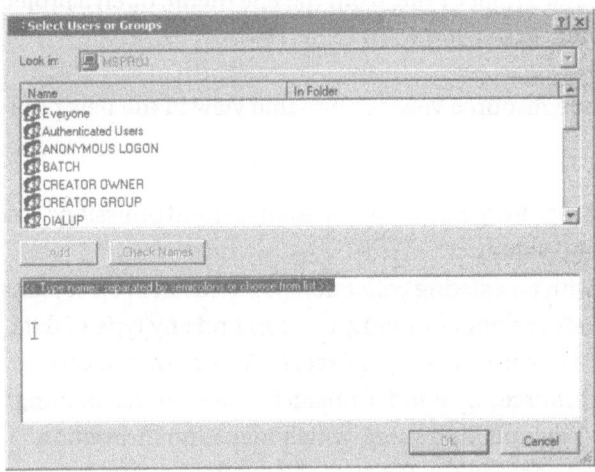

Figure 11-10. The Select Users or Groups dialog box

Connecting to the address book is a matter of making the selection from the Insert menu, as described previously. This choice opens a Select Resources dialog box that allows you to move resources from the address book to the Resource Sheet. In the upper-right corner of the dialog box, as shown in Figure 11-11, you may select from the various address books available to you on your network.

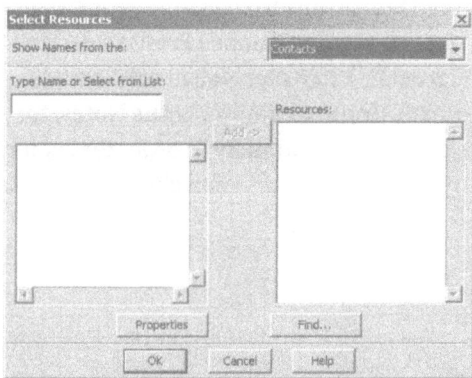

Figure 11-11. Use the Select Resources dialog box to move resources into the Resource Sheet.

Verifying a Windows Account

The importance of an accurate Windows account to the creation of a usable resource account may cause you to look at how you might merge information from more than one source. For instance, if you hope to obtain all the information you need from the company address book, and you then discover it isn't up-to-date, you have a dilemma. Is it worth obtaining the data from this source?

You can browse the Active Directory or NT domains to search for users one by one to find and fill in missing information if you import from a less than complete and accurate source. If your company has used consistent naming through the years, you can likely guess most of these, but dealing with exceptions can become a difficult task when the naming is unpredictable. Therefore, make sure that your potential data source has a valid Windows logon contained in it before you decide to use it as an import basis. If it doesn't, weigh the consequences of manual cleanup. When you use external data sources, be wary of data containing extended characters and leading and trailing spaces, with leading spaces being more troublesome. During an import, the system doesn't detect cell values from Excel that contain soft returns, for example, as bad characters in the import process but will cause database errors in production.

Project Professional provides the means to verify Windows logons by connecting to your company address book. Following this path to the address book is different from the one described in the previous topic. Adding the Windows account and e-mail address fields to the Resource Sheet view makes editing the data more convenient. To connect to the company address book, from a resource view double-click a resource to open the Resource Information dialog box. Follow these steps:

1. Click either the Windows Account or Details button to link to your global address book through your local mail client. The Choose Profile selection dialog box displays, as shown in Figure 11-12. (Note: Not all mail clients create mail profiles on a workstation during installation. Lotus Notes, for instance, must have a mail profile configured manually in order for Project to see it on the client machine. Any MAPI-compliant mail client will work.)

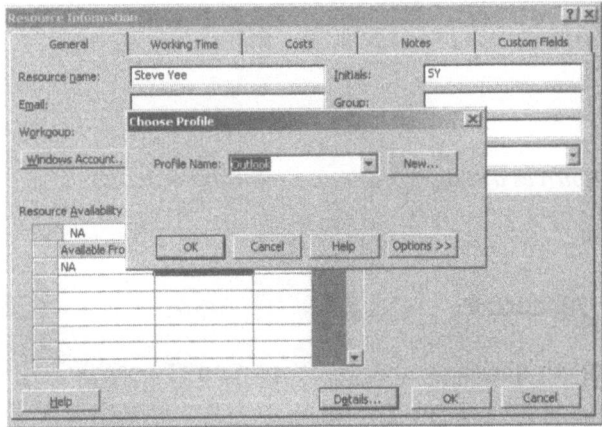

Figure 11-12. Clicking either the Windows Account or Details button opens the Choose Profile dialog box.

2. Depending on your mail client security settings, the system may prompt you for a logon. Default Outlook settings will cause a prompt for access to your Outlook client.

3. Project will attempt to match the name with an entry in the address book. The results will display in the Check Names dialog box shown in Figure 11-13.

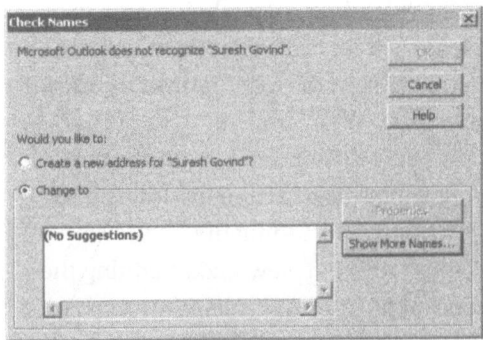

Figure 11-13. The Check Names dialog box displays matches and suggestions in the results pane.

4. Project will default to the local default address book. You can change the selection by clicking the Show More Names button in the Check Names dialog box to open the Address Book dialog box shown in Figure 11-14. The pull-down selection box in the upper-right corner of the Address Book dialog box will display all address books in your company's catalog.

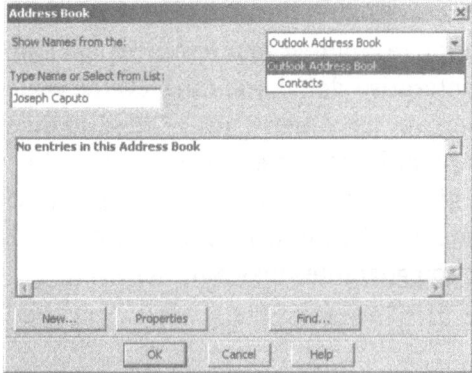

Figure 11-14. The Address Book dialog box allows you to select additional address books.

For the most part, you'll use your connection to the company address book to populate Windows accounts and SMTP e-mail addresses. The logon name in the format *domainname\logonname* or the Active Directory name is key information. It must be correct or your import will fail. A bad e-mail address won't cause an import problem, but it messes up notifications. It's not worth importing bad data, so you'll want to get it right.

Preparing Custom Field and Outline Code Data

The second hurdle in preparing your resource data after you've gathered the logon information is staging the custom outline code data. As previously mentioned, this is likely to be new to your organization, so plan for the time it takes to assign these values manually.

When importing the resource pool, Project will only map outline codes in the project to outline codes for enterprise resources. The code structures and values must match completely and exactly; however, you can map any available outline code to any available outline code, so the name you give the code and the code you select is inconsequential beyond identifying the code for your own recognition. Getting the enterprise outline code values into your source file has the added benefit of being useful when you're assigning nonrelated values as well. For instance, the skill outline code may be useful in manually setting resource cost rates, as you can use this code in your current view to sort the resources by like values. Generally, costs are consistent within these classifications.

To help build the outline codes in your file-based resource pool, you can copy the value lists from the corresponding fields that you created in your enterprise global file. Although you can't copy from one field list to another directly, you can use an intermediary application to hold the values between copying them from one outline code to another. In Project Professional, connect to your Project Server. Then open the .mpp file in which you're building your resource pool and start Microsoft Excel. After opening the enterprise global, you can view the value list of an enterprise resource outline code, copy its contents using Ctrl+C or the Copy button in the interface, paste it temporarily into Excel while you close the enterprise outline code, and open the destination outline code. Then copy the list from Excel and paste it into the destination field. The indenting of the value list is lost, so you must re-create this; however, you guarantee that your values are import-worthy during the process.

Importing Resource Information

After you have gathered, entered, and refined your resource data in the source .mpp file, you're ready to import the resources into your pool. If you've provided values for mapping all the required field values, this process will complete very quickly. To start the import wizard, log onto Project Server using Project Professional with an administrator account and select Tools ➤ Enterprise Options ➤ Import Resources to Enterprise. The Import Resources Wizard Welcome screen displays, as shown in Figure 11-15.

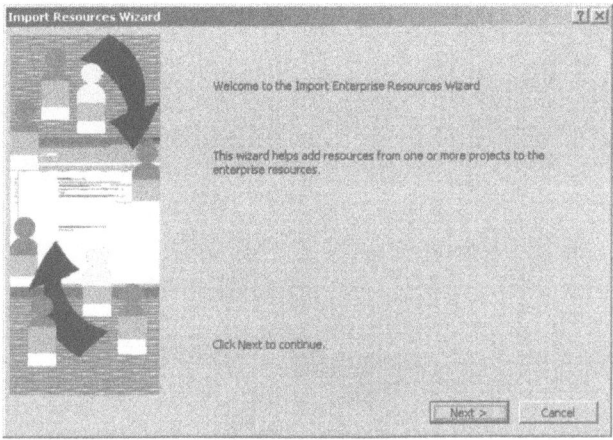

Figure 11-15. The Import Resources Wizard Welcome screen

1. Click Next and the Open from Microsoft Project Server dialog box displays, as shown in Figure 11-16.

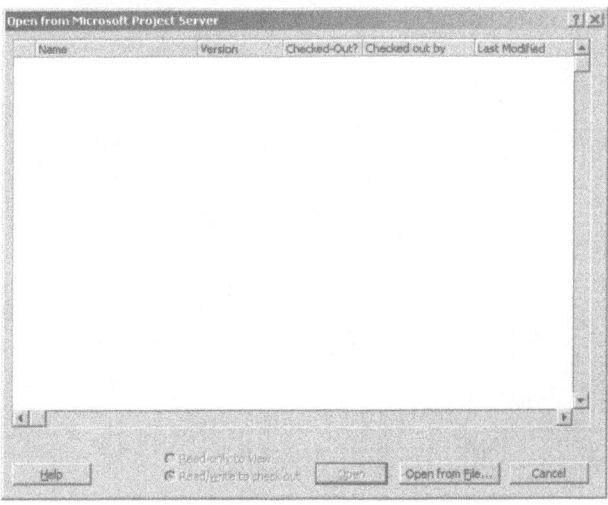

Figure 11-16. The Open from Microsoft Project Server dialog box

2. Click the Open from File button to open a standard file browser with the title Import Resources, as shown in Figure 11-17.

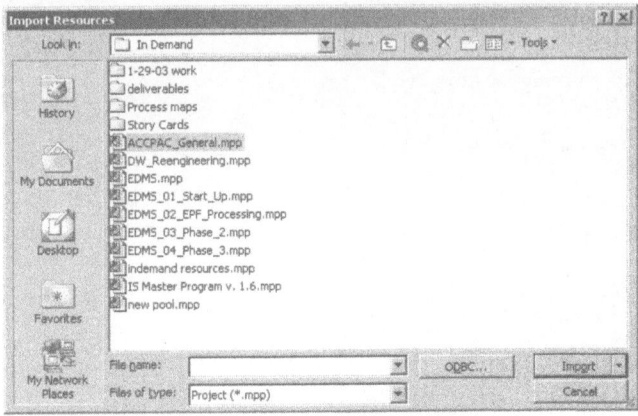

Figure 11-17. The Import Resources file browser

3. To point to a data source, such as an SQL database or another database, click the ODBC button to open the Select Data Source dialog box, where you can select an existing file or system DSN or create a new DSN as shown in Figure 11-18. Otherwise, browse to your source file and select it.

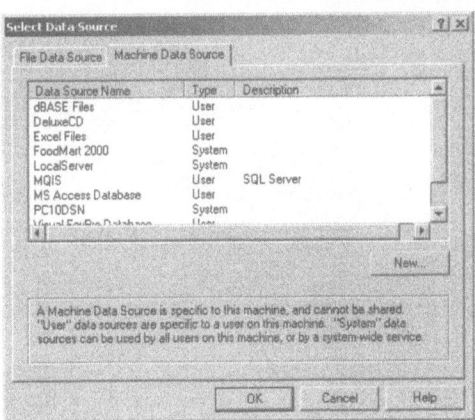

Figure 11-18. Browse to select an existing DSN or create a new one.

4. Once you've chosen a file or DSN connection to a database, the Import Resource Wizard presents the mapping screen shown in Figure 11-19. You must select each from field on the left and map it to an enterprise field on the right. You may map values contained in nonenterprise fields to enterprise fields in this screen. You must map a value for each enterprise field that's marked as required in order to continue.

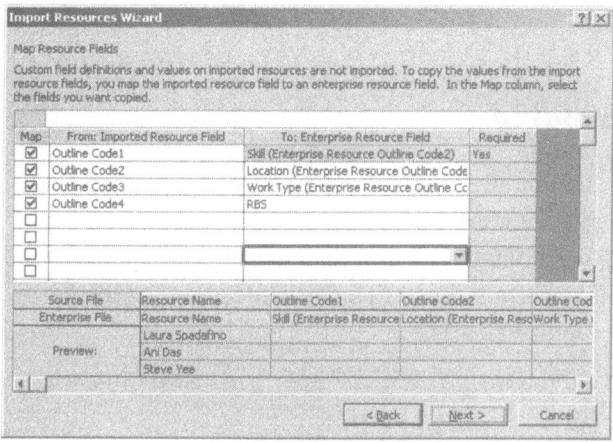

Figure 11-19. Map resource fields in the dialog box.

5. The system displays the resources and highlights any errors in the field values to be imported. The system won't allow resources with invalid required field values to be imported. These are deselected automatically, but you may provide the correct value manually. Use the horizontal scroll bar to review the field mappings and make alternate selections next to the resources with errors, as shown in Figure 11-20.

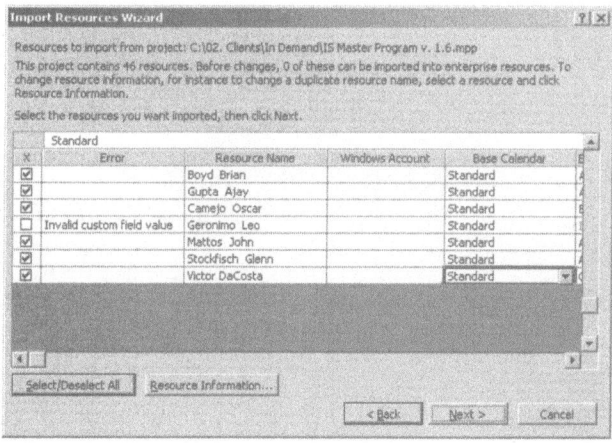

Figure 11-20. Provide correct values for required fields or the resources won't be imported.

Once you've mapped the field values correctly, click the Next button to continue. Heed any warnings displayed by the system before continuing. Upon continuing, the resources with valid required field values import to the system and the wizard reports success.

Completing the Pool Build

Whether you added resources manually or imported them, your resource pool build isn't complete until you've assigned each member to the appropriate security groups and categories. By default, all new resources become members of the Team Members group. Make certain that you have valid values in all your custom fields, especially the required fields.

Summary

You should now have a well-developed resource pool attributed in a way that delivers ease of resource selection to your project and resource managers, and delivers business intelligence by helping to shape the output of the system. Because the resource pool is central to delivering Project Server's business value, configuring it is one of the most important implementation activities.

Establishing the Project Environment and Configuring Project Server Views

If you've been using this book as a guide to building your system, you're now very close to having a fully functional implementation. With your resource pool built, all that's left is to bring your existing projects and templates into the new enterprise environment and configure your custom project views.

I saved building the views for this chapter because they're easier to validate, from a design perspective, when data is available to populate them. Because custom enterprise field names don't become available in Project Web Access until after a project has been published that carries the fields, it makes sense to configure the views after getting some projects into the environment.

In this chapter you'll finish the job of configuring your system and stage the system for your pilot launch.

Importing Projects

The Import Projects Wizard, which you access by launching Project Professional connected to Project Server and navigating to Tools ➤ Enterprise Options ➤ Import Project to Enterprise, is provided to assist you in moving your projects into the enterprise environment. The Import Projects Wizard Welcome screen is shown in Figure 12-1. Click Next to continue.

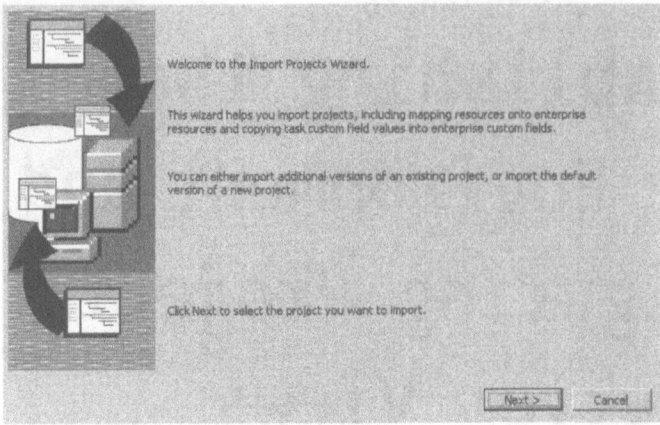

Figure 12-1. The Import Projects Wizard Welcome screen

The system displays the file browse window, shown in Figure 12-2, to allow you to browse to a directory containing the project plan to be imported or to select a project using an ODBC connection. You can point at projects stored in databases as easily as you can a file. Locate the plan and click Import to activate the import process.

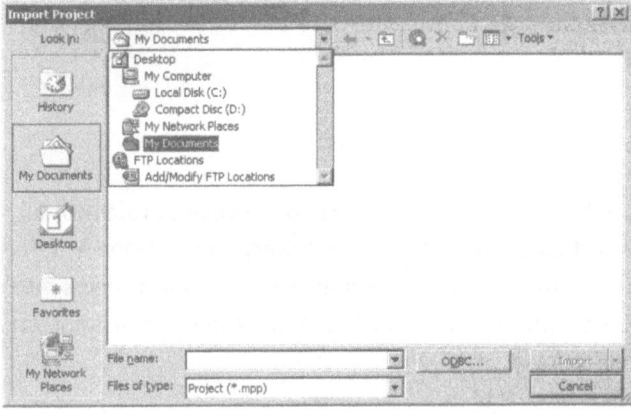

Figure 12-2. The Import Project file selection dialog box

Once you've selected your project, the system displays the first mapping dialog box shown in Figure 12-3. The dialog box enables you to insert a new name for the project, select the version, indicate whether you want to import the project as a project or a template, choose the base calendar, and input values for custom enterprise fields and outline codes. Provide the appropriate values and click Next to continue.

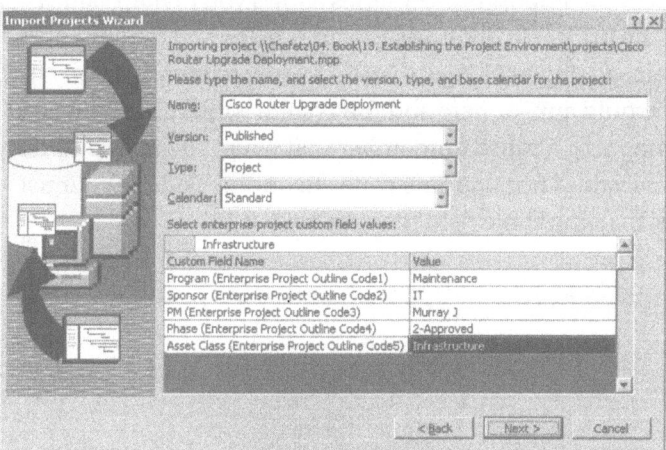

Figure 12-3. Provide custom enterprise information in the enterprise project custom field values.

After accepting the project-level information, the system displays the Map Project Resources onto Enterprise Resources dialog box, as shown in Figure 12-4. If the system finds resources in the source plan whose names match enterprise resources, it automatically maps these for you in the dialog box. Otherwise, for each resource, you choose from one of three actions: Import the resource to the enterprise, keep the resource as a local resource with a local base calendar, or map the resource to an enterprise resource. In the example in the figure, I'm mapping generic resources contained in the plan to generic resources in the enterprise resource pool.

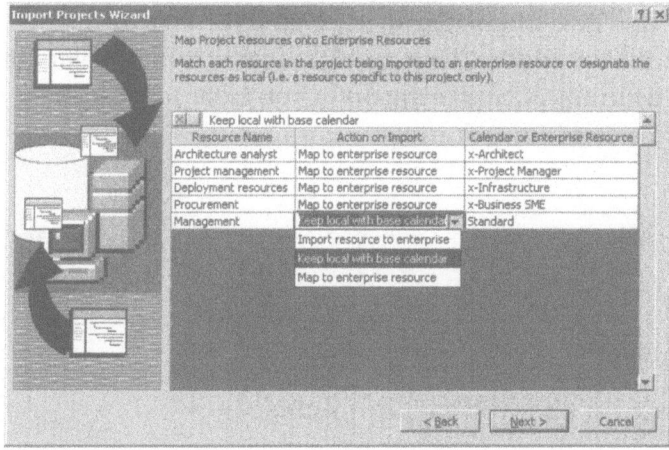

Figure 12-4. Map the resources in the project.

The next dialog box in the import project series allows you to map values contained in local fields in the project to enterprise custom fields and outline codes in the Project Server system, as shown in Figure 12-5. If you had identified any task fields as required, they would appear here and the system wouldn't let you continue further without mapping a value. Remember that when you map outline codes, you must map the values from outline codes to outline codes. You must map specific field types to compatible field types as well.

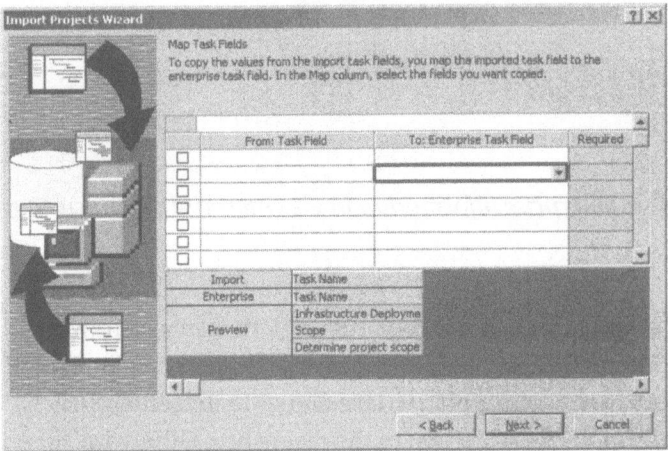

Figure 12-5. The Map Task Fields dialog box

The system next gathers the tasks and examines them for errors. It displays any errors it finds in the grid in the task summary dialog box shown in Figure 12-6. The system displays the nature of the error. To make error correction easy, the system displays a link to the Task Information dialog box, which you can activate by clicking the Task Information button. The standard Task Information dialog box launches, as shown in Figure 12-7. Click the Import button in the task summary dialog box once you've corrected any task errors.

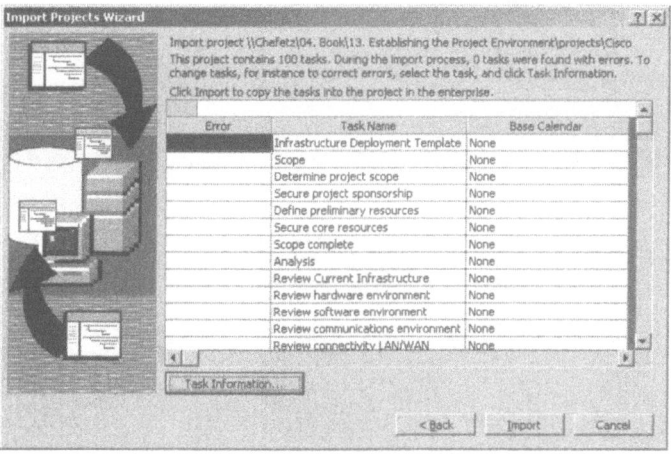

Figure 12-6. The task summary dialog box

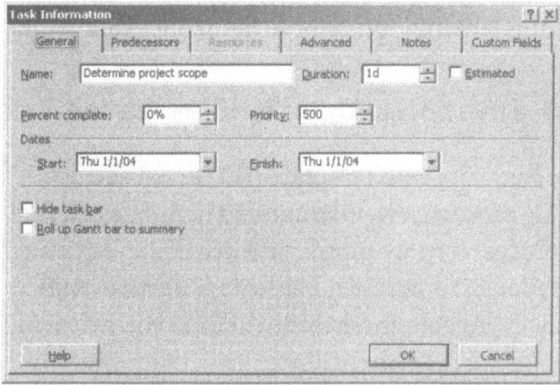

Figure 12-7. The Task Information dialog box

The system imports the project and updates the resource, task, and project information as you've instructed. When the update is complete, the Import Complete dialog box displays to report the success and give you the option to finish or import more projects, as shown in Figure 12-8.

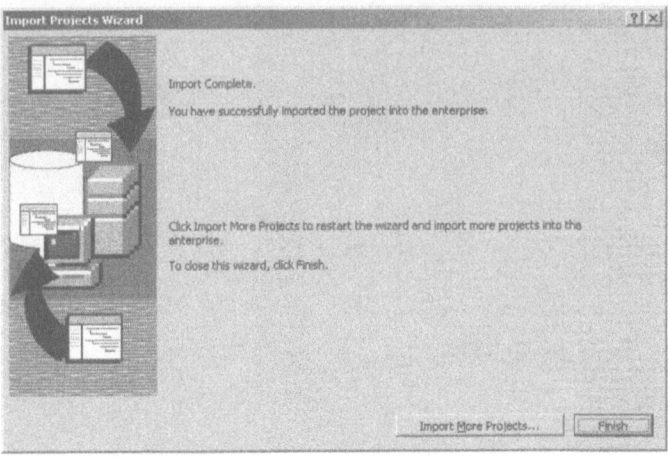

Figure 12-8. The system reports success.

Use the Import Projects Wizard to import your ongoing projects and project templates into your Project Server implementation prior to launching your pilot.

Controlling the Project Environment with Templates

An obvious and enduring benefit of working with templates is the cost savings realized by shortcutting the planning process. A well-structured template can take days or weeks out of the planning process by providing a precooked plan structure complete with a fundamental cost model. Your individual savings are determined by how easy it is to model your typical projects and how much time you invest in the process.

A less obvious reason to use templates is the opportunity they afford to take some control of the "nonenterprise" environment. I put that term in quotes because it's not a Microsoft term; it's my own. The Project Server environment templates offer the opportunity to use nonenterprise fields in an enterprise way. By embedding customizations to these with uniformity across the enterprise, you can co-opt nonenterprise fields and outline codes as pseudo-enterprise fields. The catch is that you don't really have absolute control of these. Project Professional users continue to have the ability to make changes to these, so this must be a trusted community.

Assuming that you can overcome this limitation through training and careful management, you can use templates to accomplish nonenterprise field management to a good degree. Suppose you want to get a value back from a resource at the assignment level. Because enterprise fields don't carry a discrete value at the assignment level, nonenterprise fields are the only way to capture data from users in the timesheets while preserving the data value at the assignment level. Another example is using nonenterprise fields to mirror enterprise values so that they can be exported to Project 2000 and Project 98. By defining the field customization in the template and requiring templates to initiate all projects, it's possible to distribute the customization across the enterprise.

You can also control other options through templates. You can control the settings in the Options dialog box (select Tools ➤ Options in Project Professional) through templates. Once again, this isn't a foolproof method, as users can make changes to these settings on a project-by-project basis.

Creating an Enterprise Template

An enterprise template is a template saved to the Project Server database with the type designation in the Save dialog box specified as Template. You can create an enterprise template by creating a new project from Project Professional while you're connected to a Project Server, or by importing a project or template as a template as described in the section "Importing Projects" earlier in this chapter.

To create a template directly, start Project Professional, connect to a Project Server, and begin working in Project 1. It's not until you save a project that you can indicate that it's a template. Selecting Save or Save As from the File menu opens the Save to Microsoft Project Server dialog box shown in Figure 12-9. Note the Type field in the dialog box. This is what makes a template an enterprise template.

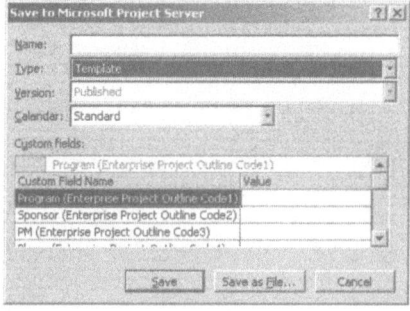

Figure 12-9. Select Template as the type in the Save to Microsoft Project Server dialog box.

TIP Use templates to build templates. If you were to modify a number of nonenterprise project fields, it might be a good idea to keep a copy of the plan with just the field customizations before building various purpose-specific templates on top of that level of customization.

Determining Timesheet (Published) Fields

You can augment information fields that display in the timesheet by adding custom fields, including standard custom fields and enterprise custom fields. Unfortunately, you may not delete or reorder the default fields provided in the system. When you add fields to the timesheet, they show up appended to the existing field display. It's typically necessary for a user to scroll the left pane of the display horizontally to the left to expose added fields.

The default fields displayed in the timesheet are the same for each tracking method; only the fields available for data entry vary. The default fields are as follows:

- Indicator

- Task Name

- Work

- % Work Complete

- Actual Work

- Remaining Work

- Start

- Finish

- Update Sent

- Project

- Assigned to

- Lead Name

To add globally available fields to the Timesheet display, first check out the enterprise global. From the Tools menu, select Customize ➤ Published Fields to open the Customize Published Fields dialog box shown in Figure 12-10. In the figure, notice that the Enterprise Date1 field has been added to the tasks view by selecting it on the left and using the right arrow button to move into the published area. Also note that this is one of many displays where custom names of enterprise fields aren't fully visible. It's always essential to have a good written record of your field customizations.

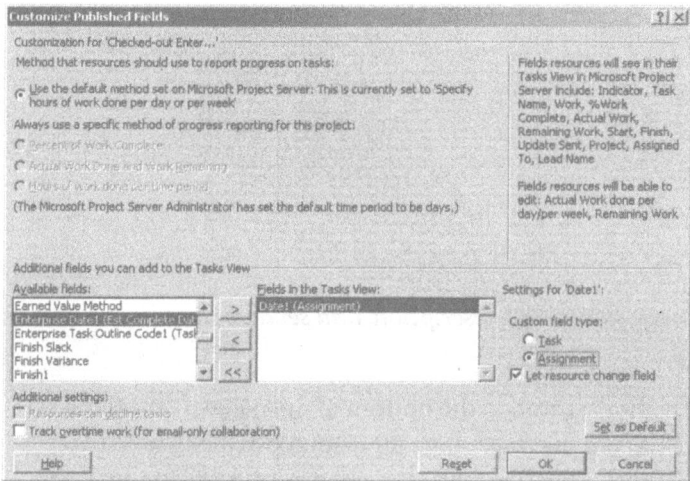

Figure 12-10. You use the Customize Published Fields dialog box to add fields to task views in Project Web Access.

Building the Cube and Publishing Resource Availability

In Chapter 9 I covered the settings related to updating resource availability and the OLAP cube. At that point in the process, prior to building the resource pool and uploading any projects, kicking off a cube build was fairly senseless. Now that you have an established pool and you've imported your projects, the time has come to launch the cube build for the first time and finalize the periodic settings for automatic cube generation.

Log onto Project Server with an administrator account and navigate to Admin ➤ Manage Enterprise Features ➤ Update resource tables and OLAP cube and scroll down past the text section. Under the "Build the OLAP cube" heading, select the "Yes, I want to update resource availability information and build an OLAP cube" radio button to reveal the options shown in Figure 12-11. When you select the radio button, the display changes to reveal the "OLAP cube name and description" section. Your Analysis Server information will prepopulate for you, but you must provide a name for your cube and an optional description. Select and set one of the date range options.

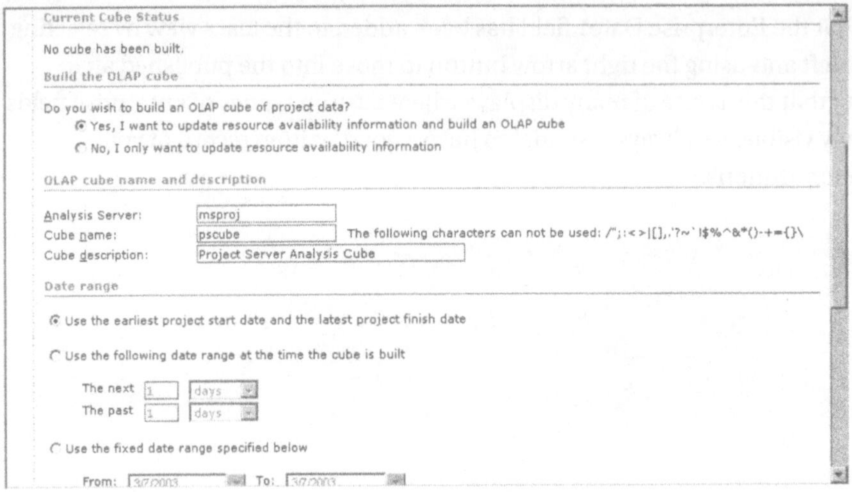

Figure 12-11. Provide a cube name and description, and set date ranges.

After you've set the options, scroll to the bottom of the page to reveal the settings shown in Figure 12-12. Set the date range for resource availability. In the "Update frequency" area, select the "Update only when specified" option. Click Save Changes and the system will confirm that the changes have been saved in an alert box.

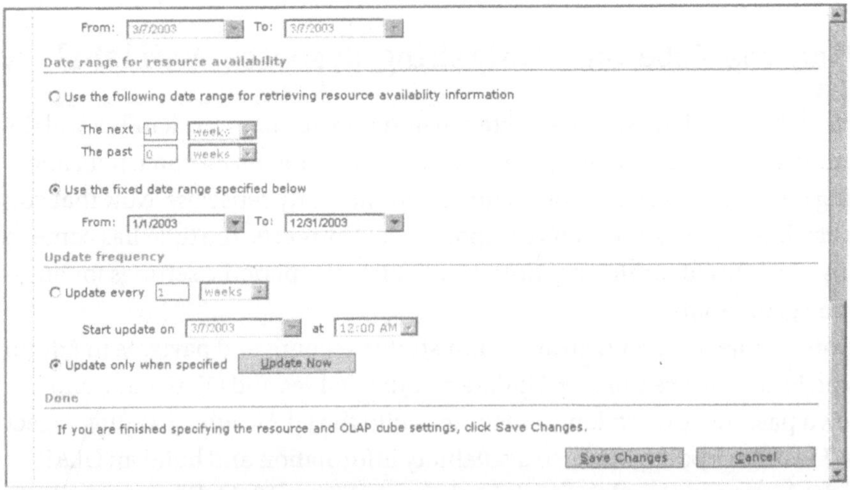

Figure 12-12. Set the resource availability date range and the update frequency.

Now that your settings have been saved, click the Update Now button to launch the cube. The system responds with the alert shown in Figure 12-13, which confirms that the cube build is in progress. Click OK.

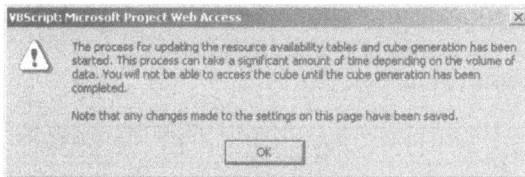

Figure 12-13. The system reports that the cube build process is in progress.

The system will return you to the top of the page. The cube build process can easily take 20 minutes or longer. Initially, you won't have any indication that anything is happening. For a while, refreshing the page will continuously report that "No cube has been built" under the Current Cube Status section of the page. Unless you're sitting at the server and can see the drive light flashing, which indicates server activity, you'll need to be patient. After a short time, when you refresh the page, the Current Cube Status section will report that the cube build is proceeding, as shown in Figure 12-14.

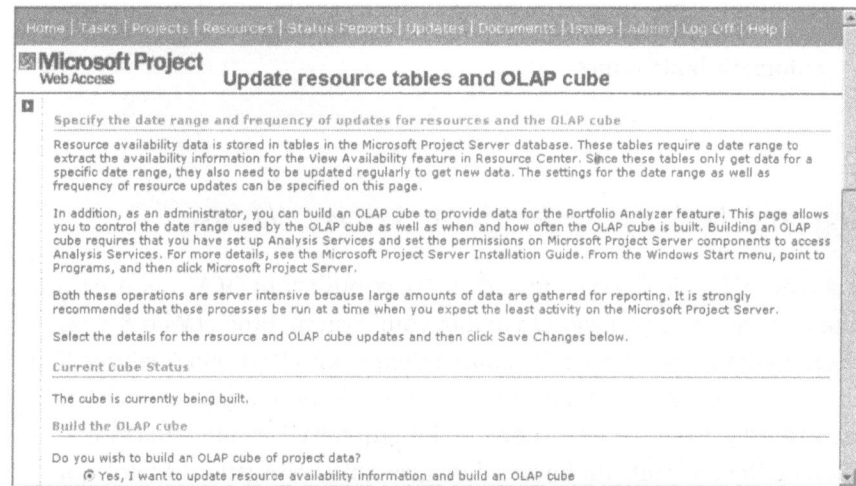

Figure 12-14. The system indicates "The cube is currently being built."

CAUTION   When you launch the cube build, the system should be idle. You shouldn't be running other applications and users should be off the system. The cube build consumes almost all of the SQL Server resources on the server running Analysis Services. If this is on a production machine serving other applications, it will essentially hose performance until the process completes.

The time the system takes to build the cube depends on the server specifications and the amount of data it needs to process. Once your cube build completes, the display under the Current Cube Status section of the page will report "The cube was successfully built on <date> at <time>." Scroll down to the bottom of the page and deselect the "Update only when specified" option and select the "Update every" radio button instead. Now set the frequency and time of your automatic cube build and click the Save Changes button. Keep in mind that your cube should be set to build when users aren't on the system and when it doesn't conflict with automatic backups.

NOTE   You use the "Update only when specified" option to build the cube for the first time because if you simply set the update frequency, your cube build won't launch until the next time the criteria for the automatic build is met.

Creating and Modifying Project Server Views

Now that you have data in the system and you have built your OLAP cube, it's time to build the custom views you want to add to your system. Project Web Access views present in the Project Center, Resource Center, and Portfolio Analyzer. You can build your Project Center and Resource Center views at any time once you've made the necessary field customizations, so I might have included this information in an earlier chapter, but having data available helps you validate your view design, and there's just no fun in building empty views! If you're like me, you'll want instant gratification for your efforts. Besides, you can't build the Analyzer views until you've built a cube.

Project Server views fall into five categories:

- *Project Center views* are portfolio-level views that display project-level information across a collection of projects. These are presented at the first level of the Project Center.

- *Project views* present information for a single project. You access them by drilling down from the Project Center. These views can display information on assignments, tasks, or resources.

- *Assignment views* present timesheet information when viewing assignments from the Resource Center.

- *Resource Center views* are displayed in the Resource Center.

- *Portfolio Analyzer views* display OLAP cube data in the form of charts and pivot tables.

Creating Gantt Chart Formats

Before you begin creating views, there are supporting customizations that you should be aware of. The Gantt chart format you apply to a view, as well as the grouping format, can be an existing format in the system or one that you customize using built-in tools. Gantt chart drawings render in Project and Assignment views in Project Web Access. Gantt charts apply to Project Center, Project views, and Assignment views. Resource Center views don't render Gantt charts. You can define up to 22 Gantt formats for use in Project Web Access views. These formats are as follows:

- Personal Gantt

- Gantt Assign Info 1

- Gantt Assign Info 2

- Gantt Assign Info 3

- Gantt Assign Info 4

- Gantt Chart (Project Center)

- Tracking (Project Center)

- Gantt Chart (Views)

- Detail Gantt (Views)

- Leveling Gantt

- Tracking Gantt

- Gantt 1–11

The Personal Gantt and Gantt Assign Info 1 through 4 formats apply to Assignment views only. You may apply the remaining Gantt formats to Project Center views and Project views. The Personal Gantt and Gantt Assign Info 1 through 4 formats display graphic representations for the following:

- Normal Task

- Delegated Task

- Milestone

- Summary Task

- Group By Summary

- Progress

Project Center views and Project views display graphic representations for the following, except that detail task information doesn't apply to Project Center views. In other words, when a Gantt chart format that includes graphic definitions for detail task information is applied to a Project Center view, task-level formatting is ignored as Project Center views display summary task and summary progress and don't include task detail.

- Normal Task

- Critical Task

- External Task

- Milestone

- Summary Task

- Project Summary

- Group By Summary

- Progress

- Summary Progress

- Baseline Task

- Baseline Summary

- Baseline Milestone

- Preleveled Task

- Preleveled Summary

- Preleveled Milestone

- Deadline

- Slippage

- Delay

- Custom Duration 1–10

- Early Schedule

- Late Schedule

- External Milestone

- Project Summary Version 1–5

For each element rendered, you determine whether the element displays, and if it does, the start and end shapes, the middle bar shape, and the color. To specify a Gantt style, in Project Web Access select Admin ➤ Customize Microsoft Project Web Access ➤ Gantt Chart formats. Figure 12-15 shows the Gantt Chart formats interface. Note that along the top the text tells that you that you can "Specify the bar styles and timescale for Gantt Charts." However, the timescale adjustment capability seems to have been left out.

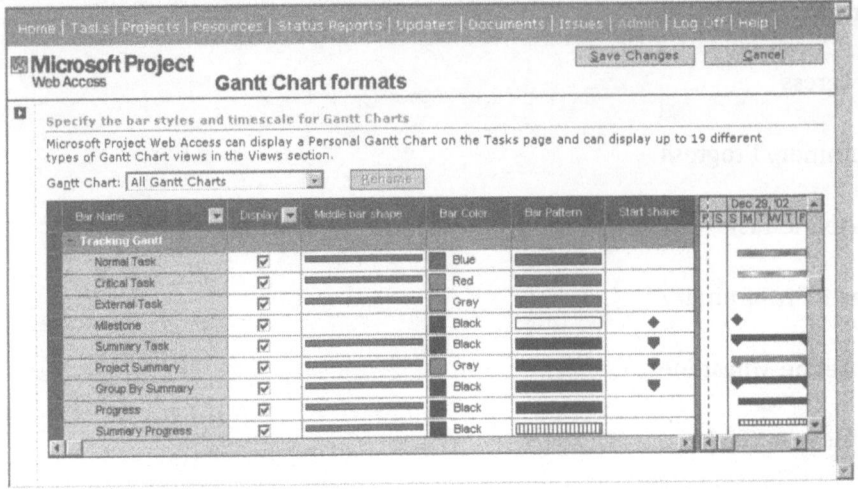

Figure 12-15. The Gantt Chart formats interface

With a selection of 11 bar styles, 14 distinct start and end shapes, and 15 colors as shown in Figure 12-16, you can create a distinctive look to offset and emphasize information as you choose.

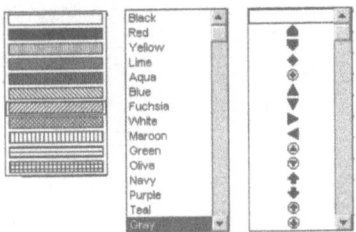

Figure 12-16. Combine bar styles, start and end shapes, and color selections to produce a unique look.

Creating Grouping Formats

Project Server allows you to apply colorful formatting to your grouping levels in views and in the timesheet. Although the timesheet has one and only one grouping format, a view in the Project Center or Resource Center as well as detailed Project and Assignment views may have any of the other ten grouping formats applied. The configurable grouping formats are as follows:

- Timesheet

- Views

- Grouping 1–9

You may determine the style of each grouping level display by selecting the following criteria:

- Cell Color

- Cell Pattern

- Font Color

- Font Style

Your color choices for cell colors and font colors for grouping formats are the same 15 basic colors offered for Gantt chart formatting. Similarly, the cell pattern styles available to you for grouping formats are identical to the bar style selections for Gantt charts. Refer back to Figure 12-16 for these selections. Because grouping styles apply to informational display, font styles are added to the pallet. Select from the standard normal, italic, bold, and bold italic styles for your grouping format.

Creating and Modifying Project Web Access Views

Selecting Manage views from the Admin menu in Project Web Access brings you to the Specify Views interface shown in Figure 12-17. The label "Specify Views" is a leftover from Project Central; don't let the inconsistency bother you. The display shows all current views in the system, grouped by view type. In order to modify or delete a particular view, you must select it in the grid and then click Modify View or Delete View. When you add a view, the system will assume that you want to add the type of view you've selected in the grid and it displays the succeeding screen accordingly. You can change the view type once in the second screen. Click the Add View button.

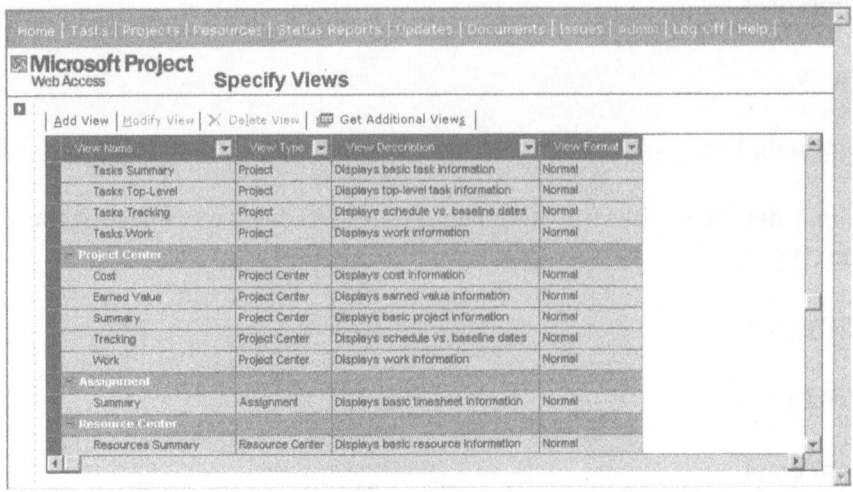

Figure 12-17. You can add or modify a Project Web Access view.

The first step in creating a new view is to choose a view type. As noted in the previous paragraph, you can preselect the type in the previous screen or select it in the Specify Views screen shown in Figure 12-18. Selecting a different type changes the field selections and other selections on the screen according to their applicability to the view type specified. For instance, the Table section applies only to Project views, which display detailed project information. Selecting a different type of view removes this section from the display. For this example, I create a Project Center view and make that selection accordingly.

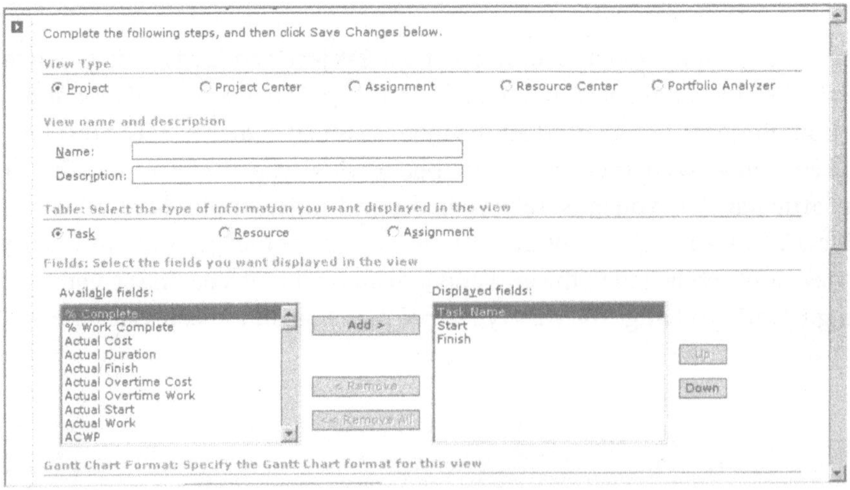

Figure 12-18. Specify the view type, name, and description.

The next step is to specify the fields that you want to appear in your new view. In Figure 12-19, I selected Enterprise Project Text1, a field that displays a graphical indicator based on budget variance. It's very important that you have your configuration document handy, as you can see that the custom name of the field isn't displayed in the interface. Each view has its own default fields that you can't remove; however, you can alter their display order by using the Up and Down buttons in the interface. Select a Gantt chart format, grouping format, and the categories to which this view belongs and click Save Changes. The system will report success.

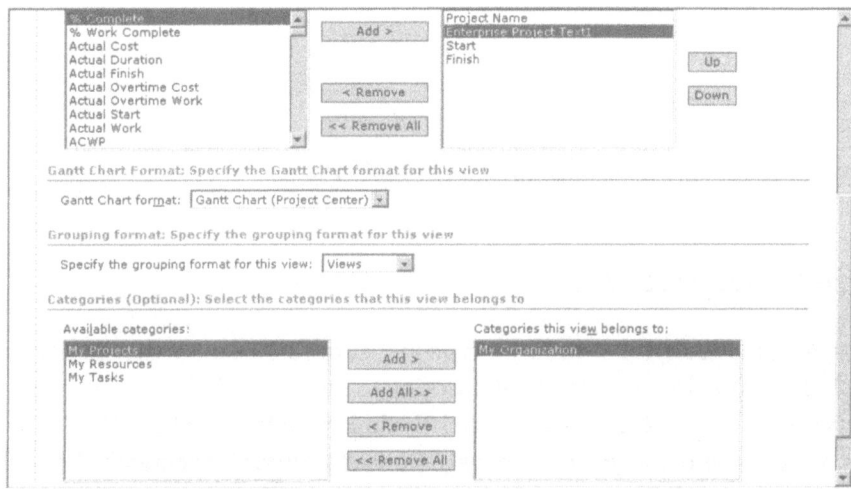

Figure 12-19. Specify fields, a Gantt chart format, a grouping style, and categories for the new view.

The system provides a section for building a filter into your view for Project views and Resource Center views. The filter builder allows you to set up to three tests for field values to filter data out of the selection. In Project views you can filter out tasks, and in Resource Center views you can filter out resources returned by the view. You may test fields for specific values with and/or conditions specified for up to three distinct tests.

The new view is now available in the Project Center, as shown in Figure 12-20. Notice that the view selection now appears in the "Choose a view" selection list and displays in the Project Center.

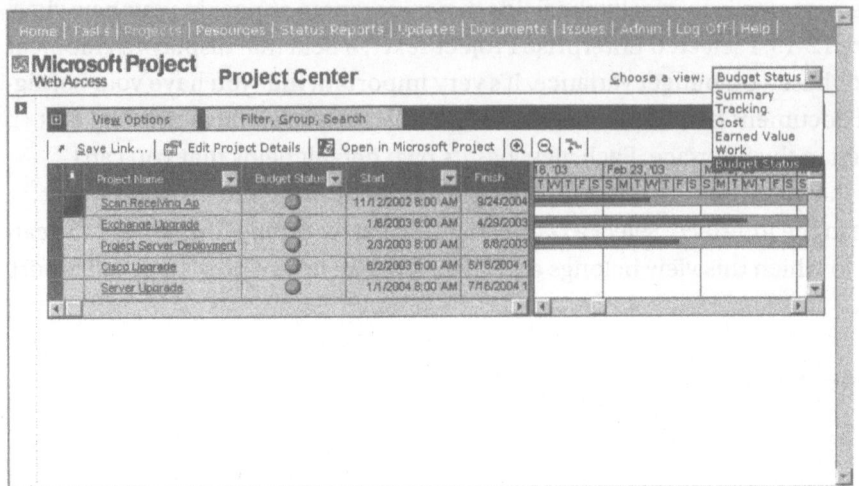

Figure 12-20. Your new view displayed in the Project Center

Creating Analyzer Views

Selecting Portfolio Analyzer as the view type in Figure 12-18 causes the display to change. If this is the first time you're attempting to create an Analyzer view, the screen shown in Figure 12-21 displays. Click the link to install the Office Web Components. Keep in mind that you must have a license for Office XP or greater, Project Standard, or Project Professional on your machine to get the fully functioning version of the Web Components activated. Otherwise, you'll get a runtime version that doesn't give you the functionality required to create Analyzer views.

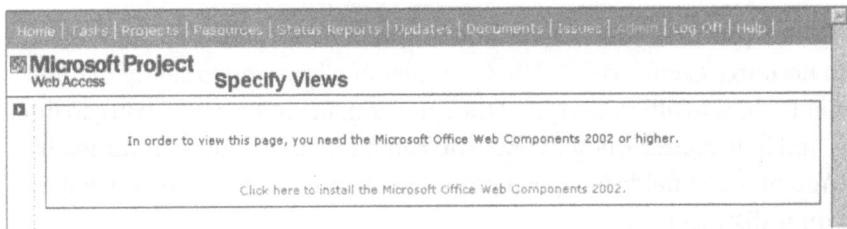

Figure 12-21. Click the link to install the Microsoft Office Web Components 2002.

A File Download dialog box appears, as shown in Figure 12-22. Select "Run this program from its current location" and click OK to continue.

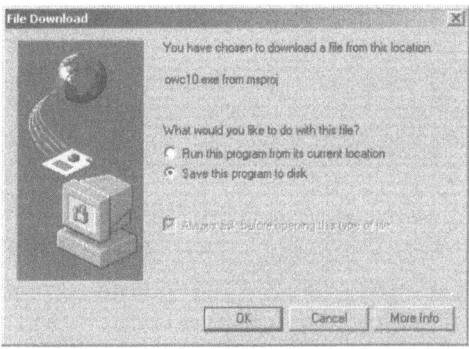

Figure 12-22. The File Download dialog box for the Office Web Components

A security warning displays. Select Yes to trust content from Microsoft. The download proceeds and the installation starts. Accept the license agreement and click the Install button. If you're running the installation from the server, rather than downloading the .exe file and then installing, the system will prompt you to close Project Web Access and any other Office program that may be running. The installation dialog box reports progress, as shown in Figure 12-23.

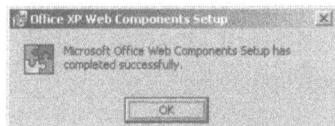

Figure 12-23. The Microsoft Office XP Web Components installer reports progress. When the installation completes, a confirmation dialog box displays.

Once the Office Web Components have been installed on the workstation you're creating the views from, you can continue to create your first Analyzer view. Because Analyzer views are highly dependent on enterprise custom data, no pre-built Analyzer views are included with the system. Once you select Portfolio Analyzer in the view type section, the display changes to accommodate an Analyzer view build, as shown in Figure 12-24. You must enter a name for the view, provide an optional description, and choose an Analyzer mode. Analyzer views may be created as PivotTable only, as Chart only, or as a combination view. You must select one of these options. The display changes according to your selection. In the figure, I've chosen to include both a chart and pivot table in the view.

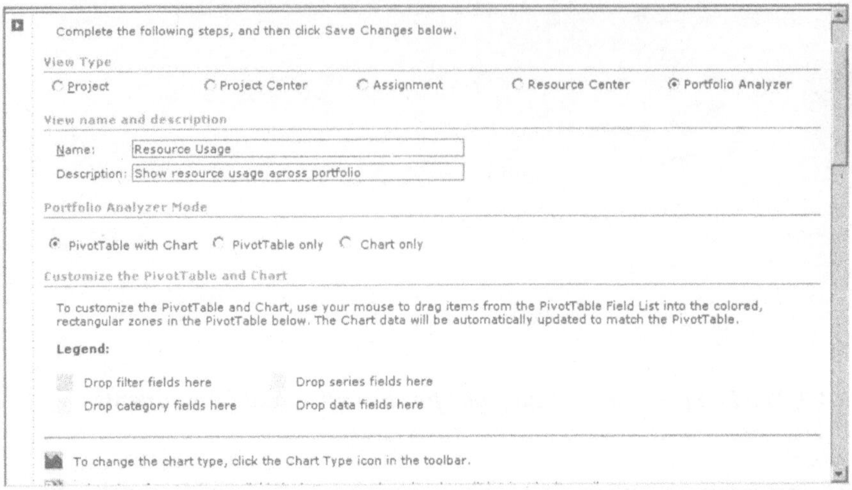

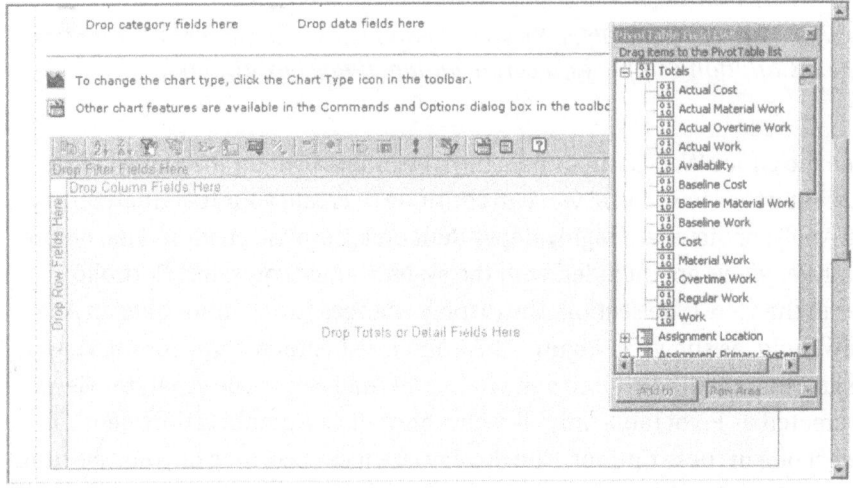

Figure 12-24. Enter a name for the view and select the Portfolio Analyzer view type.

The pivot table design area, shown in Figure 12-25, provides a design canvas for your view. Drag and drop totals and dimensions from the PivotTable Field List dialog box shown on the right side of the figure. The PivotTable Field List dialog box floats in the display, and you can send it to the background by clicking anywhere in the display behind it. To bring the dialog box forward, click the exclamation point icon on the toolbar above the design space.

Figure 12-25. The pivot table design area

Notice that there are two icon types in the PivotTable Field List dialog box. The icons resembling dominos, with the 1-0 binary pattern, are fact totals, whereas the fields identified with the grouping representation in the icon are the dimensions. The system creates four default dimensions:

- *Project dimension* contains the project names for all projects in the system.

- *Project version dimension* contains each project and version combination.

- *Time dimension* contains time settings, years, quarters, months, and days.

- *Resource dimension* contains all resource names.

All of the other dimensions you see listed in the field list dialog box are the enterprise outline codes that you created during system configuration. Here you can see the importance of these in crafting portfolio views.

The pivot table and chart design area contains drop points for fields and dimensions. The drop areas include the following:

- *Filter Fields:* Drag dimensions here to use them as filters against the data.

- *Column Fields:* Drag dimensions here to group data in columns.

- *Row Fields:* Drag dimensions here to group data in rows.

- *Data Fields:* Drag Total fields here to display data grouped by row and column dimensions.

In Figure 12-26, I first dragged the Program dimension to the Row Fields area, followed by the Project and Resource dimensions. Next, I added the Assignment Location to the Filter Fields area. Then, I dragged the Work, Actual Work, Cost, and Actual Cost totals fields into the Data Fields area. The resulting view allows the user to expand the programs and view these by project. Expanding the project then allows the user to look at the totals by resource for the project.

To change the chart type, click the Chart Type icon in the toolbar.

Other chart features are available in the Commands and Options dialog box in the toolbox.

Assignment Location ▾
All Levels

			Drop Column Fields Here			
Program ▾	Project ▾	Resource ▾	Work	Actual Work	Cost	Actual Cost
⊟ Maintenance	⊞ Cisco Upgrade.Published		2,406.0h	0.0h	182,880.00	0.00
	⊟ Exchange Upgrade.Publi	Agnetha Argueta	197.3h	125.3h	9,866.67	6,266.67
		Alberto Barcenas	248.0h	120.0h	9,920.00	4,800.00
		Alex Denisov	181.3h	85.3h	9,066.67	4,266.67
		Alic Walters	56.0h	24.0h	1,960.00	840.00
		Colleen Brosnan	444.0h	210.7h	17,760.00	8,426.67
		Edward Beiza	189.3h	125.3h	12,306.67	8,146.67
		Elaine Catlin	64.0h	64.0h	3,200.00	3,200.00
		Jeno Martin	188.0h	132.0h	9,400.00	6,600.00
		Joseph Antonelli	16.0h	0.0h	2,400.00	0.00
		Total	1,584.0h	886.7h	75,880.00	42,546.67
	⊞ Server Upgrade.Published		2,406.0h	0.0h	182,880.00	0.00
	Total					

Figure 12-26. This design provides a view of the portfolio by program, then by project and resource.

While I build the pivot table, the chart area is responding in kind because I selected to build a pivot table and chart. The resulting chart build is shown in Figure 12-27. The chart is scaled according to the largest dimension on the X or Y axis. You can see that it may not be very meaningful to attempt to display both dollars and hours on the same chart. Perhaps I should have selected PivotTable only for this Analyzer view.

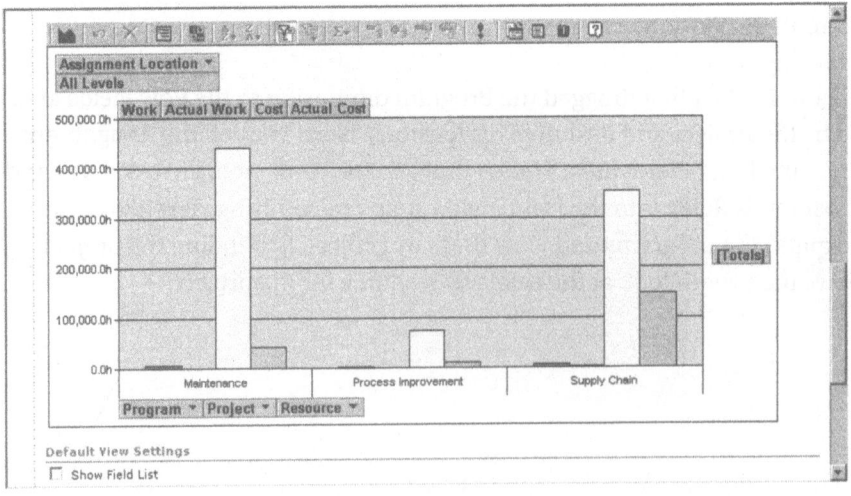

Figure 12-27. The chart updates automatically while the pivot table is constructed.

Click the Chart Type icon on the far left of the Chart toolbar, which runs across the design area, to open the Commands and Options dialog box shown in Figure 12-28. The system supports 12 chart types and their subselections. Selecting a different chart option instantly changes the display.

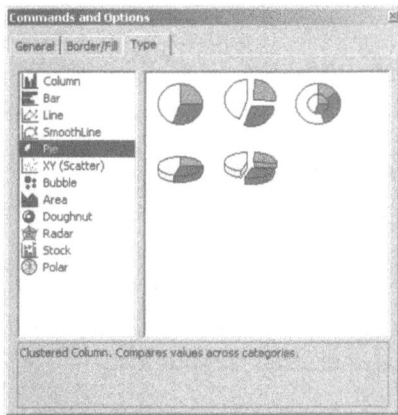

Figure 12-28. Select a chart type from the Commands and Options dialog box.

Before you save your new Analyzer view, you must select your default view settings and the categories that the new view belongs to. As shown in Figure 12-29, you can choose whether the field list and toolbars display or don't display by default when a user accesses the view from the Project Center. This refers to the default state, although users can activate these tools in the interface. These selections don't disable the tools. Select categories for the view and click Save Changes to make the view available to users. The resulting view available in the Project Center shows in Figure 12-30.

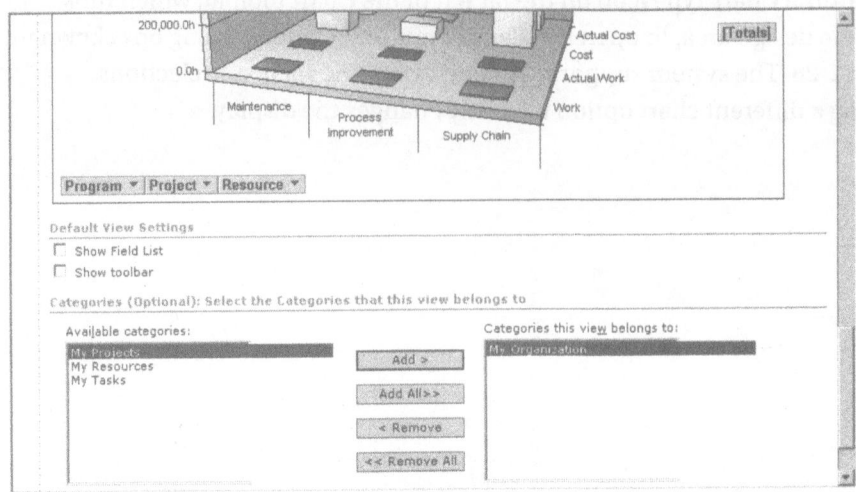

Figure 12-29. Determine default view settings and categories for your view.

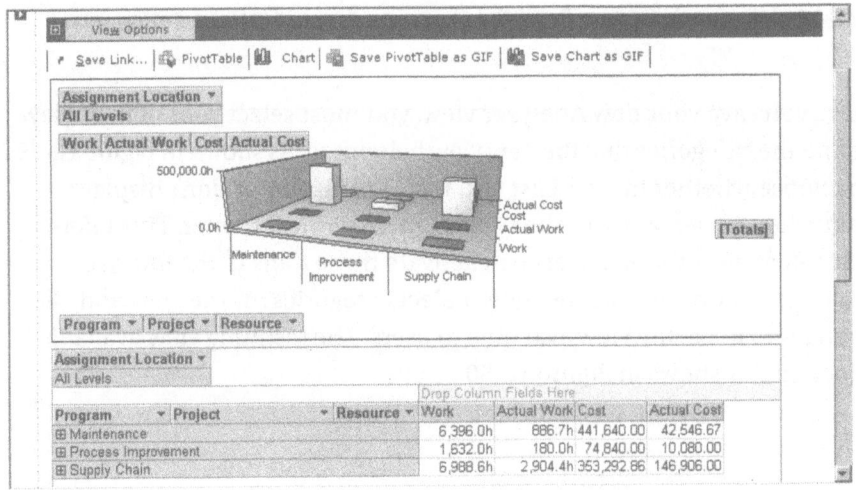

Figure 12-30. Your completed view is available from the Project Center.

Additional functionality, provided on the toolbar and shown in Figure 12-31, is useable when designing or when accessing the completed view. You can highlight a column and change the sort order by using one of the AZ icons to reverse the sort order. Next in line is the Auto Filter icon, which is active anytime you add a dimension to the filter area. The second filter icon, with the number 10 in the label, allows you to filter based on top/bottom number or percentage of items in the dataset. Add a custom total field using the calculator icon and change the display as a condition of a total display by clicking the icon labeled with the percent sign.

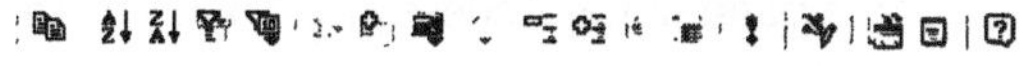

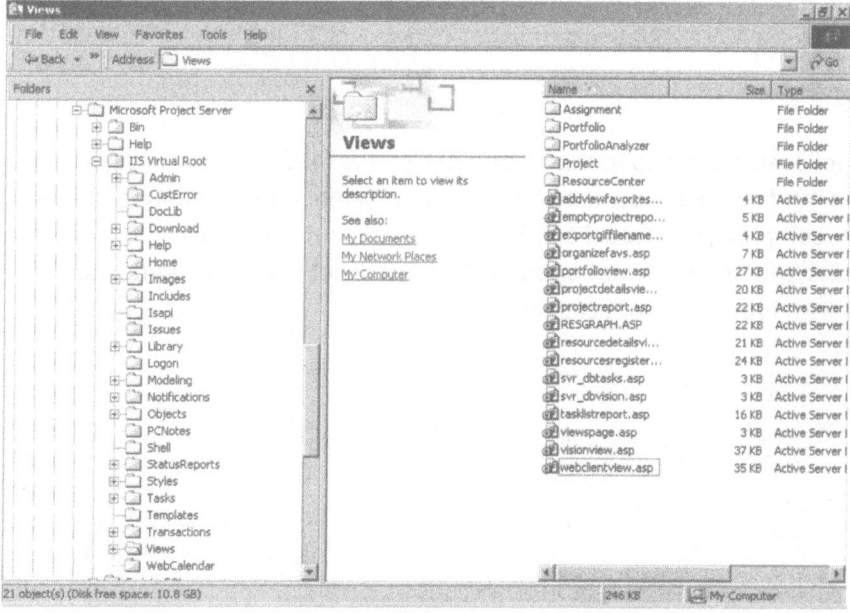

Figure 12-31. The pivot table toolbar

For users without an Office XP license, the Analyzer views that you create appear to be static. However, for users with a full Office XP license, the Analyzer views you create are starting points. When a user is armed with the full version of the Office XP Web Components, he or she can add, remove, and reshape the view with as much flexibility as you had while building it the first time.

Adding Views Created Externally to Your System

Besides the five types of views that you can create within the Project Server interface, the system also accepts HTML, ASP, and data access pages created outside the system. To add views to your Project Server installation, create them using your preferred tools. Once you've created the view page, you must deposit it in the correct folder in your Project Server virtual directory. Expand the Program Files directory on your installation drive as shown in Figure 12-32. On the right side of the explorer window, note that the five view types have their own folders under the Views folder in the Project Server virtual root. Expanding each of these reveals three subfolders: Asp, Datapage, and Html.

Figure 12-32. The Project Server IIS Virtual Root expanded

263

In my example, I've created a data access page using Access and have put the file called TestPage1.htm into the Datapage directory under the Project Center folder. From the Specify Views page, I clicked the Get Additional Views button at the top of the page. The system runs a quick routine and reports success, after which the new view is listed in the Specify Views page in the corresponding View Type category, as shown in Figure 12-33. Once you've added the view, you can delete it like any other view.

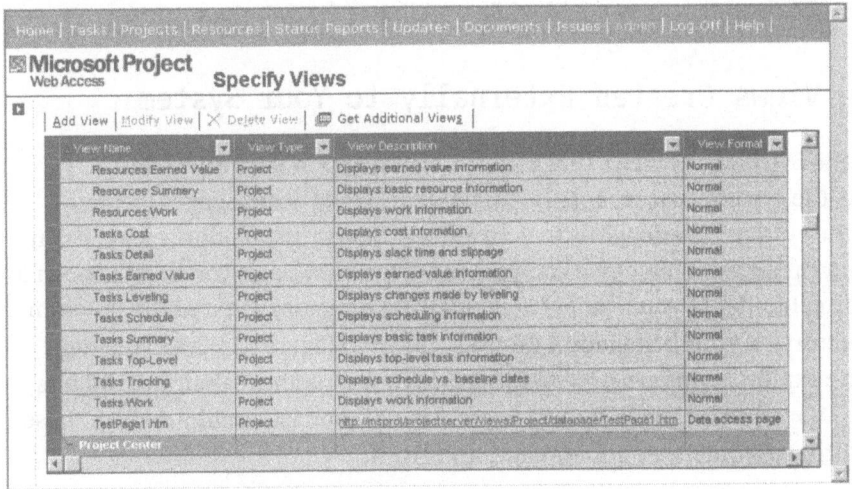

Figure 12-33. The new view added to the view list

Summary

Having followed each step in this book, once you've loaded up your projects and templates and created your custom views, your system is production ready. These activities complete your initial configuration work, but expect to tweak these configurations from time to time as you and your user population become more familiar with Project Server's capabilities.

Part Four
Project Server in Production

Building Project Plans and Project Teams

The preceding chapters focused on getting your enterprise portfolio management system ready for launch. Having made it through the first 12 chapters of planning and configuration, your system should now be ready for use.

Creating an Enterprise Project

An enterprise project is a project you create when one of the following two conditions is true:

1. You create the project with the Project Professional 2002 client connected to a Project Server with enterprise features enabled.

2. You import the project using the Import Project to Enterprise Wizard available on the Tools ➤ Enterprise Options menu in the Project Professional 2002 client when connected to a Project Server with enterprise features enabled.

To create a project under the first condition, you may begin with a blank project or with a template. When you select New Project from the File menu, the New Project pane of the Project Guide appears. From the New Project pane select General Templates. Notice that you have three selections. The Templates on My Web Sites link allows you to browse My Network Places, whereas the Templates on Microsoft.com link connects you to the Office tools on the Web section of Microsoft.com. Selecting General Templates opens the Templates dialog box shown in Figure 13-1. The dialog box has three tabs. The center tab, Enterprise Templates, is where all the templates that you've created or imported into your system will appear.

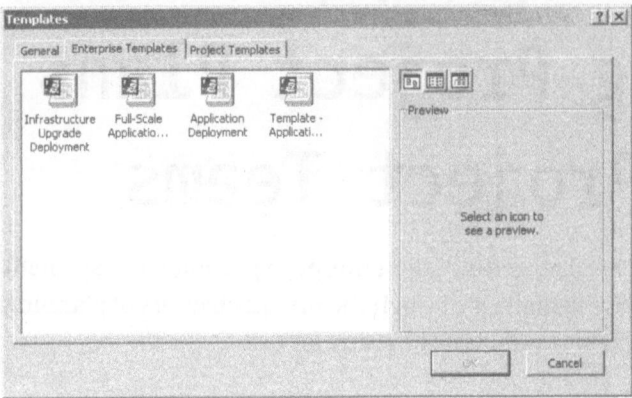

Figure 13-1. The Templates dialog box with the Enterprise Templates tab selected

Once you've selected a template, the first thing you should do is rename your new project plan and then save it to Project Server under the new name. If you save the template as a project without first changing the name, when you subsequently delete the project plan, the template will be deleted as well. This is true for installations of Project Server from the RTM release. Contact Microsoft support for a patch if you want to correct this issue. Select Save As from the File menu and rename the plan in the Save to Microsoft Project Server dialog box shown in Figure 13-2.

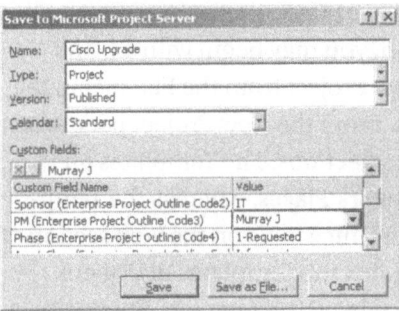

Figure 13-2. The Save to Microsoft Project Server dialog box

Opening and Closing Project Plans

It's wise to cultivate good habits when you open, save, and close project files from Project Server. Make it your practice to always use File ➤ Close to close your projects. Save your projects first or the system will prompt you to save. In my experience, clicking the "X" box in the upper-right corner of the project window leads to projects being left checked out when closed and sometimes causes file corruption. I offer this to you anecdotally and acknowledge that "this shouldn't be."

When you access File ➤ Open, the Open from Microsoft Project Server dialog box displays, as shown in Figure 13-3. Each user sees the projects that he or she has access to open. The dialog box displays the project name, version, and indicators that show whether the project is currently checked out and to whom, as well as the last modified date. At the bottom of the dialog box, notice that you may open projects as read-only or read/write. Clicking the Open from File button opens a traditional file browser. From the file browse window, it's also possible to select other supported file formats and ODBC sources.

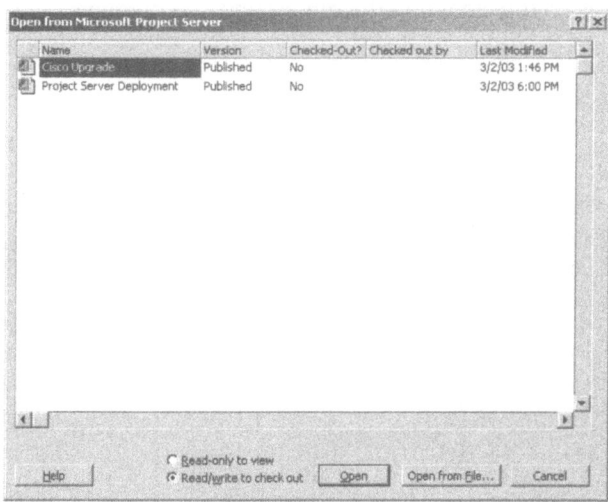

Figure 13-3. The Open from Project Server dialog box

Opening a project file marks it as checked out in the system. Any other user attempting to open the project from the server will see that another user has the plan checked out in the Open from Server dialog box and will be given the offer to open it as read-only if he or she proceeds to open it despite its being checked out.

Taking Projects on the Road

Project and Project Server allow you to take a project offline to work on. If you're a traveling project manager and need to take the project offline for updating, you must first open the plan when connected to your Project Server. To save it for updating offline, select File ➤ Save Offline. Once you've done this, the menu selection switches from Save Offline to Save Online when you next look at it. Use File ➤ Close to close the offline plan.

To save the file online again, connect to the Project Server that the file origi-
nated from. Select the file from your recent files list to open it and then select File
➤ Save Online to save the project back to the server.

Building a Team

The Build Team dialog box is a new feature in Project 2002 Professional that provides tools for searching through the enterprise resource pool to find the right
resources for your team. To open the Build Team dialog box, select Build Team
from Enterprise from the Tools menu. The Build Team dialog box, shown in
Figure 13-4, displays. The Customize filters section is expanded in the figure;
however, by default this area is collapsed when the dialog box first displays.

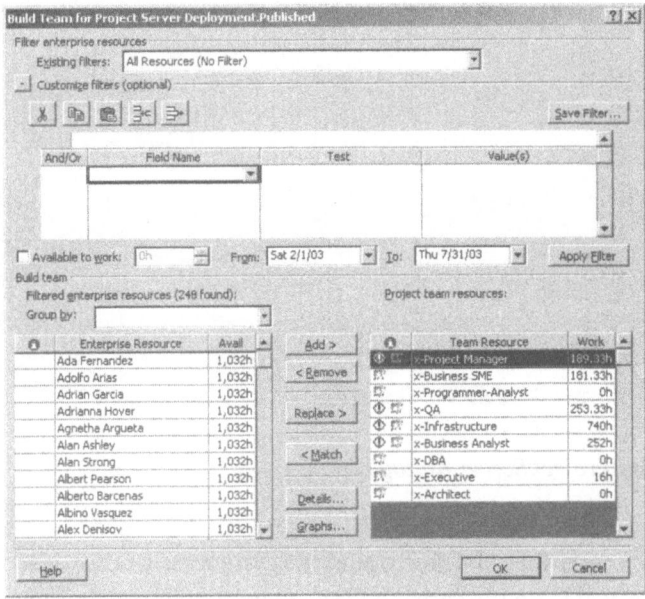

Figure 13-4. The Build Team dialog box with the Customize filters area expanded

The Build Team dialog box contains tools to slice through a large resource
pool, providing a quick way to identify resources with the skills, availability, and
other criteria for the job. Other criteria include anything you've built into resource
attribution. If your resource pool exceeds 1,000 total resources, and based on your
selection criteria 1,000 or more resources would otherwise be returned by the
dialog box, the system will prompt you to prefilter the selection in a dialog box.
The system will continue to prompt you for filters until the selection is less
than 1,000.

The Group by field just above the grid on the left side of the dialog box allows you to set a grouping on the display in the left grid. You can choose from any custom enterprise resource outline code that you created. Selecting a field will refresh the display upon selection.

Working with Filters and Grouping in the Build Team Dialog Box

One of the ways you can narrow down resource selection is using filters in the Build Team dialog box. You can specify any resource fields in Project, including your customized fields, and use them to build filters. Administrators can build and save filters that become available to all users. To set a filter, select a field by clicking in the field to activate a drop-down selector. The tests available for the filter include the following:

- equals

- does not equal

- is greater than

- is less than

- is less than or equal to

- is within

- is not within

- contains

- does not contain

- contains exactly

Unfortunately, the only drop-down values available in the values field are field names. In other words, you can set the formula to point to the value of another field. If you're using a custom outline code or field that you created, you must know a valid value and type it in. You can't look these up through the system. You should also note that the sort order of your custom fields is by their custom name in this dialog box. This isn't the way the system sorts custom fields in Project Web Access displays. In the Existing filters drop-down list the system provides a complement of precooked filters. If you're an administrator, you can save a filter and add it to the list by clicking the Save Filter button, which causes the Save Filter dialog box to display, as shown in Figure 13-5. Type in the name of your new filter and click OK to save it.

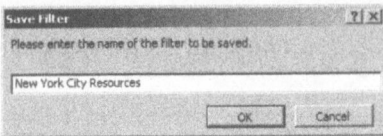

Figure 13-5. Give your filter a name to save it.

In addition to filtering on field values and grouping on custom enterprise outline codes, you can restrict resource selection by availability. An availability filter is included in addition to a field filter. Set the availability hours in the "Available to work" field and frame it with a date range.

Selecting Resources and Viewing Resource Information

In the lower portion of the Build Team screen, resources display in a grid on the left and in another grid on the right. The grid on the left displays the enterprise resources meeting any filter conditions that you set in the display and you haven't yet added to the project team. The grid on the right contains the resources that you've already added to the project team from the resource pool. The example in Figure 13-4 shows that the current project team is made up of all generic resources as far as you can see in the figure. In the example, you can see that I created all of the generic resources with "x-" preceding their names. You can also see that these are generic resources because of the double-head icon in the indicators column in the grid. Notice that other indicators also appear in this example. The (yellow) splats indicate a message. Hovering over the icon displays the message. In this case, the message indicates that the resources in the line are overallocated in the plan.

The system aids you in building the Project team by a number of functions accessed by the buttons that appear between the two grids in the lower portion of the dialog box. Use the Add button to move a resource or resources selected from the pool on the left to the team on the right. Use the Remove button to remove resources highlighted on the right. Taking this action removes the resource from the team. Use the Replace button to replace a resource high-lighted on the right with the one you highlighted on the left. After you apply prefiltering, filtering, and availability filtering, there remains one last matching criterion that the dialog box is designed to support: skill-set matching.

Use the Match button to match the skill set of a resource selected on the right to resources in the pool. When you click the Match button, only resources with an identical skill match to the resource highlighted on the right will display from within the already-filtered selection on the left. Click the Details button to display the Resource Information dialog box shown in Figure 13-6. This is the same dialog box you use to enter or edit resource information when you check out a resource for editing.

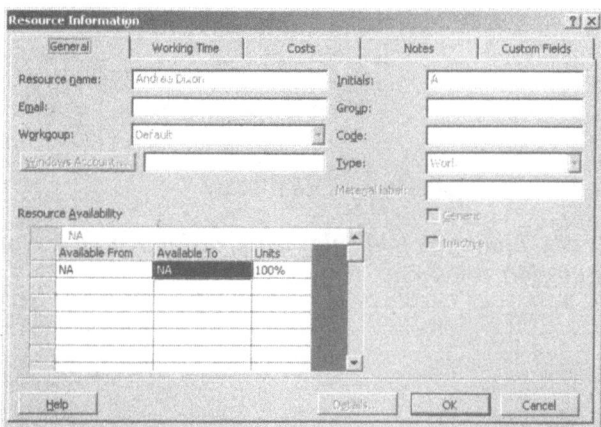

Figure 13-6. You may access the Resource Information dialog box from the Build Team dialog box.

Finally, the Build Team dialog box gives you direct access to resource availability graphs. Highlight a resource or resources and click the Graphs button to open the Graphs dialog box shown in Figure 13-7. Select Remaining Availability, Work, or Assignment Work and the system will graph your selection and display the totals across the bottom. The graph line for each selected resource will appear in the color in the legend on the right. Use the plus sign (+) and minus sign (–) magnifying glass icons to zoom in and out on the timescale displayed.

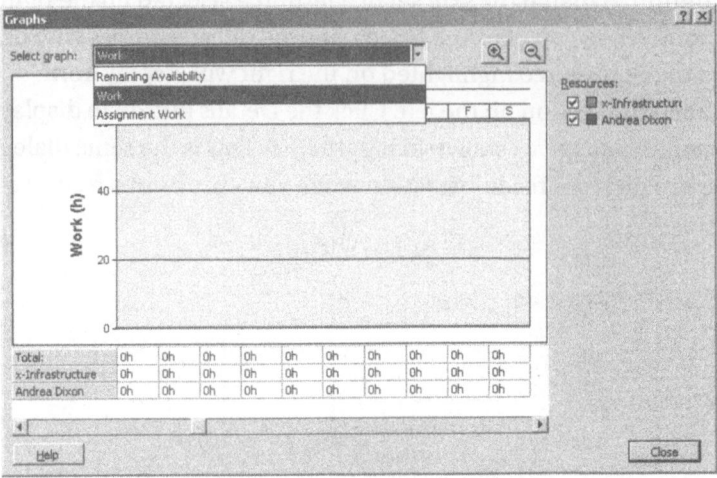

Figure 13-7. The Graphs dialog box allows you to display work, assignment work, or remaining availability for one or more resources.

Assigning Resources

Whether you're staffing a plan with generic resources or actual resources, using the Assign Resources dialog box shown in Figure 13-8 is a best practice, as it gives you the greatest control over units. Further, it exposes a functionality that's new in Project 2002: the R/D (Request or Demand) column. The Resource Substitution Wizard uses this attribute, which is why I mention it here.

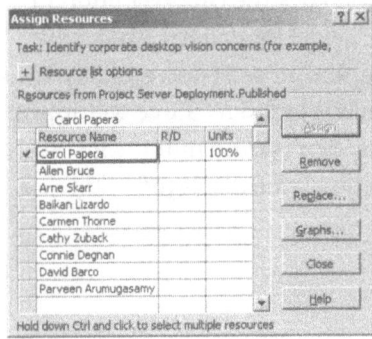

Figure 13-8. The Assign Resources dialog box

You can invoke the Assign Resources dialog box from the Tools menu or by clicking the Assign Resources icon on the toolbar as shown here:

You can select as many tasks as you want when you use the Assign Resources dialog box.

Leveling Resources

Though I consider this an area of Microsoft Project knowledge you should already have when approaching Project Server, leveling tools are integral to effectively using the new resource functionality in Project Professional 2002. This section is both a quick review and a pointer in the right direction. If you aren't familiar with using the leveling tools in Project, you should read the Help files and any other Project book you may have. Keep in mind that leveling doesn't change the resource assigned to a task; all it does is reschedule tasks.

If you want to tackle leveling manually, a couple of provided views are useful. You access the leveling Gantt from the More Views dialog box by selecting Views ➤ More Views. The Resource Allocation view also allows you to address leveling delay manually. When you're engaging in this type of activity, consider exposing the Resource Management toolbar from View ➤ Toolbars and select Resource Management. The toolbar contains links to the Resource Allocation view and the Task Entry view, and it offers you the ability to launch the Resource Substitution Wizard, find overallocations, and add users from the pool.

The system supports two types of leveling scenarios besides the native state of not leveled. You can either level a plan within the total free slack of the project or completely level the plan. You create a leveling within the free slack of the plan scenario by setting a must-finish-on constraint on a project finish task to which the critical path leads. The system will level assignments to the best of its capability within the constraint set. You can use this scenario to determine the head count your project will require in order to meet a certain date. Leveling without this constraint will produce what the system believes to be the optimum completion date.

To use the automatic leveling tool in Project Professional, select Level Resources from the Tools menu. The Resource Leveling dialog box displays, as shown in Figure 13-9. Your options occur in three categories: leveling calculations, leveling range, and resolving overallocations.

- *Leveling calculations:* You may set the calculations to Automatic or Manual. Selecting Automatic will cause the system to adjust the leveling automatically as you make further changes to the plan. Selecting Manual will cause the system to adjust leveling only when you click the Level Now button. Selecting the "Clear leveling values before leveling" option causes the system to remove any previously applied leveling before applying new leveling. Deselecting the "Clear leveling values before leveling" option causes leveling to happen on top of previous values. You can make a selection under "Look for overallocations on a <selection> basis," which allows you to control leveling precision. The choices include by minute, hour, day, week, or month.

- *Leveling range:* This category allows you to select tasks for leveling based on a date range, or you can choose to level the entire project.

- *Resolving overallocations:* The leveling order determines how Project concludes which tasks to delay or split to resolve resource allocations. Selecting ID Only causes it to split the task with the highest ID only when selecting among a number of affected tasks. If the option is set to the Standard method, the system looks at predecessors, slack, dates, task constraints, and priorities. Finally, you may select Priority, Standard, which looks first at priorities and then at the other factors of the Standard method. Selecting the "Level only within available slack" check box causes the system to honor the completion date set by a constraint on a completion task. Selecting the "Leveling can adjust individual assignments on a task" check box allows the system to make changes to one resource assigned to a task independent of another resource assigned to the same task. Selecting the "Leveling can create splits in remaining work" check box allows the system to create splits when scheduling remaining work. In other words, a task's work can be noncontiguous for one or more resources.

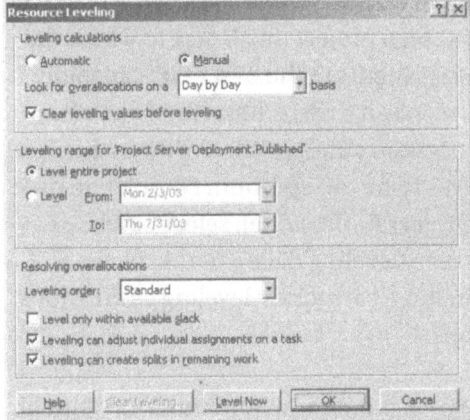

Figure 13-9. The Resource Leveling dialog box

After you select your options, click OK or Level Now. Clicking Level Now runs the leveler displaying the alert box prompt shown in Figure 13-10. Select Entire pool to run leveling on all team members with assignments in the project or choose Selected resources to level only those resources that you selected in the plan view. Click OK when you're ready, and the system performs the leveling.

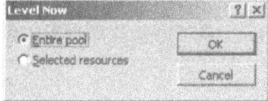

Figure 13-10. The Level Now alert

Assigning Leveling Priorities to Tasks

You can set the task priority used by the leveling system by opening the Task Information dialog box shown in Figure 13-11. You can access the Priority field from the General tab, as shown in the figure. You can set priorities to any value between 0 and 1,000, where 1,000 indicates to the system not to level and all other priorities are relative to one another. To work with priorities across many tasks, consider inserting the column into a task view such as the Gantt Chart view.

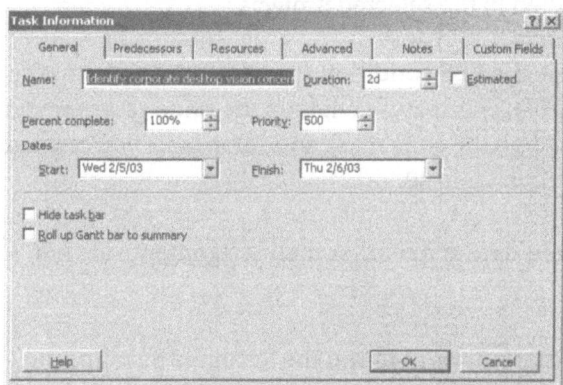

Figure 13-11. Set task priorities in the Task Information dialog box's General tab.

Using the Resource Substitution Wizard

The Resource Substitution Wizard is an automation tool that can substitute resources in one plan or across many plans, making resource substitutions based on skill code, availability, and a number of other user-defined criteria. Because you can apply the wizard's output directly to plans or save it to a file, it's equally powerful when used as a modeling tool and as a staffing tool.

The matching algorithm matches resources based on the following criteria:

- *Skill set:* The wizard is primarily used to substitute generic resources with actual resources based on a skill set. In order for this to work correctly, you must have one enterprise resource outline code defined with the "Use this code for matching generic resources" check box selected and your resources must have values set for this.

- *Availability:* The wizard matches resource availability. To get the best results from the wizard, you may want to try leveling the plan before running the wizard or running it each way.

- *Request/Demand:* The wizard honors requests when it doesn't create a resource overallocation. The wizard respects all resource assignments marked as Demand and leaves these assignments alone.

- *Priority:* The wizard weights assignments by the priority of each project identified by the user at wizard runtime.

- *Pool selection:* The wizard confines its resource selection to the restriction selected by the user at runtime. You may select specific resources, the entire pool, or only resources defined in the selected projects.

- *RBS level:* The wizard applies the RBS condition specified at runtime to the resource selection if applicable. This feature relies on the value assignments given to your resources based on the code mask and value table you created for Enterprise Resource Outline Code 30.

- *Resource freeze horizon:* Sets a date at or earlier than assignments are not touched by the wizard.

Open the project or projects that you want to run the Resource Substitution Wizard on. To launch the Resource Substitution Wizard, select Substitute Resources from the Tools menu or click the Resource Substitution Wizard icon on the Resource Management toolbar if you have it displayed. The system displays the Resource Substitution Wizard Welcome screen shown in Figure 13-12. Click Next to continue.

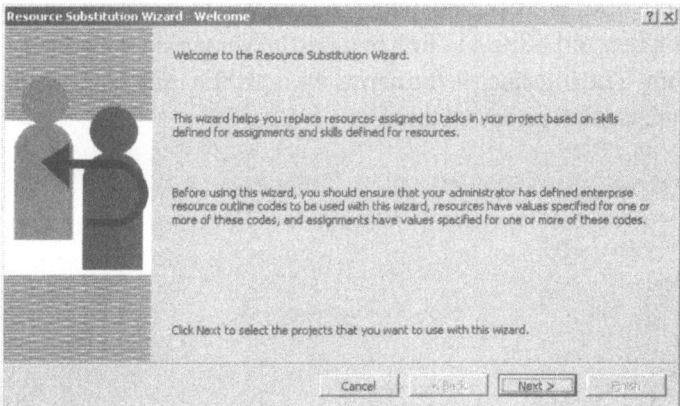

Figure 13-12. The Resource Substitution Wizard Welcome screen

The system assumes that you want to operate on all open projects, including the ubiquitous Project 1 if you haven't closed it. Deselect the projects that you don't want the wizard to consider in the Resource Substitution Wizard – Step 1 dialog box shown in Figure 13-13. Click Next to continue.

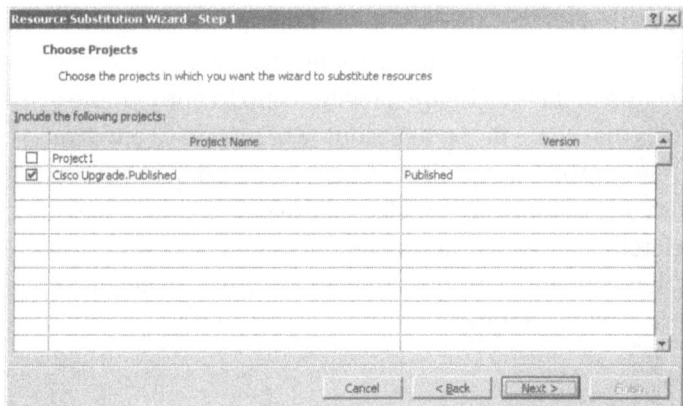

Figure 13-13. Deselect any projects that you don't want the wizard to consider.

In the next step, shown in Figure 13-14, you must choose the resources for the wizard to consider. Selecting the "In the selected projects" radio button indicates that one or more of the projects you've selected has a team already built. When you choose this option, the system will use only resources specified in the selected plans. The option "At or below the following level in the Resource Breakdown Structure" allows you to select a leaf in your RBS. The wizard will consider all resources at or below that leaf in value. The drop-down list contains the value list for your RBS. Selecting the option "Specified below" allows you to select resources from the pool by clicking the Add button to link to a partially enabled version of the Build Team dialog box. The interface is the same, without the match and substitute functions enabled. Click Next to continue.

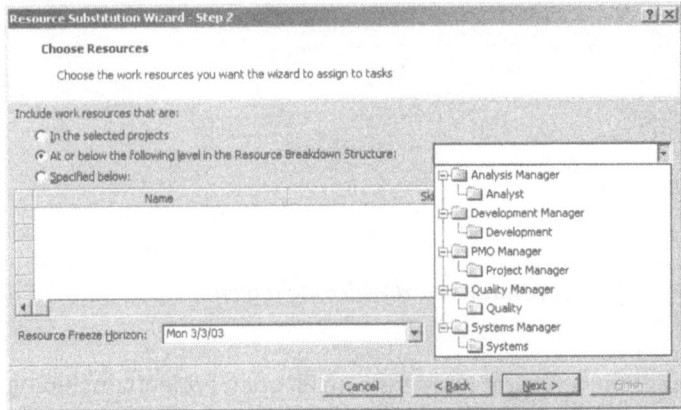

Figure 13-14. Select the resource conditions in the Resource Substitution Wizard – Step 2 dialog box.

The Resource Substitution Wizard – Step 3 dialog box, shown in Figure 13-15, displays a list of projects that either have a direct relationship with one or more of the projects in your selection or have an indirect relationship to one or more of the selected projects. Projects that share the same resource or resources are determined to have a direct relationship, and projects that share resources with projects that share resources with one or more of the selected projects are included and marked as indirectly related. In other words, the relationship is second cousin in nature. This alerts you that your substitutions could have ripple effects in the down-line projects. Click Next to continue.

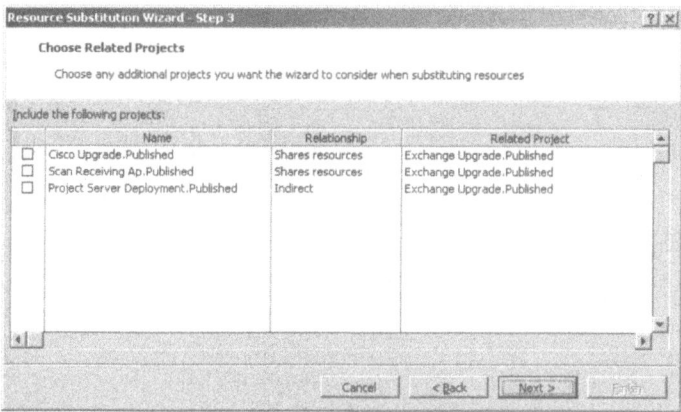

Figure 13-15. Choose additional related projects for the wizard to consider in the Resource Substitution Wizard – Step 3 dialog box.

In the Resource Substitution Wizard – Step 4 dialog box, you may set the relative priority for each selected project by increasing or decreasing the priority number of one project in relation to another. The Step 4 dialog box, shown in Figure 13-16, gives the higher-numbered project the preference between resources and their assignments. Click Next to continue.

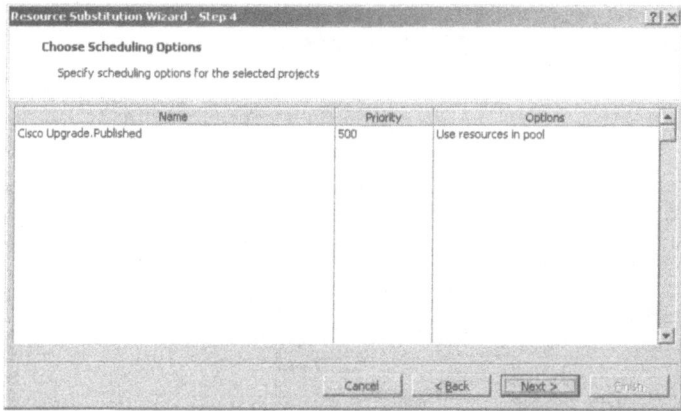

Figure 13-16. Optionally, you may set relative priorities for projects.

Before running, the system displays the Resource Substitution Wizard – Step 5 dialog box shown in Figure 13-17. This dialog box displays a textual summary of the substitution options you've chosen. If you notice a mistake here, you can either cancel the run or step back through the dialog boxes to make changes. Clicking the Run button activates the wizard.

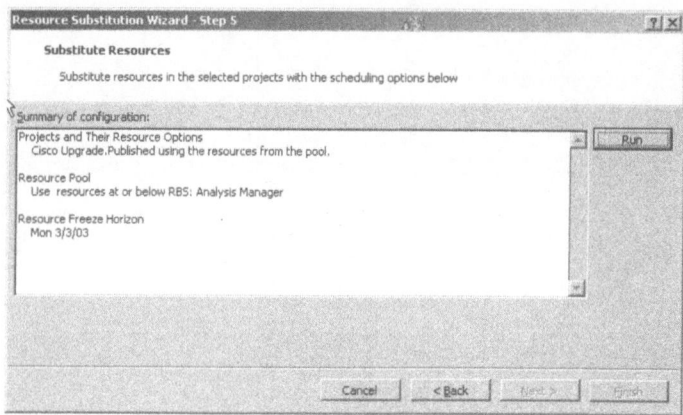

Figure 13-17. The Resource Substitution Wizard – Step 5 dialog box summarizes your selections.

After you click the Run button, click Next to display the Resource Substitution Wizard – Step 6 dialog box shown in Figure 13-18. The results of the wizard are displayed in the grid, task by task. The display contains the task name, the skill set acted upon, and the name of the new resource assigned by the wizard, as well as the original resource and the Request/Demand status of the original assignment. Click Next to continue.

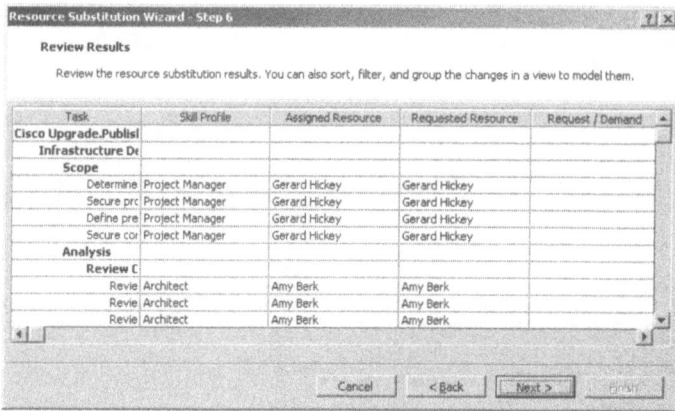

Figure 13-18. In the Resource Substitution Wizard – Step 6 dialog box, the system displays the list of assignment substitutions that it made.

The second-to-last dialog box in the series, shown in Figure 13-19, allows you to select the destination of the results. You may choose to cancel and abandon the substitutions, or you may choose to update the affected plans or store the results to a file for later consideration, or both. Click Next to continue.

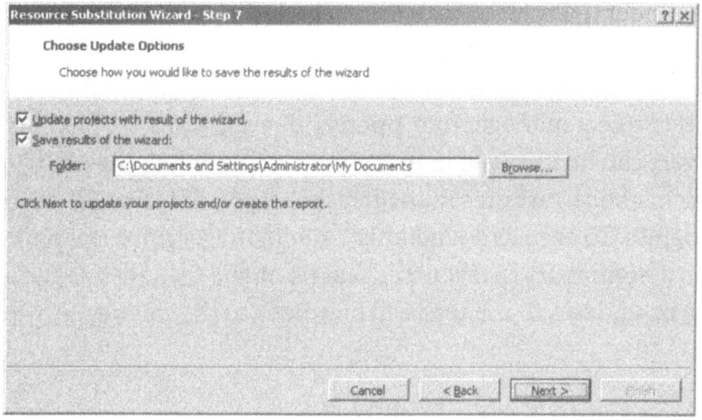

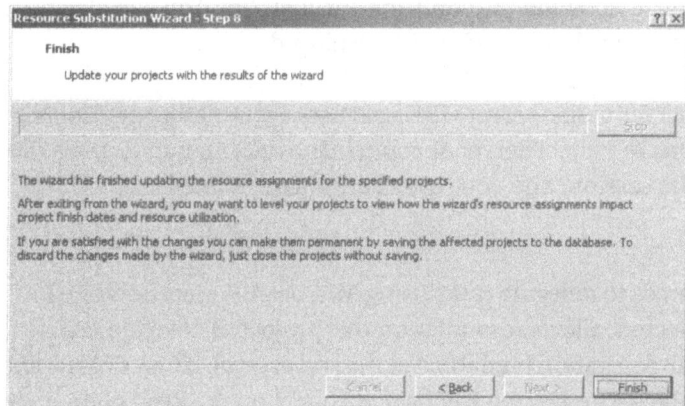

Figure 13-19. Choose the Resource Substitution Wizard update options.

Finally, the Resource Substitution Wizard – Step 8 dialog box displays, as shown in Figure 13-20, and the system makes suggestions. First it lets you know that even though the substitutions have been made in the plan per your request, these changes can still be abandoned if you don't save the plan to the database. It also suggests leveling the plan after the wizard has run.

Figure 13-20. Click Finish to make your changes permanent in the plan.

Understanding Project Server Publishing

In previous discussions, I've mentioned the concept of Project Server as a messaging system. When you save projects to the database without publishing them, project details become available in project views, but resource assignments and assignment data don't appear in Project Server views, including timesheets, until the project manager has published the assignments.

Publishing assignments controls who will receive resource updates on the tasks. Although only one project manager may open and revise a project plan at one time, many managers can be involved in managing and updating the plan. In some organizations, for instance, resource managers are responsible for assigning work and updating progress. To accommodate this, each manager must open the project and publish the assignments to resources that he or she manages. Once a manager publishes a task, updates to the task will flow back to that manager.

Controlling Default Publishing Behavior

You can control Project's default publishing behavior on a project-by-project basis by making changes on the Collaborate tab of the Options dialog box. Select Options from the Tools menu to display the Options dialog box shown in Figure 13-21. Click the Collaborate tab to expose the applicable options. As shown, the Options dialog box contains the default values for the various options.

- The "Each time I publish to Microsoft Project Server, show dialog confirming success" option is self-explanatory. Deselect this option to stop Project Server from displaying the confirmation alert box. You can also turn this option off from the alert box when it's displayed.

- You control the server name, server URL, and user account through Tools ➤ Enterprise Options ➤ Project Server Accounts. The information displayed is determined by the session, and you can't manipulate it here except for the e-mail address.

- The "Allow resources to delegate tasks using Microsoft Project Server" option, when selected, allows resources on this project to delegate tasks, provided that task delegation is enabled at the server level. If task delegation is otherwise disabled, this setting will have no effect on the local plan.

- In the ""Publish New and Changed Assignments" updates resources' assignments when" settings, selecting the "Start, Finish, % Complete or outline changes" radio button causes the system to mark the task for an update when any of these factors change. Other changes, such as changing the name of the task, won't mark the task for updating. Selecting the "Any task information changes" radio button causes the system to mark a task for updating when any information on the task changes. This is an important setting and being aware of it can spare you much grief when you're trying to understand system behavior. This feature determines what the system sees as a "changed assignment."

- The "On every save, publish the following information to Microsoft Project Server" settings allow you to automate publishing with a project save. Here you have the choice to select "New and Changed assignments" and/or "Project summary" with or without full project plan information.

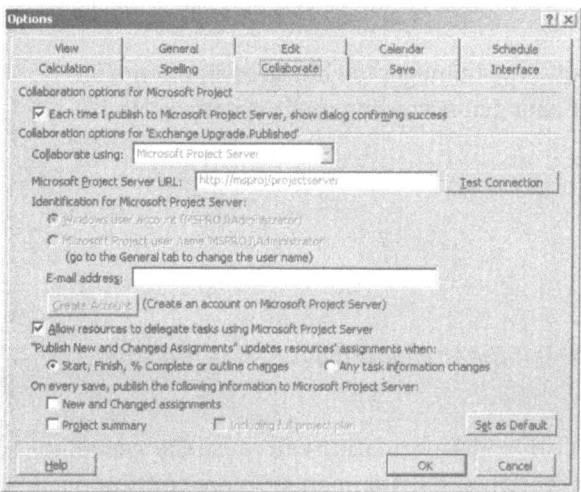

Figure 13-21. The Options dialog box with the Collaborate tab exposed

Publishing: Best Practices

Like opening and saving project plans, it's important to develop good project publishing habits. When you publish, it's best to have only one project open. Don't use publishing features on a plan you've been updating until you've saved your changes to the server. Don't open a project from the server, save it as an .mpp file, and then publish it. This series of actions will cause the creation of duplicate assignments to on the server. This is a known issue and there's a patch available from Microsoft. Until you patch your system, be very wary of this issue.

Publishing Assignments and Project Information

You activate publishing functions from Collaborate ➤ Publish, as shown in Figure 13-22. You have three publishing choices plus a republish selection. The distinction between the three publishing options is as follows:

- *All Information* automatically selects all information eligible for publishing, including new and changed assignments as well as the plan and plan details.

- *New and Changed Assignments* selects all new, not previously published assignments and any assignments that have changed according to the criteria you selected under the Collaborate tab, as described previously.

- *Project Plan* sends project information except assignments to Project Server.

- *Republish Assignments* allows the manager to choose assignments for republishing whether they changed according to the criteria or not.

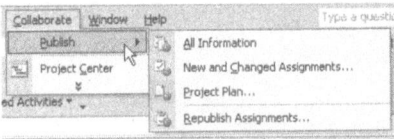

Figure 13-22. Select Collaborate ➤ Publish to choose a publishing function.

Selecting Collaborate ➤ Publish ➤ All Information will cause the system to publish all available project information and assignments. Before continuing, it will present the alert shown in Figure 13-23. You may either click OK to continue or click Cancel to stop the action. If you click OK, the publishing operation will continue without further user interface activity.

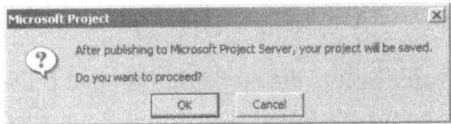

Figure 13-23. Do you want to proceed?

Selecting Collaborate ➤ Publish ➤ New and Changed Assignments first displays the same alert box shown in Figure 13-23 and then opens the Publish New and Changed Assignments dialog box shown in Figure 13-24. The system first selects all eligible task assignments and presents them in the dialog box. You may narrow down the selection by choosing Entire project, Current view, or Selected items from the pick list at the top of the dialog box. Selecting Current view limits the selection to what's visible in the current project view behind the dialog box, including any filters you've applied to the view. Choosing Selected items assumes that you've selected tasks in the plan for which to publish assignments. The figure, as shown, is grouped by resource. You can change this by selecting the Task radio button below the task list display.

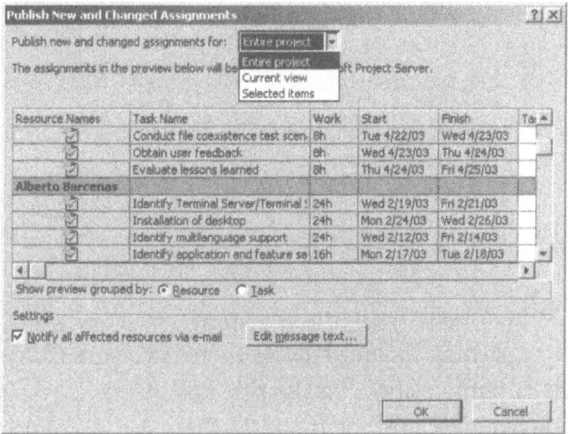

Figure 13-24. The Publish New and Changed Assignments dialog box

Normally, publishing assignments generates e-mail notifications to the resources receiving the assignments. The notification e-mails contain a link back to Project Web Access where the resources actually pick up the task information. There are times, however, when you don't want an e-mail sent. To stop the system from sending an e-mail notification, deselect the "Notify all affected resources via e-mail" check box under Settings in the dialog box. Alternately, you can personalize the message sent by clicking the "Edit message text" button to open the "Edit message text" dialog box shown in Figure 13-25. Replace the existing message or personalize it.

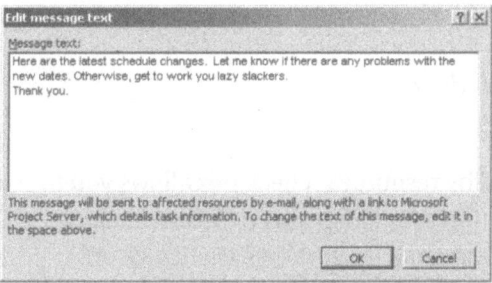

Figure 13-25. Add a personal touch to your message.

Selecting Collaborate ➤ Publish ➤ Project Plan opens the Publish Project Plan dialog box shown in Figure 13-26. Here you must select either "Summary only" or "Project plan with summary."

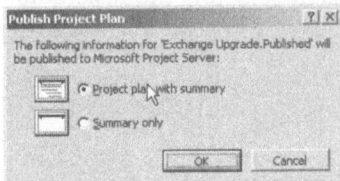

Figure 13-26. The Publish Project Plan dialog box

Republishing Assignments

Selecting Collaborate ➤ Publish ➤ Republish Assignments opens essentially the same dialog box as the one used for publishing assignments. As shown in Figure 13-27, there are, however, two important differences besides the title change to Republish Assignments. Notice the two new options in the Settings section of the dialog box.

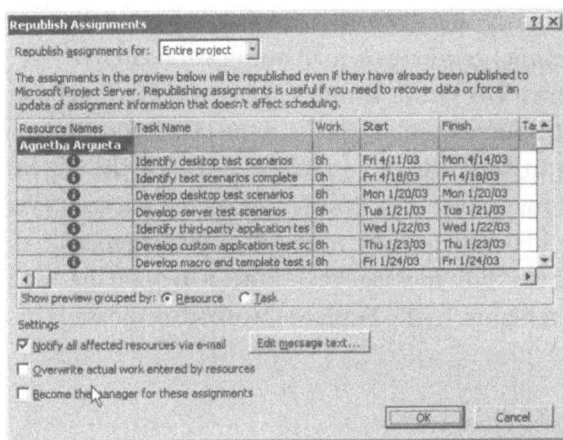

Figure 13-27. The Republish Assignments dialog box

The "Overwrite actual work entered by resources" check box allows you to push task progress back to a resource's timesheet after you've made manual updates to progress within Project Professional. If a resource is out sick on reporting day, for instance, as the project manager you may need to update the task despite not having timesheet input from the resource. After using the tracking tool in Project, you'll need to use the republish feature to synch the new actual work value and task progress with the user's timesheet. In this scenario, you must select the "Overwrite actual work entered by resources" check box to push the new values back to the timesheet.

Use the Republish Assignments dialog box to resend assignments when resources accidentally hide them or when a change occurs that doesn't trigger an update as set in your options. This function is also useful for temporarily taking over assignments for project managers who are out sick or are taking time off. To take over assignments and cause the resource updates to flow back to you instead of the original manager, open the project and select the tasks you want to take over; use the republish function, making sure that you select the "Become the manager for these assignments" check box; and choose Republish for selected tasks. If you deselect the e-mail notification check box, the updates for the tasks will now flow to you without the resource being aware of the change. When the out-of-office project manager returns, that person must take the exact same steps to return the flow back to him- or herself.

Understanding the Microsoft Project Spooler

Working behind the scenes as a silent and barely visible partner until something goes wrong is the Project spooler. The Project spooler starts when you launch Project Professional and stays active but idle until it's required. The spooler icon appears in the tray area of the taskbar, as shown here:

If an error occurs, the icon changes to include a red exclamation point next to the computer graphic and an alert box displays. The spooler functions much like the print spooler on your computer. It queues publishing jobs in the background so you can continue to work uninterrupted when the server can't immediately respond to your publishing action.

If an error occurs, the system will display an alert box like the one shown in Figure 13-28. Clicking Yes will open the spooler or you can open the spooler by double-clicking the spooler icon in the tray.

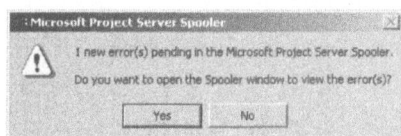

Figure 13-28. The spooler error alert box displays when an error occurs in the spooler.

You can investigate the specific error once the spooler is open, as shown in Figure 13-29. Two actions are available from the Actions menu: Retry or Undo.

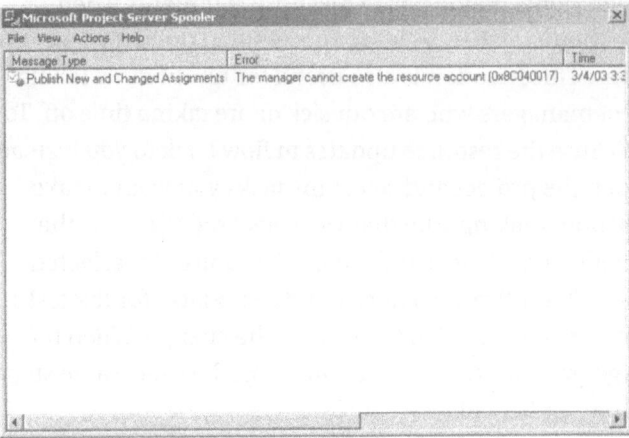

Figure 13-29. View the error detail in the Microsoft Project Server Spooler window.

Requesting Task Progress Outside the Normal Flow

In the normal flow of things, resources report progress against tasks through their timesheets based on the periodic reporting requirements established by the business. Every now and then, however, you may want to remind a resource that progress is due or receive a progress report that's out of the ordinary cycle. To accomplish this, select Request Progress Report from the Collaborate menu in Project to open the Request Progress Information dialog box shown in Figure 13-30. Typically you'll do this for specific tasks, so select the tasks first and the dialog box will automatically choose Selected items in the "Request progress information for" field.

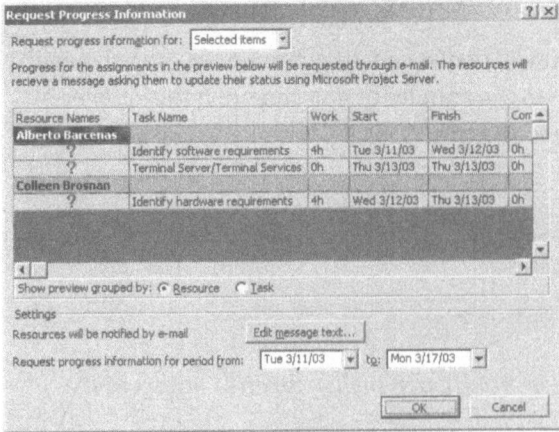

Figure 13-30. The Request Progress Information dialog box

The system actualizes this request through e-mail. It also marks the task in your plan with the following icon:

🖅

This icon appears in the indicators field in your project plan. In the user's timesheet, the task is also marked with a question mark icon, which indicates that a project manager issued a progress request for the task.

Summary

You've now learned the core task publishing workflow using Project Professional and Project Server. This chapter also covered the upper selections on the Collaborate menu in Project. The rest of the selections on the Collaborate menu, not covered in this chapter, display pages of Project Server within the Project Professional interface. I cover the functionality accessed from these pages in the next three chapters.

Tracking Progress Through Project Web Access

Now that you've learned the basics of publishing projects and assignments to Project Server, it's time to dive into the cyclical processes of maintaining your projects using the progress reporting tools in Project Server. Perhaps the most fundamental Project Server functionality is the cycle of assigning tasks to resources, pushing that information to the resources, and gathering their progress on these tasks.

In the last chapter, you learned how to build and staff a plan, and publish project and assignment information for the first time. In this chapter, you'll pick up at the receiving end of these assignments and explore the task management and tracking features of Project Server in depth.

Working with Tasks in Project Web Access

When a user logs onto Project Web Access, the home page alerts the user to any new tasks. In Figure 14-1, you can see that this particular user has quite a few new tasks. This is the result of the initial project upload. Normally you wouldn't expect to see this many tasks announced at once. It can easily happen, however, when a project manager publishes every task in a lengthy project.

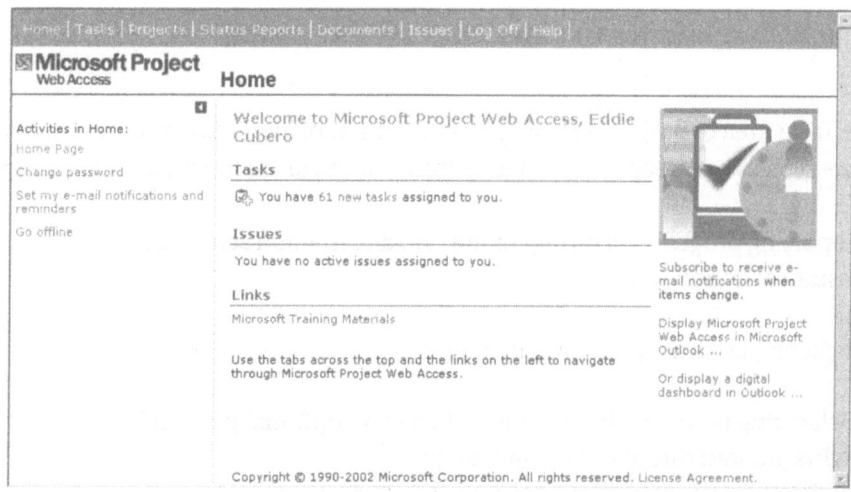

Figure 14-1. The Project Web Access home page for a user with 61 new tasks

Clicking Tasks in the menu or the link in the information center area of the page takes you to the Tasks area, which initially defaults to the timesheet view shown in Figure 14-2. In the figure, notice the navigational areas on the left side. The options in the top half allow you to choose between the personal Gantt Chart view and the Timesheet view. The lower section lists the activities available to you in the "View my tasks" page. You can access a lot of functionality from this page, which is the core for the daily work management routine for resources. The functions in the toolbar and the view options across the display tabs above the time entry grid augment the activities on the left. At the heart of this display is the time entry grid itself. This is where resources enter their time and periodically send updates to managers.

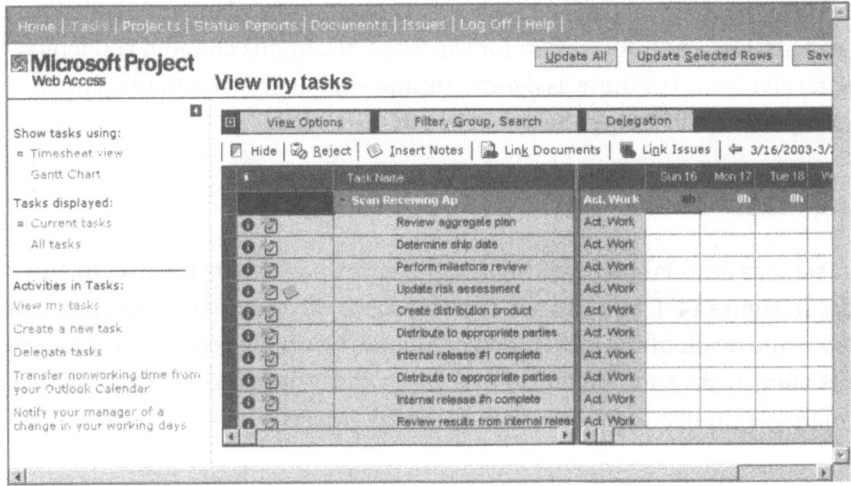

Figure 14-2. The default views are "View my tasks" and Timesheet.

The Tasks area of Project Web Access is the center of interactivity for resources. Resources access core team functionality from this page, including the following:

- Reporting progress according to the tracking method selected for the server instance or individual project

- Rejecting tasks assigned by a manager

- Delegating tasks to other resources based on optional permissions and rights granted through the application

- Transferring nonworking time from Outlook

- Sending working day changes to managers, allowing managers to react to scheduling changes

- Inserting notes on tasks to communicate additional information to the task manager

- Linking documents in the documents library to tasks

- Linking issues from the issues list to tasks that are affected by the issues

- Viewing and interacting with assignment information, and receiving updates and status alerts from managers

All of these functional areas support sharing project information. Progress reporting, task rejections, and task delegations generate immediate communication events between the resource and the manager of the affected task or tasks. Project Server routes all of these change events through the project managers, who act as a gatekeepers for all plan-changing transactions. Transferring nonworking time and work day changes have some unique effects that you should note, as I cover them later in this chapter. Inserting notes, document links, and issue links adds a more passive informational flow to the collaborative process.

Before you plunge into the reporting cycle, make certain that you're familiar with the visual and navigational elements of the Timesheet view. The next section provides a detailed examination.

Understanding the Timesheet View

All users of the system should be well versed in the Timesheet view. At the very least, make sure that anyone who has assignment work in the system knows how to use this view. My opinion is that everyone in the organization is a potential project-task-work assignee. Your organization may not see it this way, however.

Timesheet Indicators

The indicators column in the task grid at the heart of the timesheet display alerts users to task status, notes, issues, and document links as well as other timely task information. Table 14-1 contains the task indicators that you'll see in this view from time to time. Use your mouse to hover over the indicators column to bring up a brief description of the contents.

Table 14-1. Indicator Icon Descriptions

INDICATOR ICON	DESCRIPTION
🔲	Task has delegation requested
🔲	Task has linked issues
!	Task is late
☑	Task is new from a manager or a newly delegated task
📝	Task has notes
✛	Task is new and not sent to manager
📋	Task has update pending
✓	Task is complete

View Options

Select the View Options tab at the top of the timesheet display to control the data set based on standard criteria, by date range, and by type. Expanding the tab reveals the options shown in Figure 14-3. The complete list of options you control is as follows:

- *Show time with date* causes the system to display times with dates shown in the grid.

- *Show to-do lists* determines whether or not to-do list tasks are displayed in the timesheet.

- *Show summary tasks* determines whether or not summary tasks are displayed above the task assignments.

- *Show scheduled work* causes the right side of the grid to display scheduled work values in the grid along with the actual work values.

- *Show overtime work* causes the right side of the grid to display the actual overtime work field.

- *Show outline level* restricts the view to the outline level specified. For instance, if most of your tasks occur at the third level, selecting level 3 collapses everything else in the view.

- *Show Outlook tasks* and *Include completed Outlook tasks* allow you to display your Outlook tasks in your Project Web Access timesheet and selectively include completed tasks.

- The *Date range* selector fields allow you to change the date range of the display.

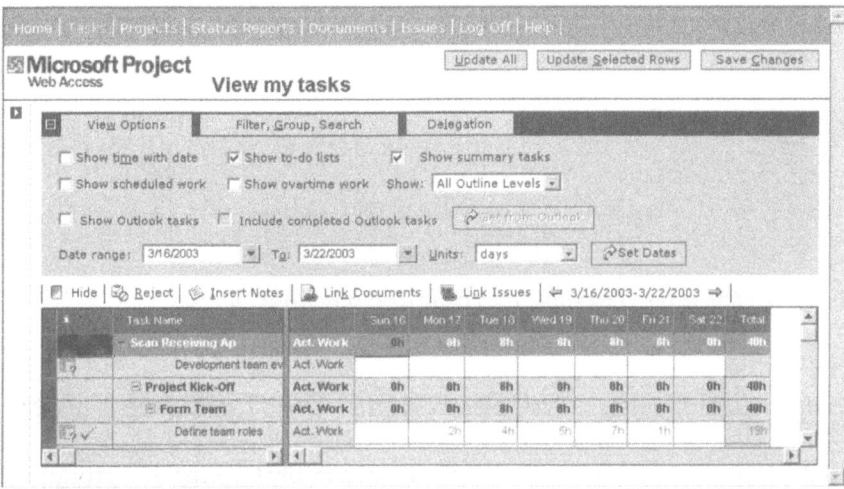

Figure 14-3. Expanded View Options tab

Opening this display introduces a couple of topics that I haven't focused on until now. The first is to-do lists and the other is the subject of Microsoft Outlook integration.

Briefly, to-do lists provide a simple way to approach informal project management of tasks that don't fall into full-scale projects in the system. Tasks can be assigned to resources and articulated through the timesheet. In the interest of keeping focused on the main tracking objective, I cover these in more depth in the next chapter. You choose whether to display your to-do list tasks by selecting or deselecting the option. Selecting the "Show time with date" option causes dates shown in the display to include or not include time. You can restrict the display of summary tasks by deselecting the "Show summary tasks" check box.

Take some time to explore the possibilities presented to you under the View Options tab and experiment with the effects of changing the settings. Finding the best way to use these capabilities is, to some extent, a personal adventure. Your organization may not recognize overtime work; then again, it may elect to collect it. Selecting both the "Show scheduled work" option and the "Show overtime work" option causes the display to change as shown in Figure 14-4.

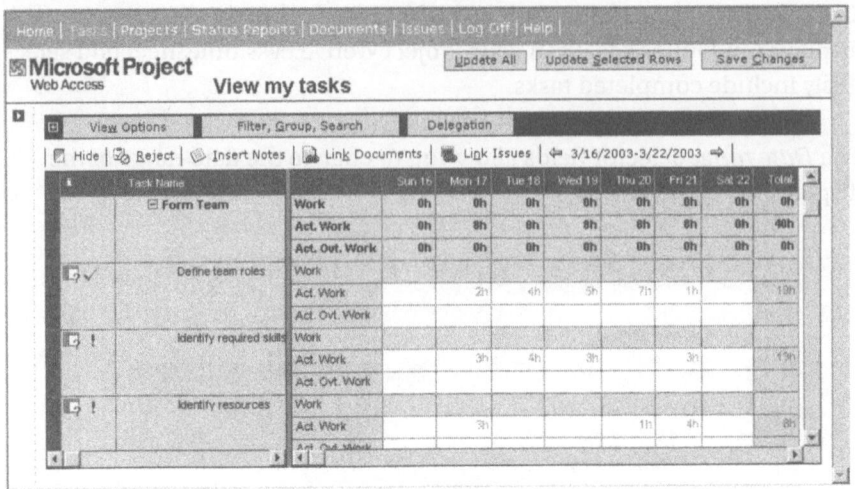

Figure 14-4. The view altered to show overtime and scheduled work

Filtering, Grouping, and Searching the Timesheet View

Besides all the view options you can control, you can apply filtering and grouping to your Timesheet view and you can search through tasks on your timesheet to quickly locate specific assignments. Expanding the Filter, Group, Search tab in the Timesheet view reveals the options shown in Figure 14-5.

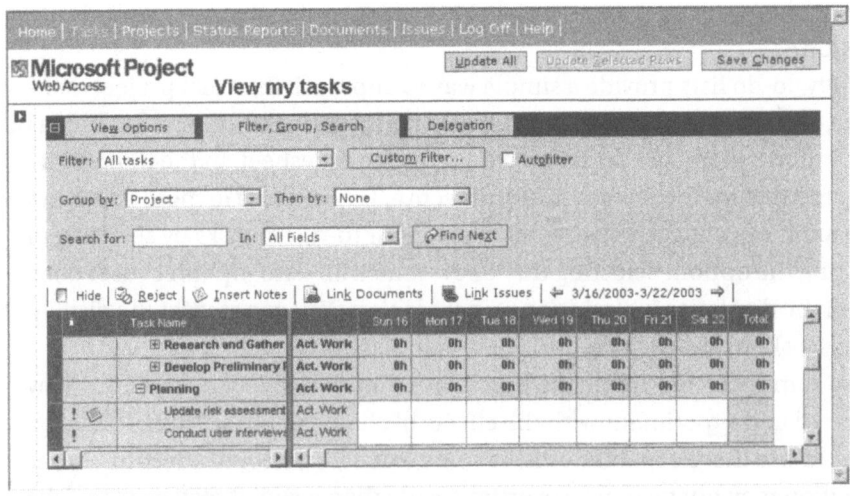

Figure 14-5. The Timesheet view with the Filter, Group, Search tab expanded

The precooked filters available to you include the following:

- All tasks (this is the default view)

- Overdue tasks

- Newly assigned tasks

- Completed tasks

- Incomplete tasks

- New tasks added by me

- Tasks deleted by manager

- Tasks changed by a manager

- Tasks pending manager's approval

- Tasks requiring progress updates

System administrators may add filters to the standard selection list. Users may click Custom Filter to create a new filter on the fly and apply it to the view. Combine up to three filter tests to restrict the view to the conditions specified in the dialog box shown in Figure 14-6.

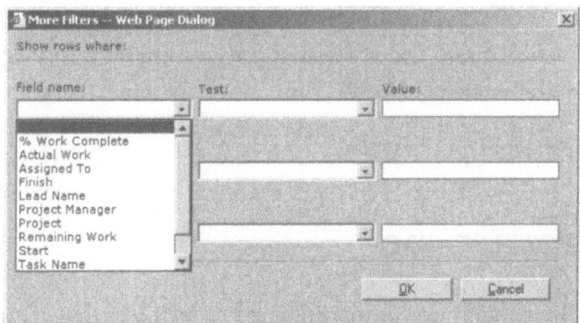

Figure 14-6. Select fields and set test values to filter the display.

The default display grouping is by project. By default, the system presents all tasks first by project and then by summary task. You can specify your own grouping requirements. The system allows you to select two levels of grouping using the following group-by selections:

- % Work Complete

- Actual Work

- Assigned To

- Finish

- Lead Name

- Project Manager

- Project

- Remaining Work

- Start

- Task Name

- Update Sent

- Work

The search feature allows you to search the timesheet textually. You can enter a sequence of characters or a word or words and search for it in the timesheet. Clicking Find Next activates the search and the system highlights each matching task instance one at a time until the user has clicked Find Next once for every match.

Opening the Task Delegation View

You expand the Delegation tab by clicking it in the Timesheet view or by selecting Delegate tasks from the Activities menu. The Delegation tab contains the necessary functions to delegate tasks, which I cover in depth later in this chapter. It also contains view options relating to delegated tasks. The "Show delegated tasks" selector allows you to select from three choices:

- All delegated tasks that I track

- All delegated tasks that I am the Lead for

- All delegated tasks that I track but am not the Lead for

Additionally, you may choose to show or not show your regular tasks along with the tasks that you've delegated. You may selectively display delegated tasks only.

Understanding the Timesheet Toolbar

The Timesheet toolbar, shown in Figure 14-7, provides access to a number of functions. In summary, these functions are as follows:

- Hide removes tasks from your timesheet.

- Reject sends a task rejection for a selected task.

- Insert Notes allows you to add notes to tasks.

- Link Documents enables users to link documents to tasks.

- Link Issues enables users to link issues to tasks.

- The date range selector allows you to set the date range for the display.

| 🗎 Hide | 🗞 Reject | 📝 Insert Notes | 📄 Link Documents | 🗐 Link Issues | ⬅ 3/16/2003-3/22/2003 ➡ |

Figure 14-7. The Timesheet toolbar

Activities Available from the View My Tasks Submenu

The activities available from the "View my tasks" submenu follow. I explore these in more depth later in this chapter.

- *View my tasks* refreshes the current view selected, either Timesheet or Gantt Chart.

- *Create a new task* opens the "Create new task" interface.

- *Transfer nonworking time from your Outlook Calendar* allows a user to transfer nonworking time from Outlook.

- *Notify your manager of a change in your working days* sends a notice to a manager or managers of a working day change.

Displaying the Gantt Chart View

The Gantt Chart selection in the "View my tasks" interface allows you to select a traditional Gantt-style presentation of your tasks, including the expected graphical representation. Shown in Figure 14-8, much of the toolbar and menu functionality available in the Timesheet view is available in this version of the view as well. The difference is mainly whether or not you can track progress in this view. Note in the figure that the update options are available. If you use the % Work Complete reporting method, you can use the Gantt presentation to update the managers. If you use hours worked by period, these inputs aren't available in this presentation.

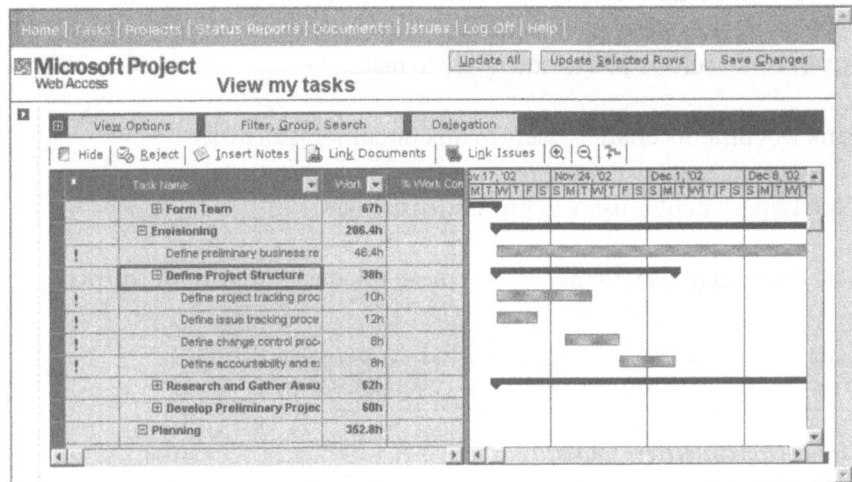

Figure 14-8. The Gantt Chart presentation in the "View my tasks" interface

Reporting Progress Through the Timesheet

The preceding overview of the Project Web Access Tasks area helps you establish a big-picture understanding of the interface. Now you'll dig deeper into the use of the key reporting features. Progress reporting along with task creation, delegation, and rejection make up the most vital active data captured through the timesheet system.

In Figure 14-9, I collapsed the navigation menu on the left side and dragged the divider bar in the timesheet display grid almost all the way to the right to expose the Remaining Work field.

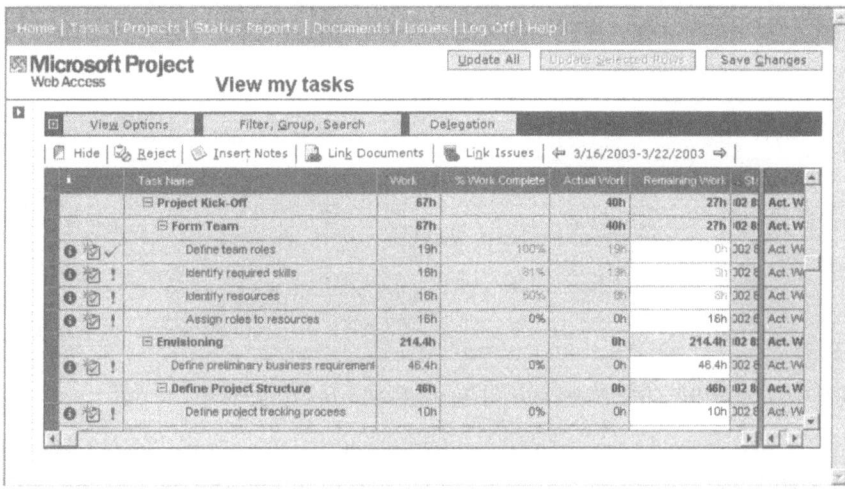

Figure 14-9. A closer look at the time reporting grid with the divider bar dragged to the right

The Remaining Work field is an available input in the timesheet regardless of the tracking method selected. Remaining work is an important input for any task that finishes with more or less work than originally predicted. Think about what percentage of tasks that implicates. If a resource doesn't report a remaining work value of zero when a task completes ahead of schedule, Project won't know that the task has completed. It will assume it can continue to calculate the remaining work figure. Similarly, as soon as a resource reports at least as much actual work as was planned, Project assumes that the task has completed. Unless the resource overrides the calculated remaining work value when a task runs late, Project assumes the task completed on time and accepts the effort entered. Do you want to allow these assumptions?

Figure 14-10 shows the same timesheet view with the divider bar dragged to the left, exposing the time entry grid. In this case, the system is set to accept time worked by day. New entries that you make in the grid appear in red, indicating that the manager hasn't accepted the update.

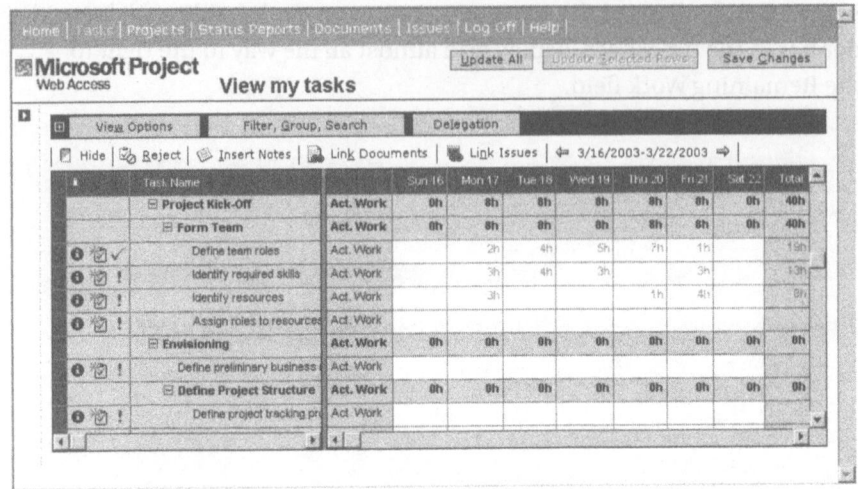

Figure 14-10. The same timesheet with the divider bar dragged to the left

To update one task or just a few selected tasks, highlight the rows in the grid and then click the Update Selected Rows button. Otherwise, click the Update All button to send all new entries to the managers. Save entries made ahead of time by using the Save Changes button. The system stores your entries until you're ready to send them. The system confirms your save, as shown in Figure 14-11.

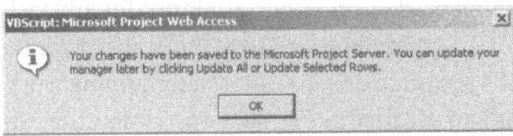

Figure 14-11. Your time entries have been saved.

 CAUTION You should verify that your manager has accepted data in your timesheet before adding new entries for the next week. Otherwise, the new entries will process along with the previous ones when the manager runs the update routines.

Rejecting a Task

Rejecting a task or tasks through the timesheet is very simple. Highlight the task rows that you want to reject and click the Reject button in the toolbar. The system displays a warning and confirmation alert, as shown in Figure 14-12. Choosing Yes to continue removes the task(s) from the timesheet and sends a notification to the project managers for the affected tasks, as shown in Figure 14-13.

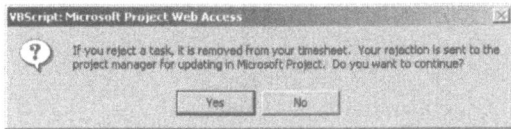

Figure 14-12. The system prompt when you reject a task

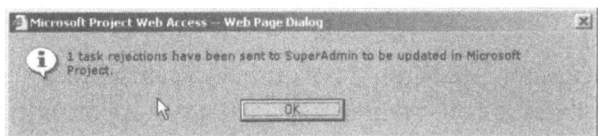

Figure 14-13. The task rejection has been sent.

Once you click the Yes button, you pass the point of no return. The system removes the task from your timesheet. Your manager may choose to reinstate your status on the assignment by republishing it to you. If the manager accepts your task rejection, from your perspective as a resource, the assignment is gone and there's nothing further for you to do.

Delegating a Task

With the Delegation tab expanded and after selecting a task in the Timesheet or Gantt Chart views, click the Delegate Task button to open the task delegation page shown in Figure 14-14. In the first step, you must select a person or persons to delegate the task to, choose to assume or not to assume the lead role, and select whether or not to continue to track the task in your timesheet. Enter any additional notes that you'd like to convey to the resource you're delegating to and to the project manager who must approve your task delegation. Click Next at the bottom of the page (not shown in the figure) to continue or Cancel to abandon the entries.

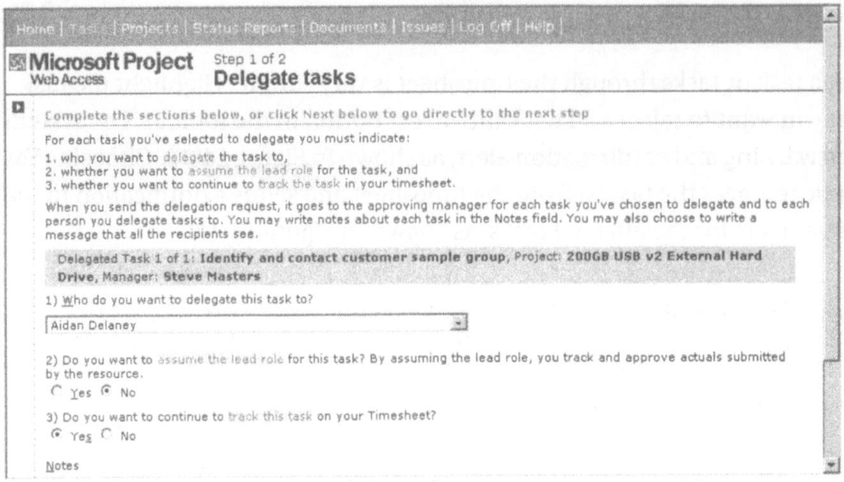

Figure 14-14. Task delegation step 1

In task delegation step 2 of 2, shown in Figure 14-15, the system displays a summary of the actions you're about to process. This page is your last opportunity to make changes to your task delegation or cancel the action entirely. Click the Send button to send the delegation proposal to the resources and the manager responsible.

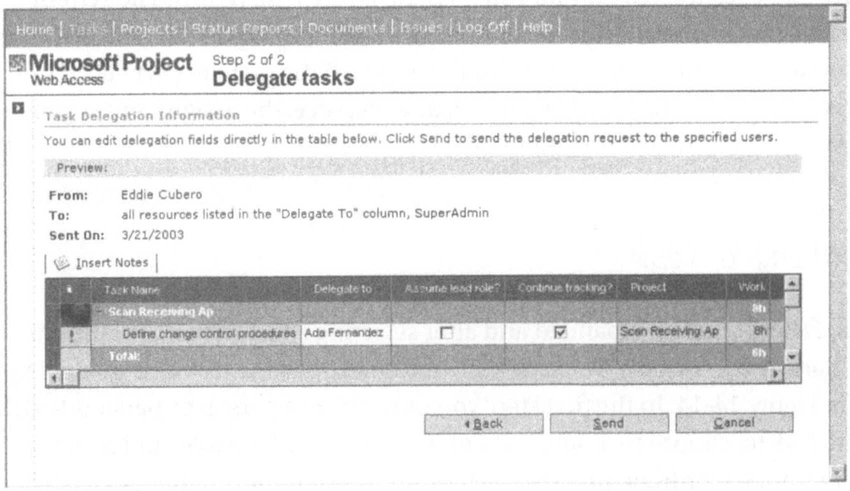

Figure 14-15. Task delegation step 2

After you click Send, the system confirms your successful options, as shown in Figure 14-16.

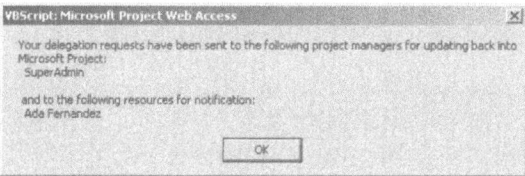

Figure 14-16. Delegation confirmation

Using Task Delegation to Take a Lead Role

Task delegation is useful for flowing work assignments to resources through team leads. If your organization uses team leads who are responsible for making work assignments to their team members and/or are responsible for monitoring their team members' work, a project manager first assigns tasks to the team leader. The team leader, in turn, uses task delegation to reassign the work to a specific resource. Selecting the "Assume lead role" option keeps the task visible on the leader's task list.

Creating a New Task

Select "Create a new task" from the Activities menu to open the "Create a new task" page, as shown in Figure 14-17. The Project drop-down list at the top of the page allows you to select an existing project or to-do list. In the second section of the page, you select the outline level for the new task. By default, the "Create the new task at the top outline level" option is selected. You may make the new task a subtask of any task already assigned to you.

Provide a task name and optional comments for your new task in the Task information section of the page. Select a proposed start date and enter a work estimate in hours or days. Indicate which value you're using by typing **h** or **d** after the number you enter. Click the Save New Tasks button to save your new task requests to your timesheet.

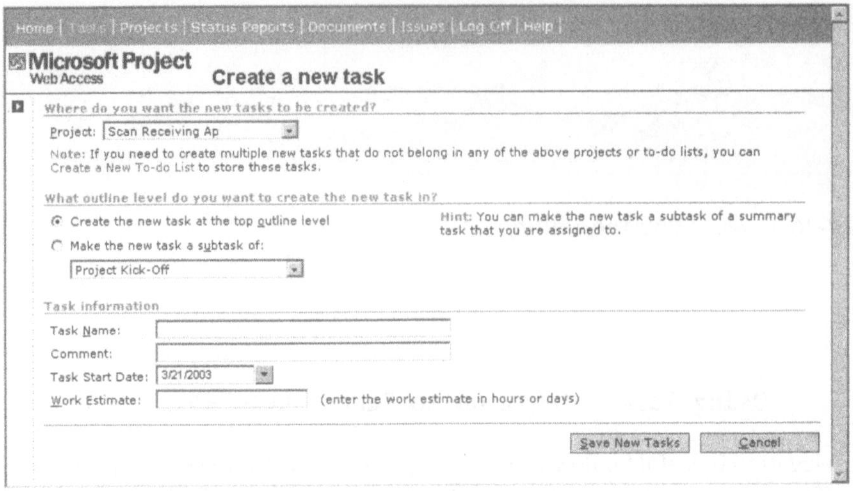

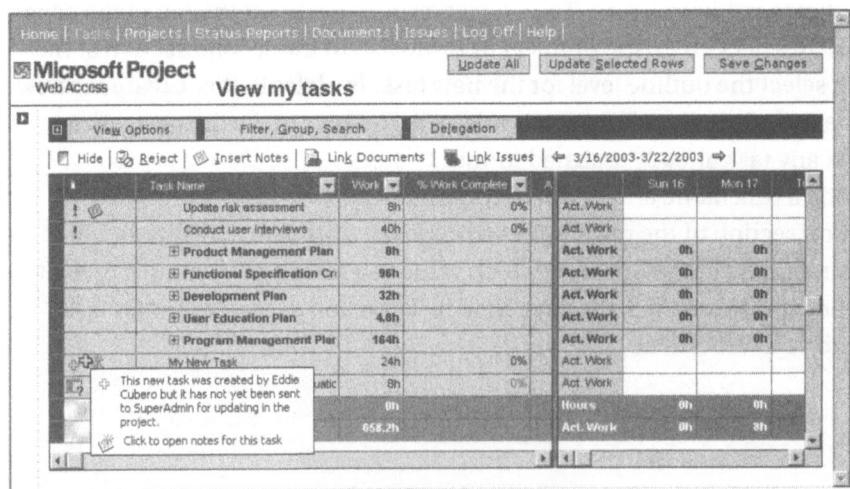

Figure 14-17. The "Create a new task" page

Saving the new tasks redisplays the Timesheet or Gantt Chart view, as previously selected when you initiated the new task page. The new task is now visible in the timesheet and contains indictors that let you know what's going on with it. For instance, in the example, I entered a note in the Note field, and the notes indicator is displayed next to the new task, as shown in Figure 14-18. Note that hovering the cursor shows that the task was added to the timesheet, but it hasn't yet been sent to the manager for updating. You must activate an update function to send this along for approval.

Figure 14-18. The new task is added to the timesheet.

Using Task Creation for Collaborative Planning

You can leverage the new task creation feature during the project planning phase to allow team leaders and team members to task out areas of the work plan. In order to allow these users to create tasks that fall below summary tasks in the plan, you must assign the user responsible for creating the tasks to the summary task to begin with. This means that you must at least dummy up this structure in your plan.

In other words, you'll need to create the summary task by both creating it as a task with an appropriate name and by adding at least one subtask to it in order to apply the indentation that, in itself, defines a task as being a summary task. Then you must assign the resource responsible for detailing the tasks below the summary task to the summary task itself.

Assigning resources to summary tasks isn't generally a good idea, because it causes work demand to be overstated. The work rollup from the summary task gets added to the resource as well as the work of the individual subtasks. This isn't a problem before you enter the phase of a project when you start tracking and for as long as you can live with overstatement of work for the resources doing the planning. Remove the resources from the summary tasks as soon as possible.

Using Other Timesheet Functions

The balance of the timesheet functionality falls outside the core reporting flow. Although information is exchanged through these actions and functions, it's not the type of information that causes progress to be updated or generates approval work for the project managers.

Transferring Nonworking Time from Outlook

Select the Transfer nonworking time from your Outlook Calendar link to open the step 1 page shown in Figure 14-19. Select whether the update will go to a manager or to your timesheet.

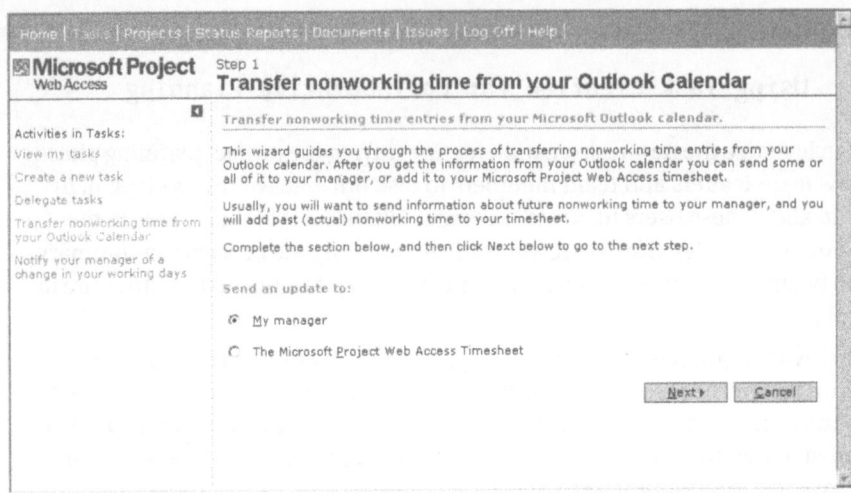

Figure 14-19. Transfer Outlook tasks step 1

Step 2, shown in Figure 14-20, displays after you click Next on the previous page. This page allows you to set a timeframe for retrieving the Outlook data. You can also set a minimum time horizon for selecting calendar entries. By default, this is limited to events of 30 minutes or longer.

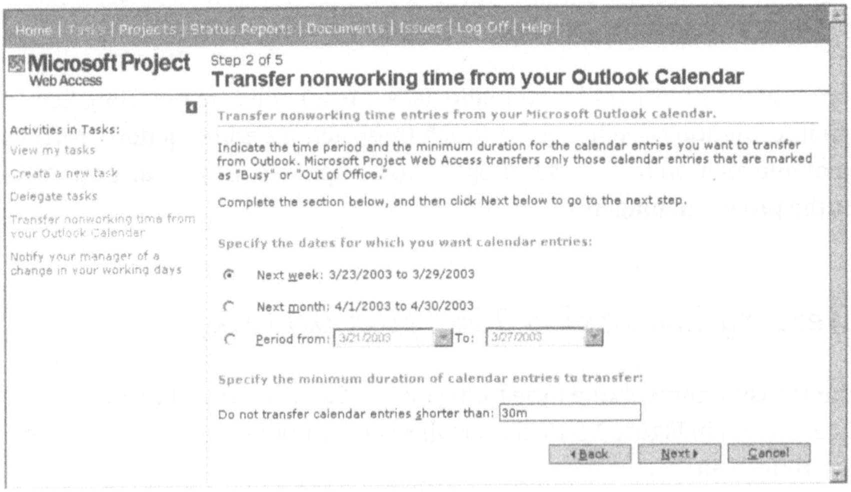

Figure 14-20. Transfer Outlook tasks step 2

CAUTION   During this process, the system may prompt you about activating ActiveX objects and it may prompt you to allow access to Outlook. These warnings are driven by your security settings. Navigate through the prompts accordingly.

Based on your selections, the system connects to Outlook and gathers the appointments that meet your specified criteria, as shown in Figure 14-21. You may deselect any appointments that you don't want to include. Once you've made your selections, click Next to continue.

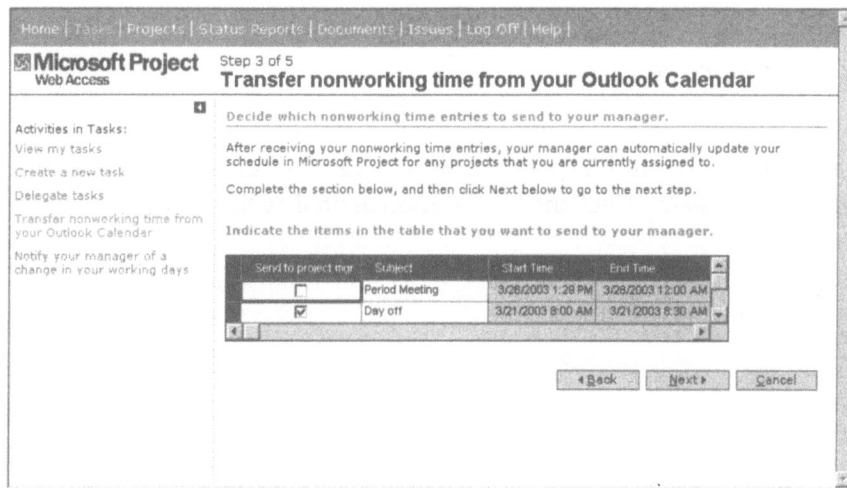

Figure 14-21. The system gathers the appointment entries meeting the criteria.

In the fourth step, shown in Figure 14-22, you must select the manager or managers to whom you wish to report the working day change. Make sure to include all the applicable managers. You're able to select only the manager or managers to whom you're already reporting task work.

Figure 14-22. Transfer Outlook tasks step 4

Finally, the system presents a summary of the action you're about to commit, as shown in Figure 14-23. Click the Send button to finalize the transfer.

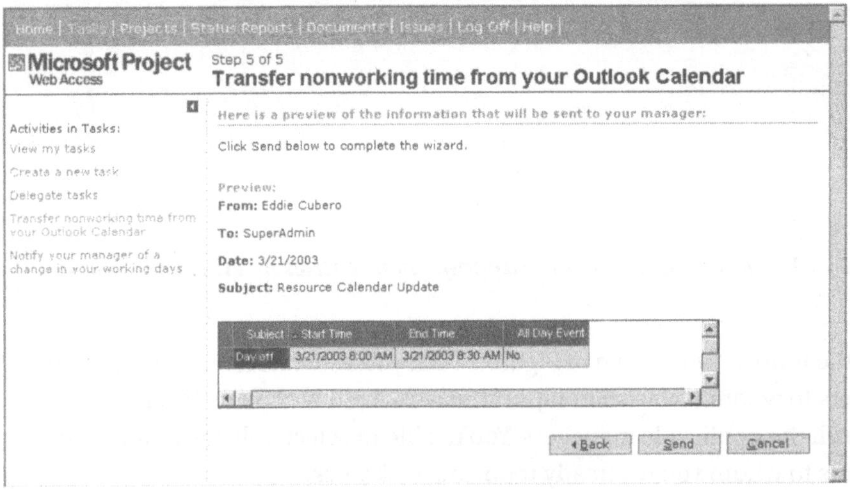

Figure 14-23. Step 5 summarizes the transfer details.

CAUTION   Consider not allowing the use of the "Transfer nonworking time from your Outlook Calendar" and the "Notify your manager of a change in your working days" features in your enterprise instance. The fatal flaw of the time transfer feature is that it doesn't communicate these changes to the entire enterprise. Instead, the information flows to individual projects based on the project managers selected by the user. A project manager creating a new project would be unaware of this change when scheduling the resource the next day. In my opinion, this isn't one of Project Server's stronger features.

Notifying Managers When Working Days Change

Rather than grabbing nonworking time from your Outlook Calendar, the "Notify your manager of a change in your working days" feature communicates changes based on your choices in three steps. Step 1, shown in Figure 14-24, allows you to select to report a working change whereby you'll be working when you previously hadn't been scheduled to work or you'll not be working when previously expected to. Select one or the other and select the period using the date picker fields. Then click Next to move on to step 2.

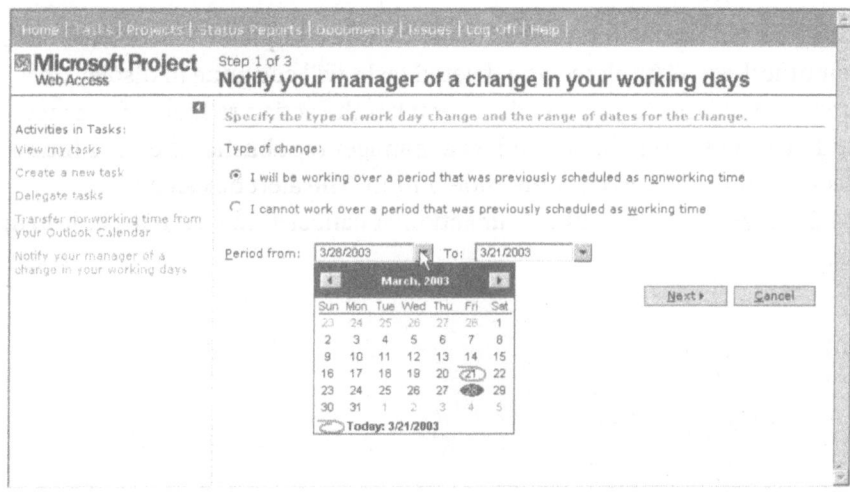

Figure 14-24. Notify your manager of a change in your working days step 1

Step 2 of the process displays the same manager selection page shown in step 4 of transfer Outlook entries in Figure 14-22 in the previous topic. Step 3 summarizes the action prior to posting, as shown in Figure 14-25.

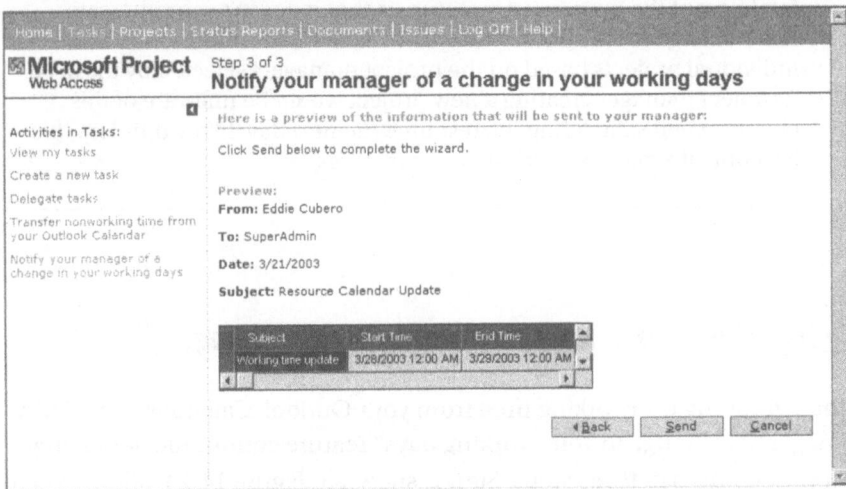

Figure 14-25. Notify your manager of a change in your working days step 3

Hiding Tasks

Hiding tasks is a feature resources need to use to hide completed and deleted tasks from their timesheet. Completed and deleted tasks will continue to display on a user's timesheet indefinitely unless the user takes the action to hide it from view. Once hidden, tasks don't redisplay unless a manager republishes them. To hide a task, select it in the grid and click the Hide button. The alert box shown in Figure 14-26 allows you to confirm your action or cancel it. Click the Yes button to continue.

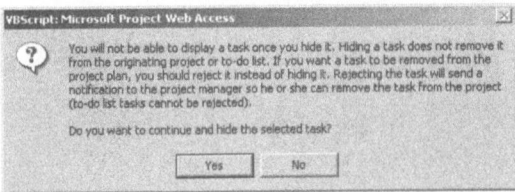

Figure 14-26. Hide a task from the timesheet.

Inserting Task Notes

Select a task and then click the Insert Notes button on the toolbar to open the Project Web Access Assignment Notes dialog box shown in Figure 14-27. The dialog box contains a current note area at the top and a history of notes already added to the task in the bottom half. You may make changes in either text area. You should make your new entry in the upper text box, as this is populated with your name to indicate that you're the one adding the note. Saving the new note automatically adds a timestamp to the record. Click OK to add the note. Your new note now appears when you reopen the Notes dialog box for the task.

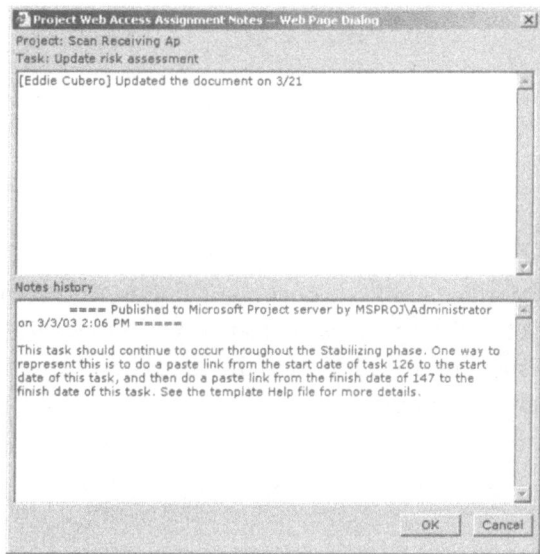

Figure 14-27. Add a note to a task in the timesheet.

Linking Documents to Tasks

You can link documents to tasks through the Tasks interface by clicking the Link Documents button on the toolbar to display the document list for the task you select in the timesheet. The Document list dialog box, shown in Figure 14-28, displays a list of documents already linked to the task if any exist. Otherwise, you can use the functional links to add documents to the project library or link the task to existing documents in the library. I cover document libraries and task linking in the next chapter.

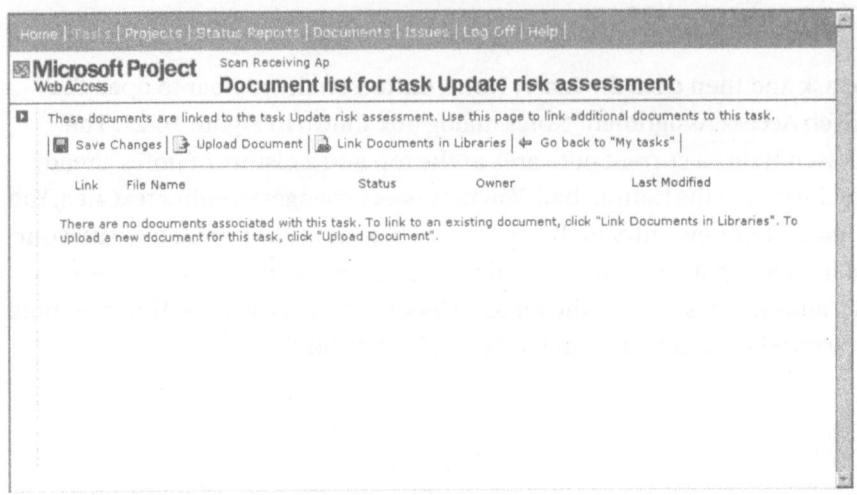

Figure 14-28. The document list for a task

Linking Issues to Tasks

Linking issues to tasks presents an interface similar to document linking, as shown in Figure 14-29. You can link the task to existing issues or create a new issue to link the task to. The page displays any issues currently linked to the task. I cover issues lists and linking issues to tasks in the next chapter.

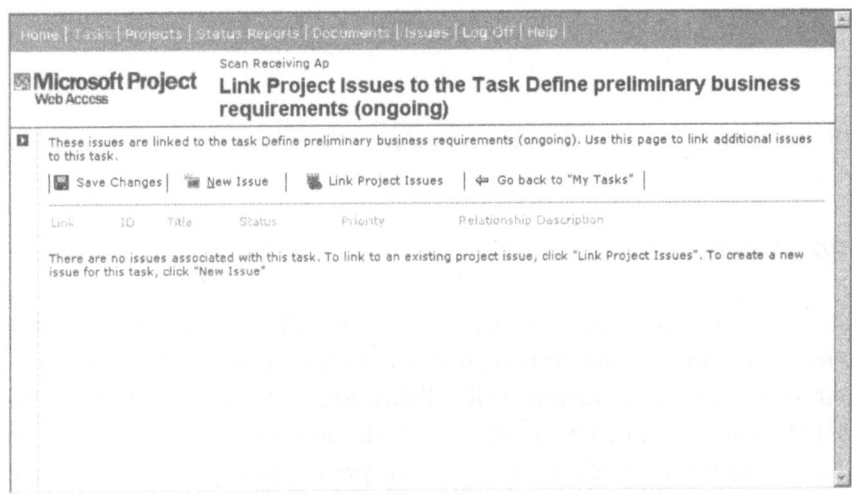

Figure 14-29. Link an issue to a task in the timesheet.

Applying Updates in Project Web Access

The reporting loop completes through the Updates section in Project Web Access. In the last chapter, you learned how a project manager pushes the task assignments from the plan to the users through Project Web Access. In this chapter, you've so far learned how resources report on assignments through the timesheet. Now it's time to accept or reject the resource reporting that flows back to you through Project Web Access. When you first log onto Project Server, the home page displays information about any new updates you may have pending in the update area. As shown in Figure 14-30, the logged-on manager has eight task changes and two calendar changes requiring responses.

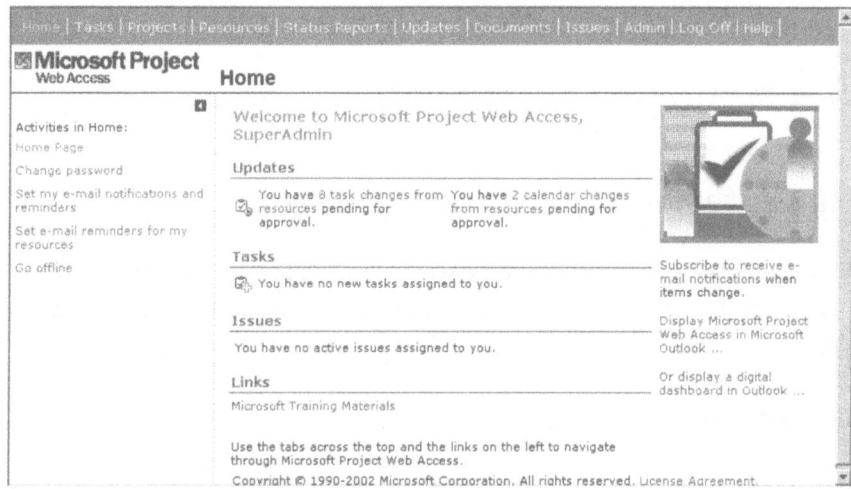

Figure 14-30. The home page displaying update activity

Click the Updates link or the Updates button in the main navigation menu to display the Updates page shown in Figure 14-31. The Updates display echoes the "View my tasks" display in many ways. Like the aforementioned area, you can choose the Timesheet or Gantt Chart formats for the view. The View Options and Filter, Group, Search sections are nearly identical to those in the "View my tasks" area. In this case, however, an Apply Rules tab replaces the Delegation tab in the Tasks view.

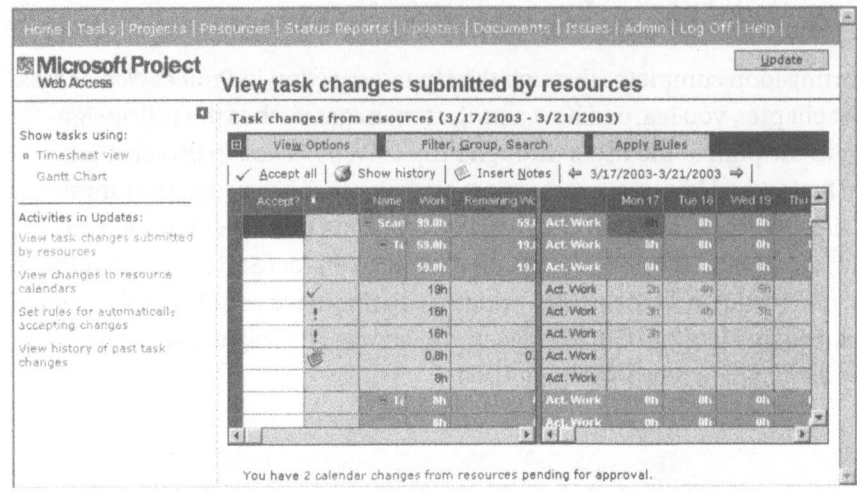

Figure 14-31. The "View task changes submitted by resources" page

Setting Filter, Group, Search Options

You build custom filters here in the same way I showed for timesheets, so I don't cover it again for this view. Expanding the Filter, Group, Search tab reveals the options shown in Figure 14-32. Precooked filters include the following:

- All task changes

- All task updates

- All new tasks

- All task delegation requests

- All resource declined tasks

- All declined task delegation requests

- All completed tasks

- All incomplete tasks

- All overdue tasks

- All tasks pending for approval

- All tasks updated into Microsoft Project

Group updates by the following criteria:

- Accept?

- From

- Project

- Task change type

- Sent date

- Work

- Remaining work

- Start

- Finish

- % Complete

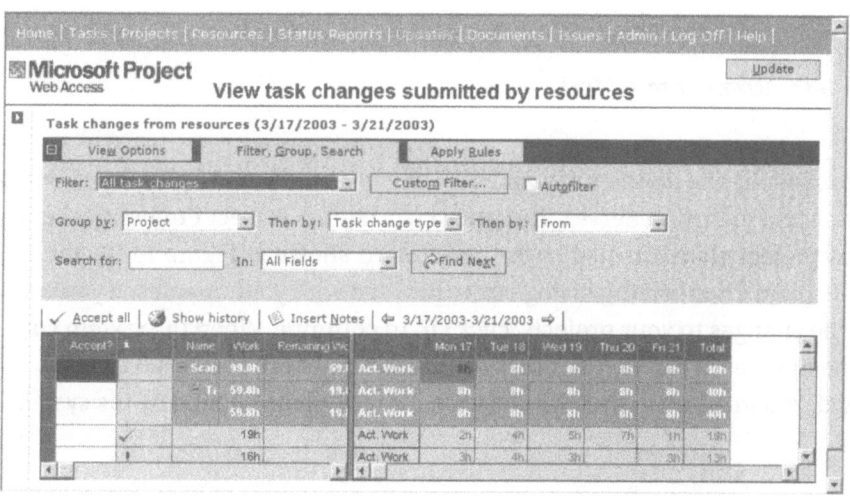

Figure 14-32. Options on the Filter, Group, Search tab

The Activities menu on the left allows you to select between viewing task changes and viewing calendar changes, and offers you the option to view historical changes. A selection for setting up rules for automatic update processing complements the Apply Rules selection on the Activities menu. Use the selection from the Activities menu to create rules, and then use the Apply Rules tab to apply the rules you create.

To accept task updates, in the leftmost column in the grid you must set each task to either Accept or Reject. Use the Accept all button in the toolbar to set all updates in the view to accept or set each one individually using the selector in the grid, as shown in Figure 14-33. Click the Update button to accept and reject according to your selections. You may see a logon screen flash briefly as the system goes to work.

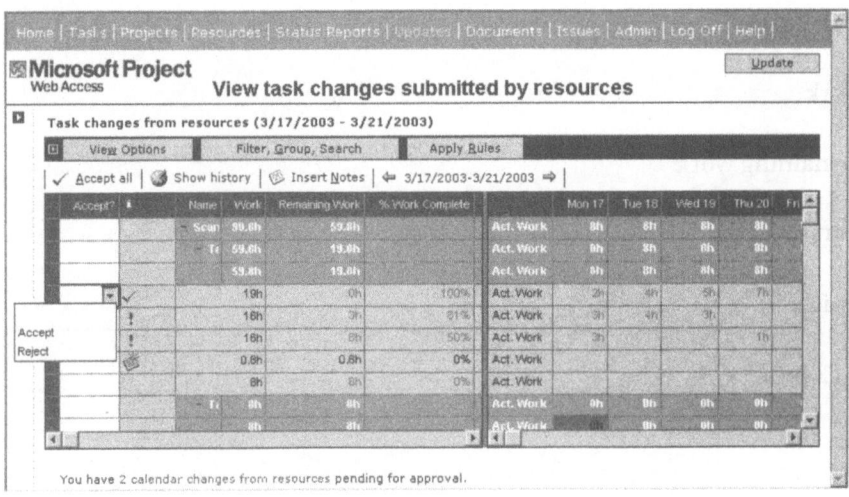

Figure 14-33. Accept or reject tasks

In processing the updates, if you don't already have Project Professional open and connected to Project Server, the system will launch Project Professional and open any project plans affected by the updates. As shown in Figure 14-34, the system displays a confirming dialog box to proceed with your updates. If you want to save the changes to your projects, click OK to continue. When the system completes the updates, it displays another confirmation that the tasks have been published. You must now save and close any project plans opened by the system.

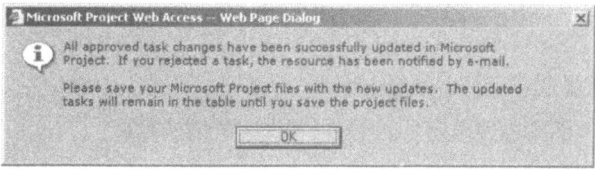

Figure 14-34. Task changes are updated.

Once all of your updates process and you've clicked OK in the final confirmation dialog box, the system redisplays the "View task changes submitted by resources" page, shown in Figure 14-35, which no longer has information to display. As soon as the next resource sends an update, the view is populated again. Notice that there are two calendar changes requiring updating as noted in the line under the blank grid display area.

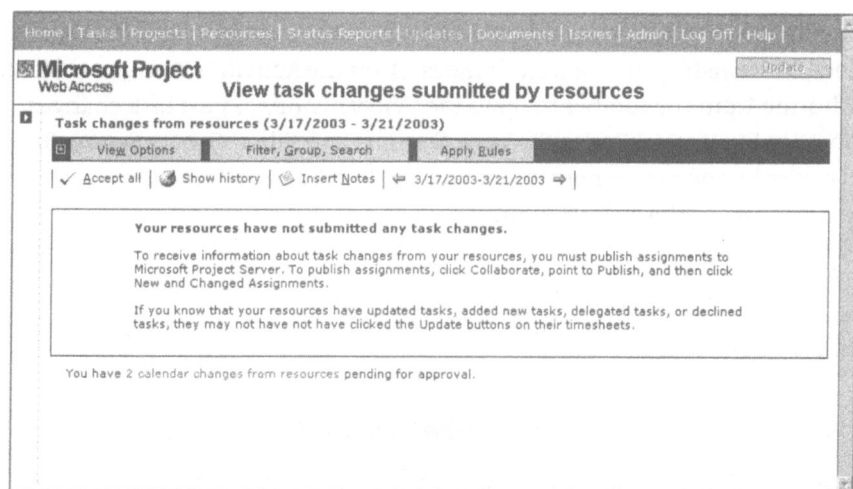

Figure 14-35. The "View task changes submitted by resources" page with no updates to tasks in the queue

Click the link at the bottom of the empty updates grid or click the link in the Activities menu to display the "View changes to resource calendars" page shown in Figure 14-36. This view has a different approach than the task updates view. Here you have the option to delete a calendar update or update all undeleted updates. Click the Update button to accept these changes into the plans affected. The system prompts you to select a project to open if one isn't already open.

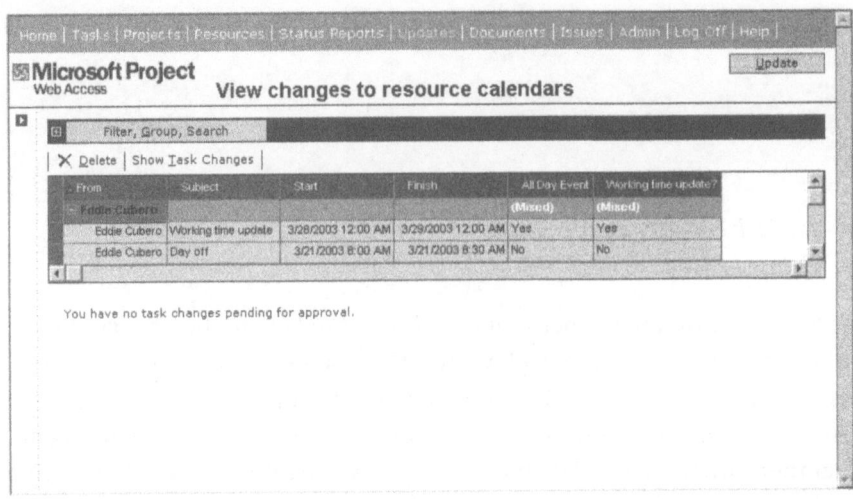

Figure 14-36. Update calendar changes.

Select "View history of past task changes" from the Activities menu or click the History button from the toolbar to open the "View history of past task changes" view shown in Figure 14-37. Use the View Options and Filter, Group, Search functions as you've learned elsewhere in this chapter to refine the data selection shown in the view as well as the presentation.

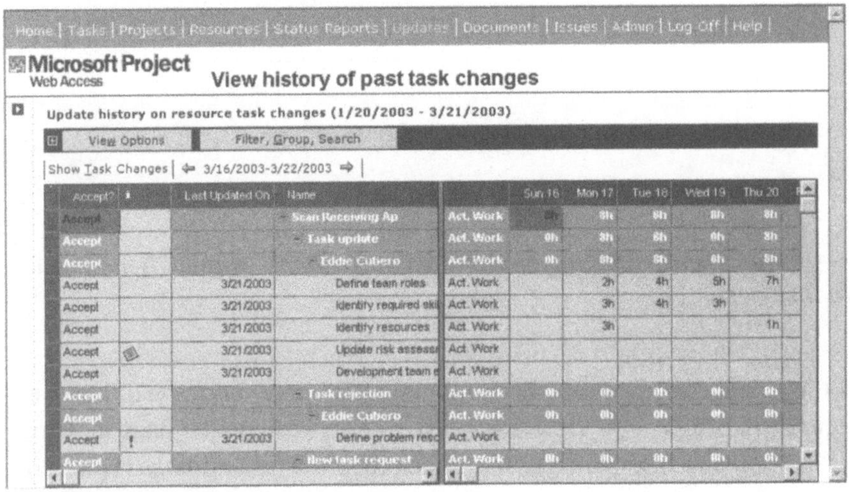

Figure 14-37. The "View history of past task changes" page

Setting Rules for Accepting Task Updates

The Set rules feature allows you to create logical rules for updating tasks to projects. Applying the rules processes task changes that meet the criteria defined in the rules. To open the "Set rules for automatically accepting changes" page, click the Set rules link in the Activities menu. The page shown in Figure 14-38 displays.

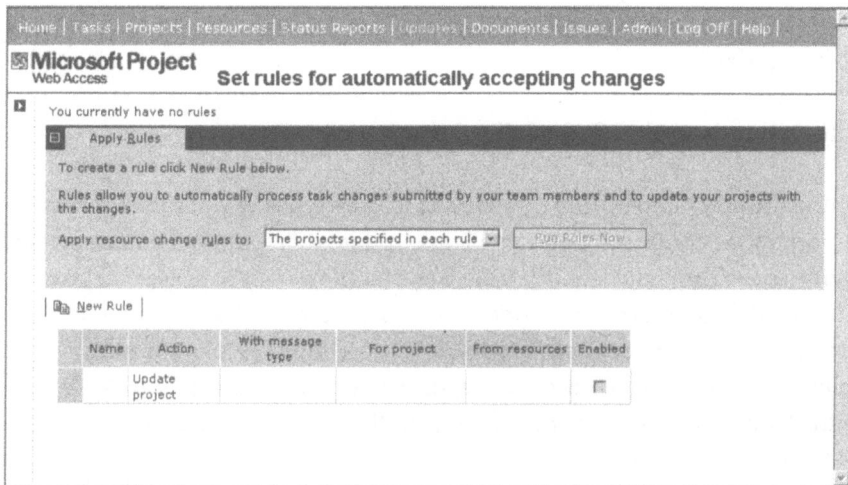

Figure 14-38. The "Set rules for automatically accepting changes" page

Click the New Rule button to open Set rules step 1, as shown in Figure 14-39.

Figure 14-39. Set rules step 1

The first step is to select the types of task changes to update automatically. Select one of the following radio buttons:

- All of the message types below

- All new task requests

- All task delegation requests

- All task updates

- Only task updates that fit the following criterion

Selecting the first radio button includes all update types. If you select this as your criterion, you're choosing to accept all task updates of all types, no matter what. Selecting one of the three succeeding radio buttons allows you to accept all task requests or task delegations or task updates automatically. You can create a rule for each separately. Create the most specific selection criterion for your new rule by selecting the last radio button and setting field-based selection tests. As shown in the figure, the new rule I'm creating applies only to update requests for tasks that are 100% complete.

Step 2 allows you to select which projects the rule should apply to. All available projects that you manage in the system display in the Available projects window on the left, as shown in Figure 14-40. Clicking the "All my current and future projects" radio button moves all available projects to the window on the right. Once you've made your project selections, click Next to continue to the last step.

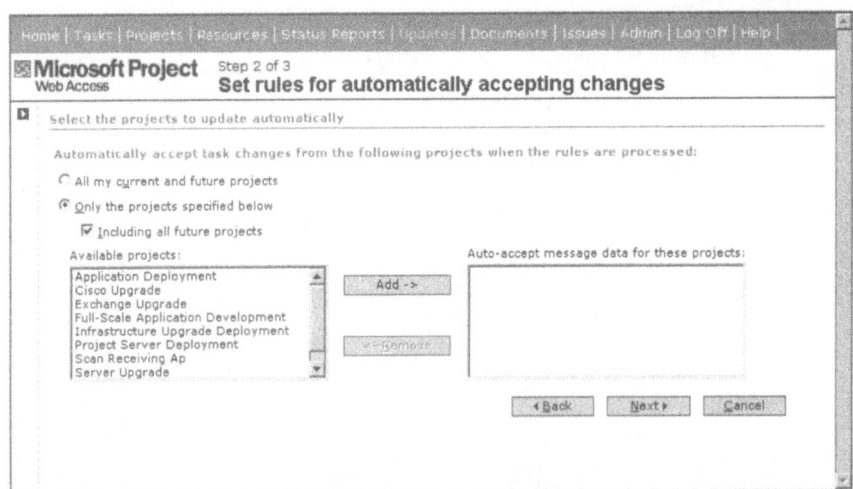

Figure 14-40. Select projects to which the new rule applies.

The last step in the new rule creation process is to select the resources that the rule applies to, as shown in Figure 14-41. As you can see, a rule can be very specific or very broad in its application. You can create a rule to update a task based on meeting specific criteria that apply to only one resource in only one project. Give your new rule a name and select the resources. Click Finish to complete the rule creation.

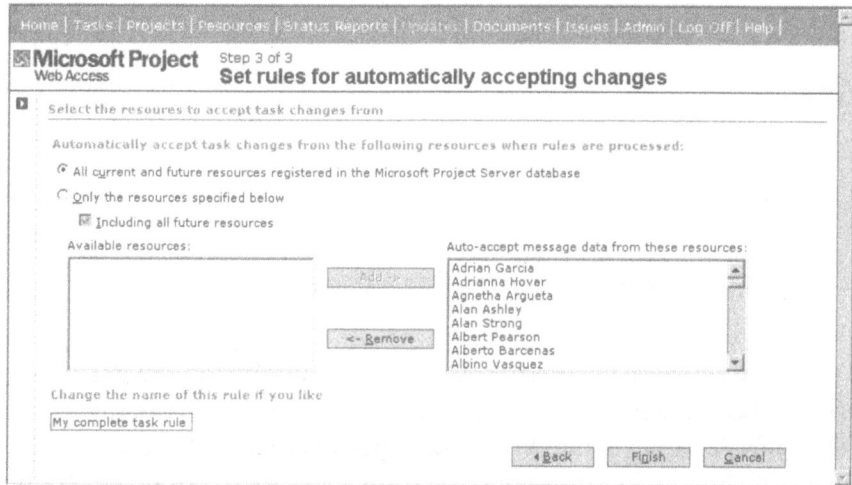

Figure 14-41. Select resources to which the new rule applies in step 3.

Once you've clicked the Finish button, the Set rules page redisplays and shows your new rule indicating an enabled state, as shown in Figure 14-42. Note that once you've created your first rule, the system reports how many rules you've created at the top of the page. The options to modify, copy, or delete the rule are now active as well, providing that you've selected a rule in the grid. Use the Copy Rule feature to create new rules based on previously created ones. Note that you can disable a rule without removing it from the system, which allows you to re-enable it later.

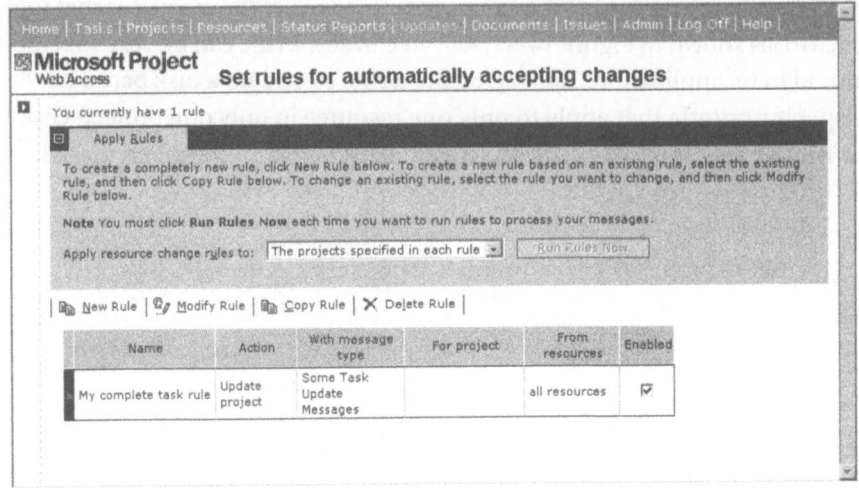

Figure 14-42. The Set rules page after a rule has been created.

The next time you have updates ready to process, run your automated rules first to accept all automatic updates that by running your rules. To run rules, expand the Apply Rules tab of the "View task changes submitted by resources" page to reveal the Run Rules Now option shown in Figure 14-43. From the "Apply resource change rules to" selector, you can choose to apply the rule to all projects or a specific project. Click the Run Rules Now button to run the rules.

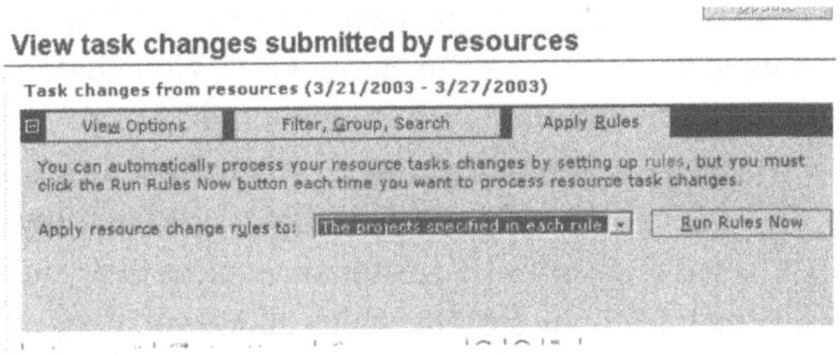

Figure 14-43. The Apply Rules tab

Summary

After mastering the topics in this chapter along with the learning from the previous chapter, you're now equipped to manage the Project Server update cycles for tracking progress in your project plans. You and your organization must make regular cyclical reporting a discipline among all resources and managers.

Everyone should enter their time and send their updates on a standard day each week. The absence of resources and managers must be tracked and managed during the update cycle. If necessary, implement surrogate processes for absent resources. Project managers enter time for absent resources directly in the project plan and then push the changes back to the resources by republishing the updated assignments. For updating purposes, managers take over tasks owned by absent managers and process the updates. Staying current with reporting and updates ensures that your system will have current data and, therefore, the respect of your user community.

Working Collaboratively Through Project Web Access

Now that you've worked through the process of publishing projects and task assignments, and you're familiar with updating progress for a project, it's time to explore the other collaborative features in Project Web Access. These include the reminders engine, document libraries, and issues lists.

These features enhance the core progress-tracking process with features that every team can use to improve intramural communications and share information pertinent to everyone's work on a project. Use these wisely to boost productivity.

Using Features from the Project Web Access Home Page

Figure 15-1 shows the home page for an administrator with a full menu of options. The Project Web Access navigation system is adaptive and displays menu selections according to a user's group membership. The main menu bar displayed across the top of the page, in this instance, shows all possible selections. If I had logged on using a project manager account, the Admin selection wouldn't be displayed. By default, team members won't see the Resources, Updates, and Admin selections on their version of the menu when they log in.

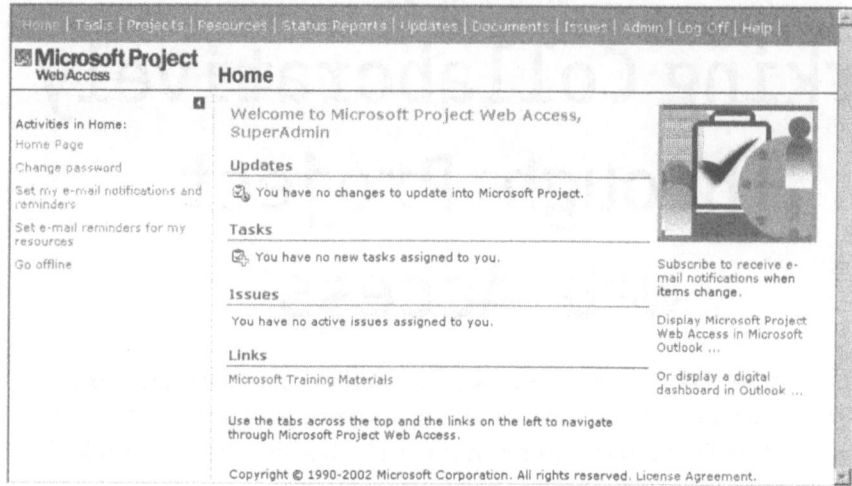

Figure 15-1. The Project Web Access home page

The menu on the left side of the page represents a submenu of selections, which change according to the main menu selection. When you're deeper into the site, this menu is often presented in two sections as you saw in the last chapter and as you'll see when you step through the various navigational areas in this chapter. Note that you can collapse this section and get it out of your way. This is particularly useful when you're accessing views.

The center section of the home page contains an at-a-glance look at the most important events of concern to a typical user: updates, tasks, and issues. Like its counterpart main menu selection, the Updates section of this page displays only for users who receive updates to project plans. Because everyone who uses the system is eligible to receive tasks and issues, these sections display for all users. The Links section (shown) and the additional home page content (not shown) appear as defined by the system administrator.

Finally, on the right side of the home page, several links are provided. Two of these links concern integration with Outlook, and the "Subscribe to receive e-mail notifications" link is redundant with the link on the left.

The activities listed in the left menu under Activities in Home are displayed according to group membership. The available selections are as follows:

- *Home Page* returns the user to the Home Page view from another activity.

- *Change password* allows a user to change his or her password.

- *Set my e-mail notifications and reminders* allows any user to set reminders for him- or herself.

- *Set e-mail reminders for my resources* allows managers to set reminders for resources they manage directly or through project plans. This section doesn't display for resources.

- *Go offline* allows a user to take his or her timesheet offline.

Changing Your Password

Only users defined with Project Server authentication can change their passwords in Project Server. Passwords for users defined with Windows Authentication must be changed according to domain policy. The system displays an error if you make this selection while logged on as a Windows authenticated user. If you're logged on with a Project Server account, making this selection displays the Change password page, as shown in Figure 15-2.

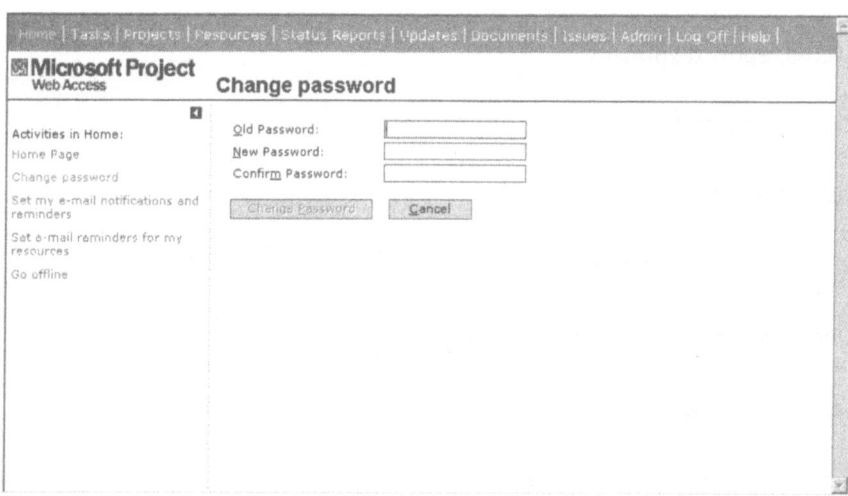

Figure 15-2. The Change password page

Setting Notifications and Reminders

The reminders and notifications engine provides automated notification based on specific events and criteria-based daily notifications based on individual selections. Users may opt out of the notifications and reminders that are user-determinable, but they may not opt out of reminders and notifications set by their managers. The following user actions can generate e-mail notifications to the resources and/or manager affected:

- Publish project plan

- Publish all information

- Request assignment status

- Publish new and changed assignments

- Delegation requests

- Delegation of lead role

- Task updates

- New task requests

- Status report requests

- Status report responses

- Open new issue

- Issue assignment

- Modify an existing issue

- Document changes (new, delete, modify)

- Task list delegation

- Rejected assignments by resource

- Rejected task updates (by manager)

- Rejected new tasks (by manager)

- Rejected calendar updates (by manager)

- Rejected task delegation requests (by manager)

- Removed from a status report (by manager)

Setting Notifications and Reminders for Yourself

When you select the "Set my e-mail notifications and reminders" option from the left menu or click the "Subscribe to receive e-mail notifications" option on the right side of the home page, the system displays the page shown in Figure 15-3. Note that many selections are turned on by default. The "my resources" section applies only to managers.

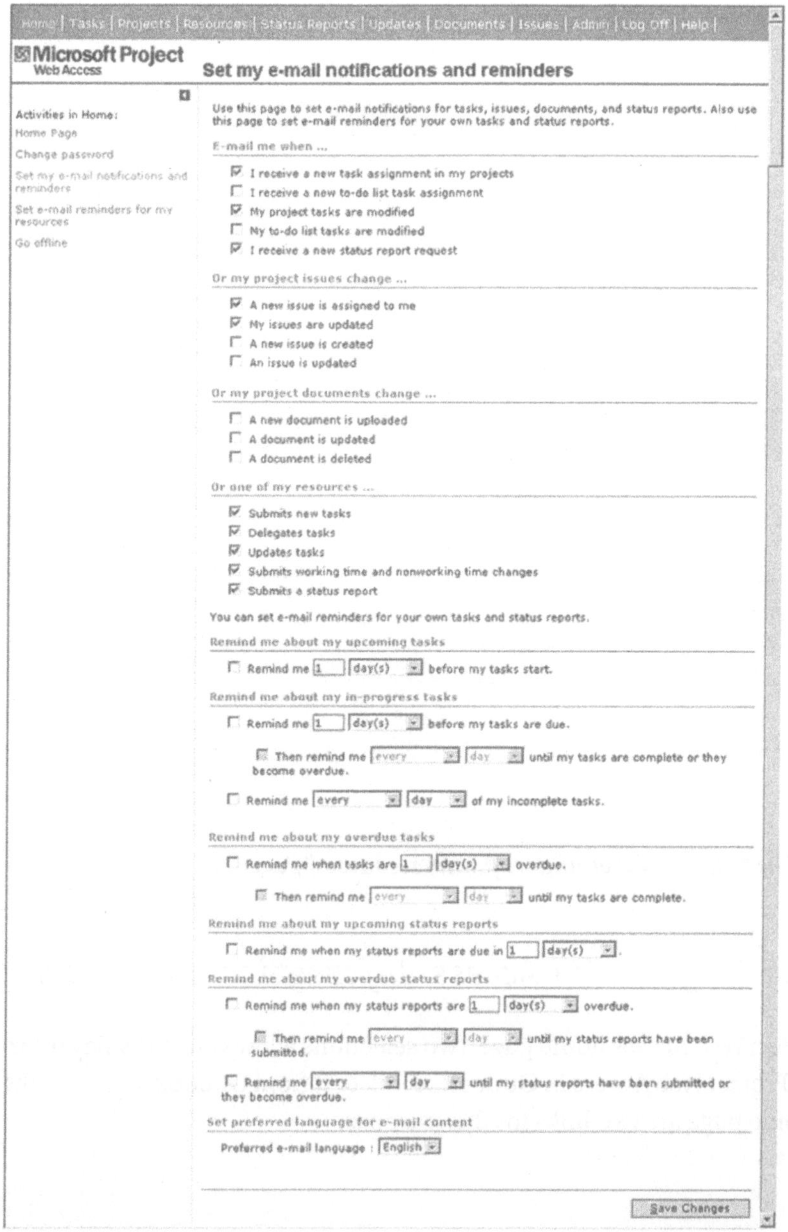

Figure 15-3. The "Set my e-mail notifications and reminders" page

Setting Reminders for Your Resources

Select the "Set e-mail reminders for my resources" option from the left menu to open the page shown in Figure 15-4. When you set reminders for your resources, you may choose to have the reminder go to your resource only, to yourself only, or to both. Keep in mind that "my resources" means that the resource is attributed with an RBS value in a subordinate leaf to your own value, or that the resource is managed by you on a project.

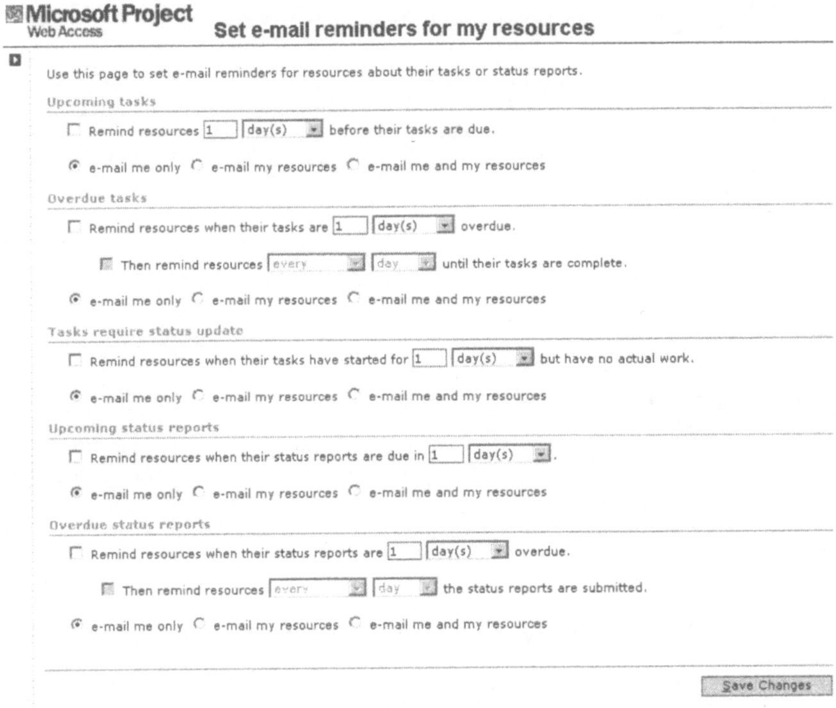

Figure 15-4. The "Set e-mail reminders for my resources" page

Displaying Project Web Access Information in Outlook

From the Project Web Access home page, two selections allow you to display information from Project Web Access in Outlook or link to it from Outlook. On the right side of the home page are two links for this purpose:

- *Display Microsoft Project Web Access in Microsoft Outlook* places a shortcut to Project Web Access in Outlook or displays a Project Web Access page as the home page of a new or existing Outlook folder.

- *Or display a digital dashboard in Outlook* allows the user to select a link for an existing digital dashboard link and create a shortcut to it in Outlook or display it as the home page of a new or existing Outlook folder.

Clicking the link "Display Microsoft Project Web Access in Microsoft Outlook" displays the dialog box shown in Figure 15-5. This dialog box automatically inserts a link or displays a Project Web Access page according to your selections. You choose the particular page to display from the drop-down list at the top of the dialog box. These selections include the following:

- Analyze projects in Portfolio Analyzer

- Analyze resources in Portfolio Analyzer

- Change Password

- Clean up Microsoft Project Server database

- Create a new personal or shared to-do list

- Create a new task

- Customize Microsoft Project Web Access

- Delegate Tasks

- Go offline

- Home Page

- Manage SharePoint Team Services

- Manage enterprise features

- Manage licenses

- Manage my to-do lists

- Manage organization

- Manage security

- Manage users and groups

- Manage views

- Miscellaneous reports

- Model Projects with Portfolio Modeler

- Notify your manager of a change in your working days

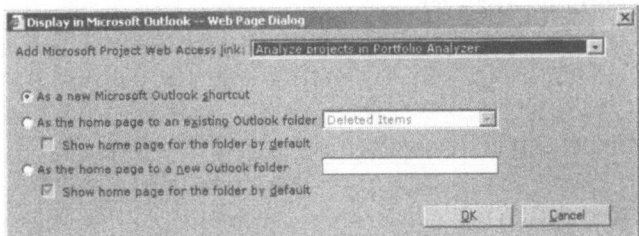

Figure 15-5. Display Project Web Access content in Outlook

Selecting the "As the home page to a new Outlook folder" radio button creates the folder in Outlook. Choose the "As the home page to an existing Outlook folder" radio button if you already have a folder in mind or have created one for this purpose. Both selections result in the selected Project Web Access page displayed in Outlook, as shown in Figure 15-6.

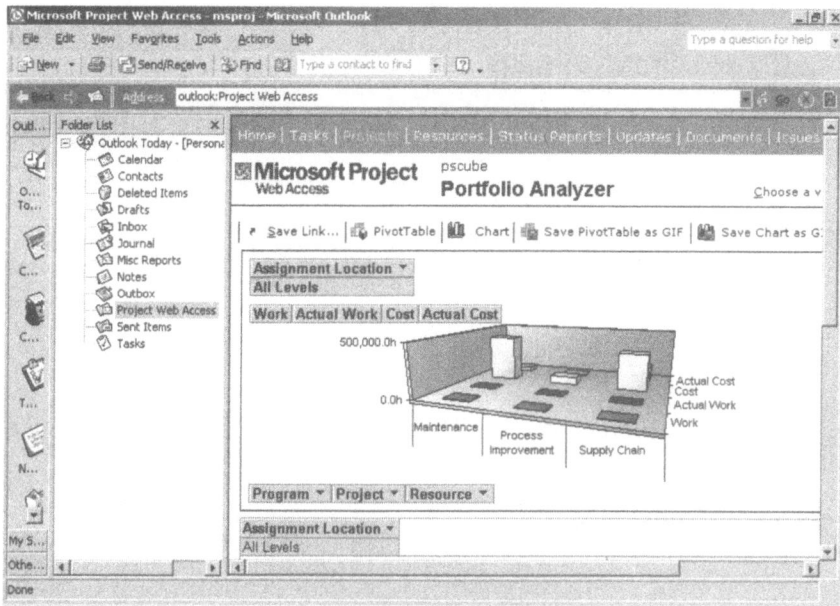

Figure 15-6. Portfolio Analyzer displayed in Outlook

Taking Project Web Access Offline

Microsoft Project Web Access leverages the offline capabilities of Internet Explorer and the operating system to provide timesheet and status report functionality offline. This is limited to a date range selected by the user and limited to entering timesheet information for later posting to the server and the editing and creation of status reports that can be later uploaded to the server. Click the Go offline link on the home page to open the Go offline page shown in Figure 15-7.

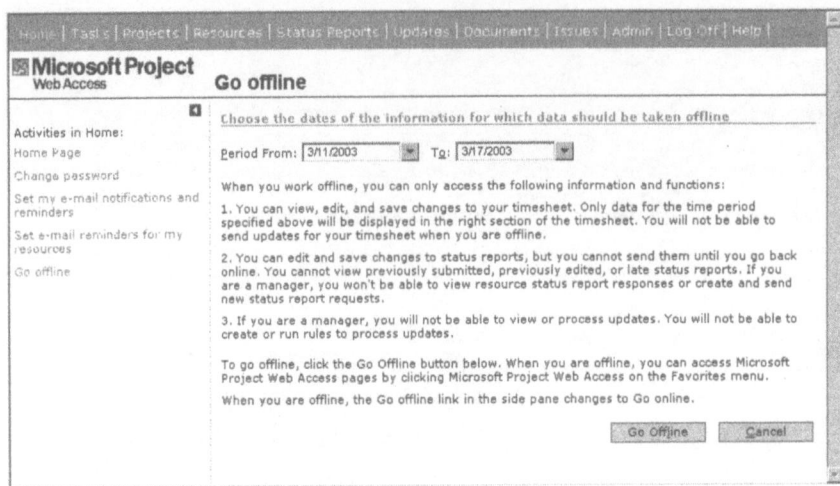

Figure 15-7. The Go offline page

Once you click the Go Offline button, the display will change while the system takes a snapshot of your Project Web Access information. The system copies this information into your offline folders. While it completes the go-offline process, the system reports saving each page. Toward the end of this process, the system displays the message shown in Figure 15-8.

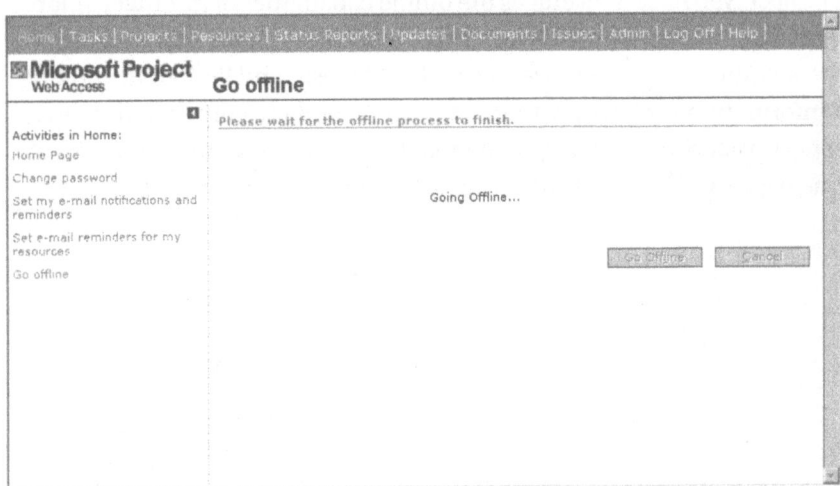

Figure 15-8. The system displays interim information while taking your pages offline.

Upon completion of the process, the system displays the confirmation alert box. Clicking OK in the alert box causes the system to redisplay the home page, which now has a very limited menu selection available, as shown in Figure 15-9. Note that the selection that once was Go offline is now Go online.

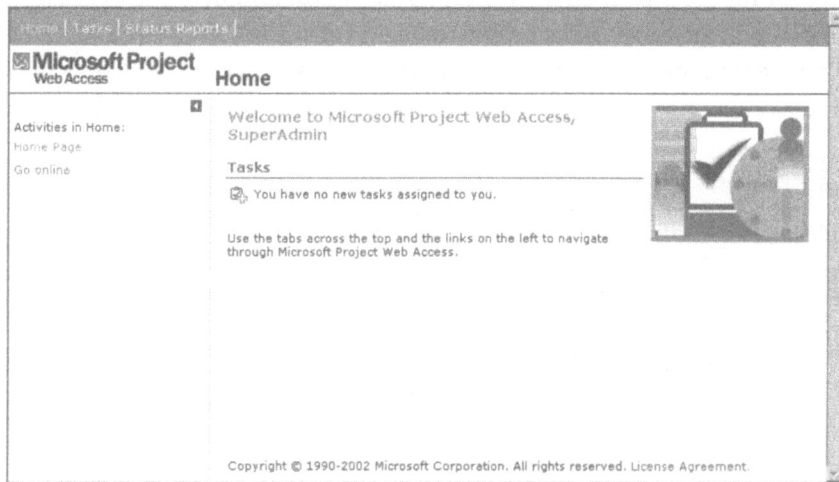

Figure 15-9. The Project Web Access offline home page

Taking Project Web Access offline adds a link to your Favorites menu, as shown in Figure 15-10. To access your offline pages, use this link. You may now add hours to your timesheet, and edit and create status reports. These remain local to your machine until you reconnect to Project Server and choose to go online.

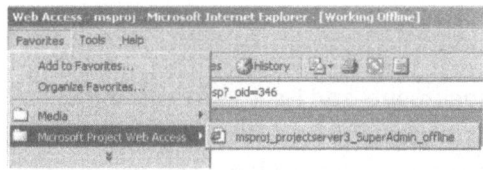

Figure 15-10. Access your offline pages from the Favorites menu in your browser.

Once you're back in the office and can establish a connection with your Project Server, you can go back online by clicking the Go online selection in the offline home page. (Refer back to Figure 15-9 to see this link.) Clicking the Go online link presents you with several choices, as shown in Figure 15-11. Click the Go Online button to update any data you've entered on your local machine and synchronize it with the server. Click the Reset button to abandon any data entered and reconnect as if you never went offline to begin with. The third selection, Stay Offline, allows you to remain offline in the odd event that you made this selection by accident.

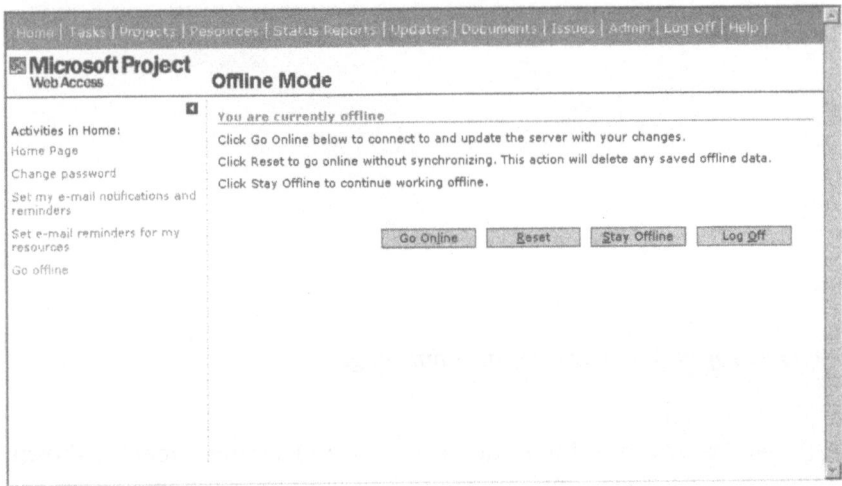

Figure 15-11. Go back online.

Working with Documents and Issues

SharePoint Team Services provides the documents and issues services in Project Server. Both services function correctly for users who have Windows credentials and who use Windows Authentication to access Project Server. Users who access Project Web Access with Project Server accounts aren't able to access these services correctly.

Working with Issues

The home page announces active issues and changes to issues when you log on. As shown in Figure 15-12, I have issues. As you saw in the previous chapter, you can link to issues through the Timesheet interface. On this page, you can either click the link in the center of the page or click the Issues selection on the main menu.

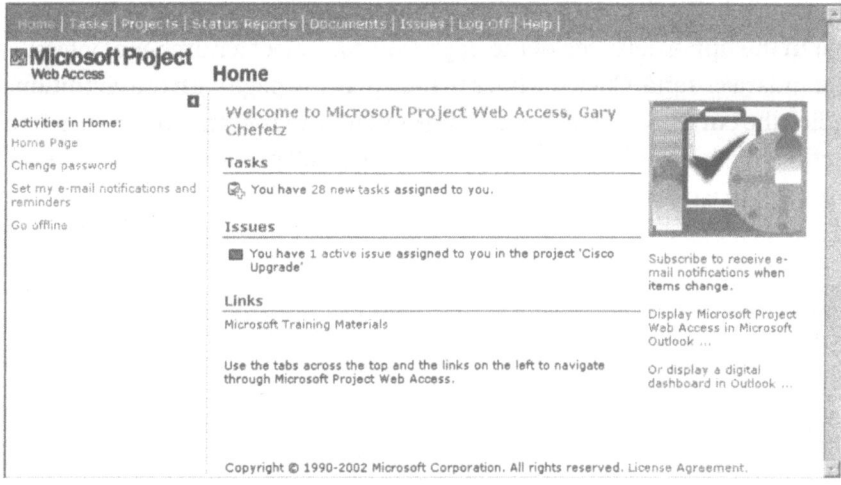

Figure 15-12. The home page with an issues information alert

In the "View and submit issues in all projects" interface, "all projects" refers to all the projects that the user has access to, defined as any project in which the user has an assignment. The system automatically grants access to the documents and issues areas to Windows users with assignments in projects. Figure 15-13 shows the "View and submit issues for all projects" interface for a user who has assignments in only one project. The grid displays one project accordingly. Note that the system summarizes issues for the project in the grid along with the current issue status. The figure shows that there's only one issue currently created for the project.

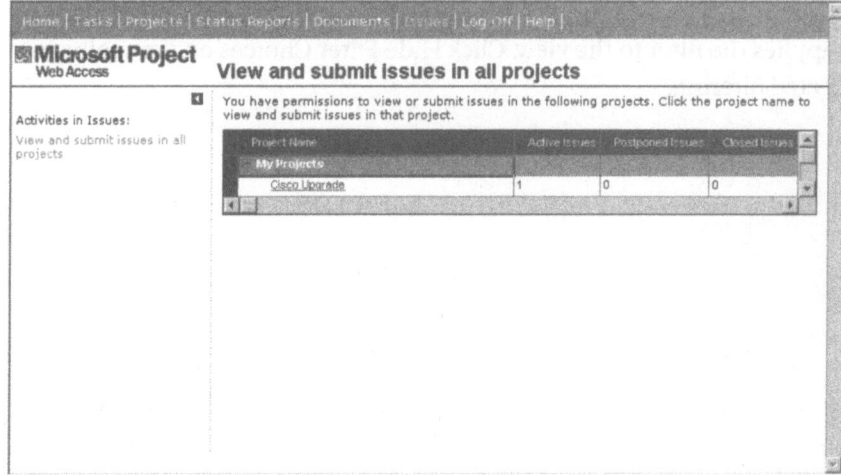

Figure 15-13. The issues home page for a user with access to one project

Clicking the project link displays the View and Submit Issues page for a single project. As shown in Figure 15-14, the project name displays above the page title. Notice that in the upper-left area of the page, you can select a number of views based on standard criteria. Click the links to redisplay the page with the conditions applied. Click the current-project-specific link in the Activities menu to return it to a full selection or click the "View and submit issues in all projects" link to select a different project to work with.

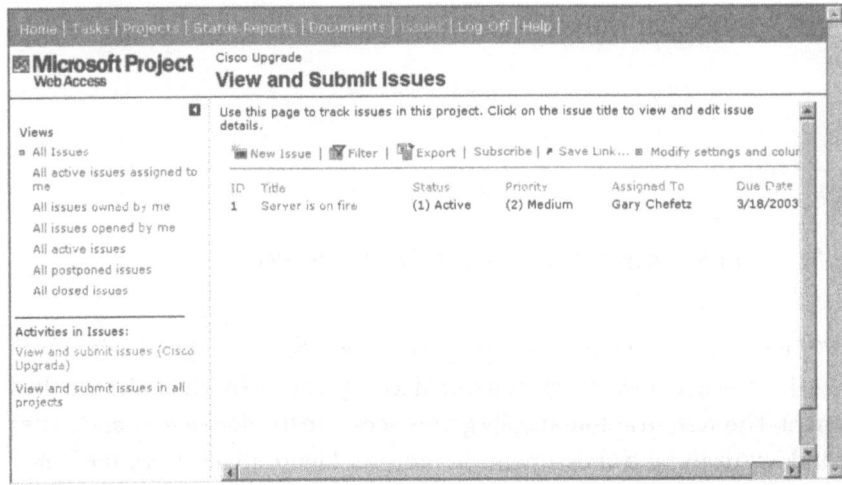

Figure 15-14. The issues page for a specific project

Use ad hoc filtering to alter the record set as well. Click the Filter link in the toolbar and the display changes, as shown in Figure 15-15. Each file in the display becomes a pick list, allowing you to set a value to filter on any column. Making a selection applies the filter to the view. Click Hide Filter Choices on the toolbar to cancel selected filtering.

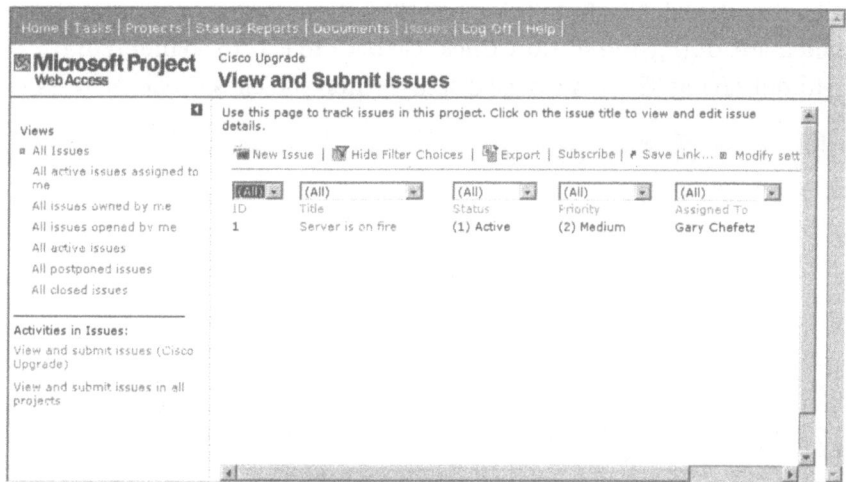

Figure 15-15. The issues page in ad hoc filter mode

Clicking the issue name in the list displays the issue details, as shown in Figure 15-16. The issue details display but you can't edit them.

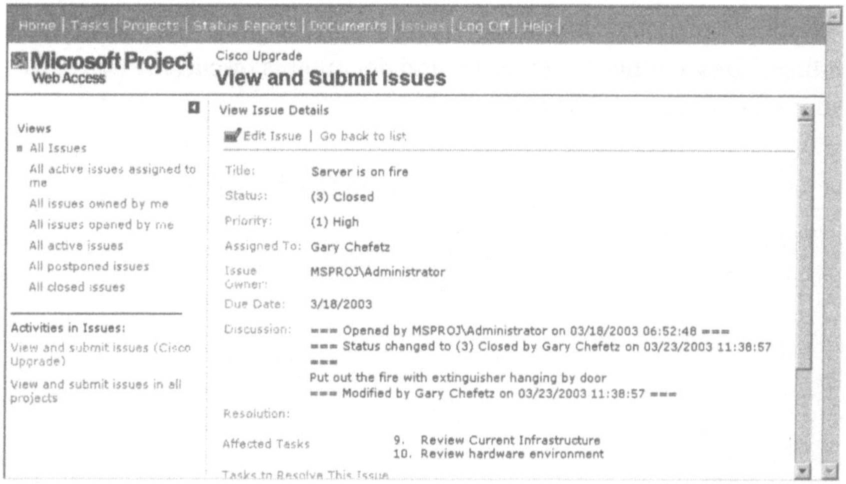

Figure 15-16. View issue details.

Click Edit Issue to open the issue for editing, as shown in Figure 15-17. Users make changes to issue details from this page. Click Save Changes to save any changes you made during the session. Click "Go back to list" to abandon the changes without saving. The same page displays when you click Create New Issue.

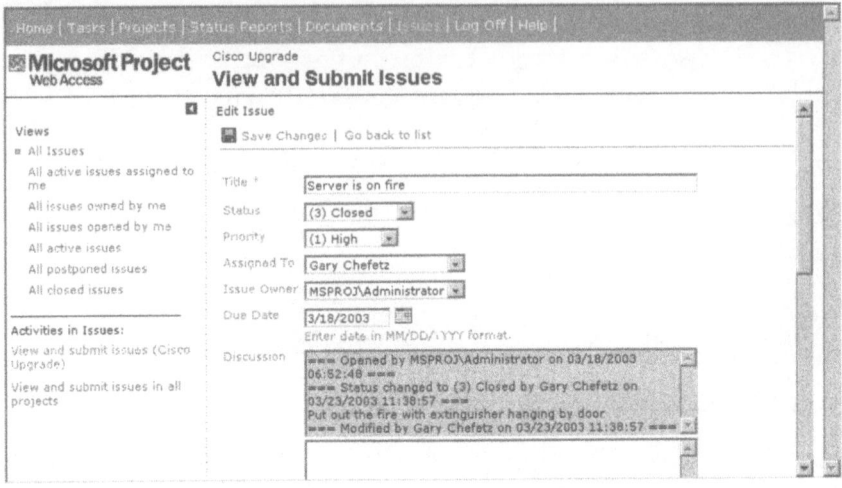

Figure 15-17. Edit issue details.

Scrolling through the edit or create new issue interface, as shown in Figure 15-18, you cross-link issues to other issues, tasks, and documents by clicking one of the link actions at the bottom of the page.

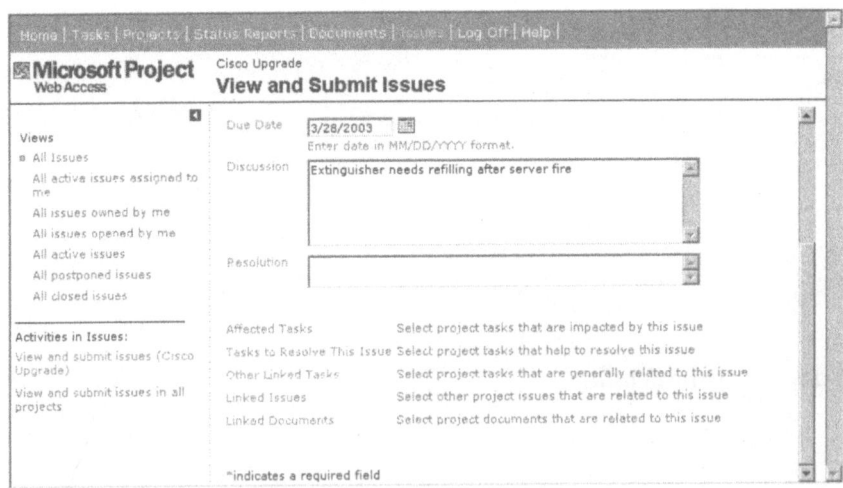

Figure 15-18. The edit issue details page scrolled to the bottom

Clicking a link opens a dialog box that displays the available selections relative to the link that you clicked. Figure 15-19 shows the "Link the issue to the selected issues" dialog box, which dynamically displays other available issues for linking. Note the filtering tools and search feature available to help you narrow the selection. Figure 15-20 shows the "Link the issue to the selected tasks" dialog box. All of these dialog boxes are very similar.

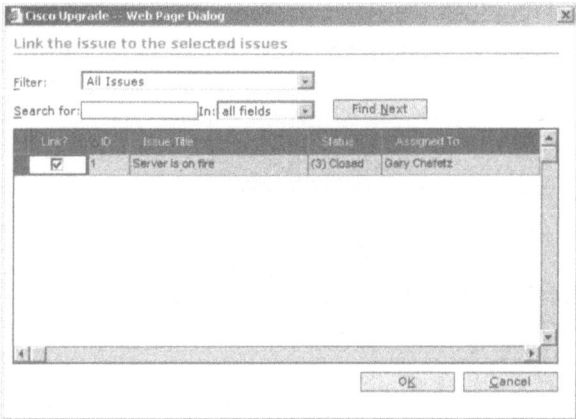

Figure 15-19. Link issues to issues.

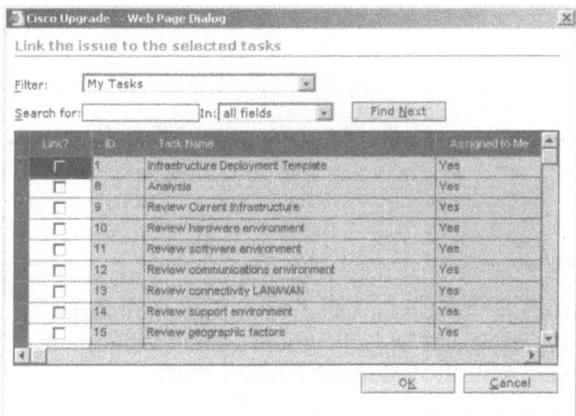

Figure 15-20. Link issues to tasks.

Clicking the Export button on the toolbar for the first time causes the system to prompt you to download a module. Accept the download and the system opens Excel, placing the list data in rows and columns in a worksheet.

Working with Document Libraries

Clicking Documents in the main navigation menu takes you to the page shown in Figure 15-21. Notice that the "View and upload documents for all projects" link displays in red to indicate that it's selected. Click this link to refresh this view at any time. Like issues, users have access to document libraries based on having a work assignment in a project. If you have an assignment in a project, you'll see it presented in the grid on this page. All Windows users in your Project Server system have access to the public documents area. System administrators have access to all libraries.

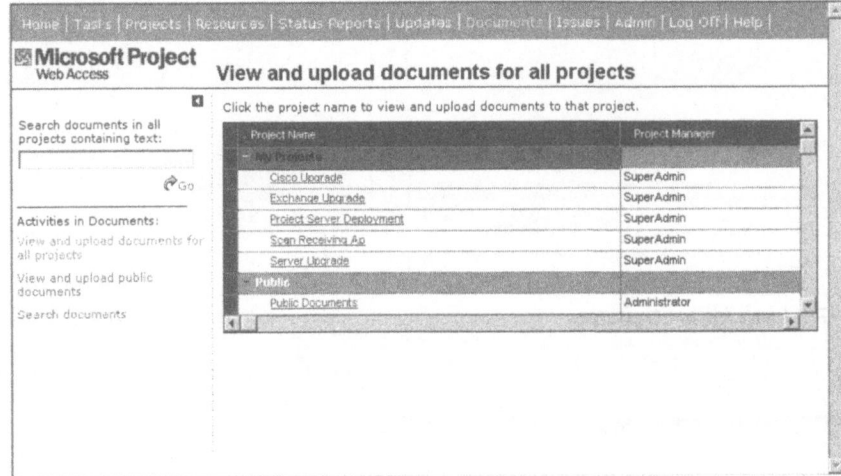

Figure 15-21. Select a project from the "View and upload documents for all projects" view.

TIP   Give Windows users in the system access to document libraries and issues lists for specific projects by giving them a small assignment in each project. These are typically tasks with a token effort.

Selecting a project link in the grid opens the document libraries home page for your project, as shown in Figure 15-22. Note that the name of the project displays above the page title. Each library contains one sublibrary indicated with a folder icon. By default, one sublibrary, Shared Documents, gets created. The documents home page displays this and any other folders that the team has added.

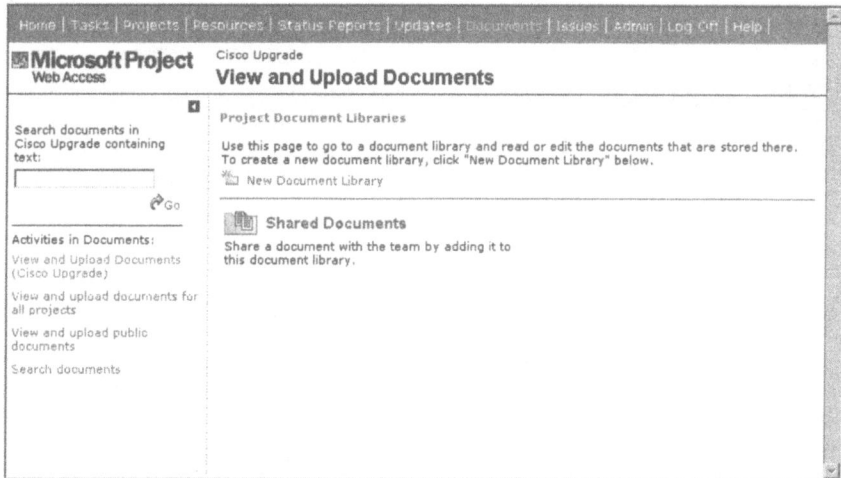

Figure 15-22. View and upload documents for a specific project.

Click the New Document Library link to create a new sublibrary in your project library. The system displays the New Document Library page shown in Figure 15-23.

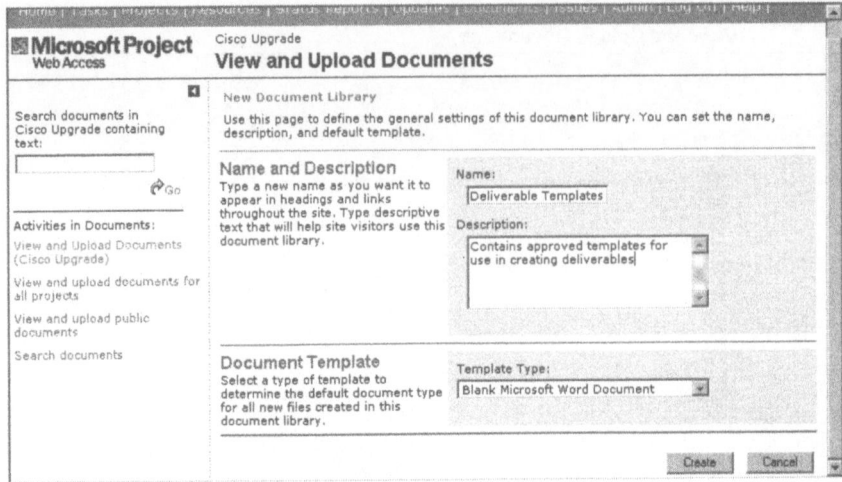

Figure 15-23. Create a new document library.

Give your new library a name and a description. Choose a template for the library from the Template Type list:

- Blank Microsoft Word Document

- Blank Microsoft FrontPage Document

- Blank Microsoft Excel Document

- Blank Microsoft PowerPoint Document

The reason for selecting a blank template relates to features available only if you have an Office XP client application license installed on your workstation. The full version of the Office XP Web Components, available only to users of Office XP, allows you to open and edit Office documents in your Web browser, thus avoiding the need to download and upload the documents each time. This feature won't work for users of earlier Office versions.

Click the Create button to create the new library and add it to your Project display, as shown in Figure 15-24.

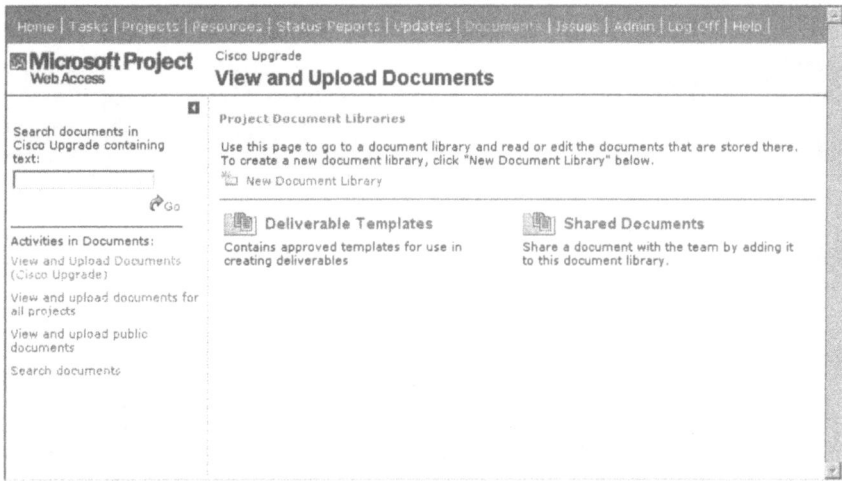

Figure 15-24. A new library is added.

Opening the shared documents library reveals the document list already available for the project. As shown in Figure 15-25, if documents contained in the library weren't available during your last session, they're flagged as new in the view. I've collapsed the left-hand navigation for better viewing. Use the New Document feature only if you have Office XP, otherwise it won't work. Similarly, click a filename to open it in your browser if you have Office XP, otherwise the system will prompt you to download the file.

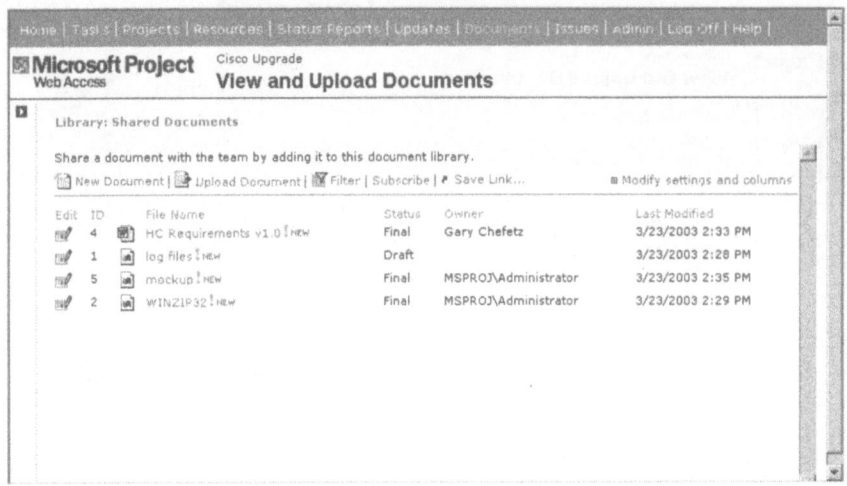

Figure 15-25. The shared documents library opened

Click the Filter link in the toolbar to change the view to expose value pickers for each field in the view to use in an ad hoc manner. Clicking the Subscribe link takes you to the "Set reminders for yourself" area of Project Web Access. Here you would make a selection under the project documents area. Click the Upload Document link on the toolbar to upload a new document to the library. Note in the upload page shown in Figure 15-26 that you can choose to overwrite a previous version of the document if you're saving it with the same name. This ability somewhat replaces the ability to edit in place for those users who don't have Office XP.

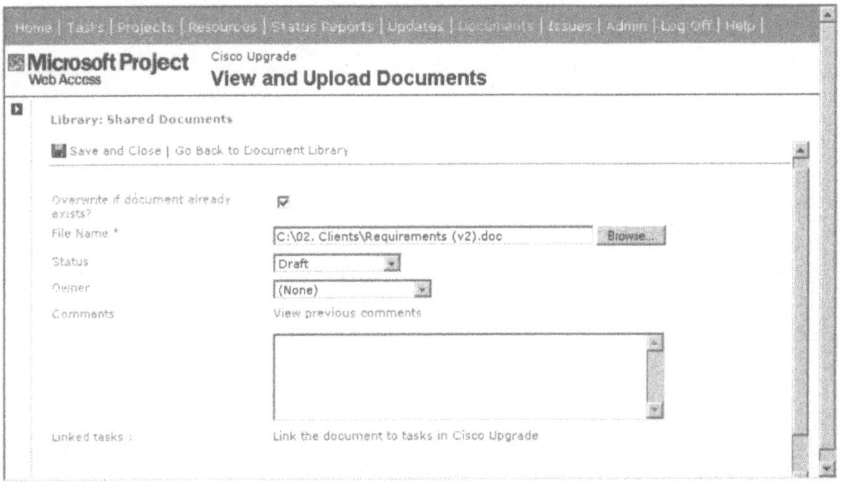

Figure 15-26. Upload a new document.

Let's say that this was a very large library and I decided to go with an ad hoc filter. I click the Filter link and choose the administrator in the Owner field to filter out all documents except those that the administrator owns. I then click Save Link on the toolbar so that I can use the filtered view again the next time I visit the page. Clicking the Save Link button presents the dialog box shown in Figure 15-27. Here I enter a name for my link and click OK.

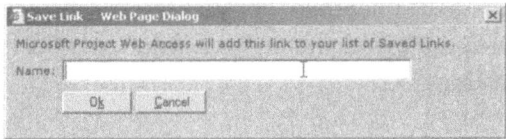

Figure 15-27. Give the link a name.

Saving the link adds a section at the top of the left navigation pane. The new Saved Links section, shown in Figure 15-28, is expanded to reveal the new link. Each time the link is clicked, the view will change to one filtered to select Administrators only.

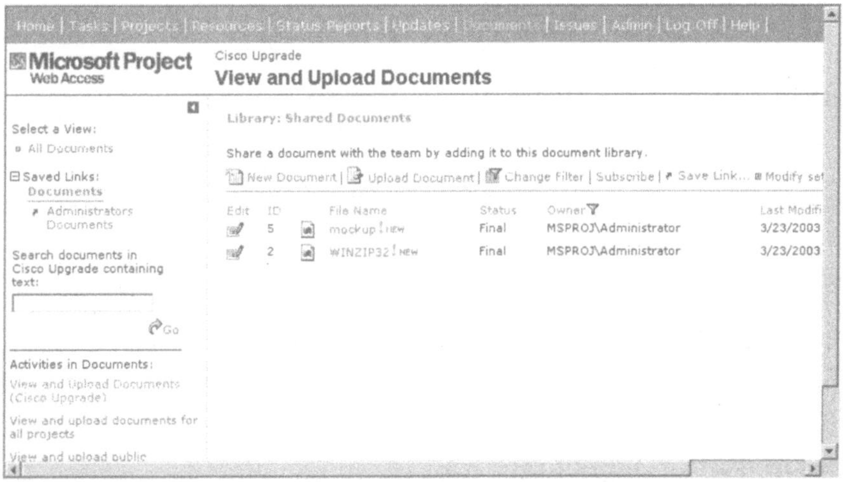

Figure 15-28. The Saved Links section now shows.

Modifying Issues Lists and Document Libraries

Both issues lists and documents libraries, at heart, are driven by the same list engine in SharePoint Team Services. The substantial difference is that one has documents attached. Otherwise, the field capture characteristics are very similar.

When you're editing them, both provide the choice to manipulate or add columns of information and to add additional views. You make modifications at the individual issues list or document library level and those modifications don't carry through to other libraries or issues lists. Unfortunately, Microsoft doesn't provide a way to make master changes through the Project Server interface. However, you can accomplish this through customization.

With all the similarities mentioned, there are some differences, too. Clicking the "Modify settings and columns" link in the document libraries toolbar displays the library design page shown in Figure 15-29. Notice that this is where you delete unwanted libraries and customize existing ones.

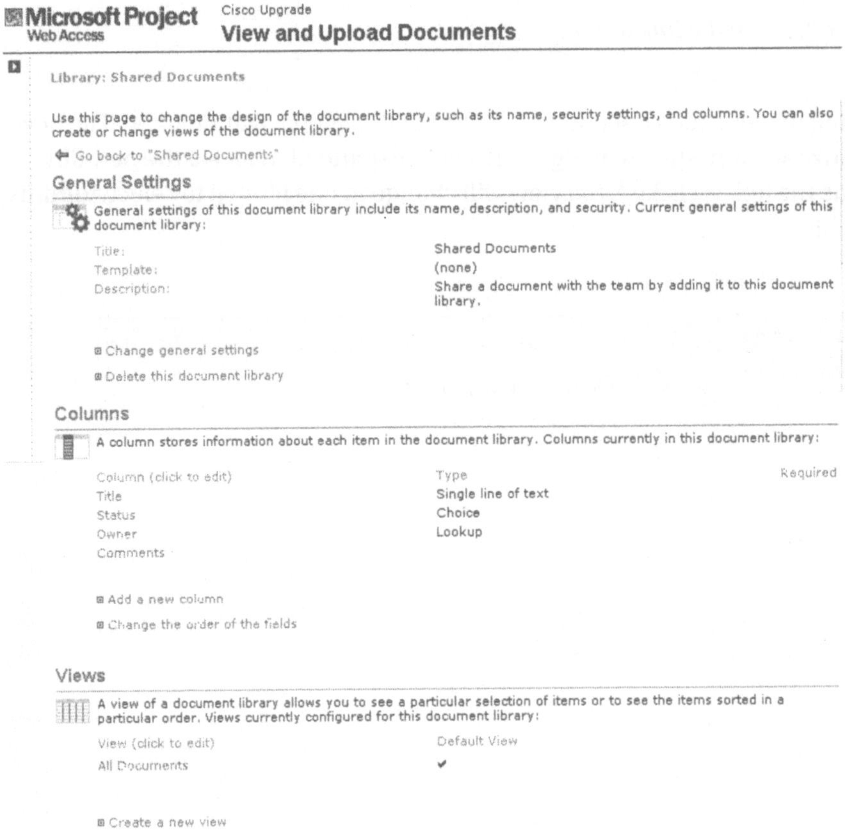

Figure 15-29. Modify the settings and columns display

Adding Columns

Whether you're working with lists or document libraries, clicking "Add a new column" displays the add column page shown in Figure 15-30. Give your new column a name and select a data type from the radio button list. Provide additional descriptive information and determine whether the field is required, has a default value, or should be restricted in size.

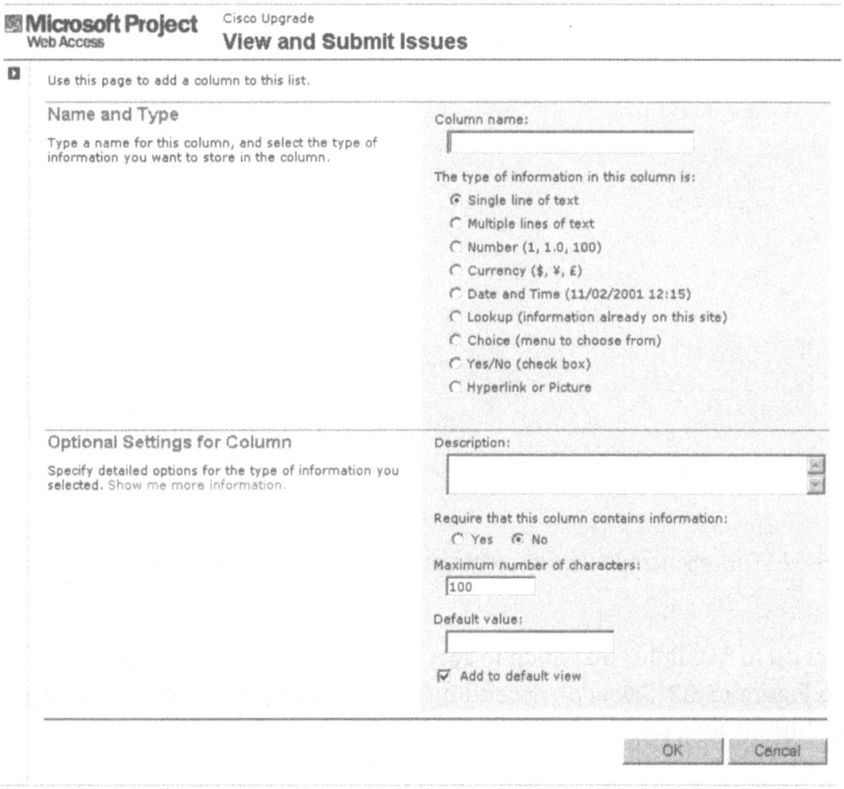

Figure 15-30. Add a column to a SharePoint Team Services list.

Adding Views

Selecting "Create a new view" in either the documents or issues page displays the add view page shown in Figure 15-31. Create a new view for your list area by giving it a new name and then selecting the columns to display and setting their display order. The system automatically enumerates these for you in the display.

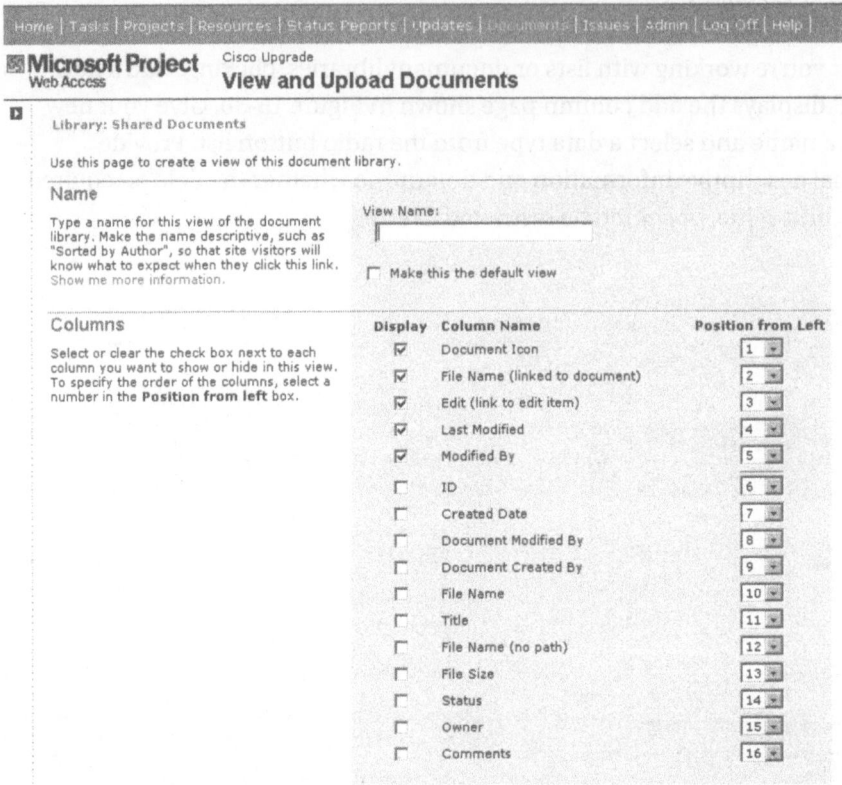

Figure 15-31. Name your view and select the columns to display.

Select up to two fields on which to sort your new view. Use the pick list fields shown in Figure 15-32. Select an ascending or descending sort order by changing the radio button selected.

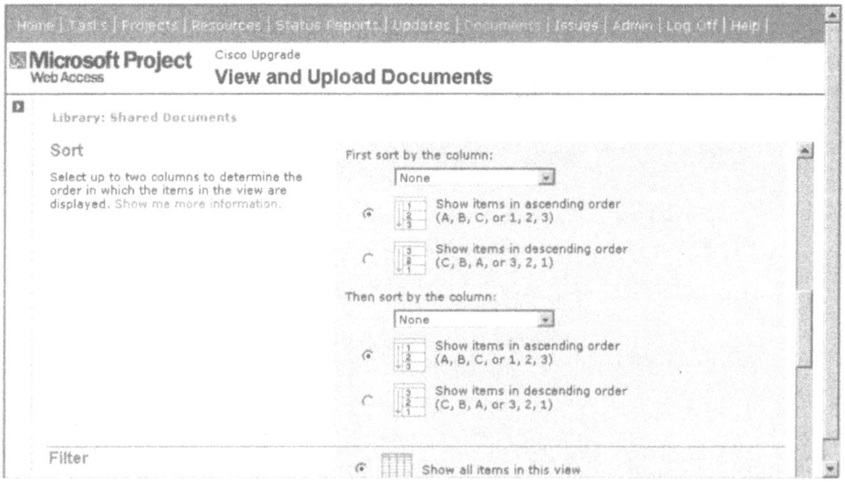

Figure 15-32. Determine the sorting for your new view.

To apply filtering to your view, change the radio button selection to show items only when the following is true, as shown in Figure 15-33. The system allows you to set an and-relationship to nest two conditions in your filter or set an or-relationship to test for alternatives. All columns in the view display in the field pick list. Set the following tests on the fields:

- is equal to

- is not equal to

- is greater than

- is less than

- is greater than or equal to

- is less than or equal to

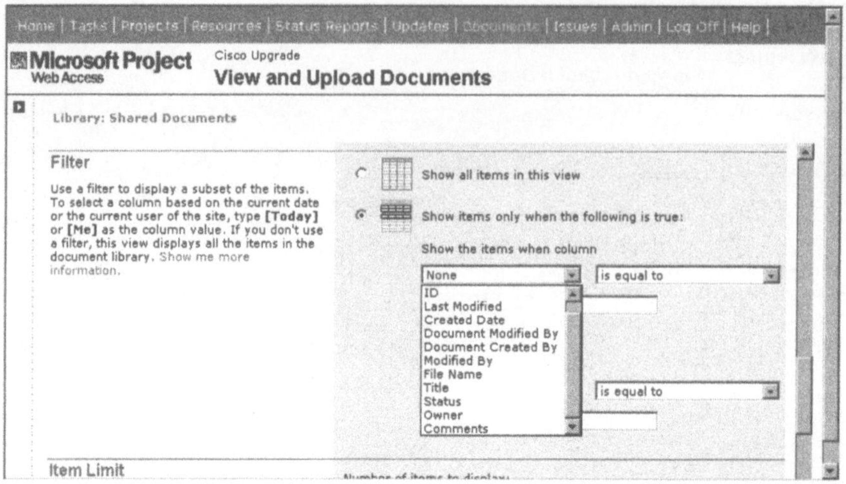

Figure 15-33. Set filtering on the view.

Finally, the system allows you to set the maximum number of records returned by a view either in total or as a batch. As shown in Figure 15-34, this setting allows you to control performance to some degree by allowing you to choose the batch size of records returned by the system or by setting a hard limit maximum. Apply hard limits only when you know they make sense, such as a view meant to show only the latest 50 additions to the library.

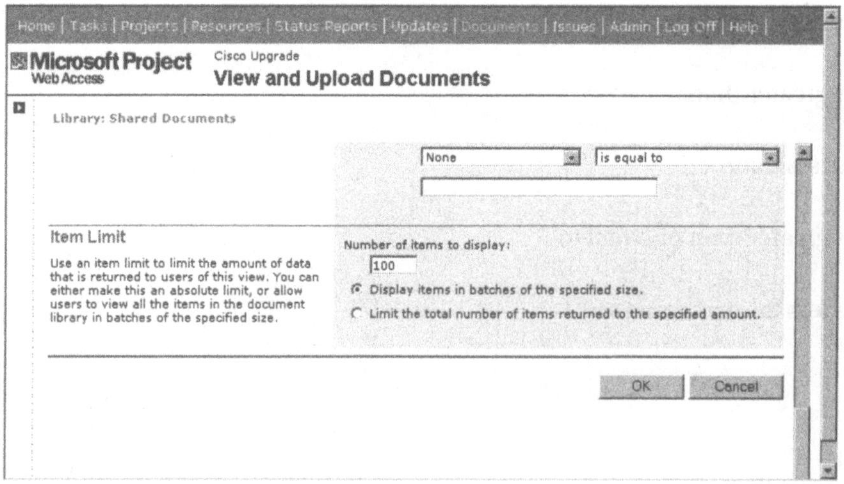

Figure 15-34. Set an item limit.

Deleting and Changing General Settings for Document Libraries

Inasmuch as the system allows you to create document libraries at will, it also gives you the opportunity to delete them or change their characteristics so that you can repurpose them from time to time. The General Settings area of the modify settings page, shown in Figure 15-35, contains a "Delete this document library" link. Clicking the link displays an alert box where the system gives you one last chance to confirm the deletion or cancel the operation. Click Cancel to abort or OK to continue. Note that a deletion isn't reversible.

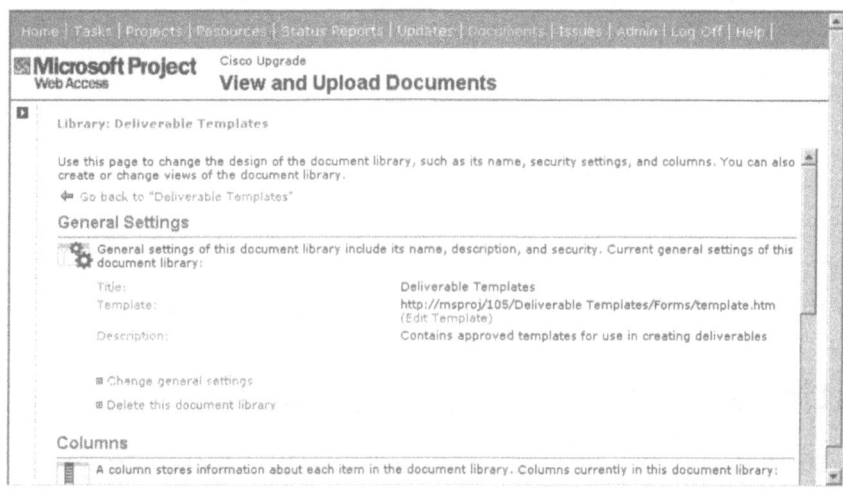

Figure 15-35. The document library General Settings area

You can change the name of a document library by clicking the "Change general settings" link in the General Settings area. Clicking the link displays the page shown in Figure 15-36. Change the name and description in the fields provided. Set the base template for the documents created within the library by setting the URL in the field provided. Determine who has permission to modify the library by accepting the default, Everyone, or restrict it to the creator of the library, the project manager who published the project plan the first time.

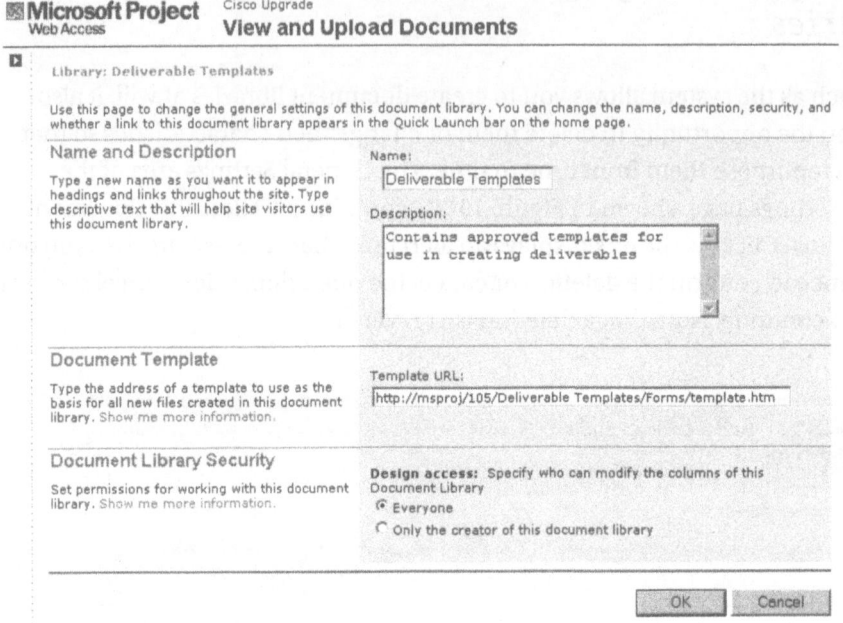

Figure 15-36. The document library settings

Requesting and Responding to Status Reports

Selecting Status Reports from the main menu in Project Web Access takes you to the "Status reports overview" page shown in Figure 15-37. Team members don't see the "Request a status report" section by default. This selection is dependent on permissions granted in groups and categories.

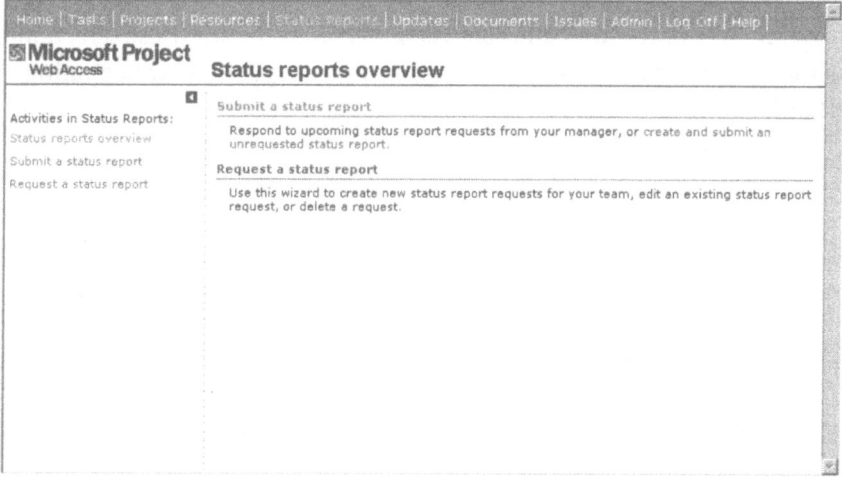

Figure 15-37. The "Status reports overview" page

Requesting a Status Report

Use the "Request a status report" feature to create periodic status reports that will be due on a regular basis. Clicking the "Request a status report" link displays the "Request a status report" page shown in Figure 15-38. Here you must select your action before selecting a status report. Assuming this is the first time you're encountering this feature, I'll begin with creating a new status report.

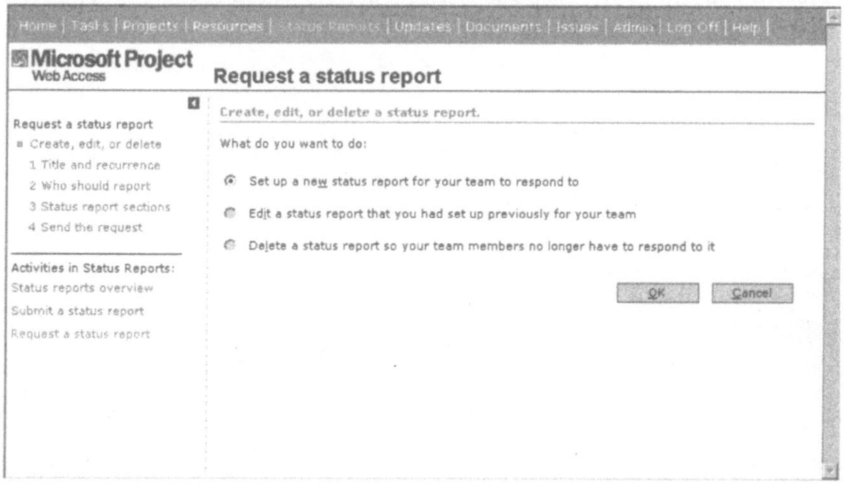

Figure 15-38. Selecting a status report action

In step 1, as shown in Figure 15-39, you give the status report a name and determine its recurrence rate and due date. As shown in the figure, these selections determine that this will be a weekly status report due every Thursday beginning March 20, 2003.

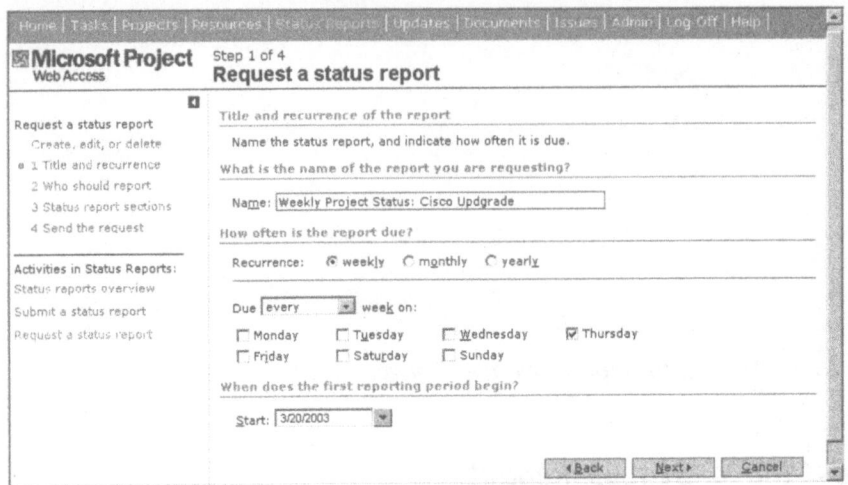

Figure 15-39. Step 1 involves entering a title and determining recurrence.

Click Next to advance to step 2, as shown in Figure 15-40. In this step, you choose the resources that are to report. Note the check box that appears next to each name on the right as you add names to the selection. The Merge box indicates that the system will merge the responses into a consolidated status report. You'll see the effect of this later in this section.

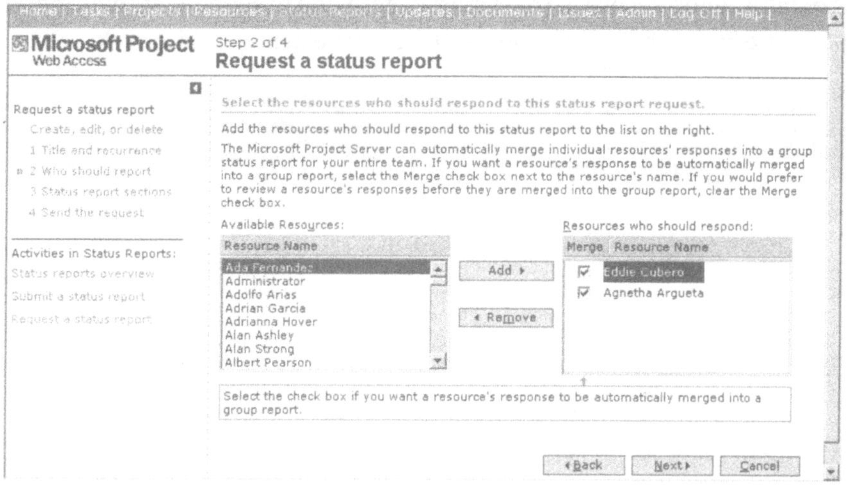

Figure 15-40. In step 2 you select the resources that must respond to the status report.

In step 3, shown in Figure 15-41, you configure the status report sections. By default, the system inserts the sections shown in the figure. You can delete them, reorder them, rename them, accept them as they are, or add to them. I'll leave the defaults.

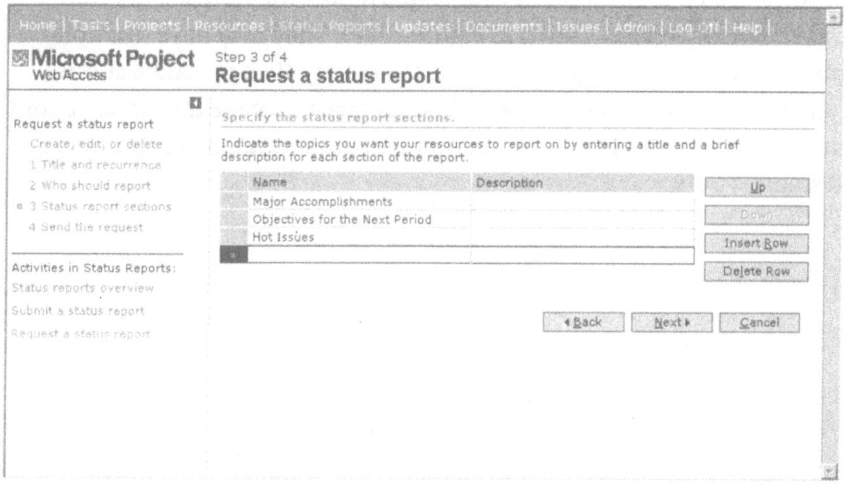

Figure 15-41. You determine status report sections in step 3.

Step 4 is simply an opportunity to go back through your selections or confirm the status report creation, as shown in Figure 15-42. Click Save to confirm and create the status report record in the system. Click Send to send the status report to the respondents immediately without waiting for the next periodic cycle.

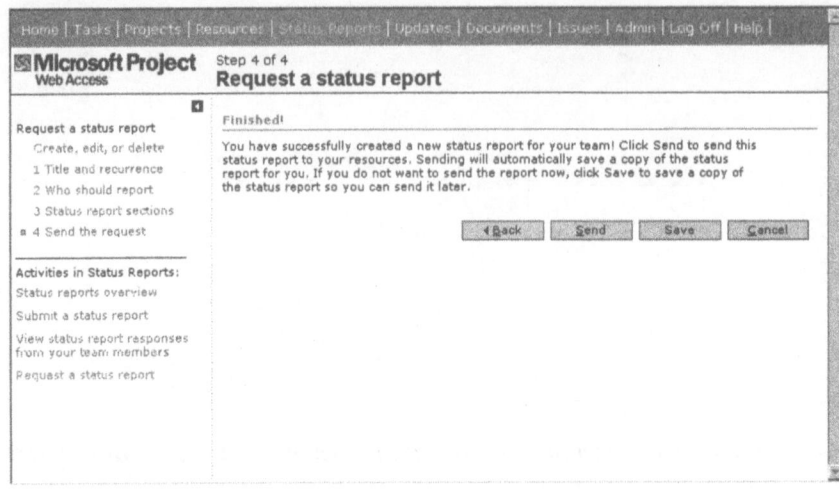

Figure 15-42. In step 4 you confirm the status report creation.

Responding to a Status Report

Users that you selected to respond to your status report will now see the status report on their home page, as shown in Figure 15-43. They may have multiple status reports created by multiple managers. Users may elect to send a status report at any time without a requirement that a request precede the status report. Creating a nonrequested status report follows the same workflow as submitting a requested status report.

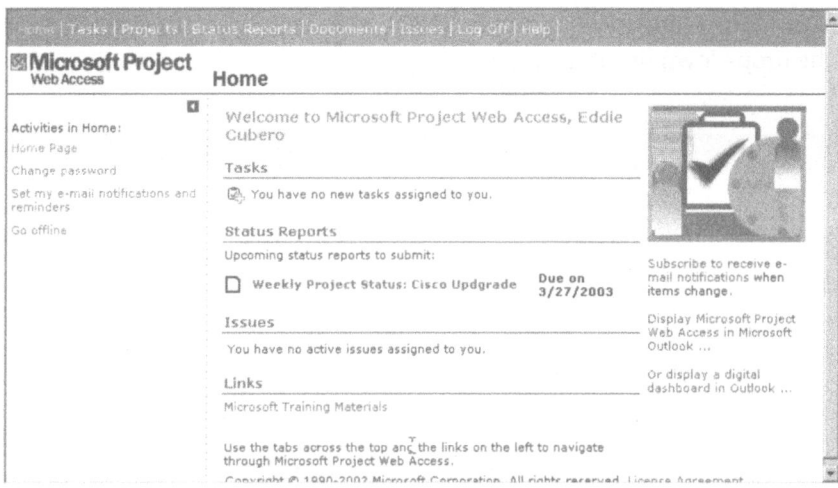

Figure 15-43. A user's home page showing an upcoming status report

Clicking Status Reports in the main menu takes the user to his or her personal status reports page, as shown in Figure 15-44. All upcoming status reports show here as well as the home page.

Figure 15-44. The status reports home page for a resource

Clicking the link for a specific status report takes the user to the "Submit a status report" page shown in Figure 15-45. Notice that the default sections I accepted when creating the status report now display as entry areas for the user to input data. Clicking into an area causes the editing toolbar to display for that section. In the figure, I've selected major accomplishments. Use the toolbar to apply rich text formatting to your entries. Select other users to cc: the status report to using the drop-down list at the top.

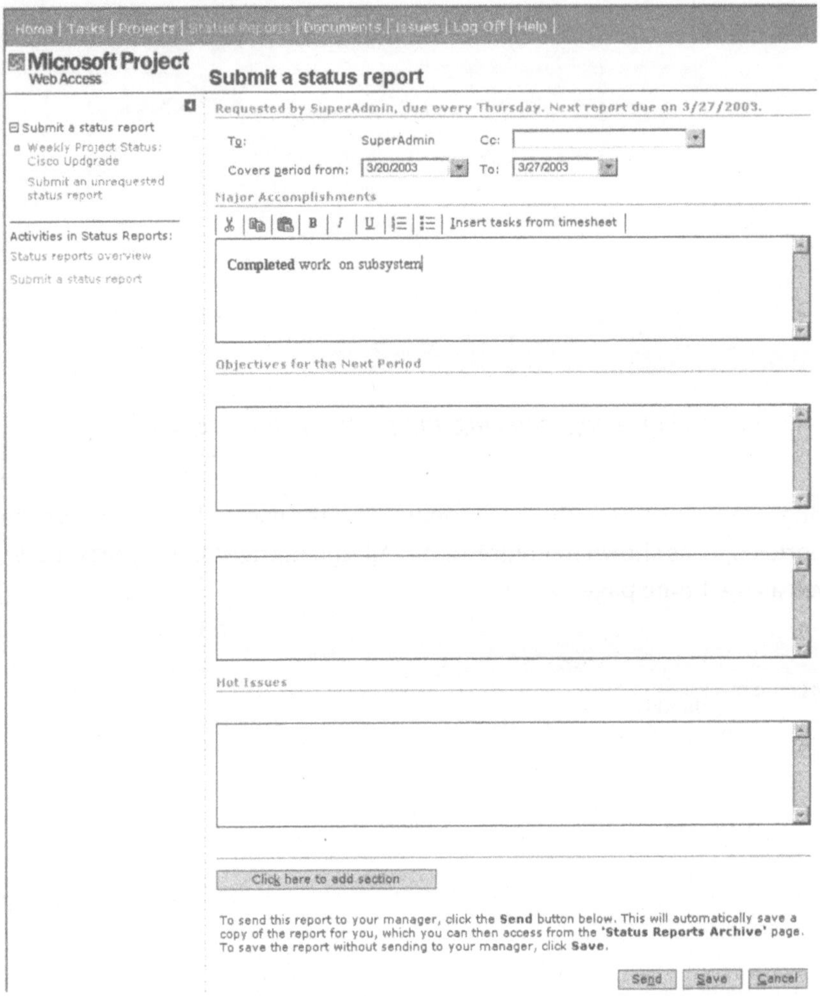

Figure 15-45. The "Submit a status report" page

Use the "Insert tasks from timesheet" link to link to timesheet tasks. Selecting tasks in the resulting display allows you to bring the task names into the status report. Click Send when you're through. Click the Save button if you prefer to save the status report and send it later.

Viewing Status Report Responses

Like other important activities, the availability of new status report responses is announced on a manager's home page, as shown in Figure 15-46.

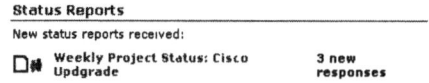

Figure 15-46. The home page section displaying status report responses

Click the link on the home page or first navigate to the status reports home page and select the specific status report to view the responses. Selecting a status report opens the "View status report responses from your team members" page shown in Figure 15-47. As weeks accrue, you see more columns in the display representing additional weeks. You can scroll through the weeks to view previously submitted reports. Note that the title of the report displays at the top of the page.

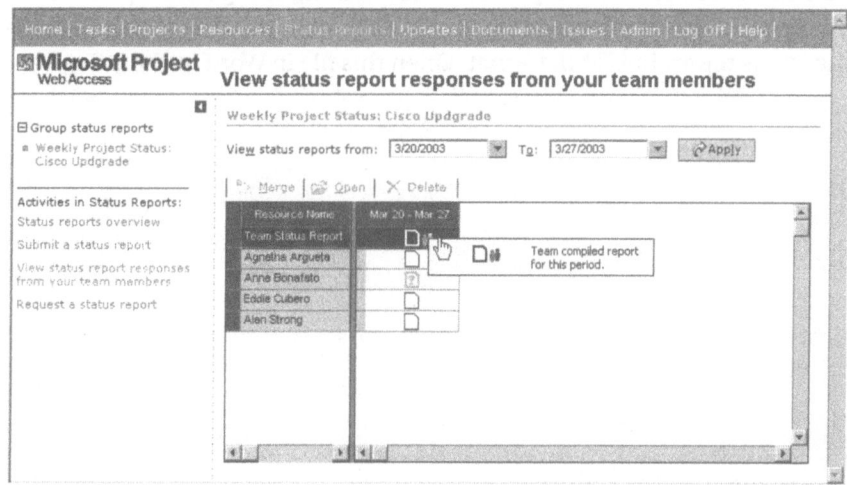

Figure 15-47. The "View status report responses from your team members" page

Click the status report icon in the date range column to open the specific report. In the display, the team status report is the automatically merged report relative to having set the option to merge the reports. Click either an individual icon or the team status icon to open the respective report. Clicking the icon for the team status report opens the report, as shown in Figure 15-48. Each section of the report displays each team member's response by name and date. Scroll down the page to read responses in all sections.

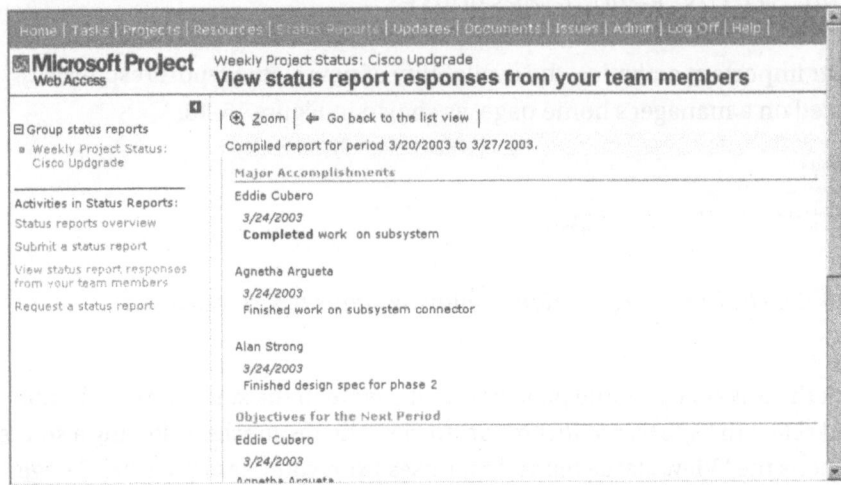

Figure 15-48. A compiled status report

Use the Zoom button at the top of the compiled status report to open the report in a new window, as shown in Figure 15-49. From here, select File ➤ Save As to save the status report in HTML format. Open this file in Word or FrontPage to edit it.

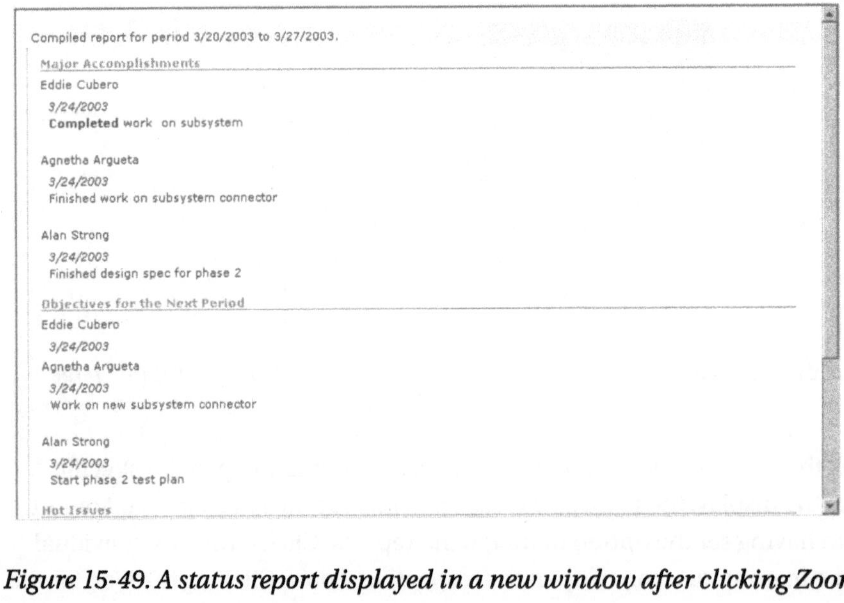

Figure 15-49. A status report displayed in a new window after clicking Zoom

TIP Upload the saved copies of the consolidated status reports to the project document library to share them with the team and stakeholders. Distribute these by e-mail as well.

Editing and Deleting Status Reports

When you select either the "Edit a status report" or "Delete a status report" radio button on the "Request a status report" page, the display changes to allow you to select an existing status report, as shown in Figure 15-50. If you select "Edit a status report," the system takes you through the status report screens and allows you to make changes. If you choose "Delete a status report," the system asks you for confirmation before deleting the status report and all responses to it in the system.

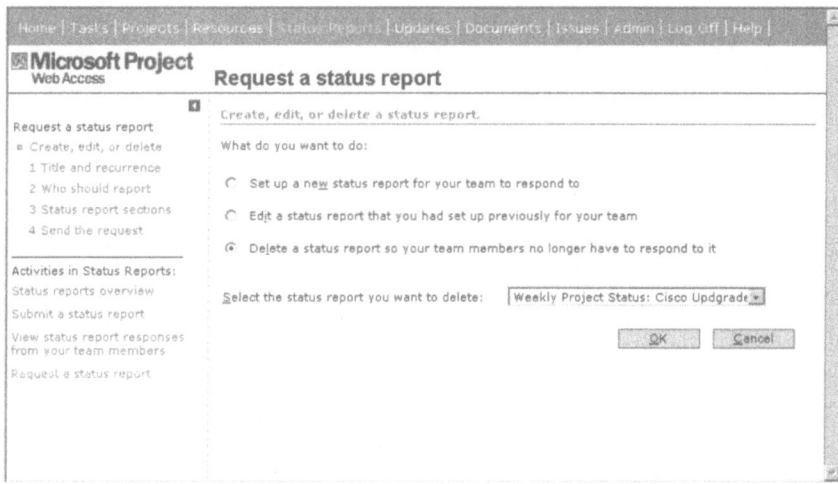

Figure 15-50. Request a status report.

Summary

Project Server provides a host of collaborative features to support team interaction on project work. The system supports collaboration with a rich reminders engine and centralized issues and project document sharing. Status reports round out the supporting cast of features that promote communication among team members.

CHAPTER 16

Viewing and Analyzing Resource and Project Information

Your new Project Server implementation is now active with projects and resources. You and your resources are tracking project progress by updating timesheets and sending updates on a periodic basis. It's now time to learn how to take advantage of the views and analysis features that provide useful information to drive your project decision-making into the future. (You may want to photocopy this chapter for your end users.)

Working in the Resource Center

Reached by clicking Resources in the main navigation menu in Project Web Access, the Resource Center displays all resources available in the enterprise resource pool. The default display, shown in Figure 16-1, lists all resources in the system. You can edit some resource details through the interface, link to the Analyzer to examine resource information in more depth, or view resource assignments from this page.

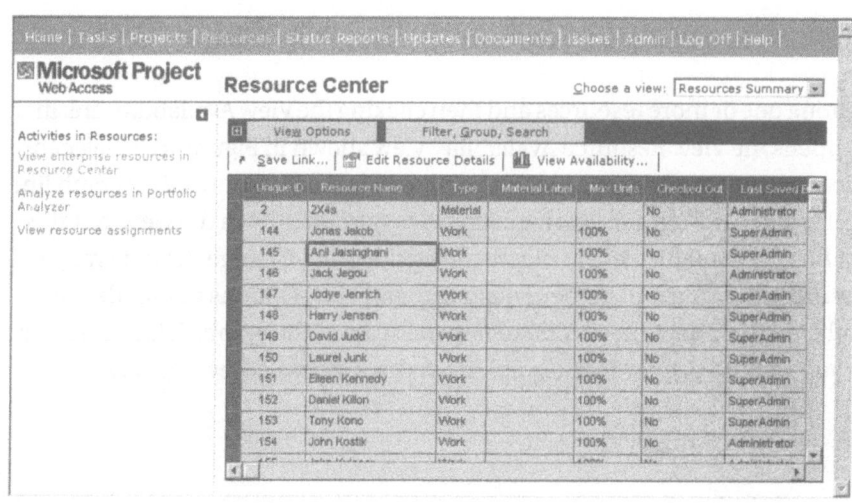

Figure 16-1. The Resource Center default view

In the upper-right corner of the page, the "Choose a view" selector allows you to select any view defined in the system for the Resource Center. The view shown in Figure 16-1 is the only view included in the Resource Center by default. Highlight a resource and then click Edit Resource Details in the toolbar to edit details for the selected resource. Clicking the link displays the view shown in Figure 16-2. You may edit only custom enterprise fields that you designed for your resource pool through this page.

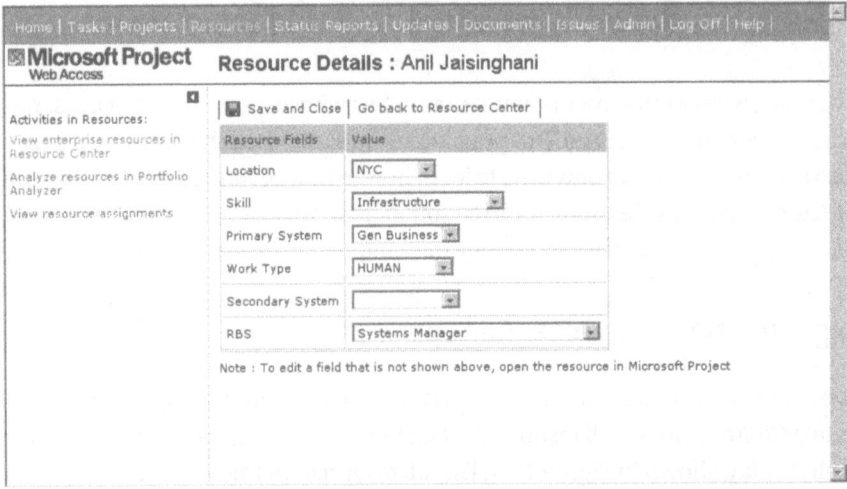

Figure 16-2. Edit resource details.

Viewing Resource Availability

Highlighting one or more resources and then clicking the View Availability link in the toolbar opens the View Resource Availability view shown in Figure 16-3. Select or deselect a resource to show or hide the graph line for that resource. The graph line for each resource is a unique color, making it easy to identify in the view, but this may not be very readable here in black-and-white print. Change the date range of the view using the date tool in the toolbar. Expand View Options to broaden or narrow the date window, thereby changing the scale of the graph. Select the information you want to display in the graph from the "Choose a view" pick list:

- Assignment Work by resource

- Assignment Work by project

- Remaining Availability

- Work

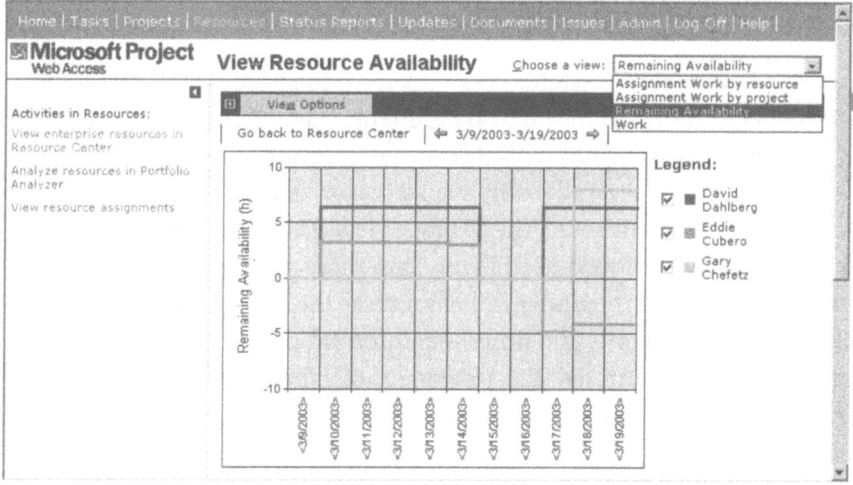

Figure 16-3. View the remaining availability for selected resources.

Selecting the "Assignment Work by project" option changes the view to show both project work assigned and remaining availability, as shown in Figure 16-4. This view makes the most sense when you're viewing data for one resource only. You can selectively change the graph by selecting and deselecting the projects that the resource is assigned to.

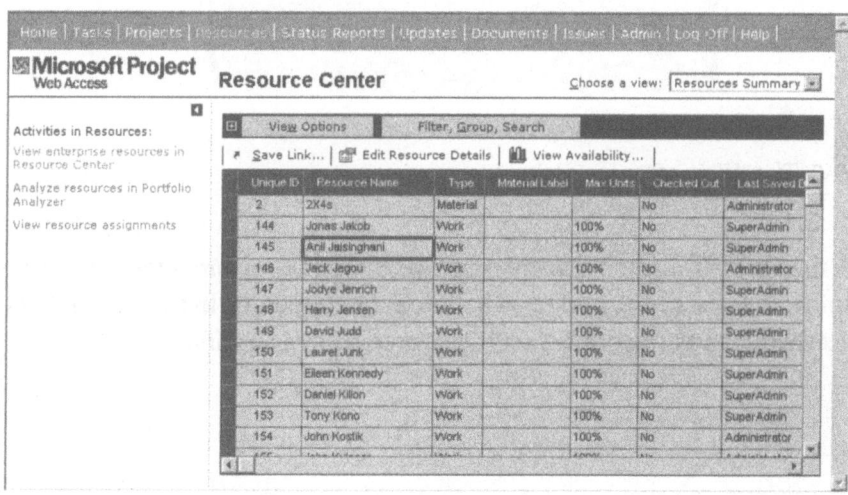

Figure 16-4. View the assignment work by project.

Viewing Resource Assignments

Selecting the "View resource assignments" link from the Resource Center Activities menu displays the "View resource assignments" view shown in Figure 16-5. The view renders with a Gantt chart display sorted by resource and then by project. By default, the Summary view is the only available view in the Assignments section unless you've added views through the Manage views interface. Notice that the task indicators you've previously seen in the Timesheet and Updates views also appear in this view. This isn't surprising inasmuch as the Assignments view is your window into user assignments and timesheet information. You can link documents and issues to tasks through this view in exactly the same way you did through the Timesheet and Updates views.

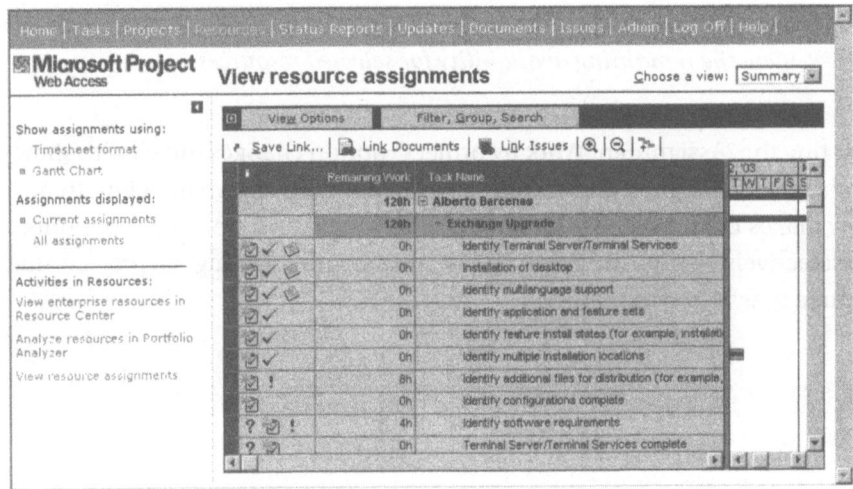

Figure 16-5. The "View resource assignments" view

Click the Filter, Group, Search tab in the view to set a custom filter or change the grouping. In Figure 16-6, I selected a custom filter opening in the More Filters dialog box shown. In the example I set the filter to show a specific resource.

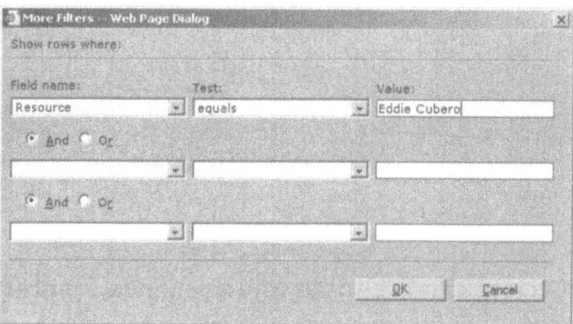

Figure 16-6. Set the filter in the More Filters dialog box.

The resulting view, shown in Figure 16-7, displays data for only the selected resource.

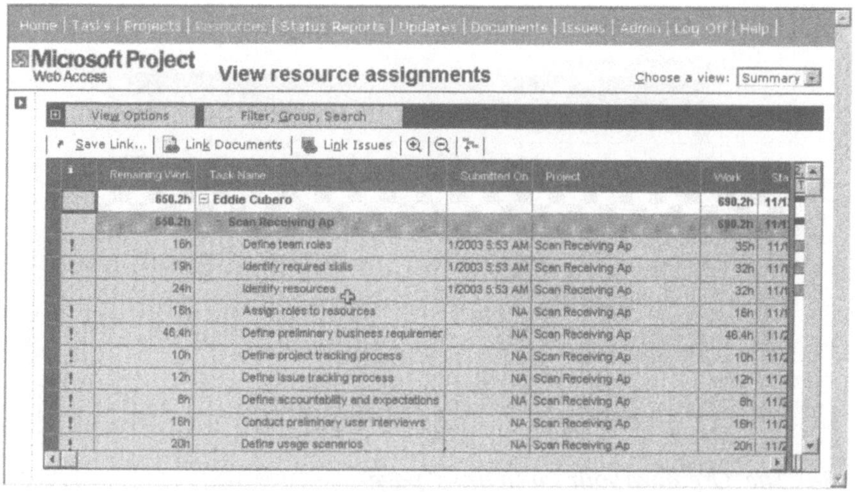

Figure 16-7. View assignments for one resource only.

Click the Save Link button on the toolbar to save a link to the view with any custom grouping you've applied. Enter a name for your new link in the Save Link dialog box shown in Figure 16-8. The system doesn't save filtering information in this view; it saves only grouping information. A Saved Links section appears in the upper-left navigation once you click Save.

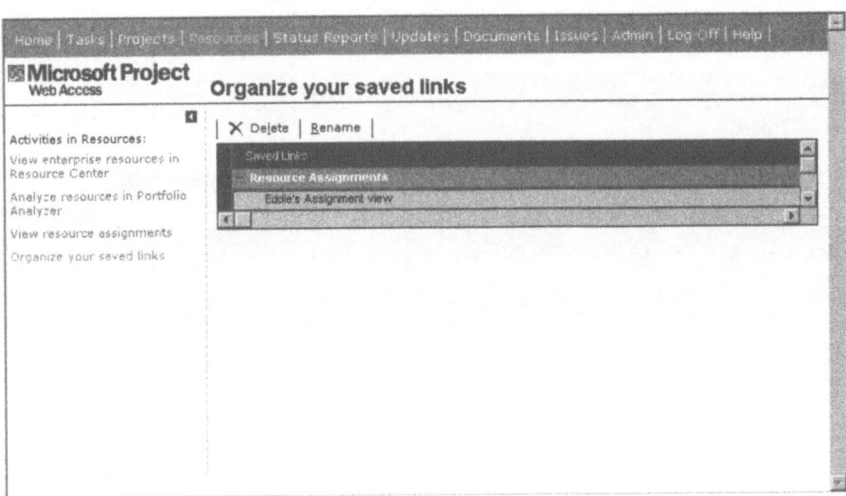

Figure 16-8. The Save Link dialog box

Any view area for which you've created links also displays a new menu item in the Activities area. "Organize your saved links" is added to the menu selections. Clicking this selection displays the "Organize your saved links" page, as shown in Figure 16-9. This behavior applies to any views area that offers saved links. Delete or modify your links from this page. Deleting a link can't be undone.

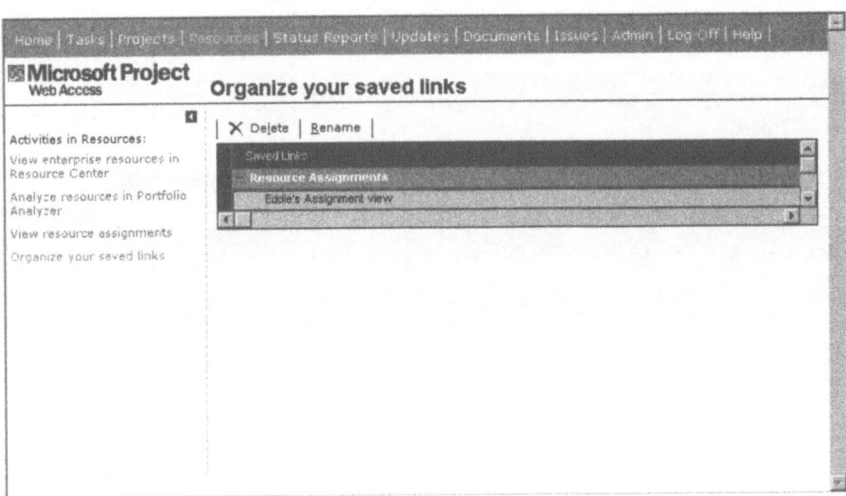

Figure 16-9. The "Organize your saved links" page

Working in the Project Center

The Project Center is the distribution hub for project information access and analysis in Project Web Access. The Project Center home page expresses portfolio-level views, and you can click a project from any Project Center view in order to access detailed project views that allow you to drill down into project detail.

You access core Project Server analysis features from the Project Center. You'll find both Analyzer views and Portfolio Modeler links on the Project Center Activities menu. Rounding out the activities in the Project Center are links for creating and managing to-do lists in Project Web Access. To-do lists are driven by Share-Point Team Services and offer what you might consider task management "lite."

Using Project Center Views

The Project Center home page is your primary source for two-dimensional presentation of your project portfolio. The system provides four standard views, all of which display a Gantt chart. In the figures included in this section, I minimized the amount of screen used by the Gantt chart.

- *Summary:* This view displays project vital statistics including start, finish, percent complete, total work, and project owner. (See Figure 16-10.)

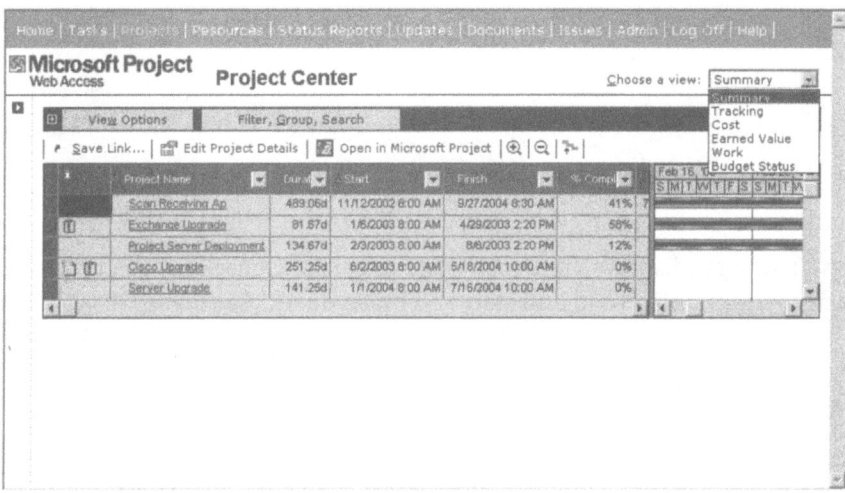

Figure 16-10. The Project Center Summary view

- *Tracking:* This view displays start, finish, actual start, actual finish, baseline start and finish, percent complete, duration, actual duration, remaining duration, actual cost, and actual work. (See Figure 16-11.)

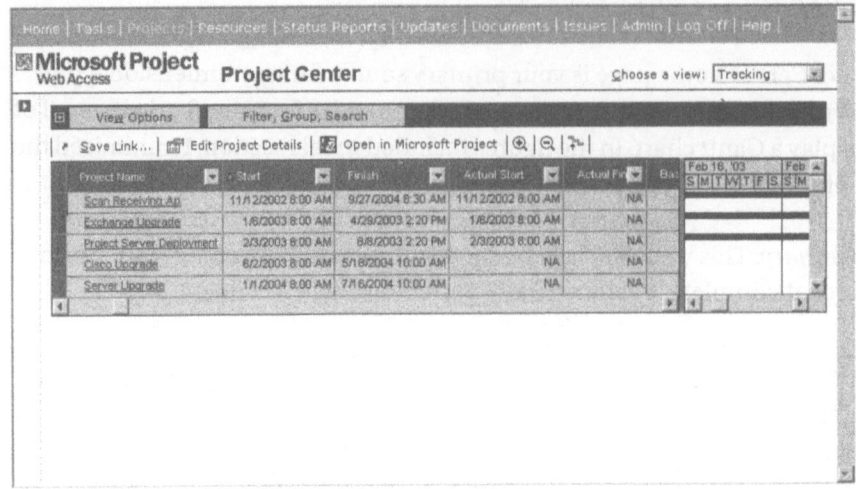

Figure 16-11. The Project Center Tracking view

- *Cost:* This view displays fixed cost, cost, actual cost, baseline cost, cost variance, remaining cost, and start and finish dates. (See Figure 16-12.)

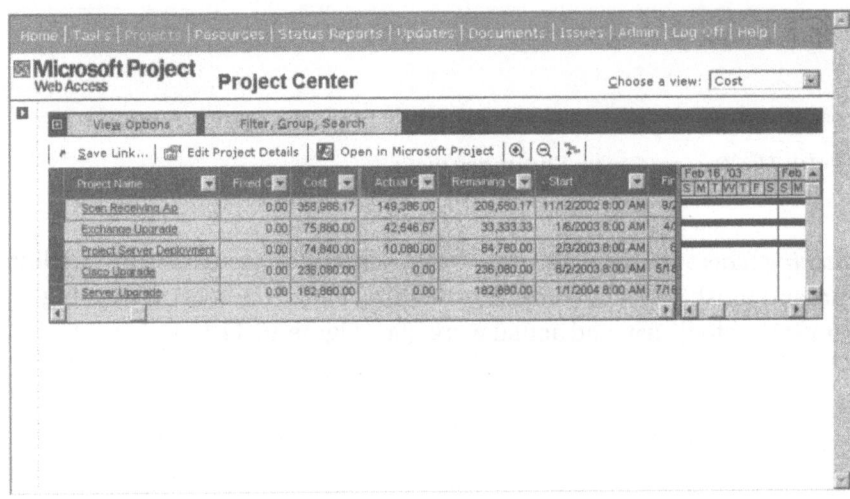

Figure 16-12. The Project Center Cost view

- *Earned Value:* This view displays calculated earned value at the project level, including BCWS, BCWP, ACWP, VAC, schedule variance, cost variance, and baseline cost, as well as start and finish dates. (See Figure 16-13.) Note that no baselines are set on the sample projects in the figure. Consequently, some totals are incorrect or missing.

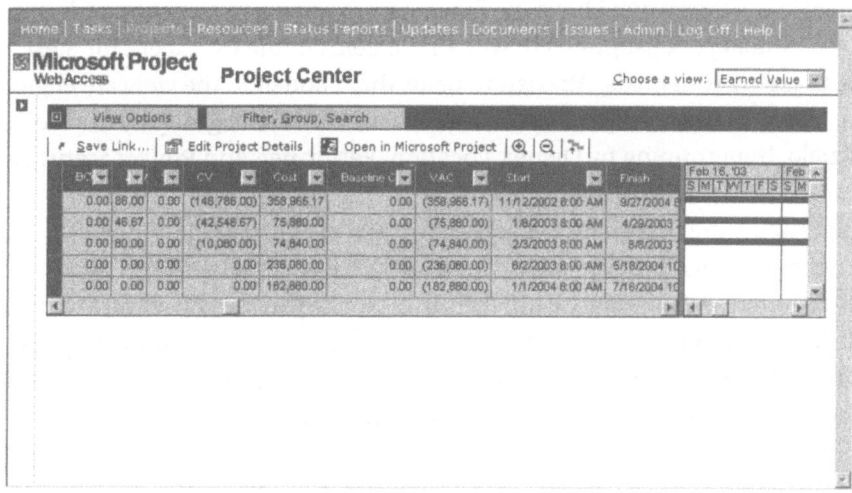

Figure 16-13. The Project Center Earned Value view

In addition to the standard views, each view that you add to the Project Center also shows up in the view pick list in the upper-right corner of the page. The Project Center is a great forum for the use of graphical indicators. It begs for them. Figure 16-14 is a view created for a Microsoft demo database called A Datum. This is the A Datum Executive Summary view, which displays two columns of red, yellow, and green stoplight icons for budget and schedule performance.

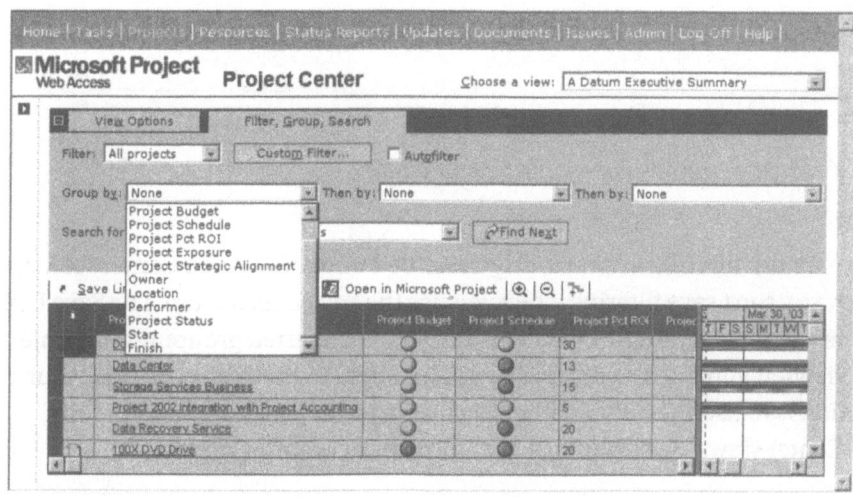

Figure 16-14. A custom Project Center view with a partial Group by pick list exposed

Notice in the figure that I have the Filter, Group, Search options expanded and the Group by field pick list pulled down. All the fields in the list except for Start and Finish are custom fields. All custom fields that I added to the view are eligible to group by. Using the example data, it wouldn't make sense to group by the Project Pct ROI field, but grouping by Owner, Location, Performer, and Project Status is very likely to yield added insight.

When I apply the project owner as the group by in Figure 16-15, Chris Preston's Project Schedule field indicators are all red and Judy Lew's second and third projects show red as well. How would seeing this make you feel if you were Chris or Judy? Recognize that this is powerful stuff. The fact that these two project managers handle the lion's share of the difficult projects from an exposure perspective, in theory, suggests to me a more systemic resource availability or performance issue in the enterprise.

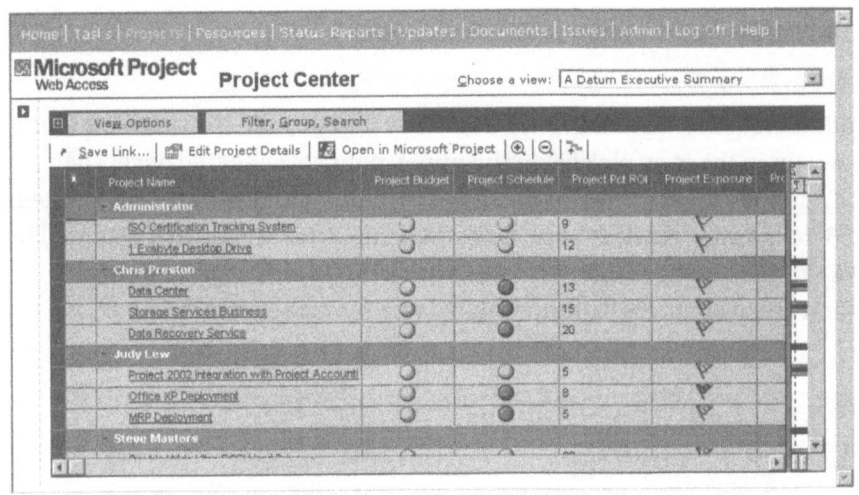

Figure 16-15. Add one level of grouping and viola!

You can use filtering as previously described under Resource Center views; however, you can't save filtering when you use the Save Link feature. The Save Link feature is a dandy way for individual users to save preferred groupings for Project Center views. If you need to provide prefiltered data to the Project Center, your best option is to use the built-in filters available when you create and modify Project Center views. See Chapter 12 to learn about building views.

Editing Project Details and Opening Projects

When you click into any single project field, the grid marks it for selection except the Project Name field, which contains a link that navigates you to detailed project views. Once you've selected a single project, clicking Edit Project Details displays the Project Details page for the current project. All applicable enterprise project fields and outline codes are displayed and editable through the interface shown in Figure 16-16 if you have the correct permissions. Enterprise project fields are the only project-level information that you can edit through Project Web Access.

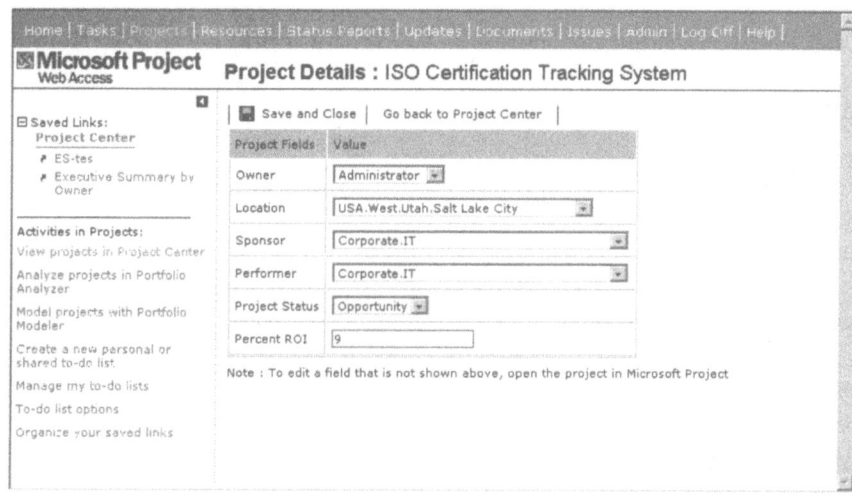

Figure 16-16. Edit project details through Project Web Access.

Clicking the Open in Microsoft Project link on the toolbar launches Microsoft Project Professional, if it isn't already started, and checks out and loads the project you selected in the grid. After completing the logon ritual according to the preferences you set, you can proceed to edit your project.

TIP Because you can access Project Center views in the Project Professional interface, you can use the Open in Microsoft Project feature to build views to help users locate files in a very large portfolio. The file open feature doesn't provide grouping or filtering capabilities, whereas Project Center views do.

Working with Detailed Project Views

Clicking the Project Name field in the grid of any Project Center view takes you to the View a Project page. The system remembers which detailed view you selected the last time you visited and defaults to that when you select a project. Project views come in three basic flavors: tasks, assignments, and resources. You get 19 views to use out of the box. In order of appearance in the "Choose a view" pick list, they are as follows:

- Tasks Summary

- Tasks Top-Level

- Tasks Detail

- Tasks Leveling

- Tasks Tracking

- Tasks Cost

- Tasks Earned Value

- Tasks Schedule

- Tasks Work

- Assignments Summary

- Assignments Detail

- Assignments Tracking

- Assignments Cost

- Assignments Earned Value

- Assignments Work

- Resources Summary

- Resources Cost

- Resources Work

- Resources Earned Value

Like Project Center views, you can use the Save Link feature to save your preferred groupings of these views. Figure 16-17 shows the Assignments Summary
view with grouping applied by resource name. Note also that the "Choose a view"
pick list is expanded. Use the plus sign (+) and minus sign (–) magnifying glass
icons to change the timescale of the Gantt chart in the display. You can walk a scale
from 15-minute intervals to years. The small connected-task icon on the toolbar is
a navigational tool that shifts the Gantt display to the record selected in the grid.

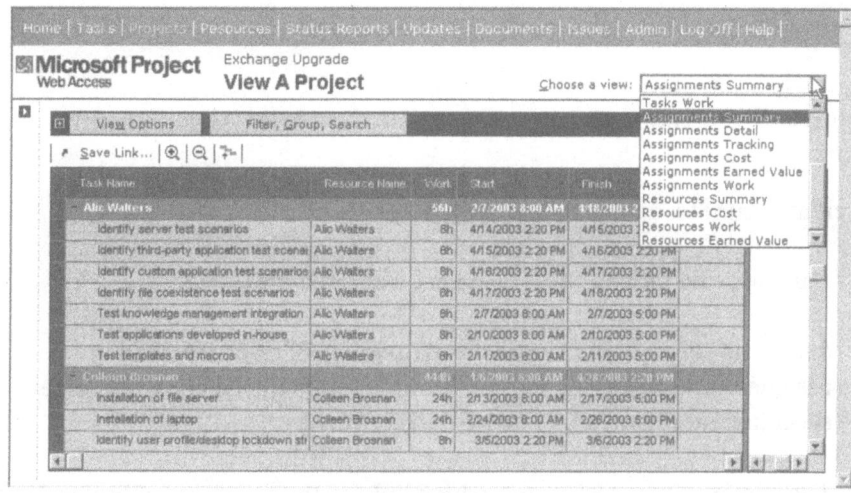

Figure 16-17. The Assignment Summary view grouped by resource name

Working with To-Do Lists

To-do lists provide an informal task management tool. They provide a flexible
forum for managing task work that's significant enough that you want to formally
record it but not formally manage it. Although tasks created on to-do lists are dis-
playable in the timesheet, they can't accept progress reporting. As shown in
Figure 16-18, clicking "Create a new personal or shared to-do list" from the Activities menu takes you the "Create a new personal or shared to-do list" page.

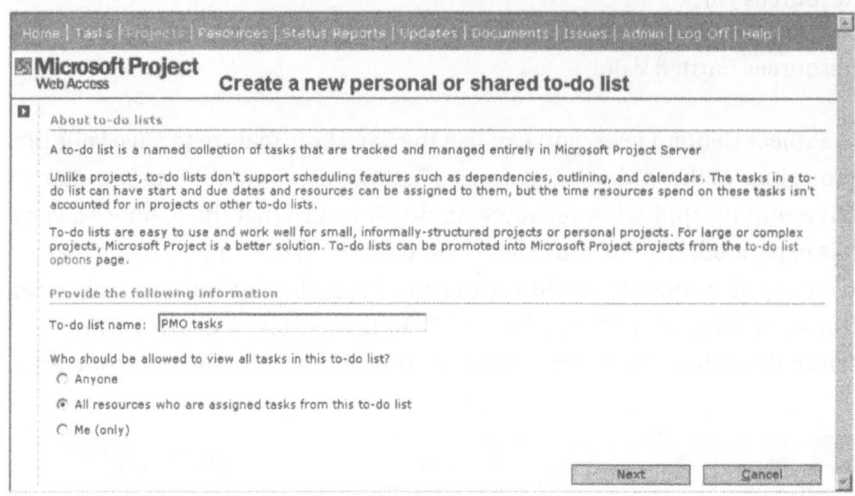

Figure 16-18. The "Create a new personal or shared to-do list" page

To create a new to-do list, follow these steps:

1. Enter a name for your new to-do list. I entered **PMO tasks**.

2. Select the access rule to apply from Anyone, All resources who are assigned tasks from this to-do list, or Me (only) by selecting the corresponding radio button. Click Next to continue.

3. The "Create a new task" page, which links to the tasks area of Project Web Access, displays as shown in Figure 16-19. This version of the page is specific to creating tasks for to-do lists. Insert and delete tasks in the grid using the corresponding tools on the toolbar. Note that you can assign a resource to a task by selecting from a pick list as shown in the figure.

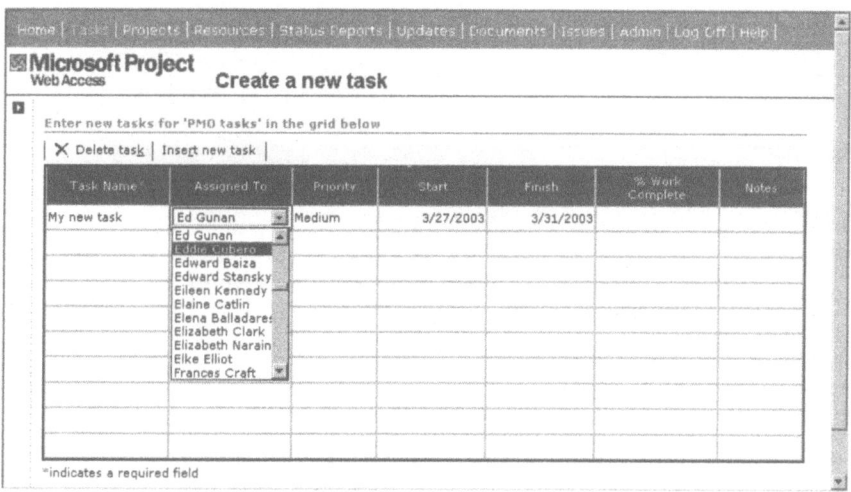

Figure 16-19. Create new to-do list tasks.

4. Click "Create new tasks" to complete your entries. The system accepts and saves your entries and displays the "Manage my to-do lists" page shown in Figure 16-20. Notice that to-do lists are represented as groupings of tasks in this view. You can also access this view directly by clicking the "Manage my to-do lists" link on the Project Center Activities menu. Notice the icons in the indicators column in the display. The stacked clipboards icon indicates it's a to-do list task. The other indicator visible indicates that the to-do task is a new assignment using the icon used in the Timesheet view. To insert notes, click the Insert Notes link in the toolbar. Clicking the New Task(s) button at the top of the page takes you to the "Create a new task" page you saw previously in Figure 16-19.

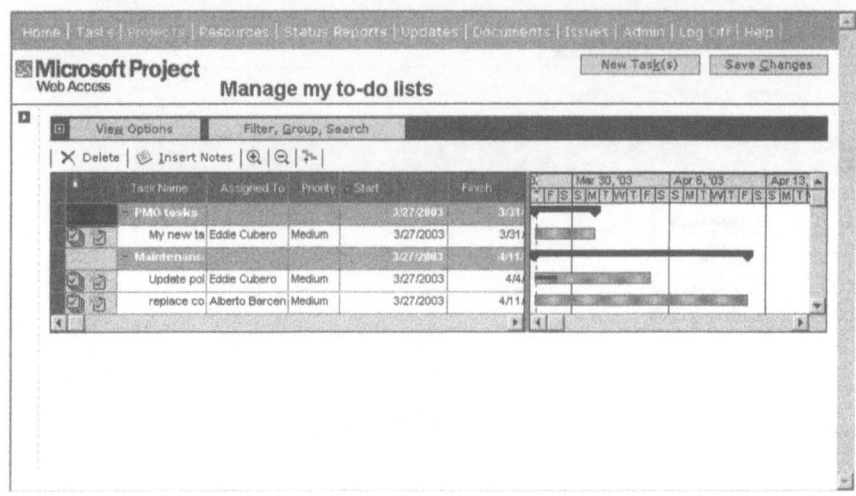

Figure 16-20. The "Manage my to-do lists" page

The remaining to-do list menu selection on the Project Center Activities menu is "To-do list options." Clicking this selection opens the "To-do list options" page shown in Figure 16-21. The following are the selections on this page:

- *Rename this to-do list* allows you to change a to-do list name.

- *Transfer this to-do list* allows you to transfer ownership of the to-do list to another system user by selecting his or her name from a pick list.

- *Promote this to-do list to a project* opens Project 2002 Professional if it's not already open and writes all the tasks and resource information in the to-do list into a new project file that you can then save to Project Server.

- *Permanently delete this to-do list* allows you to delete a to-do list.

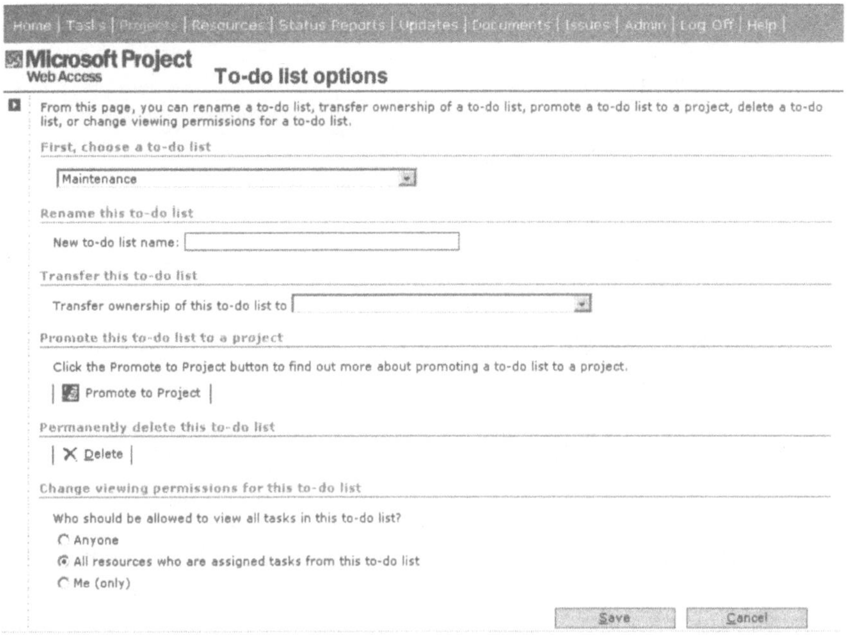

Figure 16-21. To-do list options

Note that you first select a to-do list by name from the to-do list pick list and then apply one of the previously listed actions to the list. These are simple functions and don't require much more in-depth examination.

Organizing Your Saved Links

Now that you've created some to-do lists and some saved view links, the view you get of the Project Center has changed to reflect these additions. In Figure 16-22, notice that there's now a Saved Links section above the Activities menu on the Project Center home page. You should also take note that there's a new menu selection that you haven't seen before: "Organize your saved links." In the figure, I expanded the View Options tab to show you the check box for displaying to-do lists in the particular Project Center view. To-do lists are now displayed in the Project Center view as well.

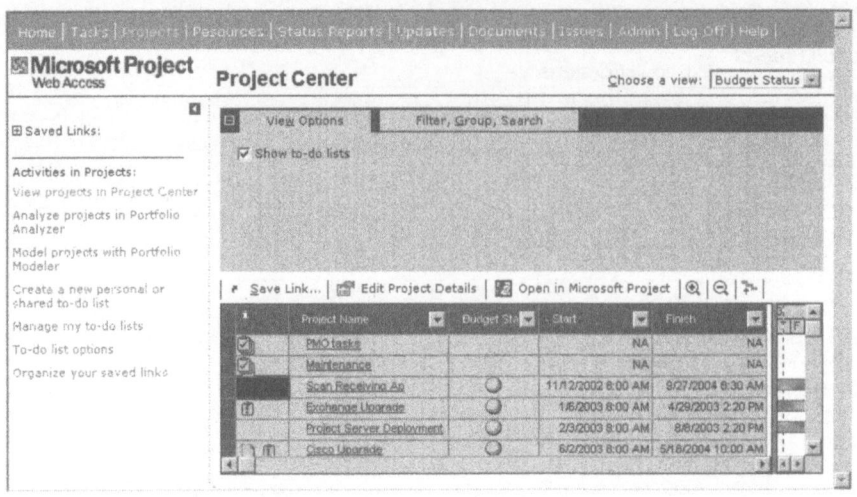

Figure 16-22. The Project Center home page displaying to-do lists along with projects

Clicking the "Organize your saved links" menu selection displays the "Organize your saved links" page shown in Figure 16-23. You can either rename a link from here or delete it entirely. Select the link name in the grid that you want to take an action on, and then click the appropriate button for your selection.

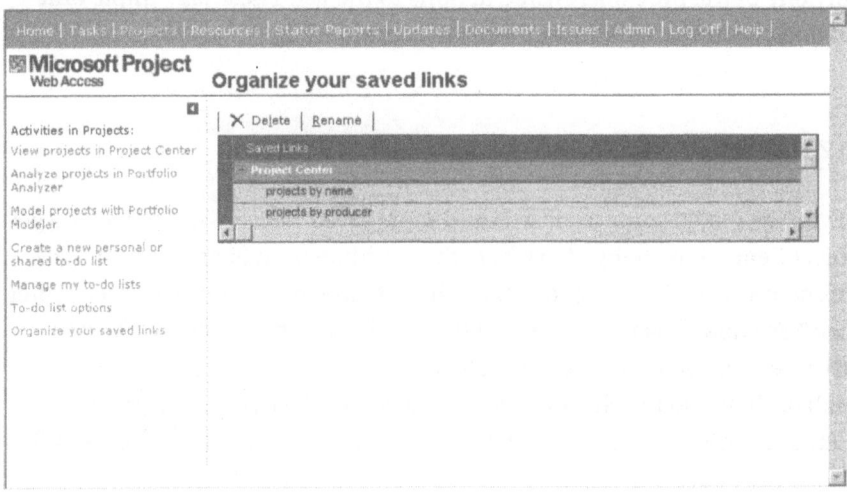

Figure 16-23. The "Organize your saved links" page

Using Portfolio Analyzer Views

Portfolio Analyzer views are always custom to the organization, as they're most useful for viewing project data by specific-to-the-business dimensions. Once you've created the first Analyzer view, the Portfolio Analyzer selection in the Project Center becomes active. As a casual user, selecting a view is as easy as choosing it from the pick list in the upper-right corner of the screen.

Using the views dynamically works exactly like creating an Analyzer view. You can literally delete everything from a view that you open and start again as if you were creating a brand-new view. Nothing is unchangeable. If it weren't for the fact that you can't save the changes you make, you're essentially enabled the same way as you are when you're creating the views. Therefore, I refer you to the section on building Analyzer views in Chapter 12.

Using the Portfolio Modeler

The Portfolio Modeler provides a workspace for "what-if" analyses for making changes to staffing and timelines for plans. It features a resource optimization engine driven by parameters you define through its interface. You build models to explore scenario-based scheduling alternatives by comparing them to each other.

To launch the Portfolio Modeler, click the "Model projects with Portfolio Modeler" link on the Project Center Activities menu. The "Model projects with Portfolio Modeler" page displays as shown in Figure 16-24.

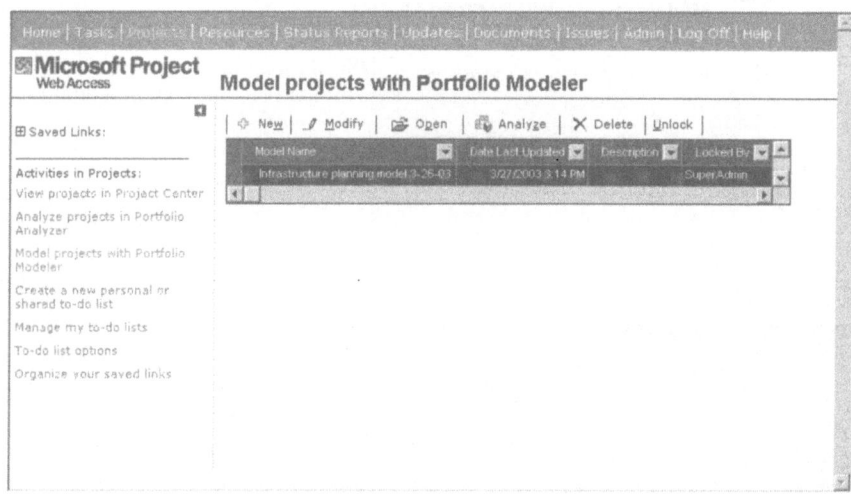

Figure 16-24. The "Model projects with Portfolio Modeler" page

In the figure, only one existing model appears in the grid. All of the functions activated from this page are on the toolbar above the grid:

- *New* launches a series of steps to create a new project.

- *Modify* allows you to make changes to the existing model you select in the grid.

- *Open* allows you to open an existing model.

- *Analyze* compares resource demand and availability in the model's plans.

- *Delete* permanently removes a model from the system.

- *Unlock* resets a locked model the way checking in resources and projects restores availability of the records for editing.

Creating a New Model

Clicking New redisplays the page with data entry fields, as shown in Figure 16-25. Enter a name for your new model and select the projects that you'd like to include in your model by selecting them on the left pane and moving them to the right using the Add button.

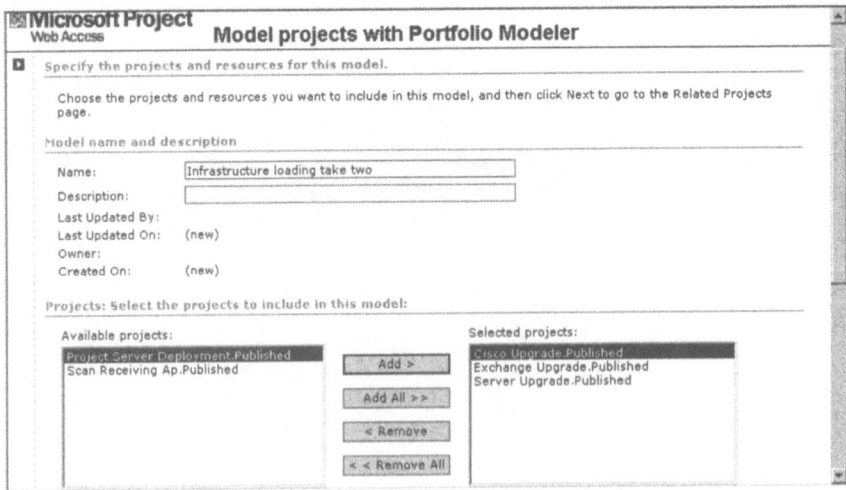

Figure 16-25. Give your model a name and select the projects to consider.

Scroll down the page, as shown in Figure 16-26, and select the resources considered in your new model. You have three choices: You can use the resources that already have assignments in the selected projects, you can select an RBS level at which the system should consider resources, or you can choose your specific resources by selecting them on the left selection pane and moving them to the right pane. In the figure, I've selected an RBS level, opening it up to the system to select a resource pool and potentially ignore the current assignments.

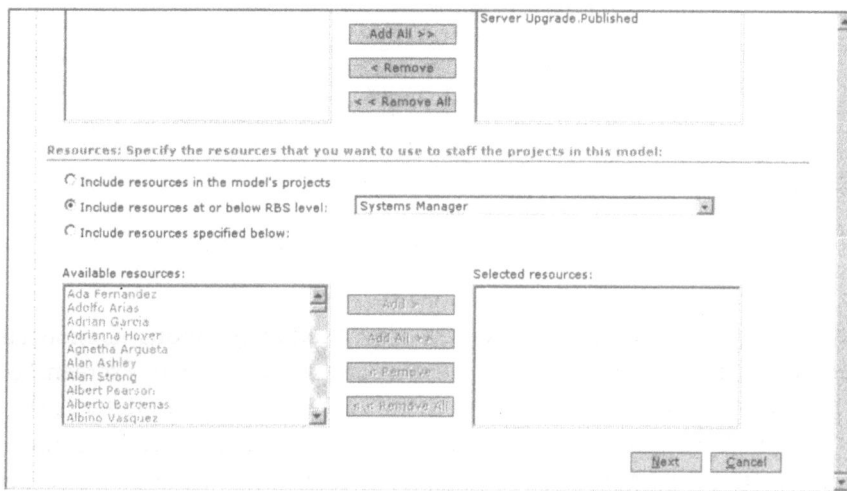

Figure 16-26. Specify the resources for use in the model.

Clicking Next takes you to the related projects page. Similar to the Resource Substitution Wizard discussed in Chapter 13, the system identifies other projects in the system with direct and indirect relationships to the plans you selected and displays them as shown in Figure 16-27. Like the Resource Substitution Wizard, one of the relationships the system identifies is sharing resources with one of your selected plans. It will highlight an indirect relationship when a project plan shares resources with a plan that shares resources with one of your selected model plans. In the figure, I didn't select either project with a direct relationship to projects in my model.

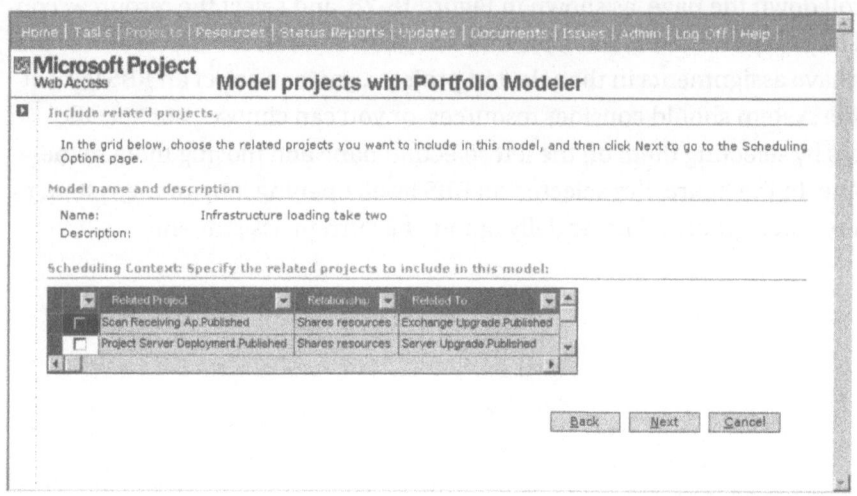

Figure 16-27. Select related projects to include in your new model.

The next step in defining your model is to set scheduling options, as shown in Figure 16-28, the page that displays after you click Next in the previous screen. You can set priority, select a scheduling option, and change project start dates in the fields in the grid. Setting relative priorities determines which project the modeler will give preference to when resolving contention for resources within the resource selection scope.

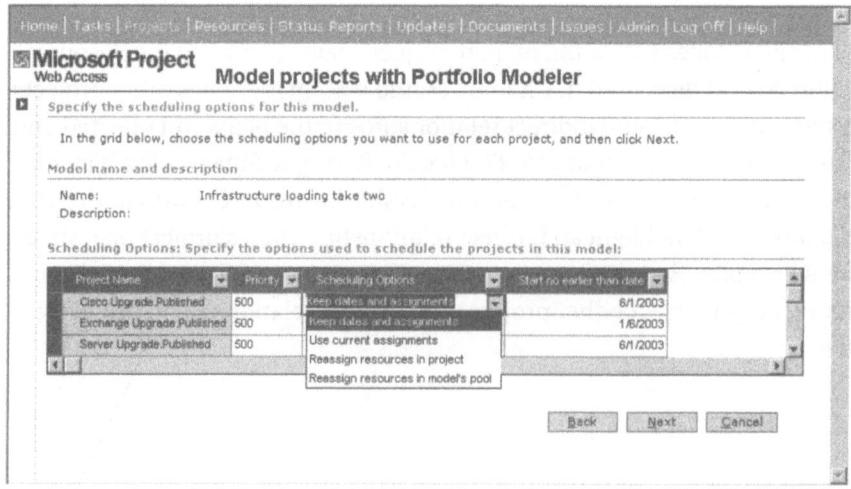

Figure 16-28. Set scheduling options, priorities, and start-date thresholds.

The scheduling options visible in the pick list in the figure allow you to select the scheduling behavior for each included project:

- *Keep dates and assignments* indicates to the modeler not to change dates and assignments in the project for which it selected. The system won't optimize dates or reassign resources to assignments.

- *Use current assignments* keeps the current assignments in the plan as set, but allows the modeler to change dates and attempt to resolve overallocated resource assignments.

- *Reassign resources in project* instructs the modeling engine that it may reassign resources from the specific project only. The modeler substitutes resources based on capacity and skill if the system is able to optimize the schedule in so doing.

- *Reassign resources in model's pool* allows the modeler to use resources included in the virtual resource pool formed by the combination of resources in the model's projects and resources included based on the combination of this selection and the steps you took in specifying resources for the model.

Start no earlier than dates allow you to set a threshold date before which the modeler doesn't attempt to reschedule the project. You can use any combination of dates here. Clicking the down arrow in the field opens a date picker.

Opening Your New Model

After you complete your entries to create the new model, the system returns to the "Model projects with Portfolio Modeler" page. Your new model now appears in the grid. If you need to refresh your memory, refer back to Figure 16-24. The model I created takes two projects, a router upgrade project scheduled to start in June 2003 and a server upgrade project scheduled to start in January 2004, and asks the question, can these be moved up to April 14, 2003? To examine the model results, open your new model. Figure 16-29 shows the model I created.

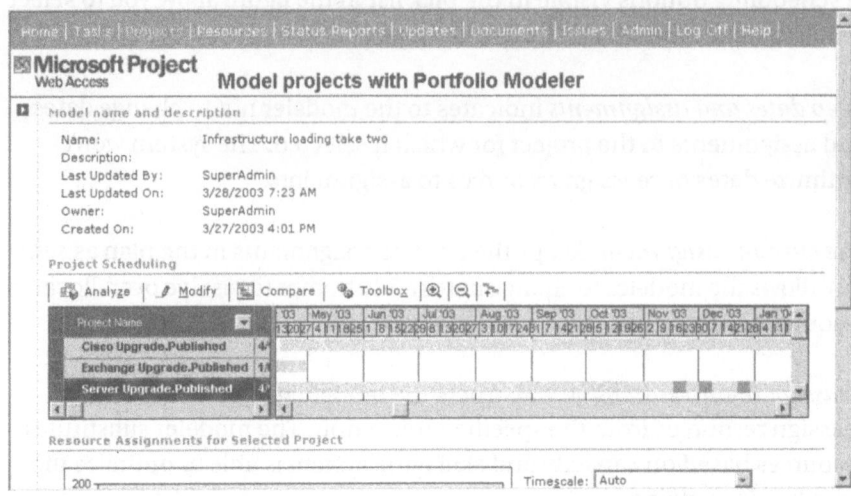

Figure 16-29. An open model

In the figure, I dragged the divider bar in the grid to the left to give myself maximum view of the chart area. The bar colors display green, yellow, or red. In the figure, all of the bars are green except for three periods in November and December 2003 for the Server Upgrade, which display red. The colors indicate overallocation of resources or lack thereof as follows:

- Green indicates that there are no resource overallocations occurring during the time period spanned.

- Yellow indicates that there are resources that are overallocated, but there are no overallocations 10% or greater over availability.

- Red indicates that there are resources overallocated at a rate of 10% or more.

In this case, the results are clear that, indeed, both projects can have their start dates moved up from a resource availability perspective. Mostly this is because my demo resource pool contains more than 300 resources, yet I've added only a handful of projects to the system. Don't expect such gratifying results when you try this at work. Looking at the bars in the figure with the three red segments in the Sever Upgrade plan only tells me that the red bars likely represent preexisting overallocations in the selected project plan. If these trouble spots were the result of resource contention between the Server Upgrade and the Cisco Router Upgrade, I'd expect to see corresponding trouble spots in the Cisco plan. In this case, both project plans share resources with the Exchange Upgrade project, but not with each other. As you can also see, the partial month overlap between the Exchange project and the other two doesn't cause resource contention problems.

Scroll down to reveal the Resource Assignments for Selected Project section of the page shown in Figure 16-30. This section of the page allows you to look at resource loading in the project to help you pinpoint the trouble spots. Use the Timescale selector, shown expanded in the figure, to set the timescale on the chart. Use the "Select the name" pane to select an individual resource to graph or a group of them using the Shift and Ctrl keys. Click the Refresh button to redisplay the graph based on any selection changes that you make.

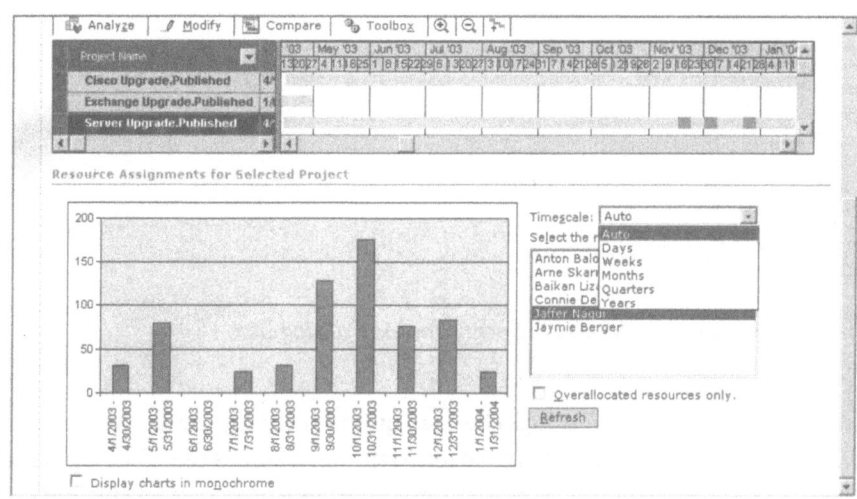

Figure 16-30. The Resource Assignments section of the model

Modifying Your Model

Whether you select Modify from the "Model projects with Portfolio Modeler" home page or you select it from the toolbar in the single model display shown in the previous two figures, the result is the same series of screens you worked through when you created your model. In other words, refer back to the "Creating a New Model" section of this chapter to learn the steps for modifying one.

Modifying Your Model with the Portfolio Model Property Toolbox

Clicking the Toolbox icon in the previous screen opens the Portfolio Model Property Toolbox dialog box shown in Figure 16-31. You can't change the name of the model using this dialog box, but you can change almost every parameter in the page-by-page modify process. In this case, you must first select a project in the grid (refer back to Figure 16-29) before you click Modify. I changed the parameters to allow the modeler to make reassignments of resources using all the resources in the model and clicked the Apply button each time.

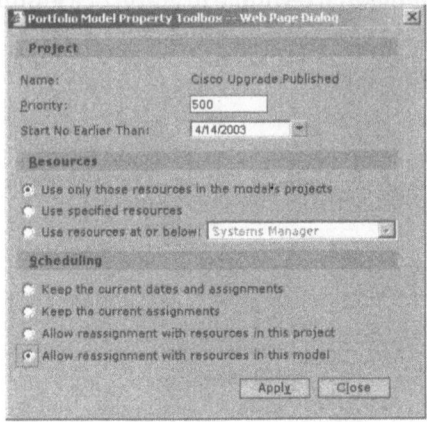

Figure 16-31. The Portfolio Model Property Toolbox dialog box

After I applied my changes, things changed quite a bit in my model, as shown in Figure 16-32. Allowing the system to make reassignments across the Cisco Upgrade and Server Upgrade projects indicates that I can complete both projects by mid-September 2003, whereas earlier both projects were completing well into calendar year 2004. You can also see that the system combined the teams. With only the Server Upgrade project selected in the figure, the list of resources has grown.

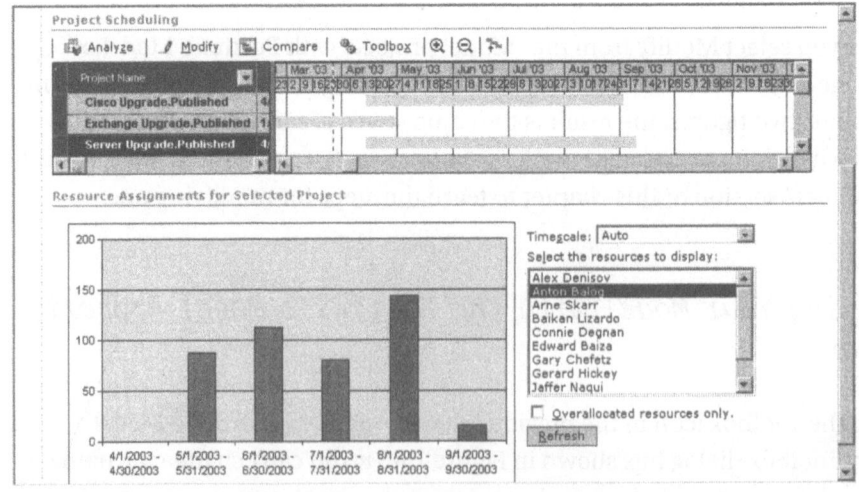

Figure 16-32. Displaying the model after making changes using the Portfolio Model Property Toolbox

Analyzing Your Model

Clicking Analyze on the toolbar displays the "Model project with Portfolio Modeler" in another incarnation, as shown in Figure 16-33.

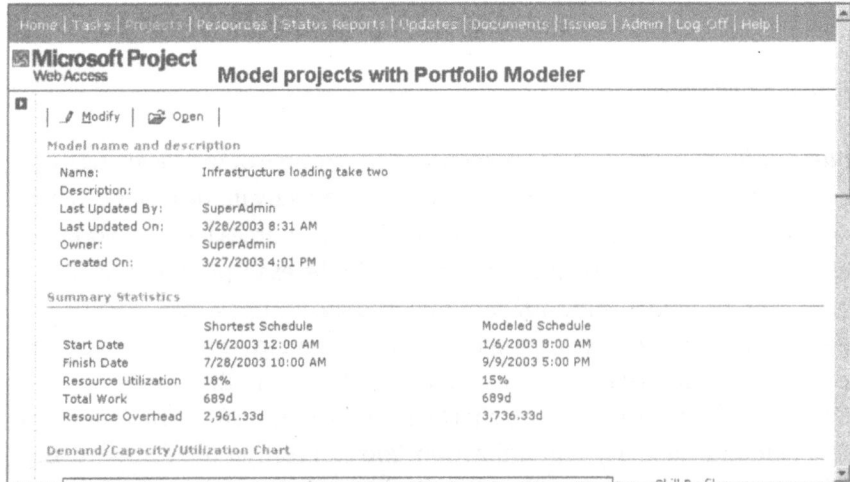

Figure 16-33. Analyze the model description and summary statistics.

At the top of the display are the model's vital statistics, including ownership and creation and modification information:

- Name

- Description

- Last Updated By (user)

- Last Updated On (date)

- Owner

- Created On (date)

The Summary Statistics are display data for the shortest possible schedule given the current set of parameters and the optimized schedule that the system is proposing. For both scenarios, the following display:

- Start Date

- Finish Date

- Resource Utilization

- Total Work

- Resource Overhead

Resource utilization refers to the percentage or resource demand versus the available capacity. *Resource overhead* refers to spare capacity in the model. In other words, resource overhead is the total availability of all resources less the workload prescribed in the projects contained in the model. In the example, the modeled schedule finishes more than a month later than the shortest possible scenario. A manager, given these alternatives, might base a decision to go with the modeled schedule in order to preserve greater resource availability for other work.

Scroll the page down to bring the chart shown in Figure 16-34 into view. The chart maps demand, capacity, and utilization. You can restrict the display using skill profiles or change the timescale of the display to days, weeks, months, quarters, and years besides the default Auto selection.

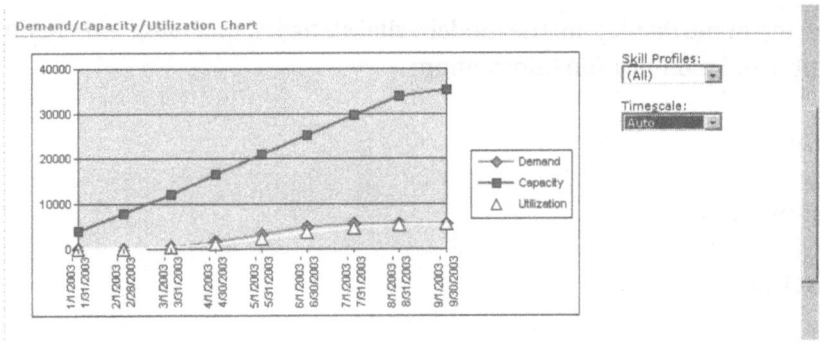

Figure 16-34. A demand, capacity, and utilization chart

Scroll to the bottom of the page to view the summarized scheduling options, as shown in Figure 16-35. Here the system enumerates the teams based on the selected scheduling options.

Model Scheduling Options
Resource Pool: Use only those resources in the model's projects
Projects:
Cisco Upgrade.Published
Priority: 500
Start No Earlier Than: 4/14/2003 12:00 AM
Project Team: Gerard Hickey, Anton Balog, Arne Skarr, Gary Chefetz, Alex Denisov, Connie Degnan, Ken Miller, Edward Baiza, Anthony Coviello, James Ziemba, Jaffer Naqui
Scheduling Options: Allow reassignment with resources in this model
Exchange Upgrade.Published
Priority: 500
Start No Earlier Than: 1/6/2003 12:00 AM
Project Team: Jeno Martin, Elaine Catlin, Alberto Barcenas, Colleen Brosnan, Alic Walters, Agnetha Argueta, Alex Denisov, Edward Baiza, Joseph Antonelli, James Ziemba
Scheduling Options: Keep the current dates and assignments
Server Upgrade.Published
Priority: 500
Start No Earlier Than: 4/14/2003 12:00 AM
Project Team: Anton Balog, Arne Skarr, Gary Chefetz, Alex Denisov, Jaffer Naqui, Connie Degnan, James Ziemba, Jaymie Berger, Gerard Hickey, Baikan Lizardo, Edward Baiza
Scheduling Options: Allow reassignment with resources in this model

Figure 16-35. Review the scheduling options and team structures for the model.

Comparing Models

Clicking the Compare link on the model toolbar displays the models to be displayed in the Portfolio Modeler selection page shown in Figure 16-36. In the example, I've selected the two versions of the model to compare. The systems displays all models that a user has access to in this display.

Microsoft Project
Web Access
Model projects with Portfolio Modeler
Specify the models to be displayed in the Portfolio Modeler page
Available models:
Selected models:
Infrastructure loading take two
Infrastructure planning model 3-26-03
Add >
Add All >>
< Remove
<< Remove All
OK
Cancel

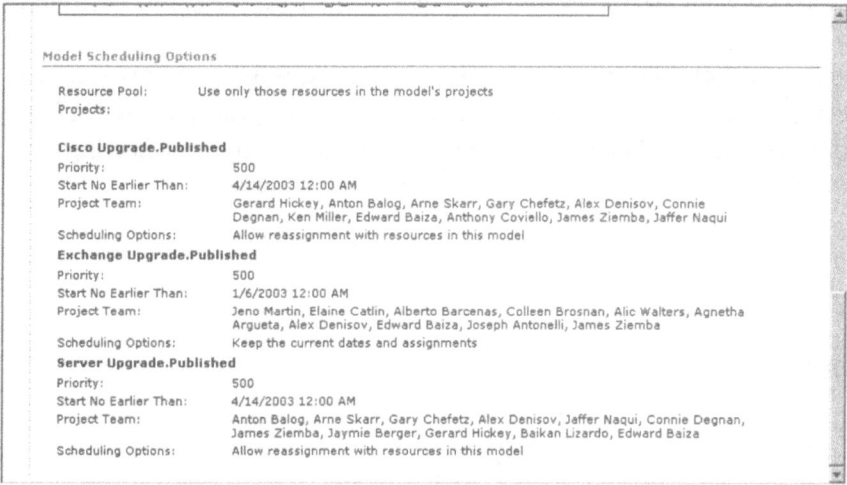

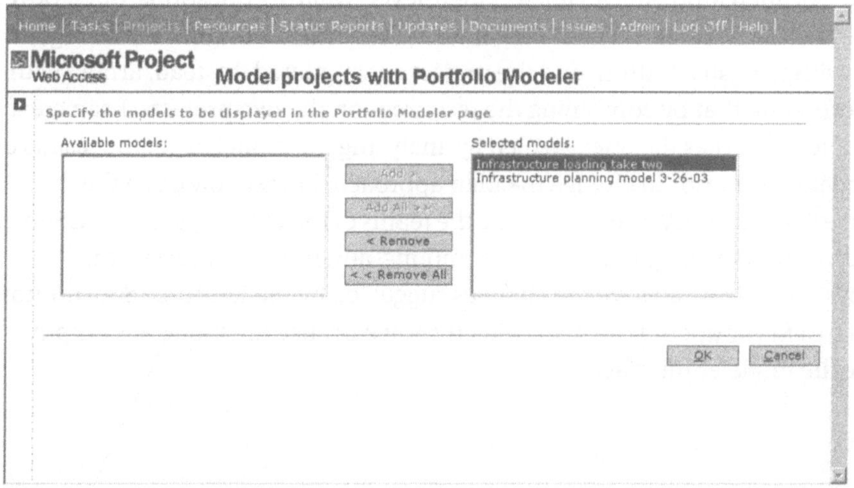

Figure 16-36. Select models to compare.

Clicking OK displays the Portfolio Modeler page with the combined details of the two models.

Scrolling further down the page reveals the Resource Assignments section, which now responds to all versions of the schedules in the grid, as shown in Figure 16-37. Use the tool the same way you used it in previous displays, selecting a project in the grid and a resource in the selection pane below.

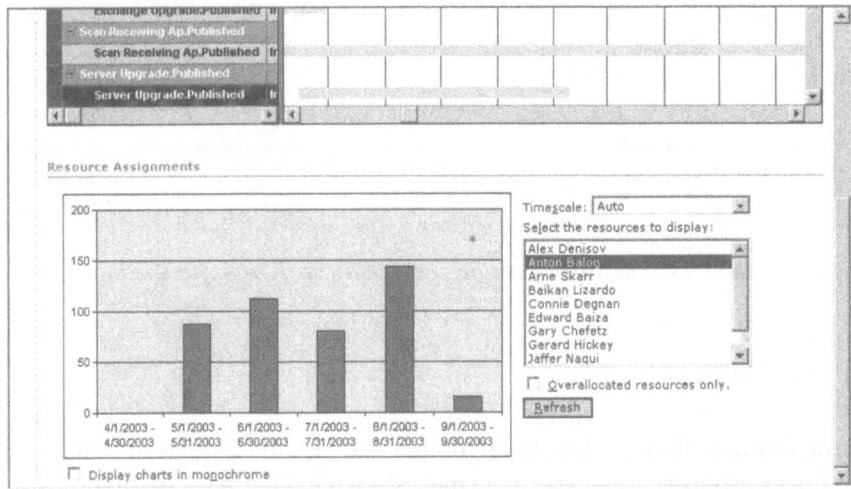

Figure 16-37. Resource Assignments in the combined model display

The Portfolio Modeler can answer high-level "what-if" questions, but it never quite reveals all its secrets. I can't take the results of the model and now say great, let's go with it, push a button, and the projects get updated. Instead, armed with the information that by combining the resources on the two projects, I can create a schedule as short as the one revealed by analyzing the model or get the results of the modeled scenario. To change the plan approach, I must now open the Resource Substitution Wizard, combine the teams of the Cisco Upgrade and Server Upgrade projects through the selection options, and then run the wizard. Remember that you can save the changes suggested by the Resource Substitution Wizard to a file or update the plans directly. You can't use the modeler's output outside the modeler interface.

Summary

The view areas of Project Web Access along with the analysis capabilities provided through Analyzer views and Portfolio models present many rewards for your efforts to maintain a managed project discipline. The information that you can synthesize from your portfolio using these tools is a necessary ingredient for improvement.

If you've taken a cover-to-cover approach to reading this book, you're now familiar with almost every inch of the application. You should certainly be comfortable with the interface.

Managing Project Server

Once it's up and running, Project Server is very stable and requires little looking after beyond your daily backup routines. Like all applications, however, Project Server may require additional attention from time to time. In this chapter you'll first dive deeper into SharePoint Team Services (STS), and I show you how to manage and exploit its administration interface and features. Then I discuss regular and preventive maintenance for Project Server. Finally, I lead you to additional resources that you can count on for the latest technical information and thinking on deploying the product.

Managing SharePoint Team Services

Although I covered using documents and issues in Chapter 15, STS administration is a topic that hasn't come up since I touched on it in Chapter 5. In your journey through the following subtopics, you'll find yourself jumping from the Project Server administration interface to various native STS administration pages. Be prepared for this. Of course, I point these out as they occur in the text. Because Project Server follows the STS theme, sometimes the differences are subtle.

Managing STS Connections

Clicking the "Manage SharePoint Team Services" link from the Project Web Access administration Activities menu takes you to the "Connect to servers" page shown in Figure 17-1. I cover connecting to STS servers in Chapter 5. I include it here for perspective only. It's the default display for STS administration in Project Web Access. The important point to remember is that although you can add STS servers, Project Server can use only one at a time for automatic subweb creation.

Figure 17-1. The "Connect to servers" page is the default display for STS administration.

Managing Subweb Provisioning Settings

Click the "Subweb provisioning settings" link in the upper part of the Options pane. As shown in Figure 17-2, I've collapsed the Options and Activities panes to maximize the display of the "SharePoint Team Services subweb provisioning settings" page. So far, you've trusted that your STS site works so you haven't had a need to look at this page, which is set to defaults.

The first section, "Specify the SharePoint Team Services server," displays your current server. The second section of the page allows you to determine whether STS subweb creation happens manually or automatically. Setting your environment to manual requires you or another administrator to extend the subweb manually for each new project.

"Grant user access to the project subwebs" is the third section of the page. Both check boxes are selected by default. The first selection tells the system to add users to roles on the new project subwebs automatically as created. This includes the project manager and team members who have assignments in the corresponding projects. The second check box selection tells the system to also add the users to the public documents library if they're not already authorized to use it.

At the very bottom of the page, you can change the STS server that's set to handle the public documents subweb. Notice that there's a link to SharePoint site administration for the server. There's a similar link in the "Specify the SharePoint Team Services server" section as well. If the two servers aren't the same, you should be careful about which one you select; otherwise, they'll take you to the same place. I'll get to this shortly.

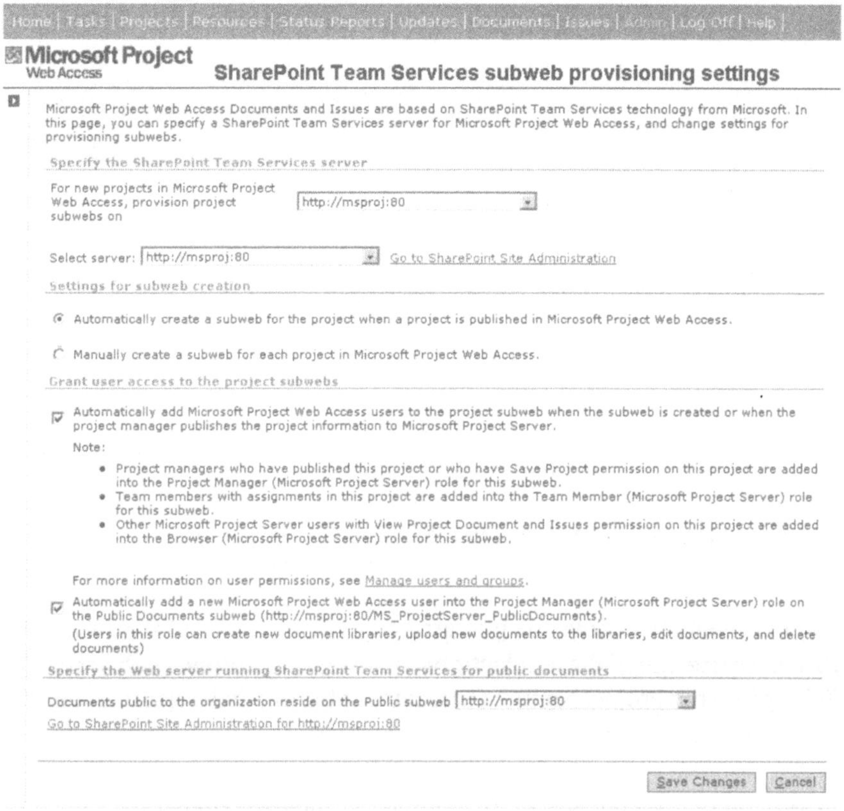

Figure 17-2. The "SharePoint Team Services subweb provisioning settings" page

Managing Subwebs

Select Manage subwebs from the Options pane to display the "Manage SharePoint Team Services subwebs" page shown in Figure 17-3. In the figure, I've collapsed the left navigation area to display more information. The top section of the screen displays a link to the server administration site. Notice that the "Manage project subwebs" section containing the grid includes a toolbar with a "Go to Web site administration" link. The former takes you to the administration page for the server, whereas the latter takes to you to the administration site for the subweb you select in the grid.

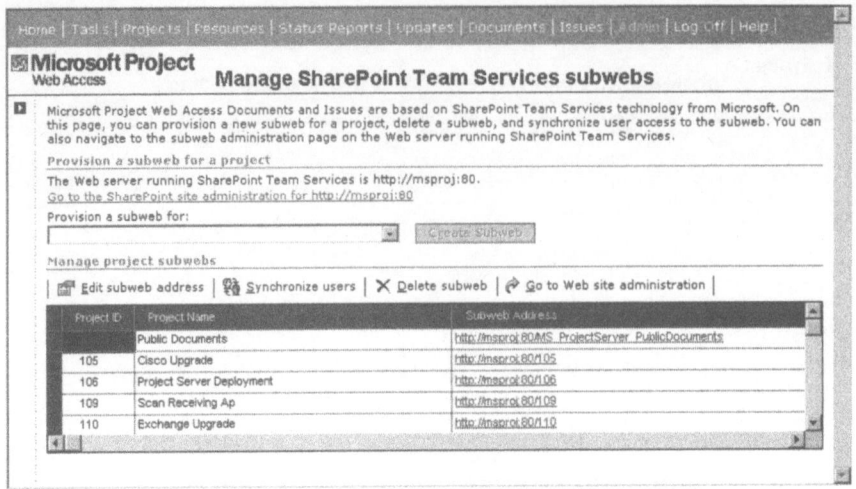

Figure 17-3. The "Manage SharePoint Team Services subwebs" page

The toolbar selections above the grid are actions that you can take on an individual subweb. To use one of these selections, first select the project subweb in the grid by clicking into the Project Name or indicator column. Clicking into a cell with a link will take you to the subweb.

- *Edit subweb address* allows you to change the subweb address for the subweb. Clicking the link opens the Edit Subweb Address dialog box shown in Figure 17-4. Select a server and enter a subweb name. Click Ok when you're done.

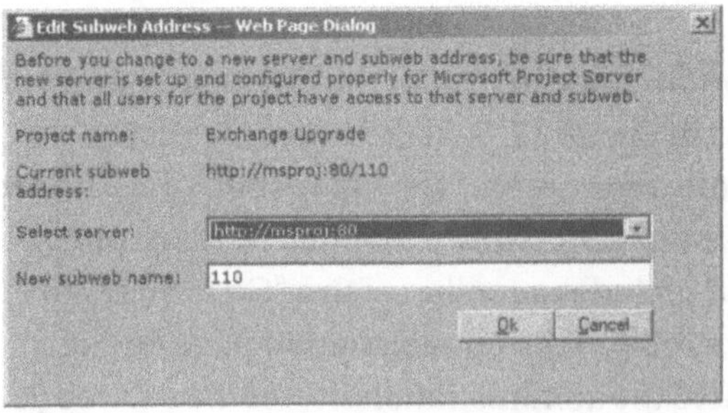

Figure 17-4. The Edit Subweb Address dialog box

- *Synchronize users* allows you to automatically resynchronize the users for the subweb with the project it represents. Selecting this link displays the alert box shown in Figure 17-5. It's important to note that running this routine will remove any manual changes you might have made to users and their roles. Consider whether this presents a problem for you before you run it. Make a backup if you're not sure.

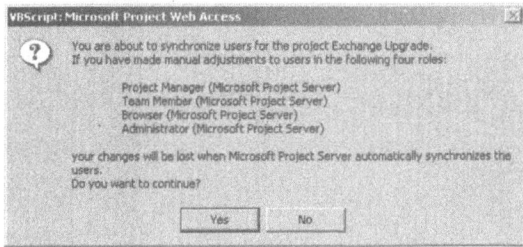

Figure 17-5. The synchronize users warning

- *Delete subweb* allows you to remove the subweb, including document libraries, documents in the libraries, and the issues list for the project. This isn't a recoverable action. When you make this selection, the system displays the warning shown in Figure 17-6.

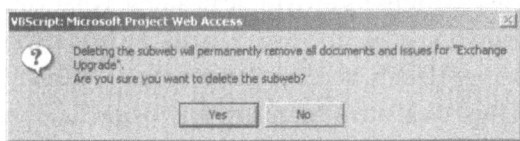

Figure 17-6. The delete subweb warning

- *Go to Web site administration* takes you out of the Project Server interface and into a native SharePoint administration page at the subweb level. As shown in Figure 17-7, the "Web site Administration" page allows you to set options specific to the selected subweb.

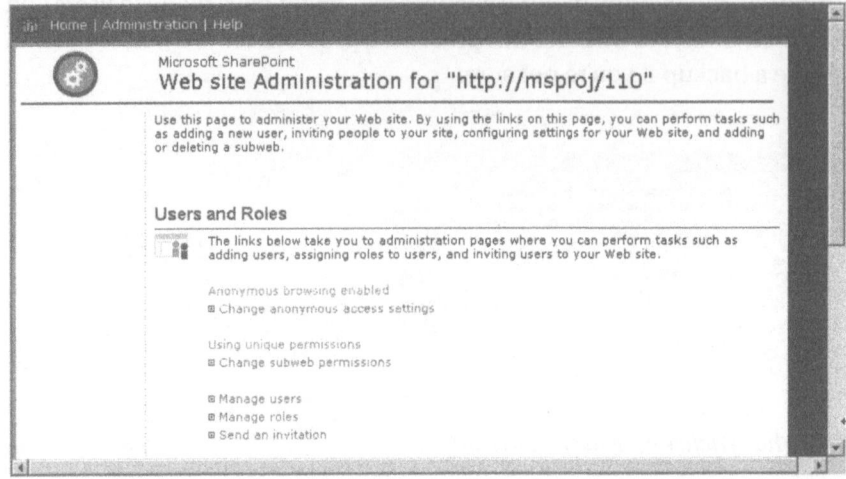

Figure 17-7. The "Web site Administration" page for a specific subweb

Using Web Site Administration for Subwebs

The last bullet point in the preceding list requires its own topic heading. What you saw in Figure 17-7 is half the picture. Scrolling down the page reveals the rest of the selections, as shown in Figure 17-8. Server Health, Version Control, and Subwebs round out the selections available on the "Web site Administration" page. You must log onto Project Server as an administrator to use these pages.

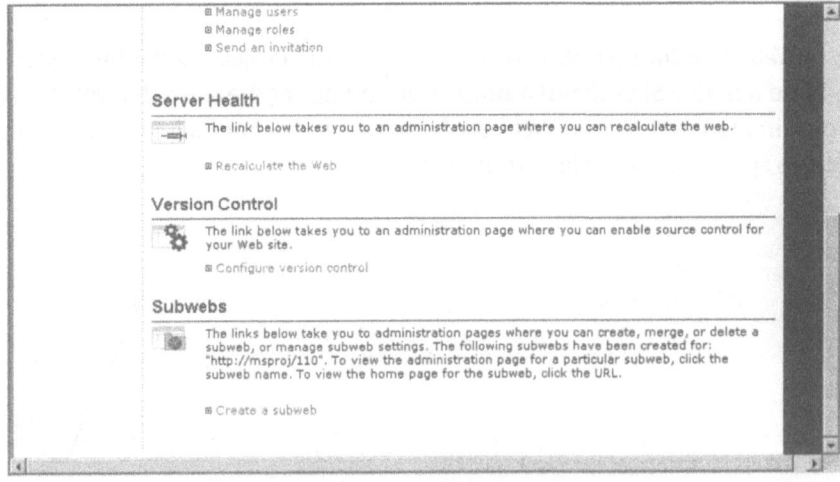

Figure 17-8. The "Web site Administration" page, part 2

Manage Users and Roles

The links listed in the Users and Roles section of the "Web site Administration" page lead you to various STS settings. Here you can make changes to anonymous settings, change subweb permissions, and manage users and roles, as well as send invitations to users. In this section you'll explore these in the order they appear on the page.

- *Change anonymous access settings* applies to users entering your subweb directly on the server without calling it through Project Server. Users accessing the documents and issues areas within Project Server must have Windows credentials or they don't gain access to the subweb and its contents. Clicking the link opens the Change Anonymous Access Settings page shown in Figure 17-9. By default, anonymous access is enabled on the subweb. This means that a user can browse to the site and use it according to the permissions granted through his or her role. (I'll explain roles in SharePoint Web sites soon). A user browsing to the site external to Project Server will see the site in its native SharePoint presentation. Figure 17-10 shows the Team Web Site home page for the project. Unfortunately, the only way for you to know which project you're looking at is to know what project "105" is, as indicated in the URL. The site doesn't tell you. The feature access for users entering this way is very restricted.

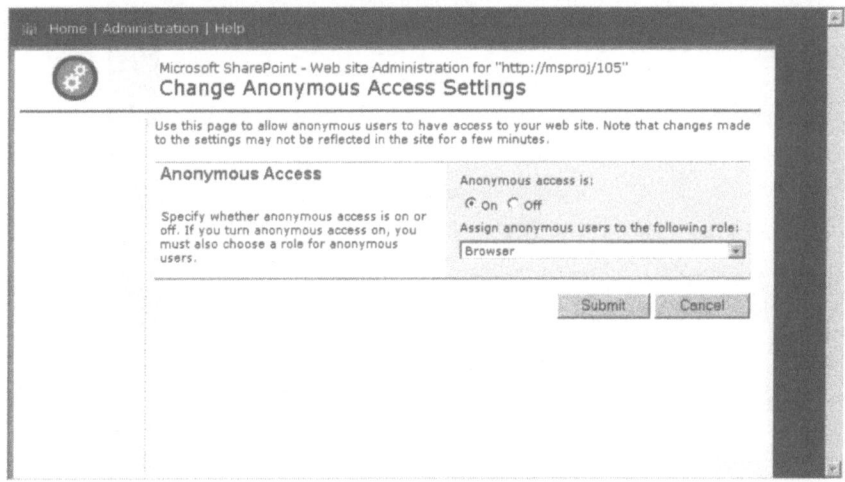

Figure 17-9. The Change Anonymous Access Settings page

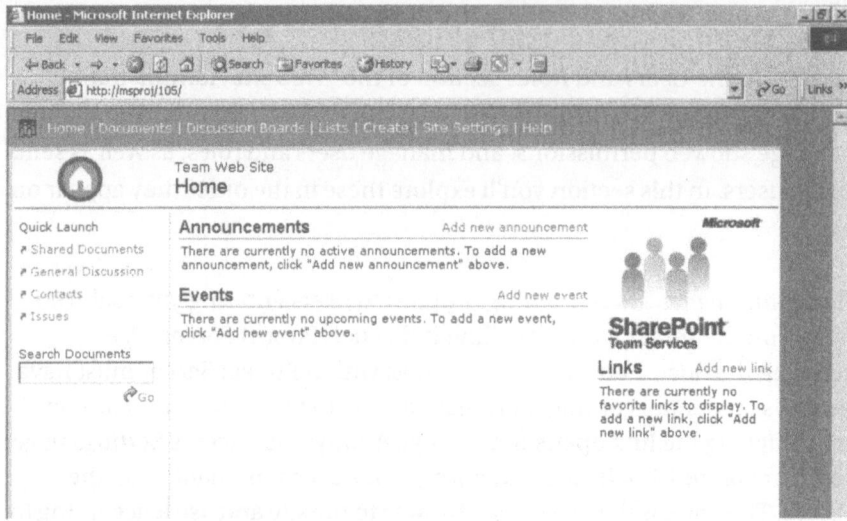

Figure 17-10. The Team Web Site home page

- *Change subweb permissions* isn't a choice you'll likely use to manage your subwebs. The default setting, shown in Figure 17-11, is to use unique permissions. Leave this as set by the system unless you created a subweb that is a subweb of the project subweb and you want to set permissions on that.

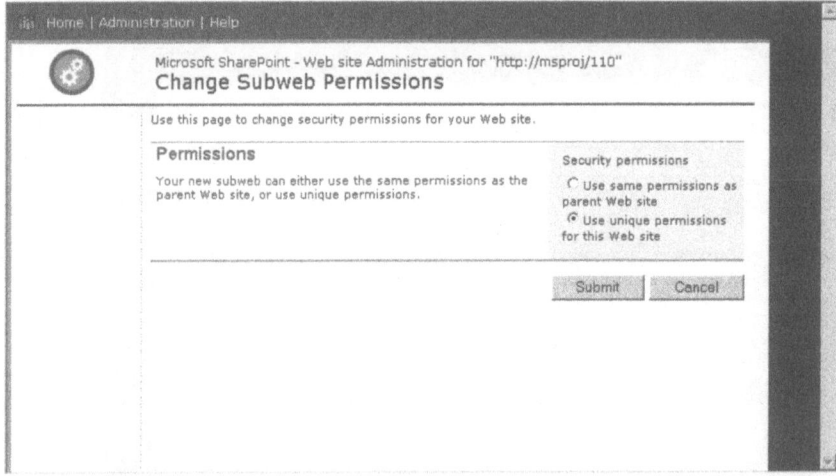

Figure 17-11. The Change Subweb Permissions page

- *Manage users* allows you to manually manage subweb users. When you open this page, shown in Figure 17-12, the system displays the current subweb users. This list includes all users in the system with assignments in the project who have Windows accounts. These will most likely be domain accounts;

however, local machine accounts can work if the users have local logon rights on the server. Select the check boxes corresponding to existing users and then click "Remove selected user(s) from all roles." The system prompts you to continue. To add a user, click Add a User and fill in the information on the Add User page. You provide a username and password and select a role.

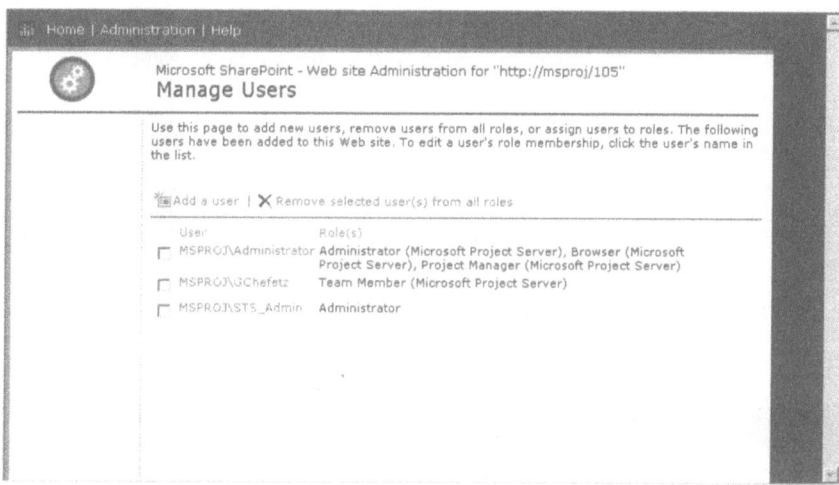

Figure 17-12. The Manage Users page

- *Manage roles* allows you to set options for roles. Roles are how permissions are managed in STS. Clicking Manage roles opens the Manage Roles page shown in Figure 17-13. The top five roles listed are built-in STS roles, and the bottom four roles are custom roles added by the Project Server installation. Clicking a role name opens the Edit Role page shown in Figure 17-14. The title of the page includes the name of the selected role. Rights define a role. Figure 17-14 shows some of the rights a role can have. You must scroll down to see all the selections. Getting into role specifics is outside the scope of this book, but I urge you to review the list of rights to learn how to control STS functionality by Project Server role.

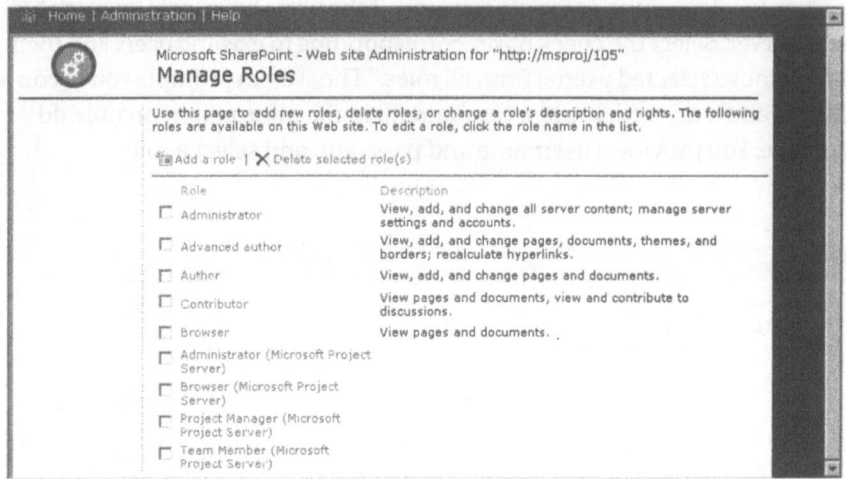

Figure 17-13. The Manage Roles page

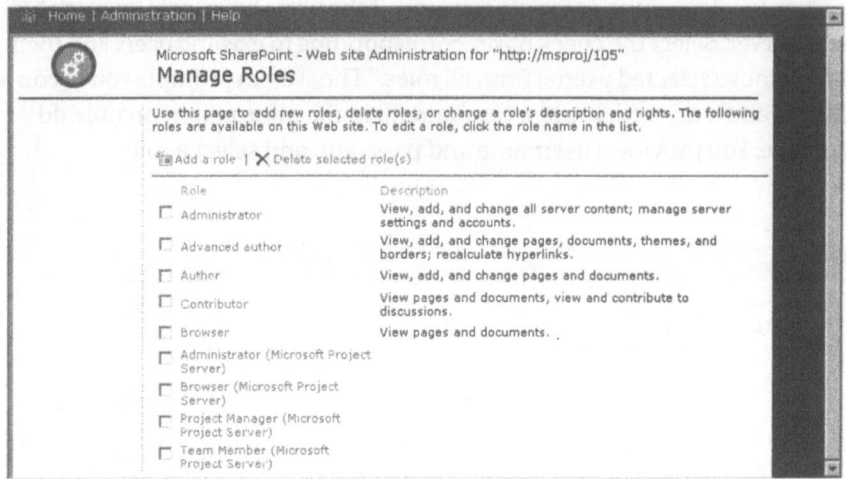

Figure 17-14. The Edit Role page

- *Send an invitation* provides a three-step process to send invitations to team members to use the site. Using this feature requires that you've set up the SMTP options in STS administration. This isn't to be confused with the SMTP setup screen for Project Server. The three pages in the send invitation process allow you to do the following:

1. Enter the e-mail address of all recipients for the invite (see Figure 17-15).

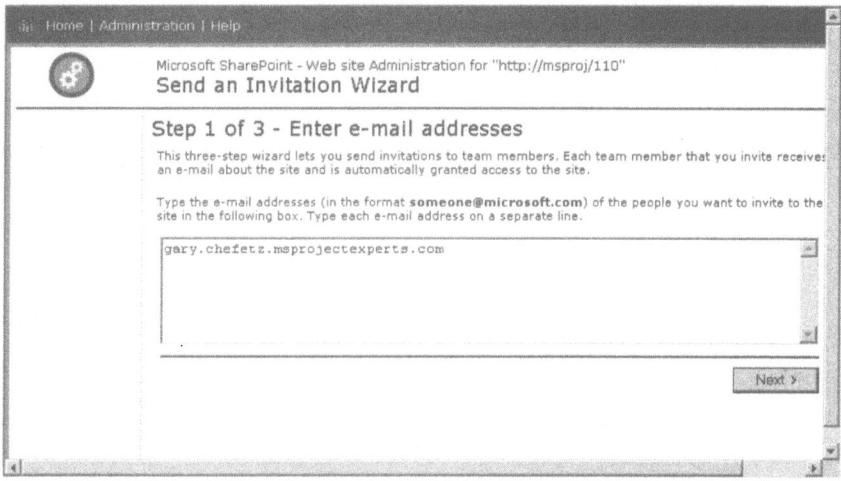

Figure 17-15. The Invitation Wizard, step 1

2. Enter user account information for the new users (see Figure 17-16).

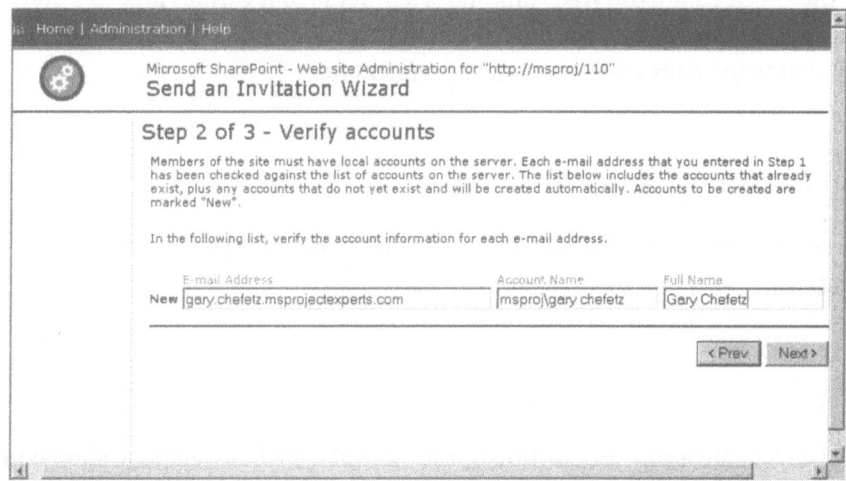

Figure 17-16. The Invitation Wizard, step 2

3. Enter a personalized greeting and choose a role for the user (see Figure 17-17).

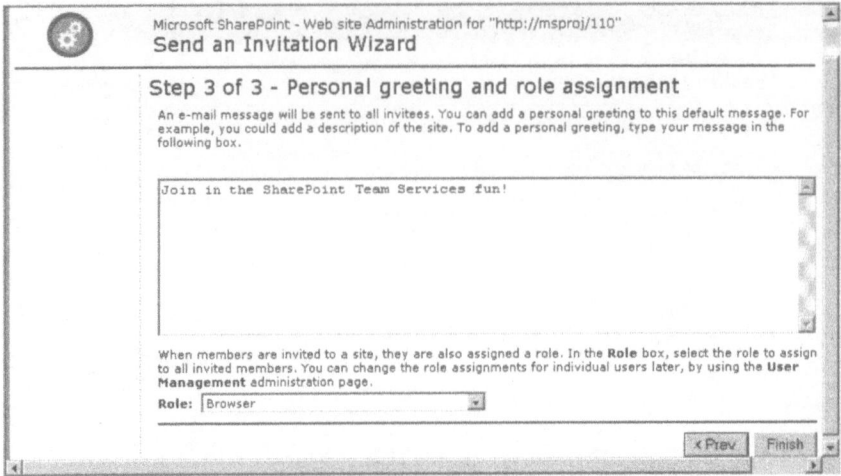

Figure 17-17. The Invitation Wizard, step 3

Server Health

Clicking the "Recalculate the Web" link starts a process that verifies link validity in the subweb and removes invalid links. It also deletes unneeded objects on the server related to the subweb to maximize performance.

Version Control

The "Configure version control" selection has no effect in Project Server configurations.

Subwebs

Selecting the "Create a subweb" option opens the Create a Subweb page shown in Figure 17-18. This feature allows you to create a new subweb as a subweb of the project subweb you're currently working in. I know this sounds like double-talk. Selecting the permissions to be the same as the parent web here makes sense. You'll want this to be a SharePoint-based Web site.

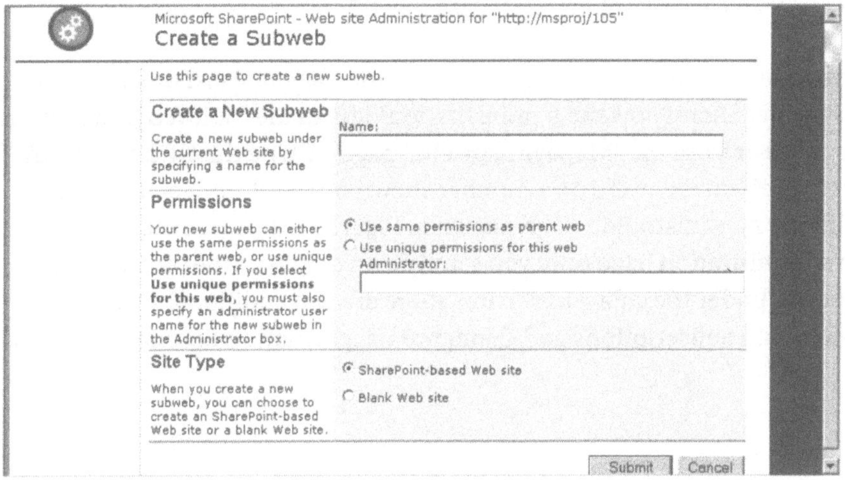

Figure 17-18. The Create a Subweb page

Synchronizing Administrators

Back now in the Project Server Admin interface, after a sojourn into the STS subweb administration pages, clicking "Synchronize administrator accounts" from the Options menu in the Manage SharePoint Team Services page opens the page shown in Figure 17-19. Clicking the Synchronize Administrators button starts the operation. While the system is processing, the usual animated gears GIF displays.

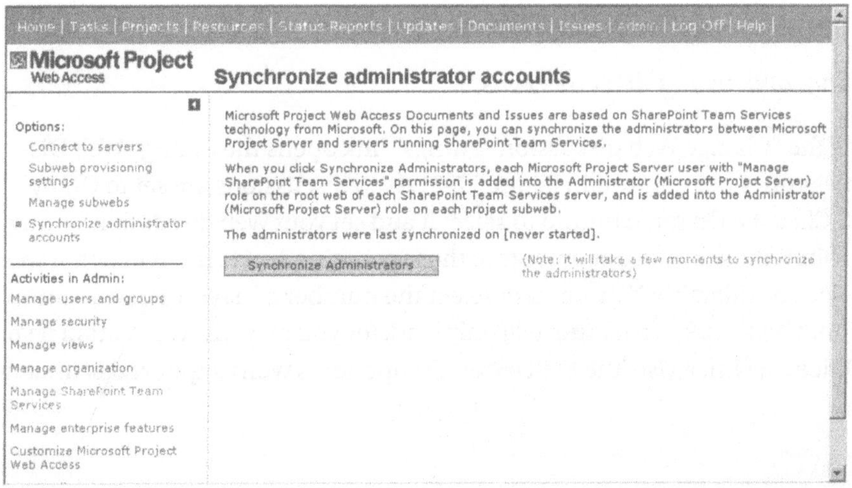

Figure 17-19. The "Synchronize administrator accounts" page

Using the STS Administration Site

Allow me to whisk you off to the STS administration site one last time. You can either click the "SharePoint site administration" link in the "Subweb provisioning settings" page or from the "Manage subwebs" page, or type the URL directly in your browser if you know the port number shown on the "Connect to servers" page. The Site Administration page, shown in Figure 17-20, looks identical to the subweb administration page until you scroll down a little further. In addition to more options under the subwebs section, there are two additional sections: Web Discussions and Subscriptions and Configure Usage Analysis Settings.

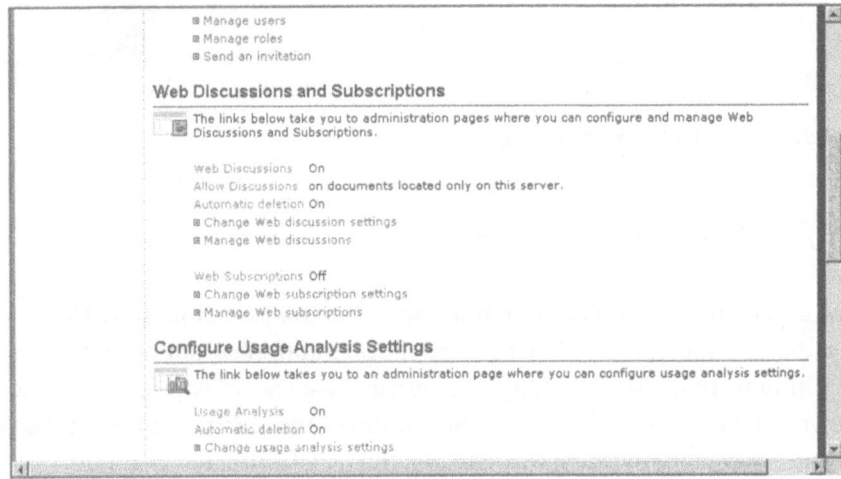

Figure 17-20. Site administration at the server level

Enabling and Using Discussions

Clicking the "Change Web discussion settings" link opens the Change Web Discussion Settings page shown in Figure 17-21. Web discussions are set to Off by default. Click the On radio button to select it and set your Web discussion settings. You can limit the scope of documents to those contained on this server or broaden the choice considerably. You can also select the number of days for discussion retention. The discussion feature will only work for you on your workstation if you have Office XP. Otherwise, the Office Web Components won't support discussions.

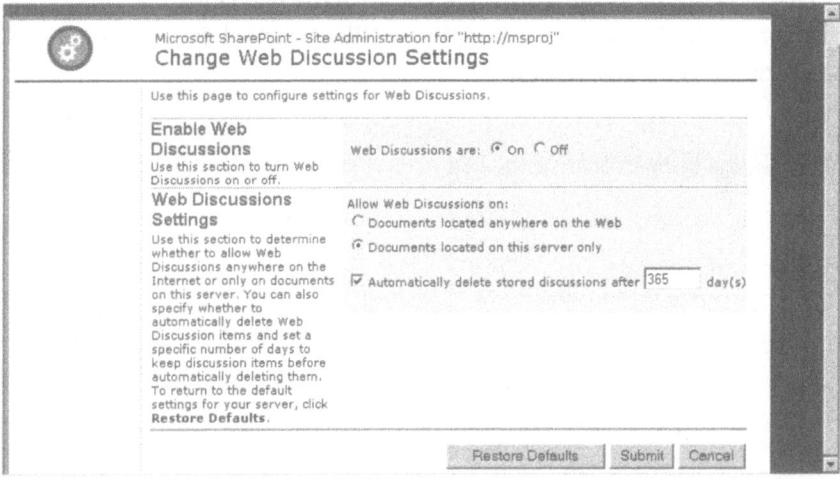

Figure 17-21. The Change Web Discussion Settings page

Once you've enabled discussions on your server, you'll be able to discuss documents in your document libraries. Click the Edit icon next to a document in the library. I've selected a Word document to demonstrate how this works. The View and Upload Documents page displays, as shown in Figure 17-22.

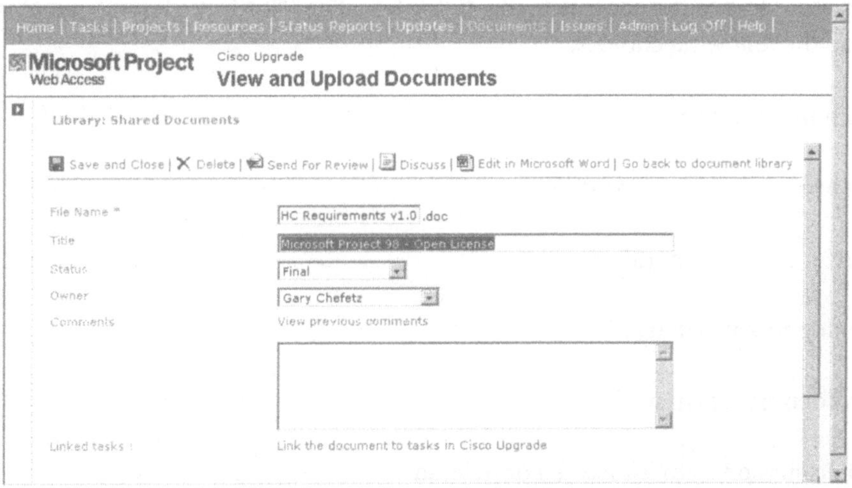

Figure 17-22. The View and Upload Documents page

Click Discuss and the system prompts you with the File Download dialog box shown in Figure 17-23. You can choose open the file or cancel the download and still make entries into the discussion.

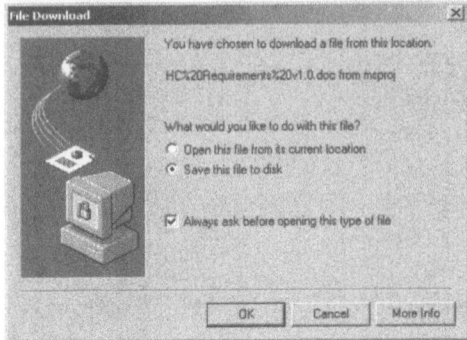

Figure 17-23. The File Download dialog box

I selected "Open this file from its current location" and clicked OK. A new browser window launches with the display split between the live document at the top and the discussion at the bottom, as shown in Figure 17-24.

Clicking the Subscribe button at the bottom of the discussion pane opens the Document Subscription dialog box shown in Figure 17-25. Set the notification options according to the choices in the dialog box. The "Notify me When" selector gives you the following choices:

- anything changes

- a new document is created

- a document is modified

- a document is deleted

- a document is moved

- a discussion item is inserted or deleted

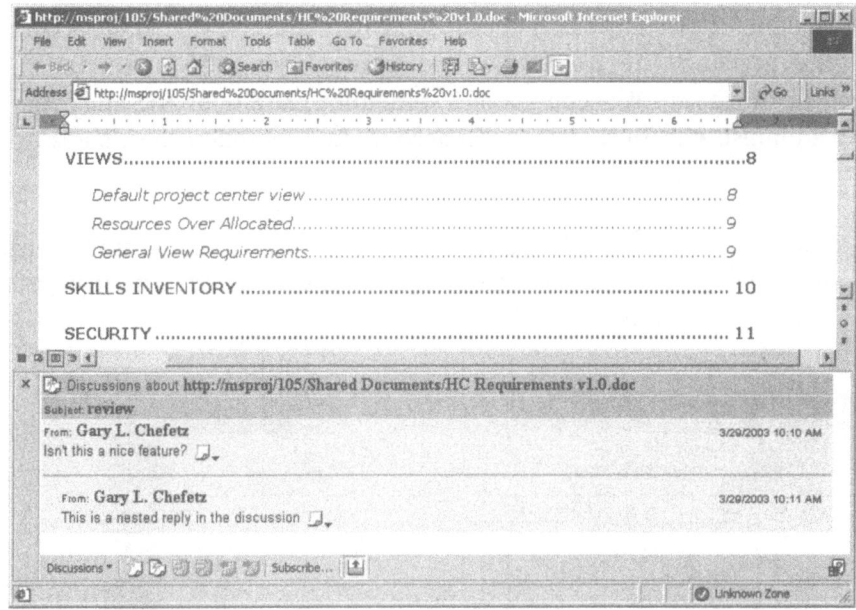

Figure 17-24. The standard split-window presentation of a document and document discussion

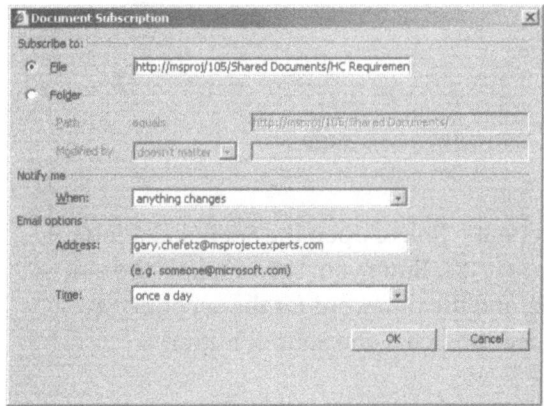

Figure 17-25. The Document Subscription dialog box

The STS SA Account Trap

You used the SA account to install STS. That's fine, because you needed to. A hidden issue remains in your STS installation. It continues to use that account for its internal connection to the database. It's not stored anywhere in the Project

Server database, but it's used in the STS connection. I suggest that you create a new SA account for this purpose. It doesn't seem to matter to STS that the account is not *"the"* SA account after it's installed and running. Using SQL Enterprise Manager, create a new SQL account. Call it something like SA_for_STS and make it a system administrator. To change the SA account for STS, follow these steps:

1. Click the Start button and select Programs ➤ Administrative Tools ➤ Microsoft SharePoint Administrator to open the Server Administration page shown in Figure 17-26. Note that the figure shows an administration page for a system with numerous STS sites.

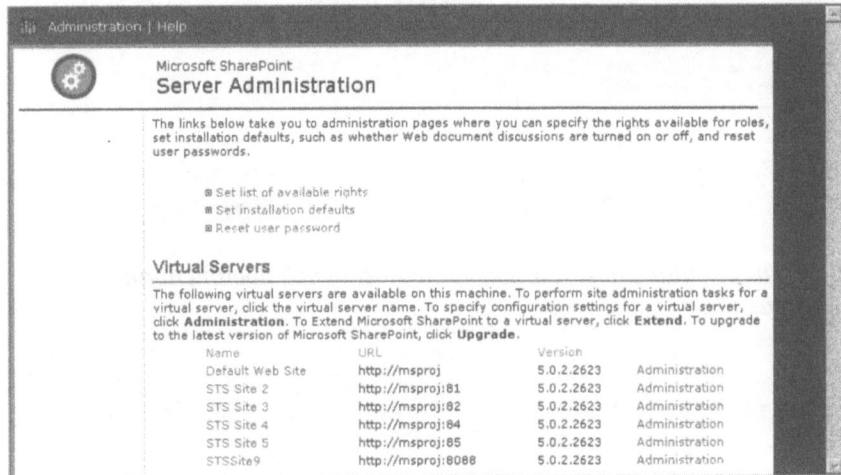

Figure 17-26. The SharePoint Server Administration page

2. Click the "Set installation defaults" link to open the Set Installation Defaults page shown in Figure 17-27. Enter your server name, the new STS SA account that you created, and the password for the account. Scroll down to the bottom of the page and click the Submit button.

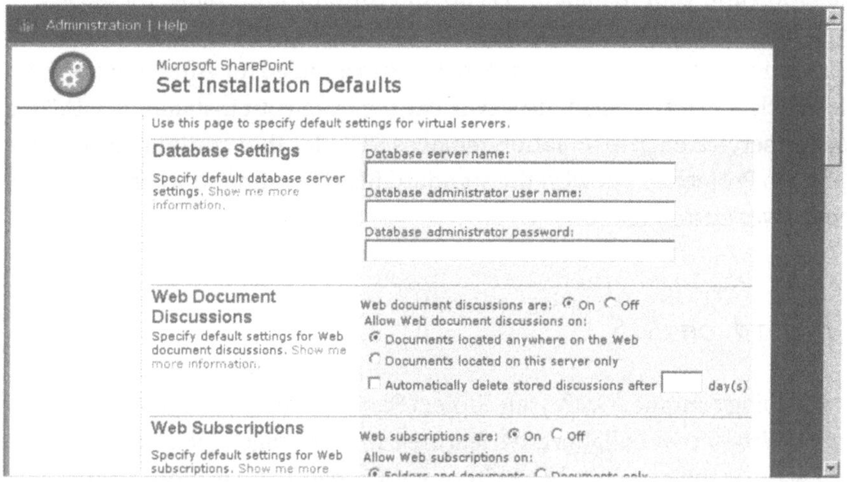

Figure 17-27. The Set Installation Defaults page

Setting Other SharePoint Installation Defaults

The Set Installation Defaults page allows you to manipulate numerous system options. Besides the database settings I showed you previously and using the page to set Web document discussions and Web subscription settings that you've already seen, you use this page to set the following options and details:

- *Usage Analysis:* Set the frequency of periodic processing and set retention periods for log data.

- *Server Health:* Set the frequency for periodic runs and the time of day for the run.

- *Mail Settings:* Enter the mail server name, the from address, and the reply to address.

- *Security Settings:* Determine whether authoring actions get logged, require SSL for authoring and administration, and allow executables to be uploaded to the STS server.

Applying Service Packs to STS

Through the course of managing your system, you may want to apply service packs to STS. Although I don't recommend doing this until after you've completed your installation and your installation is up and running and stable, there's less risk in applying the service packs. Make sure you back up your system before applying a service pack. A complete system backup is called for. After you apply an STS service pack, you must rerun the stswiz.exe file from your installation CD. This is because the service pack installation replaces STS files that contain customizations specific to Project Server with the standard files. Running stswiz.exe restores the Project Server customizations.

A Final Word on STS

The STS technology shipped with your Project Server software is at the core of many Project Web Access collaborative features. My coverage of it is cursory at best. If you want to fully exploit this technology, I suggest you explore online sources of information. At the time of this writing, there is no book available on STS 1.0. The best independent information resource I know of is the STS FAQ created and maintained by Mike Walsh, Microsoft STS Most Valuable Professional (MVP). Collutions carries a searchable version of the STS FAQ at http://www.collutions.com/Lists/FAQ/General.htm.

As always, use the resources available in the Microsoft Knowledge Base, TechNet, MSDN, and Microsoft Communities sites.

Checking in Enterprise Resources and Projects

From time to time, you'll need to check in enterprise projects and enterprise resources that get accidentally left in a checked-out state in the database. From the Project Web Access Admin menu, select Manage enterprise features ➤ Check in enterprise projects to open the "Check in enterprise projects" page shown in Figure 17-28. The familiar grid display lists projects currently checked out of the system. Make sure that someone isn't actually working on the project before you check it back in.

Figure 17-28. The "Check in enterprise projects" page

From the same Enterprise options menu, click "Check in enterprise resources" to open the "Check in enterprise resources" page shown in Figure 17-29. Select a resource in the grid and click Check-In on the toolbar. Use the Refresh option to refresh the display between deletions.

Figure 17-29. The "Check in enterprise resources" page

On occasion, you'll find that a checked-out project doesn't show up in the "Check in enterprise project" list. In such a case, you'll need to open SQL Enterprise Manager and the MSP_PROJECTS table, and set the PROJ_CHECKEDOUT field to 0 in the table row corresponding to your project. Similarly, if you need to do this for a resource, set the field RES_CHECKEDOUT in the MSP_RESOURCES table to 0.

Cleaning Up the Project Server Database

Eventually you'll need to delete data from Project Server. To accommodate your desire for tidiness, select "Clean up Microsoft Project Server database," the last entry on the Project Web Access Admin Activities menu. The "Clean up Microsoft Project Server database" page displays as shown in Figure 17-30.

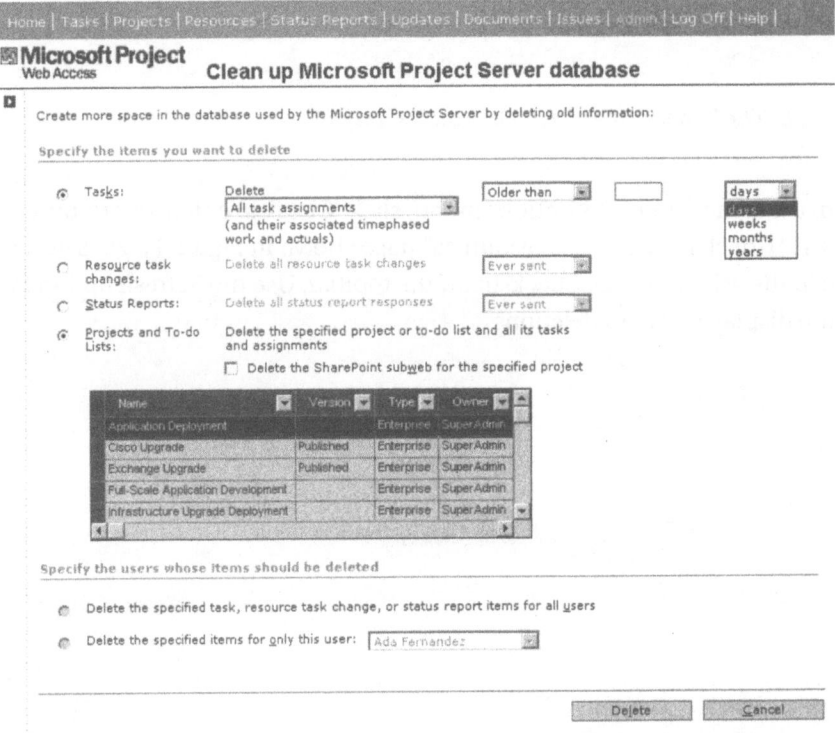

Figure 17-30. The "Clean up Microsoft Project Server database" page

You can selectively delete task assignments, resource task changes, status reports, and entire projects:

- *Tasks:* When you select Tasks, you have the option of choosing all task assignments or completed task assignments only. Choose from Older than, which exposes fields to enter a number, and choose from days, weeks, months, and years, or Ever sent or Sent between, which exposes date range fields for you to enter.

- *Resource task changes:* Deleting resource task changes deletes resource task changes based on your choice of condition: Ever sent, Older than, or Sent between dates. When you select Older than, you specify this in a number of days, weeks, months, or years, as you prefer.

- *Status Reports:* You can delete status reports based on the same selections as resource task changes: Ever sent, Older than, or Sent between dates.

- *Projects and To-do Lists:* This option allows you to delete entire projects. Select this radio button then a project in the grid below.

Selecting Tasks, Resource task changes, or Status Reports activates the radio buttons at the bottom of the page, which aren't applicable when you're deleting entire projects. Here you can specify whether to delete the selected items for one user or all applicable users.

Permanently Removing a Resource

Project Server doesn't allow you to delete enterprise resources through the Project Web Access interface. It does provide a merge user function that applies only to user accounts in the system. If you have two user accounts that you'd like to merge into one, select "Manage users and groups" from the Admin Activities menu and click Merge User Accounts to open the Merge User Accounts area of the Users page, as shown in Figure 17-31. The directions on the Users page are self-explanatory. This isn't a feature that you'll use often. To delete users from the database permanently, see the following TechNet article: "Customizing and Administering Microsoft Project Server: Microsoft Project 2002" at http://www.microsoft.com/technet/treeview/default.asp?url=/technet/prodtechnol/default.asp. The article contains instructions for creating a new stored procedure for deleting enterprise resources from the database.

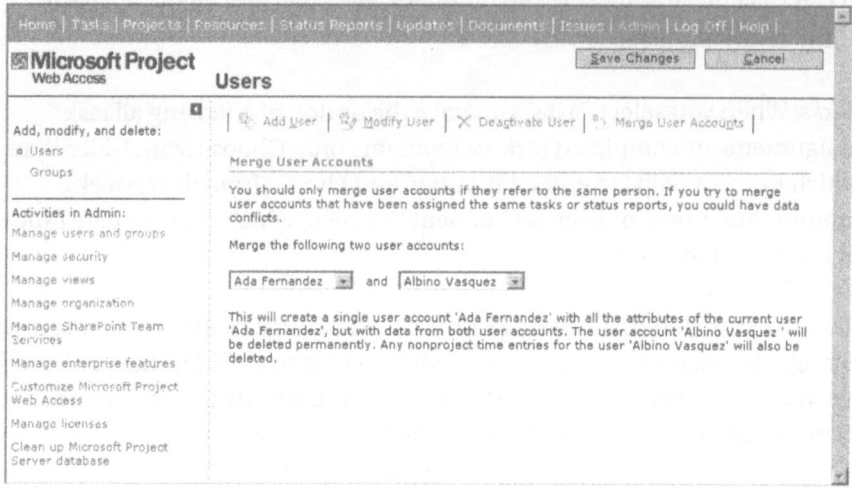

Figure 17-31. Merging users

Renaming a Project

There's no way provided in the Project Web Access interface to change the name of a project in the Project Server database. In order to accomplish this, you need to make a file backup of the project, delete the original plan and data from the server, and then import the project back into the enterprise under a new name. Once you have the plan back in the database, you republish all the assignments to restore assignments to the timesheets. Before you begin these steps, go to STS administration, navigate to Manage subwebs, and record the subweb number for the project you're about to delete. Once you've done that, here are the individual steps you'll need to perform:

1. In Project Professional open the plan you want to rename. Select File ➤ Save As, which opens the Save to Microsoft Project Server dialog box shown in Figure 17-32. Click the Save as File button.

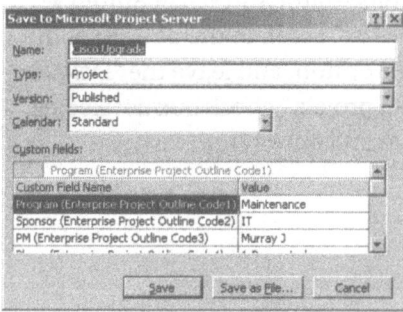

Figure 17-32. The Save to Microsoft Project Server dialog box

2. The Save As File dialog box displays as shown in Figure 17-33. Select the option to save currently loaded global items.

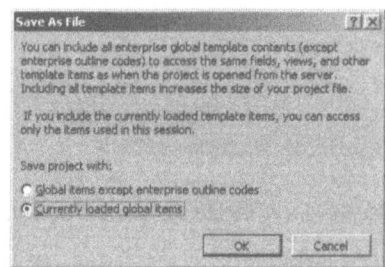

Figure 17-33. The "Save project with" options in the Save As File dialog box

3. Give the file a new name in the Save As dialog box, as shown in Figure 17-34.

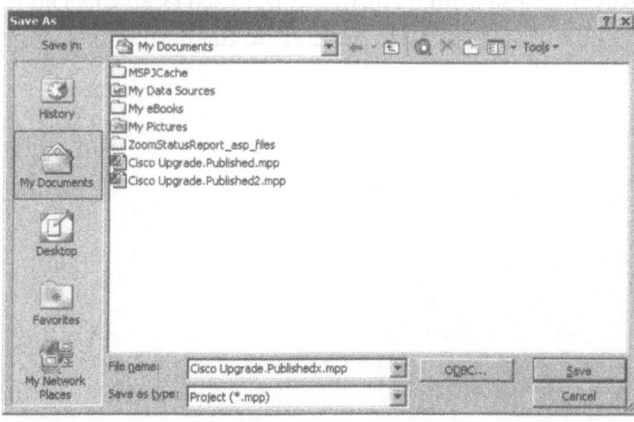

Figure 17-34. Give the file a new name in the Save As dialog box.

4. Log onto Project Web Access as an administrator and select Admin ➤ Clean up Microsoft Project Server database. Scroll to the bottom of the page, select the Projects and To-do Lists option, and leave the "Delete the SharePoint subweb for the specified project" check box deselected. Accept the delete to continue, as shown in Figure 17-35.

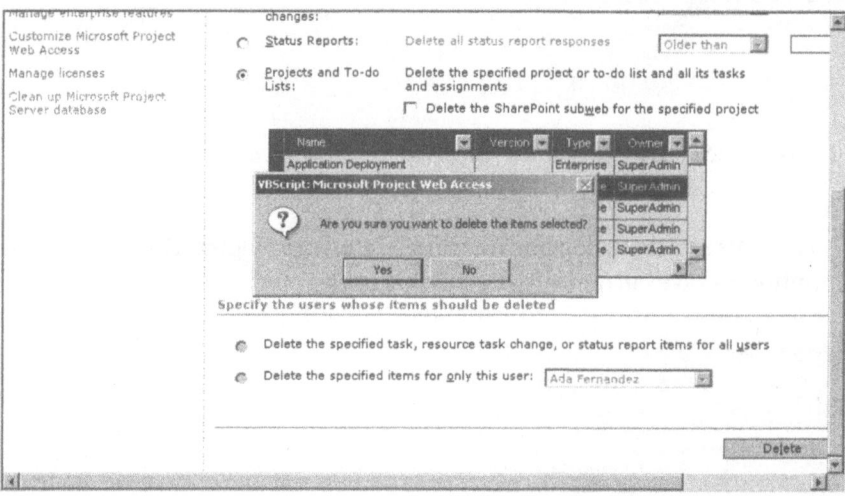

Figure 17-35. The clean up Microsoft Project Server database after delete project action

5. The system redisplays the page when it completes deleting the record.

6. In Project Professional, select Tools ➤ Enterprise Options ➤ Import project to enterprise. Click the Next button on the welcome screen. Select the file you saved in step 3 and click Import. The Import Projects Wizard initial screen displays, as shown in Figure 17-36. In the figure, I've renamed the project **Cisco Router Upgrade** from its former title, **Cisco Upgrade**. Did I really go through all this to add the word "Router" to the name?

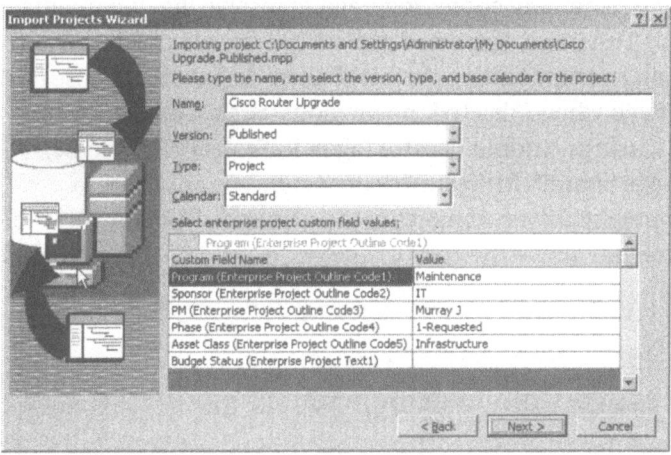

Figure 17-36. The first page of the Import Projects Wizard

7. In the next screen (see Figure 17-37), the system maps all the resources in the plan to the enterprise resources. In other words, it maps the resources back to themselves.

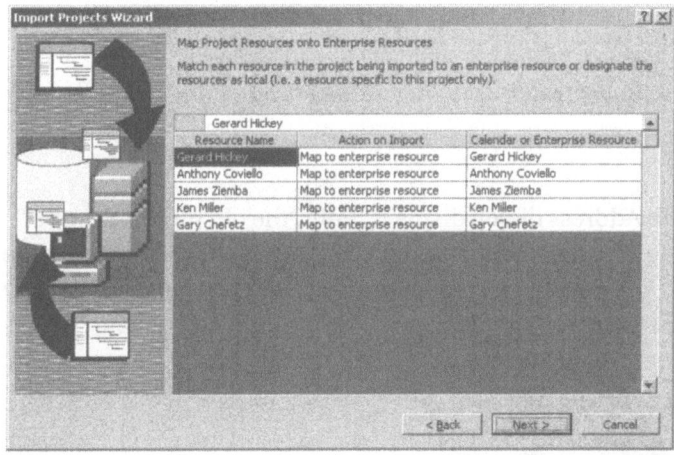

Figure 17-37. Mapping resources in the Import Projects Wizard

8. Because I covered the Import Projects Wizard in Chapter 12, I'll skip to the end at this point. After completing the import process, you close and reopen the plan from Project Server. Go to Collaborate ➤ Publish ➤ Republish Assignments and republish all the assignments in the plan.

9. Now you have one remaining chore: You need to resolve the documents and issues library. The newly imported project has its own newly created blank subweb using its new unique project ID. Remember that I chose not to delete the subweb when I deleted the previous version of the project. What I now do is, using an administrator logon in Project Web Access, navigate to Manage SharePoint Team Services subwebs as shown in Figure 17-38. Highlight the new project in the grid and click Edit Subweb address on the toolbar above the grid.

Figure 17-38. Editing the subweb address in the "Manage SharePoint Team Services subwebs" page

10. The Edit Subweb Address dialog displays. Enter the old project number here, as shown in Figure 17-39. I entered **105** instead of **115** to redirect the new project to a previously created team site. Click Ok when you're ready to record the changes.

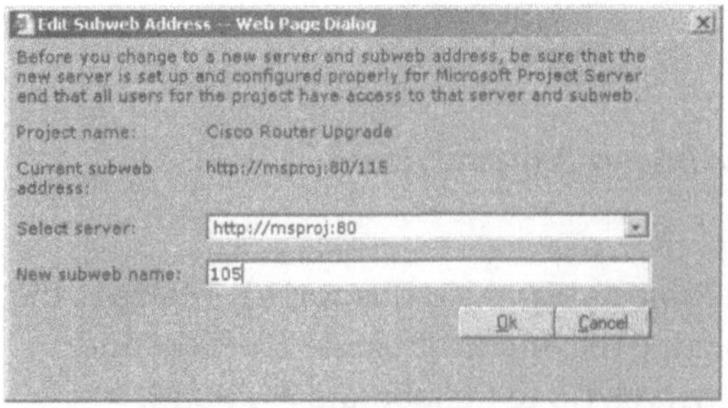

Figure 17-39. The Edit Subweb Address dialog box

The new project now points to the old SharePoint team site. At this point, you can go to the SharePoint Web administration site you explored at the beginning of this chapter and delete the subweb that the system created for the newly imported project.

The preceding is what it takes to make a change to a project name in Project Server. I included this section so that you can see how to use the various administrative interfaces you've learned about in concert to achieve certain tasks that aren't provided for in the default administration interface.

Monitoring Your Server

The most important monitoring you can do of your active Project Server system is routinely reviewing the event logs on the servers. Checking on the machine(s) that are running Project Web Access can reveal application errors that indicate problems on the server. Right-click the My Computer icon on your server, select Manage, expand the Event Viewer, and highlight the application log, as shown in Figure 17-40.

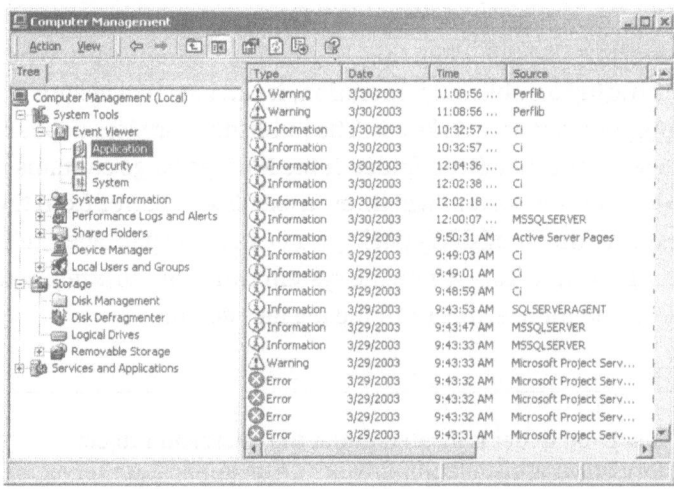

Figure 17-40. The Computer Management console exposing the Event Viewer and application log

Double-click an error to open it in the Event Viewer, as shown in Figure 17-41. The 0x80004005 error indicates an authentication issue on the process.

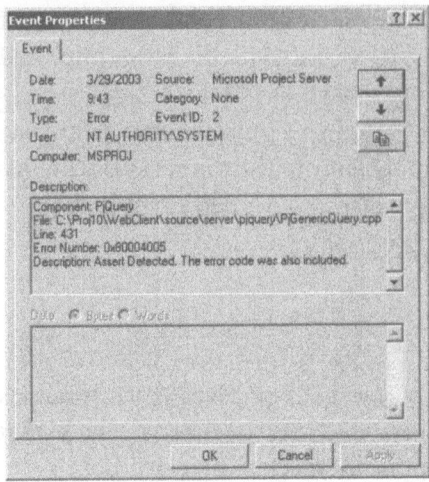

Figure 17-41. The Event Properties window

When the server continuously throws errors like this, one of the things that can happen is that the log files fill up and denigrate server performance. You should seek to eliminate errors like this when they begin to occur frequently. When this type of error occurs during a publishing operation, it can lead to a vicious error cycle that can bring your server to its knees. The publishing process deposits XML transaction packages in the ViewDrop folder. If the XML package contains unauthorized user credentials, the system will throw a 0x80004005 error from the component trying to execute the publishing package. Because the package can't be processed, it remains in the directory where the system continues to attempt to process it, throwing more and more errors until the log files get full.

NOTE The ViewDrop folder is located under the Microsoft Project Server directory on your installation drive or on an application server that you designated.

Keep an eye on the ViewDrop folder during your periodic server inspections, especially if you see errors in the application log. If you find lingering XML packages in the directory, remove them from this folder and copy them to another folder for further investigation.

The most common cause of this is when users attempt to publish project plans without being in a domain environment. It can also happen when there are problems on your network. Sometimes a bad network segment can cause a server to be unable to contact the domain. This will wreak havoc on your system.

Use the System Monitor tool to set up monitors for your system and review these periodically. From the Control Panel, select Administrative Tools and double-click the Performance icon to open the System Monitor, as shown in Figure 17-42. See the Windows 2000 Help files for assistance on using the System Monitor. Use it to monitor your system and application processes running on your system.

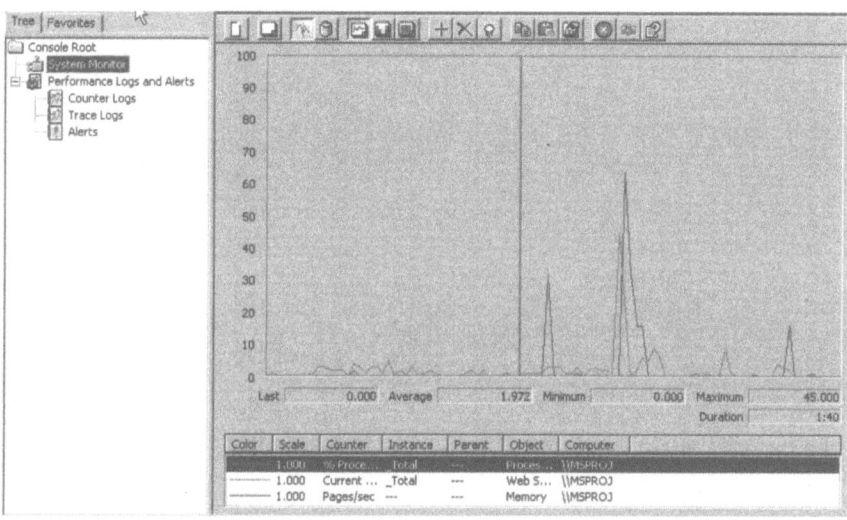

Figure 17-42. The System Monitor

Lastly, keep an eye on your SQL server and logs. You may need to shrink your SQL logs from time to time.

Summary

After reading through this chapter and completing the entire book, you should be ready to manage your own Project Server system. Refer back to topics in the book as you need them and find me online in the Microsoft Communities if you have any questions. In the next chapter, you'll explore customizing the project guide.

Customizing the Project Guide

by David Gage, Microsoft Project MVP

The Project Guide is a new feature in Microsoft Project 2002 Standard and Professional editions. Its purpose is to assist users through the process of building a project plan. In its standard form, the Project Guide steps users through the common tasks that project managers typically execute in creating new projects, including adding tasks, specifying resources, assigning resources to tasks, and tracking and reporting progress. The interface for the Project Guide provides intuitive assistance without being overbearing.

Introduction to the Project Guide

The Project Guide design takes a generic approach in order to be useful to the greatest number of users. It's meant to work with stand-alone instances of Microsoft Project and enterprise configurations using Project Server. Customizing the Project Guide to follow your organization's project management standards and methodologies can add a lot of value for your users. Popular customizations include incorporating steps for project initiation, working with enterprise templates, and setting application options. You can also use the Project Guide as a training tool in your project environment.

You can add customizations to the existing Project Guide or you can create a completely new Project Guide. In this chapter, I'll focus on modifying the current Project Guide. Although you'll gain the knowledge necessary to create your own Project Guides, I suggest you approach your customizations in incremental steps.

I present examples that touch on many technologies related to Microsoft Project and Project Server, such as the Project Data Service (PDS), Extensible Markup Language (XML), Simple Object Access Protocol (SOAP), and JavaScript, as well as some Microsoft Project intrinsic functions.

Components of the Project Guide

The Project Guide uses three primary display components, as shown in Figure 18-1.

Project Guide Toolbar

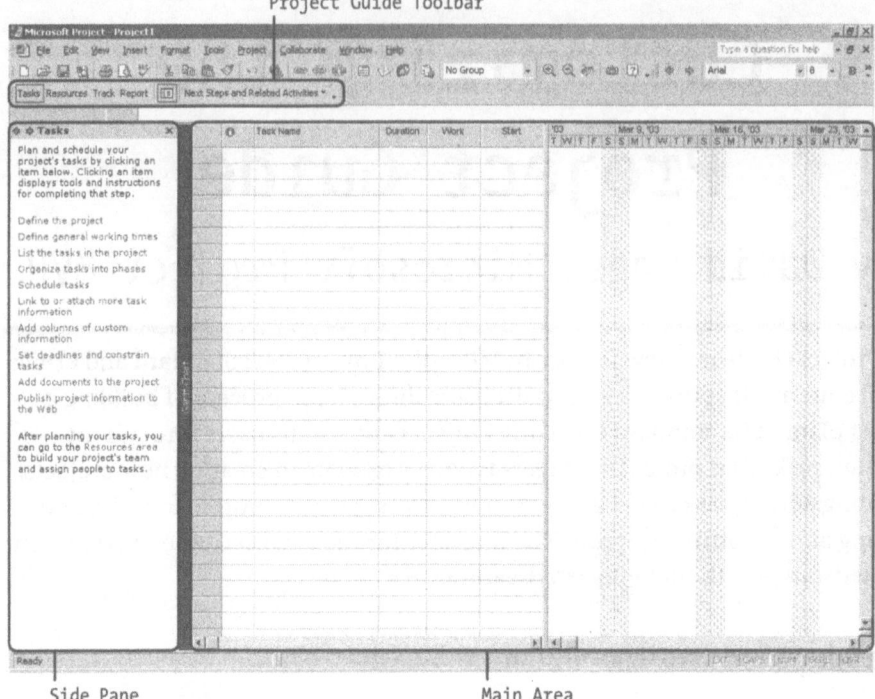

Side Pane   Main Area

Figure 18-1. Components of the Project Guide

The Project Guide toolbar, side pane, and main area are the three components of the view that interact with the Project Guide.

- *Project Guide toolbar:* The Project Guide toolbar is an additional toolbar that provides top-level navigation to the different sections of the Project Guide. Each section or goal area contains goals or tasks a user might want to perform. The Project Guide toolbar included with Microsoft Project contains four goal areas: Tasks, Resources, Track, and Report. These areas correspond to the major phases of managing a project.

- *Side pane:* The side pane is the primary interface for users working with the Project Guide. Each goal area in the Project Guide toolbar has a corresponding list of goals in the side pane. When a goal is selected in the side pane, a new page will appear with information or steps to accomplish the desired task.

- *Main area:* The main area is the view area to the right of the Project Guide where Microsoft Project views are shown. The main area may change views depending on which goal area and goal are selected in the side pane. For example, a user working with Tasks may see the Gantt Chart view, but if the user switches to the

Resources goal, the view may change to the Resource Sheet view. Changing the view may change the goal area shown in the side pane.

The Project Guide in Action

The Project Guide is flexible in its capability to assist users with tasks in Microsoft Project; it uses task pages and wizards to present assistance to users performing tasks within Microsoft Project. In this section, I show you some of the features of the Project Guide. In later sections, you'll learn how to implement these features and capabilities into your own custom Project Guide.

Goal Pages

Figure 18-2 shows a typical goal page that contains all the information pertinent to a specific task. Select the third item in the Tasks goal area, "List the tasks in the project." This page highlights some of the features of a task page such as the Hint option and the More Information option, as shown in Figure 18-2. Note that this is a normal view and not a wizard; there are no step numbers listed at the bottom of the side pane.

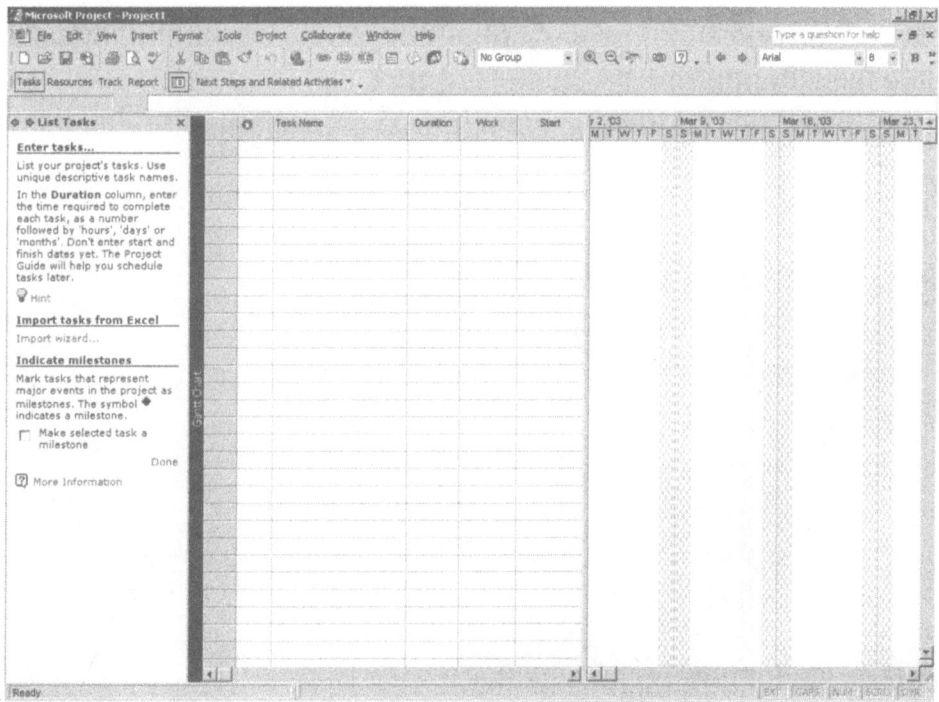

Figure 18-2. List the tasks in the project goal.

Click Hint to get a hint or tip on entering tasks. *Hints* are short messages embedded within the task page that expand to give extra information about the current task. Hints are intended for short messages. You should add more detailed information using the More Information item, which I cover next.

On this page, the Import Wizard shows you how you can use the Project Guide to call Microsoft Project methods. You learn how to call Microsoft Project functions later in this chapter. Click More Information to get additional information for the selected task. You use the More Information option to open a related page with more comprehensive help. Click Done when you're finished with this task view and you're taken back to the list of goals for the currently selected goal area.

Wizard Pages

Click "Define the project," which is the first item of the Tasks goal area. This displays the wizard interface provided by the Project Guide as shown in Figure 18-3. Wizards are meant to guide users through a series of steps required to complete a certain goal or task. The current step and the total number of steps required to complete the goal are listed at the bottom of the side pane.

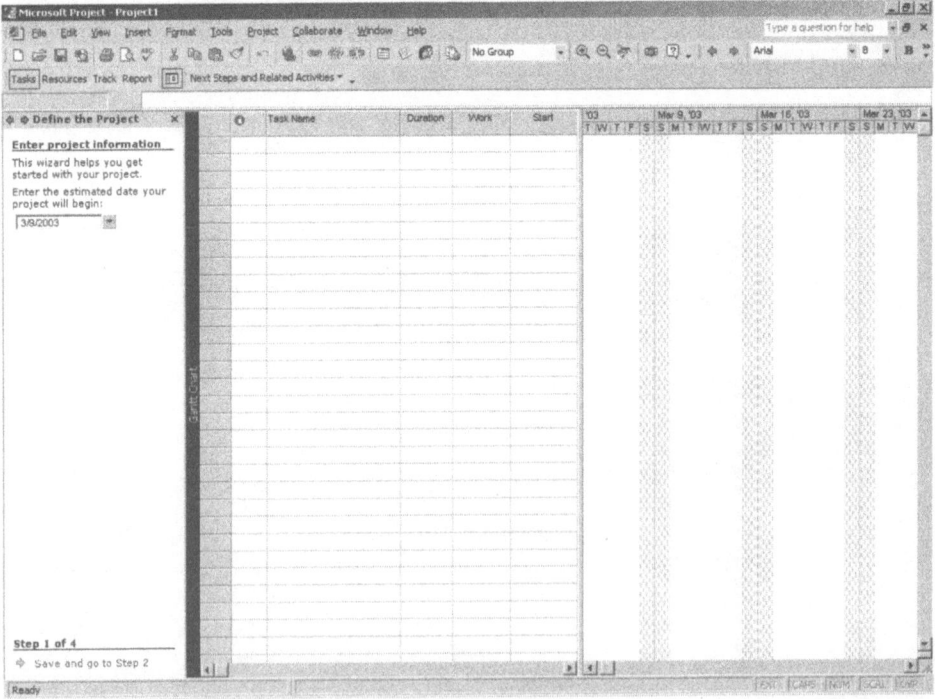

Figure 18-3. The Define the Project Wizard

Without completing the wizard, click the Tasks section of the Project Guide toolbar to display the Tasks goal area in the side pane. Notice that you receive a warning message if you don't complete all steps of a goal wizard, as shown in Figure 18-4.

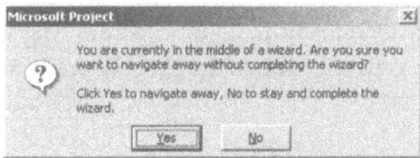

Figure 18-4. Warning you receive when you leave an incomplete wizard

Views and the Project Guide

An important Project Guide objective is to always deliver relevant information in the side pane in context with the action the user is taking in Microsoft Project. To accomplish this, the Project Guide keeps a list of relevant views for each goal area or task. This is important for you to understand because you won't see the Tasks goal area when you're looking at a resource view. Instead, you'll see information pertinent to resource actions. Although this division follows a rule of thumb, there are some views, such as the Gantt Chart view, that are applicable to both tasks and resources. To see this in action, perform the following steps:

1. To see the Project Guide change in the main area view, click the Resource tab in the Project Guide toolbar and select "Define working times for resources," the second goal in the Resources goal area. Notice that the view automatically changes to the Resource Sheet view.

2. To see the Project Guide goal area change based on the Microsoft Project view selected, while you're in the Resource Sheet view select the Gantt Chart view from the Views menu and notice that the goal area changes to the Tasks goal area.

3. To see the Project Server pages selected change the Project Guide side pane goal area, select the Project Center page (select Collaborate ➤ Project Center) and notice that a new page displays. In this instance, the page change selected a specific task instead of a goal area.

Project Guide Architecture

Figure 18-5 shows the Microsoft Project Options dialog box (select Tools ➤ Options). Click the Interface tab to look at the options for the Project Guide. The settings at the bottom of the tab that relate to the Project Guide are in the Project Guide Functionality and Layout Page section and the Project Guide Content section. I discuss these two setting areas in the next section. If you click the "Use a custom page" and "Use custom content" radio buttons, notice the gbui:// prefix in the URLs/filenames.

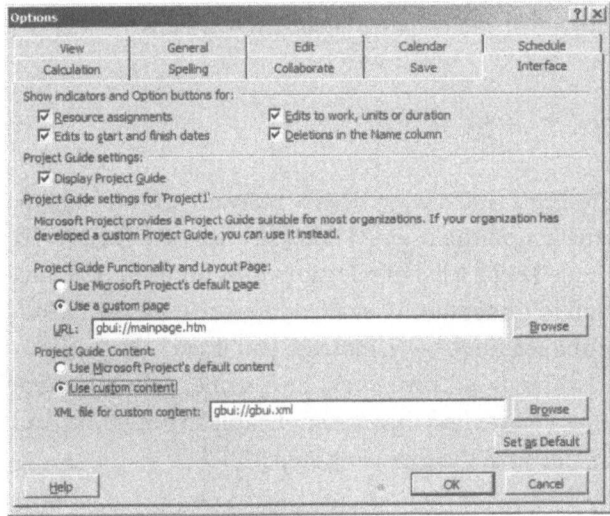

Figure 18-5. The Interface tab of the Microsoft Project Options dialog box

gbui Protocol

Microsoft Project uses a special protocol called gbui to serve Project Guide data. All of the files for the Project Guide, across all languages, are compiled into the Pj10intl.dll file and accessed using the gbui protocol. Microsoft Project knows to go to Pj10intl.dll to find any pages requested with the gbui:// prefix. The communication mechanism is very similar to HTML, except that gbui gets data from a specific file instead of a Web server.

You create most custom content using HTML, ASP, JavaScript, or other, similar Web technologies, and you store this content on your local machine or on a Web server. Because the Pj10intl.dll file is installed by Microsoft Project, you can include original Project Guide content within your custom Project Guides by using the gbui:// prefix. This allows you to slowly evolve a custom Project Guide instead of creating your own Project Guide from scratch.

Project Guide Functionality and Layout Page

One starting point for creating custom Project Guides is the Project Guide Functionality and Layout page. By default, this file is gbui://mainpage.htm and you use it to lay out the Project Guide side pane and main area views. You won't be working with this page in this chapter, as it controls more of the fundamental functions and internal architecture of the Project Guide. For more information on customizing the main page, see the article "Customizing the Microsoft Project Guide" in the Microsoft Project 2002 Software Development Kit (http://msdn.microsoft.com/library/en-us/pdr/PDR_Overview_3338.asp).

Project Guide Content

A second starting point for customizing the Project Guide is to create custom content within the existing Project Guide framework. When you create a custom Project Guide, you create a properly formatted Project Guide XML file. The Project Guide XML content file contains the hierarchical representation of information and specifications for features such as view changes and help displays.

In this section I show you the Project Guide XML content file structure. The Project Guide XML content file has three main sections:

- ViewChanges

- PageChanges

- GoalArea

The ViewChanges area determines the goal area displayed when you change a view in Microsoft Project. The PageChanges section specifies the Project Guide goal area or goal task presented when you connect to a Project Server page within Microsoft Project. The final section, GoalArea, is the hierarchical representation of information for the Project Guide and the section on which I focus most of this chapter.

ViewChanges

The ViewChanges section determines how the Project Guide will react to Microsoft Project view changes. The ViewChanges section is made up of one or more ViewChange elements, as shown in Listing 18-1. Within each ViewChange element is a ViewType, ViewScreen, or ViewName element, which relates to the type of view within Microsoft Project, and a GoalAreaID, which represents a corresponding goal area. Table 18-1 lists ViewType values, which represent an entire category of views. Table 18-2 lists the ViewScreen and corresponding ViewName values.

 NOTE ViewChanges applies only to goal areas. ViewChanges doesn't work with goal tasks.

Listing 18-1. The ViewChanges Structure in the Project Guide XML Content File

```
<ViewChanges>
    <ViewChange>
        <ViewType> 0 </ViewType>
        <GoalAreaID> 1 </GoalAreaID>
    </ViewChange>
    <ViewChange>
        <ViewScreen> 7 </ViewScreen>
        <GoalAreaID> 2 </GoalAreaID>
    </ViewChange>
    <ViewChange>
        <ViewName> Resource Usage </ViewName>
        <GoalAreaID> 3 </GoalAreaID>
    </ViewChange>
</ViewChanges>
```

Table 18-1. ViewType Value List

VALUE	VIEWTYPE DESCRIPTION
0	Task views
1	Resource views
−1	Neither task nor resource views (applies to Microsoft Project Web Access or other Web pages displayed within Microsoft Project)

Table 18-2. ViewScreen and ViewName Value List

VIEWSCREEN	VIEWNAME	MICROSOFT PROJECT ENUMERATION
1	Gantt Chart	pjGantt
2	Network Diagram	pjNetworkDiagram
3	Relationship Diagram	pjRelationshipDiagram
4	Task Form	pjTaskForm

Table 18-2. ViewScreen and ViewName Value List (Continued)

VIEWSCREEN	VIEWNAME	MICROSOFT PROJECT ENUMERATION
5	Task Sheet	pjTaskSheet
6	Resource Form	pjResourceForm
7	Resource Sheet	pjResourceSheet
8	Resource Graph	pjResourceGraph
10	Task Details Form	pjTaskDetailsForm
11	Task Name Form	pjTaskNameForm
12	Resource Name Form	pjResourceNameForm
13	Calendar	pjCalendar
14	Task Usage	pjTaskUsage
15	Resource Usage	pjResourceUsage

The example in Listing 18-1 has three ViewChange sections. The first section specifies that a view change to a task type view will change the Project Guide to goal area 1 (Tasks). The second ViewChange group specifies that switching to the Resource Sheet will result in a switch to goal area 2 (Resources). The final ViewChange element specifies goal area 3 (Track) will be selected when the Resource Usage view is chosen.

If you go through the example in Listing 18-1, you may notice the Project Guide doesn't always change goal areas as expected. The reason for this is that the ViewChange event won't fire unless the Project Guide goal area is irrelevant to the newly selected Microsoft Project view. The following series of steps shows how the Project Guide reacts to Microsoft Project view changes. Start with the Resource Sheet selected.

1. Select the Gantt Chart view, which is of the Tasks view type, and notice the Project Guide switches to the Tasks goal area (GoalAreaID 1).

2. Select the Resource Sheet and the Resources goal area (GoalAreaID 2) becomes active.

3. Select the Resource Usage view and notice that the Project Guide doesn't change to the Track goal area (GoalAreaID 3) as you might expect.

4. Select the Gantt Chart view.

5. Select the Resource Usage view again and the Project Guide displays changes to the Track goal area as you might have expected in step 3.

The reason the Project Guide didn't change to the Track goal area in step 3 is because the Resource Sheet and Resource Usage view are both relevant to the Resource goal area. Switching to the Gantt Chart view, which is a task type view, and then to the Resource Usage view produces the expected change to the Track goal area. The relevant views for a task are specified in the RelevantViews section of each goal area, which I cover in the GoalArea section of this chapter.

PageChanges

PageChanges actions are very similar to ViewChanges actions, except they react to changes to Microsoft Project Web Access pages instead of Microsoft Project views. The PageChanges section consists of one or more PageChange elements, as shown in Listing 18-2. Within each PageChange element is a ProjectServerPageID element and a GoalAreaID or TaskID element.

The example in Listing 18-2 shows a PageChange element applying to a TaskID and a GoalAreaID. As mentioned in the Note in the previous section, PageChange can move to a TaskID or a GoalAreaID, whereas ViewChange only applies to GoalAreaID. The first PageChange section shown represents a change to the Updates page (select Collaborate ➤ Update Project Progress) and corresponds to Project Guide TaskID 19. The second PageChange group changes to the Resource goal area when you select the Resource Center page in Microsoft Project.

 NOTE PageChanges can change to Project Guide goal areas or goal area tasks. ViewChanges only apply to goal areas.

Listing 18-2. The PageChanges Structure in the Project Guide XML Content File

```
<PageChanges>
    <PageChange>
        <ProjectServerPageID> 1 </ProjectServerPageID>
        <TaskID> 19 </TaskID>
    </PageChange>
    <PageChange>
        <ProjectServerPageID> 5 </ProjectServerPageID>
        <GoalAreaID> 2 </GoalAreaID>
    </PageChange>
</PageChanges>
```

Table 18-3 contains a list of all available ProjectServerPageIDs.

Table 18-3. Project Server Page Value List

PROJECTSERVERPAGEID	PAGE DESCRIPTION
1	Updates page showing updates for the active project
2	Document library page for the active project
3	Issues page for the active project
4	Project Center page
5	Resource Center page
6	Portfolio Analyzer
7	Portfolio Modeler

GoalArea

The GoalArea section of the Project Guide XML content file is the hierarchical representation of information for the Project Guide. The GoalArea section contains groupings of goal area elements with further groupings of goal task elements. Each goal area element may consist of one or more goal task elements.

GoalArea Element

Each section of the Project Guide is represented by a goal area and is specified in the Project Guide XML content file, as shown in Listing 18-3.

Listing 18-3. GoalArea Element Structure

```
<GoalArea>
    <GoalAreaID> 1 </GoalAreaID>
    <GoalAreaName> Tasks </GoalAreaName>
    <GoalAreaDescription> Plan and schedule your project's tasks.
        </GoalAreaDescription>
    <URL> gbui://tasks_main.htm </URL>
    <RelevantViews>
        <ViewType>1</ViewType>
        <ViewScreen>14</ViewScreen>
        <ViewName> Resource Sheet <ViewName>
    </RelevantViews>
    <GoalAreaTask>
        <-- NOTE: Goal area tasks will be covered in the next section -->
    </GoalAreaTask>
</GoalArea>
```

Here's a description of each item in the GoalArea element:

- *GoalAreaID:* Each goal area must have a unique ID.

- *GoalAreaName:* This is the name of the goal area. You should keep this name short because it's the name shown at the top of the Project Guide side pane.

- *GoalAreaDescription:* The description of the goal area is shown just below the side pane title and above all of the goal tasks.

- *URL:* This is the URL for the HTML page associated with each goal area. This page is displayed when the goal area is selected.

- *RelevantViews:* This element defines the Microsoft Project views relevant to the goal area. The valid options are ViewType, ViewScreen, and ViewName, as addressed in the "ViewChanges" section earlier in this chapter.

- *GoalAreaTask:* This element represents one or more goal tasks within the goal area.

GoalAreaTask Element

Each goal area is represented by one or more goal area tasks. Listing 18-4 represents the Project Guide XML content structure of the GoalAreaTask element.

Listing 18-4. GoalAreaTask Element Structure

```
<GoalAreaTask>
    <TaskID> 11 </TaskID>
    <Title> Select Enterprise Resources </Title>
    <TaskName> Specify people and equipment from Microsoft Project Server
        </TaskName>
    <URL> file://C:\CustomPG\...\EnterpriseTeamBuilder.htm </URL>
    <TaskHelp>
        <HelpName> More Information </HelpName>
        <URL> file://C:\CustomPG\...\EnterpriseTeamBuilder_Help.htm </URL>
    </TaskHelp>
    <RelevantViews>
        <ViewType> 1 </ViewType>
        <ViewScreen> 7 </ViewScreen>
        <ViewName> Resource Form </ViewName>
    </RelevantViews>
    <RelatedActivity>
        <ActivityName> Enterprise Team Builder </ActivityName >
```

```
            <VBAMethod> EnterpriseTeamBuilder </VBAMethod>
        </RelatedActivity>
        <RelatedTask>
            <TaskID> 13 </TaskID>
        </RelatedTask>
    </GoalAreaTask>
</GoalAreaTask>
```

The GoalAreaTask element contains the following elements:

- *TaskID:* Each goal area task must have a unique ID.

- *Title:* This is the title shown at the top of the Project Guide side pane. You should keep this name short because it's the name shown at the top of the Project Guide side pane.

- *TaskName:* This is the text shown in the goal area in the list of tasks.

- *URL:* This is the URL for the HTML page associated with each goal task. This page is displayed when the goal task is selected.

- *TaskHelp:* This section specifies the help page associated with a goal area task.

- *HelpName:* This is the name for the help link shown at the bottom of a goal task.

- *URL:* This is the URL for the HTML page associated with each goal task help. This page is displayed when the goal task help is selected.

- *RelevantViews:* This element defines the Microsoft Project views relevant to the goal task. The valid options are ViewType, ViewScreen, and ViewName, as addressed in the "ViewChanges" section earlier in this chapter.

- *RelatedActivity:* This section specifies other activities to be shown in the Next Steps and Related Activities button on the Project Guide toolbar.

- *ActivityName:* This is the name shown on the Next Steps and Related Activities button.

- *VBAMethod:* This is the name of the Microsoft Project VBA method for the given activity.

- *RelatedTasks:* This section specifies tasks related to this goal task to be shown in the Next Steps and Related Activities button on the Project Guide toolbar.

- *TaskID:* This is the TaskID of a related task.

Customizing the Project Guide

Now that you have the lay of land, you'll explore three different examples of modifying the Project Guide. In the first example, you'll replace the default "Specify people and equipment for the project" goal with a Microsoft Project Server–centric "Specify people and equipment from Microsoft Project Server," including how to specify relevant views, and help files. In the second example, you'll look at how to add a new goal area to the Project Guide. In the third and final customization example, you'll create a goal task wizard, which shows you what you can accomplish with custom development work. You'll work with Project Server embedded technologies, including the PDS, SOAP, XML, JavaScript, and Microsoft Project functions.

All files for these examples are available on the Web site for this book (`http://www.projectserverexperts.com`). You may also want to download the sample Project Guide files available in the article "Customizing the Microsoft Project Guide" in the Microsoft Project 2002 Software Development Kit (`http://msdn.microsoft.com/library/en-us/pdr/PDR_Overview_3338.asp`).

Modifying an Existing Project Guide Goal Task

In this example, you change the default "Specify people and equipment for the project" goal with a Project Server–centric version. This will force Project Guide users to specify resources using the Build Team from Enterprise dialog box only.

Here are the steps required for changing or adding a goal to an existing goal area:

1. Modify the Project Guide XML content file.

2. Create a Web page for the goal task.

3. Create a Web page for the goal task help (if applicable).

4. Create scripts as needed for custom functionality.

5. Specify the Project Guide content file.

Modify the Project Guide XML Content File

The first step in creating a custom Project Guide is to modify the Project Guide XML content file. The code for this example is shown in Listing 18-5.

NOTE The URLs specified in Listing 18-5 are hard-coded to the local machine. Make sure to put the files in the same location or modify the URLs in the listing.

Listing 18-5. Project Guide XML Content for the First Example

```
<GoalAreaTask>
    <TaskID> 11 </TaskID>
    <Title> Select Enterprise Resources </Title>
    <TaskName> Specify people and equipment from Microsoft Project Server
        </TaskName>
    <URL> file://C:\CustomPG\Project Server
        Book\EnterpriseTeamBuilder\EnterpriseTeamBuilder.htm </URL>
    <TaskHelp>
        <HelpName> More Information </HelpName>
        <URL> file://C:\CustomPG\Project Server
            Book\EnterpriseTeamBuilder\EnterpriseTeamBuilder_Help.htm </URL>
    </TaskHelp>
    <RelevantViews>
        <ViewType> 1 </ViewType>
    </RelevantViews>
</GoalAreaTask>
```

I've covered all the items in Listing 18-5, so there shouldn't be any surprises for you there. Pay attention to the note in this section that states files are hard-coded to the local machine in the example. You must put the files in the same location or modify the URLs in the code. When you deploy your customized Project Guide within an organization, you'll most likely put these files on an internal Web server.

NOTE Set the Web site holding the Project Guide pages as a Trusted Site in Internet Explorer.

Create a Web Page for the Goal Task

The code in Listing 18-6 presents an HTML page for the goal task. In this example are sections including the header, body header, task header, divMain section, and the divContent SidepaneData data section. I cover each of these in more detail in this section.

Listing 18-6. Enterprise Team Builder.htm

```
<html>
<head>
<meta http-equiv="content-type" content="text/html; charset=Windows-1252">
<script src="file:\\C:\CustomPG\Project Server
Book\EnterpriseTeamBuilder\EnterpriseTeamBuilder.js" language="JScript">
    </script>
<script src="gbui://util.js" language="JScript"></script>
<link rel="stylesheet" href="gbui://ProjIE.css" type="text/css" />
</head>

<!-- The body should always have an onLoad call to handleResize() -->
<body onLoad="handleResize(); setupView()">
    <!-- Display the Task Header -->
    <script language="JScript">
        // pDisplayTaskHeader should always be called before pSetupSidepane
        pDisplayTaskHeader();
        pSetupSidepane();
    </script>

    <div id=divMain class="divMain" onResize="handleResize();">
        <div id=divContent class="Sidepanedata">
            <p>
            Click the link below to bring up a list of all the resources on the
            Microsoft Project Server:
            </p>
            <p>
                <a class="trigger" href="#" onClick="EnterpriseTeamBuilder()">
                Build Team from Enterprise...</a>
            </p>
            <p>
                In the dialog that is brought up, use filters to display the
                appropriate users, and click
                the <b>Add</b> button to add these users to the project.
            </p>
            <!-- Separator line -->
```

```
<hr width=95% align=center>
<p>
    <b>Generic Resources</b>
</p>
<p>

    If you are using generic resources in your templates, you
    might want to use the <b>Replace</b> button.  Select the
    generic resource in the Project Team Resources list (right
    list) in the Build Team dialog.  Then select the resource
    from the Enterprise Resource list (left list) who is to take
    over the work assigned to the generic resource. Finally,
    click the <b>Replace</b> button and the enterprise resource
    will now be assigned to all of the tasks previously assigned
    to the  generic resource.
</p>
<p class="rightAlign">
    <!-- pNavigate(goalAreaID, taskID, elementID) -->
    <!--            * goalAreaID - goal area to go back to -->
    <!--            * taskID - task ID to go back to (-1 for goal
        area menu) -->
    <!--            * elementID - 'GoBack' takes you back to the
        previous location -->
    <!--    In this instance we are going back to the Goal Area
        2 main menu -->
    <a title="Done" id="GoBack" class="trigger" href="#" onClick=
        "parent.navigate(2,-1,'GoBack')">Done</a>
</p>

    <!-- Display the Task Footer -->
    <script language="JScript">
        pDisplayTaskFooter();
    </script>

    </div> <!--divContent   - Sidepanedata-->
    </div> <!-- divMain -->
</body>
</html>
```

The header of the Enterprise Team Builder file provides some very important pointers to related files with needed functionality. The first script file is Enterprise Team Builder.js, which has the JavaScript functions necessary to implement behaviors for the Enterprise Team Builder goal task. The next file, Util.js, is a Project Guide file that provides several functions, such as displaying the task header and setting up the side pane. This file is included as part of the download for the Microsoft article "Customizing the Microsoft Project Guide" if you'd like to study this file in more detail. The final part of the header is a link to the ProjIE.css style sheet, which gives the Project Guide a consistent appearance.

The body section begins with an important call in the onLoad event. Call the `<body onLoad="handleResize()">` event first in every Project Guide HTML file, as it handles any size changes to the Project Guide side pane. The call after `handleResize()` is `setupView()`, a function I created to change the view to the Resource Sheet. I cover this function call in the Enterprise Team Builder.js file. If you want code to run before the Web page loads, such as a customized data retrieval task, you put these function calls in the `<body onLoad=` event as well. The next call is `pDisplayTaskHeader();`, which displays the title and forward/backward buttons in the side pane header. The final function call in the top of the body section is `pSetupSidePane();`, which updates the Goal Bar based on the new content. The `pDisplayTaskHeader();` function call should always be called before the `pSetupSidePane();` function.

The divMain section of the HTML page applies to content in the main area of Microsoft Project. You put content in this section if you want to modify the content on the right or call a Web page in the main area. As I am primarily working with the side pane, I don't have any calls in the divMain section.

The divContent section represents all of the information to be shown in the side pane for the goal task. For this example, I have several paragraphs with text, but the most important section is the link represented by `<a class="trigger" href="#" onClick="EnterpriseTeamBuilder()">Build Team from Enterprise...</a>`. When this link is clicked, it calls the `EnterpriseTeamBuilder()` function that I created in the Enterprise Team Builder.js file (I cover this later in this example). The `<a title="Done" id="GoBack" class="trigger" href="#" onClick="parent.navigate(2,-1,'GoBack')">Done</a>` link puts a Done link at the bottom of the goal task page. The `parent.navigate` call in this instance returns to the Resources goal area (2) main menu (–1). At the bottom of the divContent section is the function call `pDisplayTaskFooter();` that sets up the task footer and establishes a task help link if specified.

Create a Web Page for the Goal Task Help

The code in Listing 18-7 represents the HTML page for the goal task help. In this example, the page is very similar to the Enterprise Team Builder.htm page I covered in the previous section. There are three primary differences between this page and the goal task page. The first difference is the call to `pDisplayTaskHelpHeader();` instead of `pDisplayTaskHeader();`. A second variation is that the Done link navigates back to the goal task (11) instead of the goal area menu (–1). The final distinction between the two pages is that the `pDisplayTaskFooter();` shouldn't be called because I don't want a help link on the help page.

Listing 18-7. Enterprise Team Builder_Help.htm

```html
<html>
<head>
<meta http-equiv="content-type" content="text/html; charset=utf-8">
<meta http-equiv="MSThemeCompatible" content="Yes">
<title> Microsoft Project </title>
<script src="gbui://util.js" language="JScript"></script>
<link rel="stylesheet" href="gbui://ProjIE.css" type="text/css" />
</head>

<!-- The body should always have a onLoad call to handleResize() -->
<body onLoad="handleResize()" onContextMenu="return false" tabIndex=1>
    <script language="JScript">
        // pDisplayTaskHeader should always be called before pSetupSidepane
        pDisplayTaskHeader();
        pSetupSidepane();
    </script>
    <div id=divMain class="divMain" onResize="handleResize();">
        <div class="SidepaneData">
            <div class="heading_over">
                <p>
                    Generic Resources
                </p>
            </div>
            <p>
                You should use generic resources when possible as they have
                several benefits:
                    <li>
                        act as placeholders for resource assignments
                    </li>
                    <li>
                        all task assignments are replaced when a resource is
                        assigned using <b>Replace</b>
                    </li>
                    <li>
                        allow preliminary reporting before the project plan
                        is complete
                    </li>
            </p>
            <p class="rightAlign">
                <!-- pNavigate(goalAreaID, taskID, elementID) -->
                <!--          * goalAreaID - goal area to go back to -->
                <!--          * taskID - task ID to go back to (-1 for
```

```
                                                goal area menu) -->
                           <!--              * elementID - 'GoBack' takes you back to
                                     the previous location -->
                           <!--        In this instance we are going back to the
                                     calling page Goal Area 2 and TaskID 11 -->
                           <a title="Done" id="GoBack" class="trigger" href="#"
                                 onClick="pNavigate(2,11,'GoBack')"> Done </a>
                    </p>
                    <!-- Don't put a setup footer because we don't want to
                           include a More Information link on the help page -->
             </div> <!-- SidepaneData -->
          </div> <!-- divMain -->
      </body>
      </html>
```

Create Scripts for the Goal Task

The code in Listing 18-8 shows the Enterprise Team Builder.js page with the JavaScript functions necessary to give the goal area task added functionality. The first function, setupView(), changes Microsoft Project to the Resource Sheet if it isn't already the current view. The EnterpriseTeamBuilder function gets an object link to the Microsoft Project application using var application = window.external.Application; and then it calls the Microsoft Project EnterpriseTeamBuilder function. You can find the command for this feature by looking in the Microsoft Project VBA help file, VBAPJ10.CHM, or by recording a macro and then selecting Build Team from Enterprise from the Tools menu.

Listing 18-8. Enterprise Team Builder.js

```
//*********************************************************************
// This jscript file has functions needed by the EnterpriseTeamBuilder
// task page htm file
//*********************************************************************


var RESOURCE_SHEET = "Resource Sheet";


//*********************************************************************
// NAME: setupView
// PURPOSE: This function sets the current view to the Resource Sheet
// PARAMETERS: None
// RETURN: None
//*********************************************************************
function setupView()
```

```
{
    try
    {
        var application = window.external.application;
        var script = pscript();

        //Make sure Resource Sheet view applied
        if (application.activeproject.currentview != RESOURCE_SHEET)
        {
            script.applyNewView(RESOURCE_SHEET);
        }
    }
    catch(err)
    {
        alert("Error applying view!");
    }
}


//**************************************************************************
// NAME: EnterpriseTeamBuilder
// PURPOSE: This function calls the EnterpriseTeamBuilder Microsoft
// Project function.
// PARAMETERS: None
// RETURN: None
//**************************************************************************
function EnterpriseTeamBuilder()
{
    try
    {
        // Create the application object in memory
        // Set the application object so we can access Microsoft Project
        // functions
        var application = window.external.Application;

        // Call the EnterpriseTeamBuilder function
        // This was found using VBAPJ10.CHM, which is an
        // install option for Microsoft Project
        application.EnterpriseTeamBuilder;
    }
    catch(exp)
    {
        alert("Error calling EnterpriseTeamBuilder function!")
    }
}
```

Specify the Project Guide Content File

You've now created a customized Project Guide that changes the standard resource selection to allow selecting resources from Microsoft Project Server only. The last step is to open up the Options dialog box (select Tools ➤ Options) and specify the Project Guide Content XML file for custom content. Then go to the Resources goal area and take a look at the customized "Specify people and equipment from Microsoft Project Server."

TIP   When you test a custom Project Guide, press Ctrl+R to refresh updated Project Guide data in Microsoft Project.

Creating a New Project Guide Goal Area

In this example, I create a brand-new goal area called Project, which will be the first goal in the Project Guide. This new goal area contains a simple page specified for project templates. In the following example, I add a goal task wizard to the Project goal area.

Here are the steps required to add a new goal area:

1. Modify the Project Guide XML content file.

2. Create a Web page for the goal area page.

3. Create scripts as needed for custom functionality.

4. Specify the Project Guide content file.

Modify the Project Guide XML Content File

Once again I want to add a new goal area to the Project Guide XML content file. Listing 18-9 shows the code to add the new goal area and a new goal task.

NOTE The URLs specified in Listing 18-9 are hard-coded to the local machine. Make sure to put the files in the same location or modify the URLs in the listing.

Listing 18-9. ProjectGuideArea.xml Content for the Goal Area Page

```
<GoalArea>
    <GoalAreaID> 10 </GoalAreaID>
    <GoalAreaName> Project </GoalAreaName>
    <GoalAreaDescription> Follow the steps below to create a new project
        </GoalAreaDescription>
    <URL> file://C:\CustomPG\Project Server Book\Project Goal Area\
        Project_Main.htm </URL>
    <RelevantViews>
        <ViewType> 0 </ViewType>
    </RelevantViews>

    <GoalAreaTask>
        <TaskID> 101 </TaskID>
        <Title> Project Templates </Title>
        <TaskName> Use project templates </TaskName>
        <URL> file://C:\CustomPG\Project Server Book\Project Goal Area\Project
                Templates\Project_Templates.htm </URL>
    </GoalAreaTask>
</GoalArea>
```

I've already covered the details of this code. As you can see, creating a goal area is very similar to creating a goal area task entry. Be aware that the GoalAreaID for Project is 10; however, I put this section in front of the Project goal area with a GoalAreaID of 1. The Project goal area will show up first if it's specified first in the XML file. The GoalAreaID doesn't determine the order of goal areas, and the same applies to goal tasks. Make certain that each goal area or goal task has a unique ID within its group.

Create a Web Page for the Goal Area Page

The code in Listing 18-10 shows the HTML page for the Project goal area page. There are several differences between a goal area page and a goal task page. The first difference is making the pDisplayGoalAreaTasks(); function call to display the goal area tasks. The next function call displays the goal area footer, but the pDisplayGoalAreaFooter(); function isn't used in the Project Guide at this time. The last variation contains a link to navigate to the next goal area at the bottom of the side pane.

Listing 18-10. Project_Main.htm

```
<!-- This is the goal area page for the Project Goal Area -->

<html>
<head>
<meta http-equiv="MSThemeCompatible" content="Yes">
<script src="gbui://tasks_main.js" language="JScript"></script>
<script src="gbui://util.js" language="JScript"></script>
<link rel="stylesheet" href="gbui://ProjIE.css" type="text/css" />
</head>
<!-- The body should always have a onLoad call to handleResize() -->
<body onLoad="handleResize();" onContextMenu="return false" tabIndex=1>
    <script language="JScript">
        // pDisplayTaskHeader should always be called before pSetupSidepane
        pDisplayTaskHeader();
        pSetupSidepane();
    </script>
    <div id=divMain class="divMain" onResize="handleResize();">
        <div class="SidepaneData">
            <script language="JScript">
                <!-- Display the Goal Area tasks as listed in the XML file -->
                pDisplayGoalAreaTasks();
            </script>
            <script language="JScript">
            <!-- Display the Goal Area footer, which is not currently used -->
            pDisplayGoalAreaFooter();
            </script>
            <!-- Place a link to the next Goal Area here -->
            <!-- Navigate to Goal Area ID 1 (Tasks area) -->
            <p>
                After completing the initial project setup, you can go to the
                <a title="TasksArea" id="GoToTasks" class="trigger" href="#"
                    onClick="pNavigate(1)"> Tasks area </a>
                to create tasks in your project.
            </p>
        </div> <!-- SidepaneData -->
    </div> <!-- divMain -->
</body>
</html>
```

Specify the Project Guide Content File

I don't cover the creation of the Project_Templates.htm file in this chapter, as the process to do so is very similar to the process to create the goal task page you created in the first example. All of the files are available for download from http://projectserverexperts.com. Once you specify the new content, you have a new goal area in your Project Guide.

Creating a New Project Guide Goal Task Wizard

In this example, you'll focus on building a goal task wizard page that introduces some new behind-the-scene technologies. I cover these technologies briefly.

The steps required to create a new goal task wizard are as follows:

1. Modify the Project Guide XML content file.

2. Create a Web page for the goal task wizard page.

3. Create a script page for wizard functionality.

4. Specify the Project Guide content file.

Modify the Project Guide XML Content File

Once again, you're working with the Project Guide XML content file to add a new goal area to your Project Guide. Listing 18-11 shows the XML code to add to the Project Guide content file for the new goal task wizard.

 NOTE   The URLs specified in Listing 18-11 are hard-coded to the local machine. Make sure to put the files in the same location or modify the URLs in the listing.

Listing 18-11. ProjectGuideArea.xml Content for the Goal Task Wizard Page

```
<GoalAreaTask>
    <TaskID> 102 </TaskID>
    <Title> Project Parameters </Title>
    <TaskName> Enter project parameters </TaskName>
```

```
<URL> file://C:\CustomPG\Project Server Book\Project Goal Area\Project
    Initiation Wizard\Project_Initiation.htm </URL>
<RelevantViews>
    <ViewType> 1 </ViewType>
</RelevantViews>
</GoalAreaTask>
```

Create a Web Page for the Goal Task Wizard Page

Listing 18-12 shows the HTML page for the goal task wizard page. Although the overall structure is very similar to customizations you made to the goal task and goal area pages, there are several new items to explore in detail. The first is the new set of calls in the body onLoad and onUnload events. A second major difference is that I've introduced SidepaneData sections for each wizard step. Finally, the wizard footer navigation allows the goal task to move between the different steps that make up the wizard page.

Listing 18-12. Project_Initiation.htm

```html
<html>
<head>
<meta http-equiv="content-type" content="text/html; charset=utf-8">
<meta http-equiv="MSThemeCompatible" content="Yes">
<title> Microsoft Project </title>
<script src="file://C:\CustomPG\Project Server Book\Project Goal Area\Project
    Initiation Wizard\Project_Initiation.js" language="JScript"></script>
<script src="file://C:\CustomPG\Project Server Book\Project Goal Area\Project
    Initiation Wizard\Project_Initiation_Wizard.js" language="JScript"></script>
<script src="file://C:\CustomPG\Project Server Book\Project Goal Area\Project
    Initiation Wizard\PDS_SOAP.js" language="JScript"></script>
<script src="file://C:\CustomPG\Project Server Book\Project Goal Area\Project
    Initiation Wizard\XML_OutlineCodes.js" language="JScript"></script>
<script src="gbui://util.js" language="JScript"></script>
<link rel="stylesheet" href="gbui://ProjIE.css" type="text/css" />
</head>

<body onLoad="handleResize(); initWizardScripts(); ProjectInitiation_Main();"
        onUnload="cleanupWizardScripts();"
        onContextMenu="return false" tabIndex=1>
    <script language="JScript">
        // pDisplayTaskHeader should always be called before pSetupSidepane
        pDisplayTaskHeader();
        pSetupSidepane();
    </script>
```

```
<div id=divMain class="wizardMain" onResize="handleResize();">


        <!----------------------------------->
        <!---First wizard step-->
        <!----------------------------------->
        <div class="SidepaneData" id="Step1" style="display:none">
            <div class="heading_over">
                <p>
                        Project ID
                </p>
            </div>
            <div>

                <p>
                        Contact the Project Management Office to receive your
                        Project ID.  The Project ID allows reports to include data
                        from Microsoft Project Server and the accounting
                        system.
                </p>
                <p>
                        Project ID:  <input type="text" name="ProjectID">
                </p>
            </div>
        </div>


        <!----------------------------------->
        <!--Second wizard step-->
        <!----------------------------------->
        <div class="SidepaneData" id="Step2" style="display:none">
            <div class="heading_over">
                <p>
                        Sponsor Organization
                </p>
            </div>
            <div>

                <p>
                        Select the sponsor organization for this project from
                        the list below.
                </p>
                <p>
                        <select id="lstOutlineCodes" ></select>
                </p>
            </div>
        </div>
    </div> <!-- divMain -->
```

```
<!--------------------------------------------------------------->
<!-- Wizard footer navigation ----------------------------------->
<!-- The functions below sets up the Wizard footer         -->
<!-- navigation as "Step i of n".  There should be one      -->
<!-- write_WizardFooter for each wizard step.               -->
<!-- write_WizardFooter(A, B, C, D)                         -->
<!--      A - is the step number                            -->
<!--      B - is the number of steps                        -->
<!--      C - is the previous step number                   -->
<!--      D - is the next step number                       -->
<!--------------------------------------------------------------->
<div id="divWizFooter" class="SidepaneData">
    <script language="JScript">
        try
        {
            var script = pscript();
            script.write_WizardFooter(1, 2, 0, 2);
            script.write_WizardFooter(2, 2, 1, 0);
        }
        catch(exp) {}
    </script>
</div>
</body>
</html>
```

Note the two calls in the <body> section of the HTML page: onLoad="initWizardScripts();" and onUnload="cleanupWizardScripts();". The initWizardScripts(); function initializes the wizard environment and sets up environment items such as putting the Project Guide into wizard mode and setting up the wizard footer. onUnload="cleanupWizardScripts(); resets the Project Guide from wizard mode and cleans up any resources the wizard was using.

Wizard content is found in each of the wizard steps, which are specified by the SidepaneData groups for each step. Notice the ID for each SidepaneData divisor is Step#, which tells the Project Guide to get content for the current step. There is a SidepaneData grouping for each wizard step.

The final item is the WizardFooter navigation function call. There is a Wizard-Footer call for each wizard step. The format for the function call is pscript.write_WizardFooter(step#, # of steps, prevStep, nextStep);.

Create a Script Page for Wizard Functionality

The content in Listing 18-13 shows some functions that I added to make data validation easier to implement. Most of the code for this wizard script page isn't shown here. You can download the full code sample from http://www.projectserverexeperts.com.

Listing 18-13. Project_Initiation_Wizard.js

```javascript
var stepCount = 2;  // Here's the total number of steps in the wizard.
var goalAreaID = 10; // Project Goal Area ID of the parent goal area
//*********************************************************************
// NAME: stepValidation
// PURPOSE: This handler validates data in the step we are leaving.
// This event will be ignored if the next step is not prevStep + 1.
// This event also ignores the initial entry with prevStep = 0.
// PARAMETERS:
// prevStep -- ID number of the step we're leaving
// nextStep -- ID number of the step we're going to
// RETURN: None
//*********************************************************************
function stepValidation(prevStep,nextStep)
{
    try
    {
        // Validate when going to the next step only
        if ((nextStep == prevStep + 1) && (prevStep != 0))
        {
            // Select the step to validate
            switch(prevStep)
            {
                case 1:
                    // Make sure a value was entered for ProjectID
                    if (ProjectID.value.length ==0)
                    {
                        alert("Please enter a valid Project ID!");
                        return false;
                    }
                case 2:
                    // Enter validation code here
            }
        }
    }
    catch(err)
```

```
        {
            alert("Error in wizard stepValidation at step#: " + prevStep);
        }
    }


//***********************************************************************
// NAME: wizardCompleteSuccess
// PURPOSE: This handler will fire when the wizard is completed
// successfully.  This will usually be used to store wizard data values.
// PARAMETERS: None
// RETURN: None
//***********************************************************************
function wizardCompleteSuccess()
{
    // Store the Project ID and Outline Code entries
    storeValues();
}
```

Specify the Project Guide Content File

Besides the Project Guide XML content, the two main requirements are a goal task wizard HTML page and a goal task wizard JavaScript page. I mention JavaScript, but VBScript is also an option. I chose JavaScript for these examples, however, because it's the primary language Microsoft used in the creation of the Microsoft Project Server Web content. Although I've covered the requirements for a goal task wizard, this example won't work without several other files. I go over these files and the technologies used in the next section.

Overview of the Technologies Used in the Goal Task Wizard

I've covered the main requirements in creating a goal task wizard page, but I haven't addressed all of the files included with the Project Initiation Wizard example. Several new technologies are incorporated into this example: PDS, SOAP, XML, and several Microsoft Project intrinsic functions. I cover each of these items in the following sections.

Requirements of the Project Initiation Wizard Example

To successfully run the Project Initiation Wizard, you must ensure the following requirements are met:

- The Project Initiation Wizard example requires Microsoft Project Professional and Microsoft Project Server.

- You must be able to connect to Microsoft Project Server for this example to work.

> **NOTE** Microsoft Project will display a message box asking whether you want to run ActiveX controls on the current page. This message is created by the ActiveX SOAP client connecting to Microsoft Project Server to communicate with the PDS. Click Yes to allow the Project Initiation Wizard to work correctly. If you click No or if your security settings disallow the running of ActiveX controls, the Project Initiation Wizard won't work.

- The Project Initiation Wizard uses the Enterprise Project Text1 and Enterprise Project Outline Code1 custom fields. You must define both of these in the enterprise global template. To set up Enterprise Project Text1, rename it to **ProjectID**. To set up the Enterprise Project Outline Code1, you name it, specify a code mask, and input a list of valid values. For this example I named the outline code **Sponsor Organization**, specified a character code mask, and inserted the following lookup values: HR, Engineering, Finance, and IT.

- You may need to resize the side pane if the outline code data is too wide.

Project Initiation Code

Most of the magic behind the scenes of the Project Initiation Wizard example is organized by the Project_Initiation.js file. This file has three functions, ProjectInitiation_Main(), FillOutlineCodeList(), and storeValues(), as shown in Listing 18-14. The ProjectInitiation_Main() function marshals calls to other functions to connect to Microsoft Project Server, get a login cookie, set up an XML request string, make the PDS SOAP call, get the XML response, and pull out the outline code values. The FillOutlineCodeList() function takes an arrayed list of outline values and uses them to populate a list box. The storeValues() function takes the values entered into the wizard and assigns them to the active project.

Listing 18-14. Project_Initiation.js

```
//***********************************************************************
// This jscript file is the main jscript file for the Project
// Initiation task page.  This page stores the variables that need
// to be changed for the PDS calls to function correctly.
//***********************************************************************


//***********************************************************************
// Set the variables below
//***********************************************************************
var intUserType = 1; //1 for Project Server and 2 for Windows Authenticated users
var strPServer_url = "http://pserver/projectserver/";  //Project Server address
var strUID = "PM";  //Provide a username and password for Project Server users
var strPWD = "PM";  //Provide a username and password for Project Server users
// Stores the XML XPath search string for nodes to return
var strXML_XPath = "Reply/OutlineCodes/OutlineCode/Values/Value/ValueFull";


//***********************************************************************
// NAME: ProjectInitiation_Main
// PURPOSE: This is the main function for the Project Initiation that
// calls other functions to connect to Project Server, get a cookie,
// make the PDS SOAP call, get the XML response, and get the Outline
// Code values.
// PARAMETERS: None
// RETURN: None
//***********************************************************************
function ProjectInitiation_Main()
{
     var strPServerLogin_url;  // Stores the complete Project Server Login URL
     var strPServerPDS_url; // Stores the Project Server PDS URL
     var strCookie;  // Stores the login cookie from Project Server
     var strXMLRequest;  // Stores the XML request for PDS
     var strXMLResponse;  // Stores the XML response for PDS
     var astrValues = new Array(); // Stores the Outline Code values returned
          from Project Server

     // Check the Project Server url for a / (slash) at the end
     strPServer_url = CheckPServer_url(strPServer_url);

     // Get the Project Server login url based on the user authentication type
```

```
        strPServerLogin_url = PServerLogin_url(intUserType, strPServer_url, strUID,
            strPWD);


        // Get the Project Server PDS url
        strPServerPDS_url = PServerPDS_url(strPServer_url);


        // Get the Project Server login cookie
        strCookie = GetPServerCookie(strPServerLogin_url);


        // Setup the PDS SOAP request for Enterprise Project Outline Code 1
        //       CODETYPE 0 corresponds to project enterprise outline codes
        //       CONV_VALUE 188744589 for Enterprise Project Outline Code 1
        //           found in MSP_CONVERSIONS database table:
        //       STRING_TYPE_ID      105
        //       CONV_VALUE          188744589
        //       CONV_LANG_ID        1033
        //       CONV_STRING         Task Enterprise Project Outline Code1
        strXMLRequest = EnterpriseOutlineCodes_XMLRequest(0, 188744589);


        // Make the SOAP call to Project Server
        strXMLResponse = SoapCall(strPServerPDS_url, strCookie, strXMLRequest);


        // Get the list of values from the last SOAP call
        // Pass in the XML Response string and the XML XPath search string
        astrValues = GetXMLValues(strXMLResponse, strXML_XPath)


        // Sort the array of values
        astrValues.sort();


        // Fill the Outline Code list
        FillOutlineCodeList(lstOutlineCodes, astrValues);
}
//**********************************************************************
// NAME: FillOutlineCodeList
// PURPOSE: This function fills the list object with the list of valid
// outline code values.
// PARAMETERS:
// lstOutlineCodes - A link to the list object on the html page
// astrValues - The array of valid outline code values
// RETURN: None
//**********************************************************************
 function FillOutlineCodeList(lstOutlineCodes, astrValues)
 {
     try
```

```
        {
            var objOption;  // New option to add to the list

            // Loop through the array and add an option in the pulldown for each
            for (i = 0; i < astrValues.length; i++)
            {
                // Create a new option object
                objOption = document.createElement("option");

                // Set the option text value from the array
                objOption.text = astrValues[i];

                // Add the option to the list
                lstOutlineCodes.options.add(objOption);
            }
            lstOutlineCodes.selectedIndex = 0;
            lstOutlineCodes.style.display = "";
        }
        catch(err)
        {
            alert("Error in FillOutlineCodeList!");
        }
}
//************************************************************************
// NAME: storeValues
// PURPOSE: This stores the values given in the Project Initiation wizard.
// PARAMETERS: None
// RETURN: None
//************************************************************************
function storeValues()
{
    try
    {
        var application = window.external.Application;
        var strProjectIDValue;
        var strOutlineCodeValue;

        // Get the ProjectID and Outline Code values from the text and list boxes
        strProjectIDValue = ProjectID.value;
        strOutlineCodeValue =
lstOutlineCodes.options[lstOutlineCodes.selectedIndex].text;

        // Set the Enterprise Project Outline Code1 value
        // See above for information on how to find the code value
```

```
            application.ActiveProject.ProjectSummaryTask.SetField(188744729,
                strProjectIDValue);

            // Set the Enterprise Project Outline Code1 value
            // See above for information on how to find the code value
            application.ActiveProject.ProjectSummaryTask.SetField(188744589,
                strOutlineCodeValue);
        }
        catch(err)
        {
            alert("Error trying to store values!");
        }
    }
}
```

The first section of the `ProjectInitiation_Main()` function has constant variables that you must set accurately for the Project Initiation Wizard to work properly. These variables include the authentication type for Project Server users, either Project Server or Windows Authentication. You must specify the URL for the Microsoft Project Server. For Project Server authenticated users, you specify a username and password to use. Finally, you input a valid XPath search path for the desired XML element. The XPath specified by default will return the ValueFull parameter from the enterprise outline codes.

I recommend you look at each function called by the `ProjectInitiation_Main()` function to better understand how the PDS function call handles getting the outline code values. PDS_SOAP.js and XML_OutineCodes.js are the main files used by the `ProjectInitiation_Main()` function. The primary steps in a PDS call are as follows:

1. Get the Project Server URL with the correct authentication type and login page.

2. Get the Project Server PDS URL.

3. Connect to Microsoft Project Server and retrieve a login cookie.

4. Build an XML request string to send to the PDS.

5. Make the PDS SOAP call to Microsoft Project Server.

6. Get the XML response from the PDS SOAP call.

7. Manipulate the XML response as needed to get usable data.

Deploying Project Guides

There are two primary challenges to implementing a customized Project Guide. The first challenge is deploying the custom Project Guide content to make it accessible to users. The second challenge is getting all the users pointing to the new custom Project Guide.

One option for content deployment is to put the custom content on a central Web server and have everyone's machine point to the Web server. The second alternative is to put the custom Project Guide files on each workstation. If you have many users, it may be difficult to administer content changes on each machine. If you go the route of a Web server, you need to make sure the Web server is a member of Internet Explorer's Trusted Sites on each user's machine.

Once you have the content available to each user, you have to set Microsoft Project to use the custom Project Guide content. You have a few choices in how you tackle this task. The easiest method for most people using Microsoft Project Server enterprise features is to put a macro in the enterprise global template that sets the ProjectGuide parameters (see ActiveProject.ProjectGuide* in the Microsoft Project VBA environment) automatically upon login. Another choice is to set up system policies for Microsoft Project, a topic addressed in the Microsoft Project 2002 Resource Kit (http://www.microsoft.com/technet/prodtechnol/ project/project2002/reskit/default.asp). A third option is to manually set the registry settings on each Microsoft Project installation.

Summary

You can access many resources on the Internet to learn more about customizing the Project Guide and the Project Data Service (PDS). I recommend you study the Microsoft Project 2002 Software Development Kit (SDK) (http:// msdn.microsoft.com/library/en-us/pdr/PDR_Overview_3338.asp). The SDK contains great articles covering all aspects of customizing Microsoft Project and Project Server.

INDEX

S

X